MOVING IN AND OUT OF ISLAM

MOVING IN AND OUT OF ISLAM

EDITED BY KARIN VAN NIEUWKERK

UNIVERSITY OF TEXAS PRESS
Austin

Printed in the United States of America
First edition, 2018

Requests for permission to reproduce material from this work should be sent to:
Permissions
University of Texas Press
P.O. Box 7819
Austin, TX 78713-7819
utpress.utexas.edu/rp-form

♾ The paper used in this book meets the minimum requirements of ANSI/NISO Z39.48-1992 (R1997) (Permanence of Paper).

Library of Congress Cataloging-in-Publication Data

Names: Nieuwkerk, Karin van, 1960– editor.
Title: Moving in and out of Islam / edited by Karin van Nieuwkerk.
Description: First edition.
Austin : University of Texas Press, 2018.
Includes bibliographical references and index.
Identifiers: LCCN 2018001353
ISBN 978-1-4773-1747-1 (cloth : alk. paper)
ISBN 978-1-4773-1748-8 (pbk. : alk. paper)
ISBN 978-1-4773-1749-5 (library e-book)
ISBN 978-1-4773-1750-1 (non-library e-book)
Subjects: LCSH: Conversion—Islam. | Apostasy—Islam.
Islam—Social aspects. | Religion and culture.
Classification: LCC BP170.5 .N54 2018 | DDC 297.5/74—dc22
LC record available at https://lccn.loc.gov/2018001353

doi:10.7560/317471

CONTENTS

MOVING IN AND OUT OF ISLAM

INTRODUCTION

Moving In and Out of Islam[1]

KARIN VAN NIEUWKERK

Peter,[2] a former convert to Islam and now active in founding an ex-Muslim platform in Germany, told me his story over coffee. Being raised as a practicing Catholic, he met his Egyptian wife-to-be at the university. They felt attracted to each other, and when he eventually asked her to marry him she inquired about his willingness to convert. He agreed because "Islam" for him was "his wife." She was a calm person who would never challenge people, a real likable person, "a person you like to be close to. If she is like that and she is a Muslim then it cannot be wrong." They married in Egypt and Peter took his *shahada* as part of the marriage ceremony. He learned how to pray, obtained some Arabic, and knew several verses of the Qur'an necessary for religious rituals but did not undertake a systematic study of the Qur'an. Neither Peter nor his wife observed fasting. Although faith was self-evidently present and they decided to give their older children an Islamic upbringing, due to their busy work schedules Islamic rituals became a rather marginal element in their everyday life. When his youngest son started asking questions about Islam and the Qur'an, Peter tried to answer his son's queries. However, this needed a more systematic inquiry. His son raised questions about Islamic law, particularly the legal position of women and the "killing of apostates." Parallel to his son's investigations, Peter said that he discovered that many negative images about Islam's perceived lack of concern with human rights and gender issues were actually based on a literal reading of the scriptures and were accordingly enabled by religion. Relativism or context-based argumentation lacked a profound insight into what the Qur'an actually authorizes, according to Peter. The more he read, particularly about the character of the Prophet, the more he realized he could not digest it anymore. He felt the urge to publicize his newfound insights in order to open up the Muslim community, as well as left-wing intellectual relativist defenses of Islam, to the "true nature of Islam." Of course this brought huge tensions within his marriage, but his wife tries to deny and avoid this new reality. He still loves his wife but no longer Islam.

This is just one of the many conversion and deconversion stories that we will encounter in this volume. It tries to make sense of the various narratives and experiences of processes of moving in and out of Islam—and sometimes both of them in the same life story. Personal stories open up an understanding of larger social, political, and religious tendencies. By bringing together the trajectories of embracing Islam and leaving the faith, the chapters explore the different theoretical approaches to as well as reception of the two processes. The processes are not identical but share common grounds. Many conceptual issues need clarification—and these will not be settled—but it is suggested that the notion of "moving in and out of religion" most clearly expresses the ongoing nature of religious transformation processes.

In this introduction I will locate this book within the larger field of studies on religious transformation processes among Muslims and explain how it tries to advance new approaches to "conversion" and "apostasy." Next, I will deal with the reason why it can be illuminating to bring the processes of moving in and out together and look into the commonalities as well as the differences between the two processes at a general level. Finally, I will briefly introduce the individual chapters and the arrangement of this volume, which chooses not to have completely separate sections on moving in and out because the trajectories are more complexly intertwined than such an order would suggest. Conversion cannot entail only a deconversion component, but apostasy from Islam is not a final stage either. Peter has been looking into the Bible, and although he is not convinced by the Bible either, his spiritual journey is ongoing.

STUDYING RELIGIOUS TRANSFORMATION PROCESSES

The study of religious transformation in general, and with regard to Islam in particular, faces certain gaps and divides that this book tries to bridge, such as moving in and out of religion; believing and belonging; as well as the politics and embodiment of the "secular" versus the "religious."

First, the study of conversion and deconversion (or "apostasy") is until now rather disconnected. At the time of publication it can be said that the study of conversion is generally well developed, as it is with regard to conversion to Islam (Allievi 1998; Roald 2004; Van Nieuwkerk, ed., 2006; McGinty 2006; Gooren 2010; Özyürek 2015).[3] Initially the question of *why* people—

particularly women—embraced Islam captured the attention of scholars. Female converts' motives and narratives were illuminated, as were their gender discourses. By now research has turned to everyday lived realities of converted Muslims—to the ways they embody Islam and try to fashion a pious self—as well as to how they organize themselves in order to gain and transmit Islamic knowledge. This developing field of study reflects the fact that converts have taken root within Europe and the Unites States.

Although the way in which converts develop a European or American Islam has been reflected upon previously, how this shaping of a "native" Islam positions converts vis-à-vis born-Muslim communities has hardly been explored. This will be the focus of several contributions dealing with ethnicity, race, and religion (Özyürek, Pirický, and Shanneik, all in this volume). Also, the conversions to Shiʿa Islam (see Shanneik, this volume) and Sufism (see Yarosh, this volume) have been relatively neglected fields within conversion studies. In addition, less attention has been paid to conversion in Central and Eastern Europe. Therefore this volume also includes case studies on conversion in postcommunist Central Europe such as Poland, Lithuania, Slovakia, and the Czech Republic (see Barylo; Račius; and Pirický, all in this volume).

It is interesting to observe that, in general, moving in has received more attention than moving out. Whereas the rise of "nones" in the West and movements like New Atheism have not yet received much scholarly attention, this is even more the case for similar developments in the Middle East. Research has been conducted on the social and legal consequences rather than the motives and process itself. Particularly the theological discussion on whether apostasy is punishable by death and some particular legal cases have received scholarly attention (Peters and De Vries 1976–1977; Berger 2003; O'Sullivan 2003; Olsson 2008; Adang et al. 2016).

Despite the sensitive nature of leaving Islam, a growing number of nonbelievers do speak out, both in the Middle East and among Muslim communities in the West. This relatively new development, however, has hardly been examined (exceptions are Cottee 2015; Schielke 2012, 2013; Whitaker 2015). This inattentiveness can be related not only to the general lack of notice to the study of atheism and nonbelieving but also to perceptions of Islam as a solid, inerasable personal and political force. The study of Muslim societies suffers from an overemphasis on religion as the most important factor in the lives of Muslims (Bowen 2012).

This book therefore fills a gap in studying nonbelieving in different regional contexts such as Sweden (Enstedt, this volume), the UK (Alyedreessy; Cottee, both in this volume), Canada (Cottee, this volume), Egypt (Van Nieuwkerk, this volume), and Iran (Pauha and Aghaee, this volume). It includes the perspective of different actors, including ex-Muslims as well as voices from within the Muslim community, such as those of imams (Larsson, this volume) and converts (Račius, this volume).

In addition, this book examines ambiguity and "in-betweenness" of believing and belonging during the process of moving in and out of Islam. These religious transformation processes are usually not linear or experienced as straightforward delineated episodes, although they might be sometimes narrated as such. Since the 1990s, the study of piety movements have been growing (Mahmood 2005; Hirschkind 2006; Hafez 2011; Van Nieuwkerk 2013), as well as Salafi groups' attraction for born Muslims and converts (Inge 2016; Jawad, this volume). These groups, and most of the research on them, have put emphasis on exemplary conduct of the pious individuals, who are totally dedicated to perfect their religious lifestyles. Lately, this focus has been criticized for reproducing ideals rather than reality and for not representing the ambiguous everyday reality of ordinary people (Schielke 2009). It has produced a distortion toward the "grand schemes" of Islam (Schielke and Debevec 2012) as a totalizing force in which moments of religious skepticism, uncertainties, contradiction, or religious indifference have no place. Religious doubt has hardly been touched upon, which can also be understood in light of its notoriously complex nature. Convictions, whether strong belief or firm nonbelief, are easier to capture than trajectories of doubt because "doubt tends to vanish with articulation" and "doubt is always on the move" (Pelkmans 2013: 5, 15).

This volume looks into ambiguity, doubts, and nonlinear trajectories of both moving in and out of Islam. Whereas the *shahada* is often understood as a clearly demarcated point of entry into the faith, Galonnier (this volume) observes a wide range of experiences of converts. Whereas for some it was the pinnacle of conversion, for others it was a rather insignificant moment, not pronounced for years after they actually believed to have become Muslims. Some declared the *shahada* several times due to a state of in-betweenness and the ambiguous nature of what "becoming Muslim" entailed for them. Yarosh (this volume) describes a small number of Sufi converts in Berlin who can be described as, using the classification of Taylor (1999), "awkward," that is, "converts who participate in rituals, festivals, pilgrimages of one religion while worshipping another religion" (Taylor 1999: 48). This "in-between traffic" sits ill with most approaches toward conversion.

Another facet of in-betweenness that this book looks at is the ambiguous relationship between believing and belonging. Several contributions investigate the complex relationship between race, ethnicity, and religious membership of a community. Whereas the concept of believing without belonging has long entered the field of religious studies to classify nonaffiliated believers, in this book we come across the opposite case. Some ex-Muslims no longer believe but feel attached to the community. Quite often they try to pass as a Muslim in order not to be excommunicated. Coming out of the closet can sever the ties with loved ones (see Cottee, this volume). In yet another case, native Muslim Tatars in Poland cannot leave the faith as this is considered to be the core and inseparable component of Tatar ethnic identity (Górak-Sosnowska and Łyszczarz, this volume).

Several other contributions discuss the intricate belonging of converts within the Muslim communities and the various strategies of inclusion and exclusion adopted. German converts have to deal with a dramatic loss of status in society, yet they also do not fit in the existing Muslim community. German converts resist this double exclusion, first by claiming that they as converts can be better Muslims than immigrant Muslims because they live a pure Islam not contaminated by cultural practices. Second, they try to connect to the lost ideals of the German Enlightenment and European ideals of tolerance (Özyürek, this volume). Czech and Slovak converts to Islam also try to inscribe themselves into local histories by putting an Islamic frame around local heroes and symbols in order to ground their belonging to the nation. Shanneik (this volume) discusses the politics of exclusion and inclusion with regard to Shiʿa converts in the UK, who simultaneously act as spokeswomen for the outside public while being denied real authority within the community.

The third theme to which this book contributes is the embodiment and politics of the "secular" and the "religious." The idea that religious and secular systems of governance and values are contradictory and opposed to each other has been questioned by anthropologists (Asad 2003; Hafez 2011; Mahmood 2009). They go beyond the deadlock of the secular-religious binary and show that these notions co-constitute each other. Asad and Mahmood have argued that a secular worldview produces certain notions of religion and circumscribes its appropriate place, regulating it by disciplinary power. The same can be said about a religious worldview and the ways it defines and governs the secular. The religious and the secular are thus not opposed to each other but intricately related. People are formed both by the discursive opposition as well as by the mutual implication of the religious in the secular and vice versa.

In this book we will introduce many people crossing the religious-secular divide in their lives, changing some of their ideas, sensibilities, and embodied ways of everyday life. They enact the newfound ideas and realities in multiple and ambiguous fashion and experience various (disciplinary) reactions to their move. Whereas for conversion studies go beyond the cognitive and ideological level by analyzing the embodiment of Islam with regard to veiling, rituals and fashioning a pious self (Bourque 2006; Van Nieuwkerk 2014), the field of leaving Islam is not yet very rich in this respect. As Hirschkind (2010) observed, there is generally not yet much insight in secular sensibilities, affects, and dispositions. This is due to the fact that it is "the water in which we swim" and therefore almost invisible. Studying moving out in its embodied dimensions is for that reason a potentially rich field for exploring secular sensibilities. As Enstedt (this volume) and Cottee (this volume) demonstrate, leaving the faith has complex dimensions of learning and unlearning habits, tastes, way of dressing, and interacting with people. Due to the sensitive nature of leaving the faith, nonbelievers can also uphold daily religious practices they do not adhere to anymore, thus mixing the eating of pork and drinking of alcohol with an occasional Friday prayer.

This brings us to the political context of studying moving in and out of Islam. In the West, particularly after 9/11 and the Global War on Terror, Islam largely has become a security issue. The securitization of Islam has also put converts to Islam, particularly those embracing Salafi groups, under surveillance (de Koning, this volume). Studies on radicalization and the development of policies to deradicalize Muslim youth have become a top priority. Haifaa Jawad (this volume) looks into one particular effort of the public intellectual Hamza Yusuf to counter radicalization among born and converted Muslim youths by providing them with the teaching of "traditional Islam." Traditional "tolerant" Islam is perceived as the antidote to radicalization. The surveillance of "radical" Islam is buttressed by the embrace of "moderate Islam" (Mahmood 2009). Not only "moderate Muslims" but also those moving out of Islam or "secular Muslims" are encouraged to publicly testify to the need for reform. Testimonials of ex-Muslims, like those of Hirsi Ali (2006, 2007) and Wafa Sultan[4] (2009; see also Ibn Warraq 1995, 2003), have been received as the "authentic" accounts of Islam from within. Their personal stories, for instance, of abuse, violence, or intolerance within Islam are received as "native" and accordingly "accurate" narratives of Islam (Mahmood 2009).

These debates on radicalization, moderation, and "enlightened" Islam form an important backdrop to the reception and perception of processes of moving in and out of Islam. How this plays out in diverse media is not straightforward. In some media the liberal voices (for instance, imams) speaking out against the death penalty for apostasy (Larsson, this volume) are downplayed for opinions that bolster the harsh face of Islam; in other media the liberal, secular nonbelievers are provided a platform to criticize Islam for its "obscurantist" or "violent" character. Both trends converge in reinforcing the commonly held view that Islam is in urgent need of reform.

In many countries of the Muslim world, political Islam is under siege as well. Traditional and cultural forms of tolerant Islam are also reinvigorated in many parts of the Islamic world. The "traditional Islam" is deployed to counter literal and "purified" interpretations and ensuing ways of (political) acting. This can take the form of promoting Sufi Islam or supporting the traditional centers of learning as the preserves of true Islam. Yet, contrary to the West, secular Muslims—let alone atheists—evidently do not receive a favorable treatment and are silenced.

Processes of secularization also gained an important, albeit severely contested, foothold in the Muslim world. However, especially since the Islamic Revival of the 1970s, the conflation—as assumed in the West—of the religious with the private and the secular with the public realm have almost been inversed (Krämer 2013). The public sphere is ruled largely by religious-moral norms, while critics, skeptics, or nonbelievers are relegated to the private sphere or even secrecy. Nonbelievers in Egypt, for instance (see Van Nieuwkerk, this volume), are perceived as a threat to public moral order. They are perceived not only as traitors or foreign agents but also as corrupting society and public morality. The powerful intertwinement of religion, politics, and morality makes nonbelieving an extremely sensitive issue. For that reason not only political Islam but also unbelief are a matter of state security.

Due to the contrasting political reception—on the one hand of moving in and out of Islam, and on the other hand of these two trajectories in the West and the Muslim world at large—it is especially insightful to compare and contextualize these religious transformation processes.

COMPARING MOVING IN AND OUT OF ISLAM

Combining the two processes can accordingly prevent them from being hijacked by polarizing debates about Islam and enable us to contextualize and deconstruct how moving in and out are perceived and analyzed in different settings. It can also help to develop new dynamic approaches to embracing and leaving Islam. I will compare moving in and out with regard to terminology; the developmental process; the salience of transformation and its embodiment; as well as the consequences.

It is interesting to observe that the semantic field around conversion is imbued with more favorable connotations than leaving the faith. Atheism, unbelief, agnosticism, and related terminology suffer from negative connotations (Zuckerman 2009). This holds true even in the field of sociology of religion where notions such as apostates, disaffiliates, or defectors reveal a religious hegemony (Cragun and Hammer 2011). Being a nonbeliever is constructed as a deviant identity. This is also strongly the case for the Arabic equivalences, such as *kufr* (unbelief), *ilhad* (atheism), and *ridah* or *īrtidad* (apostasy). They all convey strong negative overtones, which makes using these concepts rather problematic.

The concept of conversion has also been criticized for its Christian paradigm, and most "converts" to Islam strongly dislike the notion. They either prefer the label "revert" or descriptive terms such as "embracing Islam" or "becoming Muslim" (see Van Nieuwkerk 2006). Yet the term "revert" is ideologically charged, and descriptive terms are often not sufficiently concise. So, despite the critical notes, the term "conversion" is used in this volume together with more descriptive labels.

The conceptual issues with regard to moving out are even more complex. Not many people will identify with labels such as "apostate" or *kafir* (unbeliever). People can use the terms "atheist" (*mulhid*) or "ex-Muslim," but many do not feel comfortable with such a label either because it does not cover their convictions (atheism) or it still attaches them to the label they have tried to cast off (Muslim). Also, closeted nonbelievers, who identify with the Muslim community, are hesitant to label themselves in clear-cut terms. Yet, apostasy is a widely used concept, particularly in the context of legal matters within Islamic studies; it is also used by some authors in this volume because of its clear resonance and familiarity. "Deconversion" is another term discussed by some authors. Following Streib and Keller (2004), it can be utilized as a synonym for apostasy or be used in the more specific case of converts who later on decide to leave Islam, such as Peter, whose story was introduced at the beginning of this chapter (see also Pauha and Aghaee; Račius, all in this this volume).

In the introduction and the title of the book, the concept of moving in and out of Islam has been chosen for several reasons. First, it brings the two fields of study in closer semantic and substantive contact. They are not perceived as unrelated fields of research, although the trajectories under study can be in opposite directions. Yet, as mentioned before, conversion to a new religion often entails deconversion from another, and people can convert and later on deconvert from the same religion. Second, the terminology of "moving" has no negative connotations, nor does it privilege one direction over the other. In addition, it highlights the dynamic character of the trajectories of embracing and leaving Islam. Instead of focusing on the "destination"—that is, the "state" of conversion or apostasy—the concept of moving draws attention to the journey itself. It also highlights the possibility of an ongoing trajectory between different worldviews. Moreover, it opens up space to reverse the attention from religion as a system defining people's behavior to the idea that it is people who make sense of and move from, to, between, and out of (non)religious positions and worldviews. This process takes place at the level of ideas but also, and particularly, at the level of everyday practices in which ideas, morality, and sensibilities are embodied and enacted. Finally, related to the focus on the people rather than the "religious stuff," biographical methodologies are well positioned to study these trajectories, approaches many of the authors in this volume have used (see also Rambo 2014).

Nevertheless, the concept of moving in and out of Islam is not perfect either. Despite the importance of "persons who move," the notion delineates the process rather than the people. The open and indeterminate character of the concept makes it for that reason particularly useful in combination with other concise notions (see also Barylo, this volume).

Previous studies that facilitate a comparison of the process of moving in and out particularly developed comparative stage models (Ebaugh 1988; Rambo 1993; Streib and Keller 2004; Roald 2004, 2006; Streib 2014). Gooren (2010) introduced the concept of "conversion careers" in order to include both affiliation and disaffiliation. Particularly Rambo's and Ebaugh's stage models have been applied to different cases (see also Alyedreessy, this volume). Whereas Rambo distinguishes several stages in his conversion model, including (1) context; (2) crisis; (3) quest; (4) encounter; (5) interaction; (6) committing; and (7) consequences, Ebaugh discerns the following stages in the process of exiting: (1) first doubts; (2) seeking and weighing role alternatives; (3) a turning point; and (4) establishing an ex-role identity. Both authors consider a crisis experience or a turning point pivotal in the transformation process (see also Wohlrab-Sahr 2006). Whereas this often plays a major role, alternative routes without major crises experiences or ruptures take place as well. Streib and Keller for that reason characterize the deconversion trajectory as existing of (1) loss of specific religious experiences; (2) intellectual doubts; (3) moral criticism; (4) emotional suffering; and (5) finally disaffiliation, pointing toward the experiential, ideological, ritualistic, and consequential dimension respectively.

Despite convergences and overlap in some of the stages and accompanying experiences, Ebaugh points out some important differences as well between the processes of affiliation and disaffiliation, engagement and disengagement, or identification and disidentification. Not only is the "ex-role" explicitly linked to the previous identity and not to the new identity, "exiters" are also clearly aware of the communities' expectations. This makes trying to pass as Muslim for nonbelievers, emotionally difficult, perhaps, but practically viable. For converts this new lifestyle and the expectations from the Muslim community often are an uncharted terrain. Also, the direction of change that converts move toward, a new belief system, appears to be more clearly demarcated than the process of moving out that not necessarily has a new clear destination. It can be a newfound belief, nonbelief, or something in between. Yet this observation needs to be nuanced as well. As we have seen in the beginning of this introduction, Peter was more convinced and determined in his stage of moving out than he was in his phase of moving in.

The relevance of stage-model approaches is that they make clear that we need a dynamic, long-term approach. However, we should not take the stages as fixed phases leading to a final destination but rather study the ongoing journey. In a small research project I conducted, I was able to trace half of the female converts I interviewed in the late 1990s. It was highly interesting to see the different trajectories and metaphors of change they deployed for their ongoing journey with Islam. Whereas some had slowly grown into a greater understanding of Islam through Islamic knowledge, others had witnessed huge highs and lows in life that reflected on their relationship with Islam. Most hang on to Islam and felt that it had helped them through these vicissitudes, but some eventually left Islam. Most of my previous interlocutors developed their own understanding of Islam, quite often of a more spiritual or personal kind than the literal or perfectionist understanding with which they started.

Also among my interlocutors who left Islam—converts and born Muslims—different trajectories are discernable. For some of them the mere realization that a verse in the Qur'an is not compatible with science or that there are contradictions in the Qur'an was enough to radically fall out of the faith. The belief in the holy and perfect nature of the Qur'an is completely blown up the moment a small "error" is observed. For others Islam slowly faded out of their life, and they were in a state of doubt or of neglect.

Accordingly, in addition to the long-term perspective on different trajectories of moving in and out of Islam, it is important to look into the salience of the experience. Also, the extent to which these experiences are expressed, ritualized, and embodied varies greatly. It is in the nature of the study of conversion and deconversion to expect this to be a major life event, which quite often is the case but not necessarily so. As mentioned, the processes of moving in and out are not necessarily accompanied by crises experiences and clear turning points. In addition, the salience of the experience usually changes over time.

Whereas some converts and ex-Muslims exactly remember the day and moment they decided to change faith, for many it is an extended and fuzzy period with no clear beginning or ending. Conversion is generally characterized by a more clearly delineated threshold—professing the *shahada*—whereas no formal ritual exists for leaving the faith. Yet not only do some converts feel or become Muslim without a formal *shahada*; ex-Muslims can ritually mark their new identity by, for instance, drinking alcohol or eating pork (see Galonnier; Cottee; and Enstedt, all in this volume).

In both processes of moving in and out of Islam strategies have to be developed for hiding or showing aspects of the new identity. Depending on personal circumstances and convictions people can change their name, behavior, and appearance upon both conversion and leaving the faith. A female convert to Islam can decide to veil, and an ex-Muslim woman can decide to unveil, but they can also decide not to change their appearances. This can be related to personal circumstances—not being able or willing to confront the environment and relatives with the changes in worldview—personal beliefs—this is not an important element of the new conviction—or stickiness and the comfort of old habits.

Whereas many converts were eager to tell their stories in the beginning of their new journey, some long-term converts became weary to tell the same story again. They felt they were more than just a "convert." It was just a small part of their personality that they did not want to flag. Those leaving Islam were mostly hesitant to highlight this trajectory, in order not to embarrass or hurt their relatives and communities, and not to put themselves in potentially dangerous situations. However, some ex-Muslims became vocal and outspoken activists, opening Facebook pages and YouTube channels to testify their atheism and, sometimes, anti-Islam ideas, as Peter had. For others, not "coming out" was also due to the fact that it was not "an issue" to them. They preferred to engage themselves with more important social and political matters. A long-term perspective on the salience of the experience can uncover that initially the experience of the loss of faith can be overwhelming, whereas a few years later it perhaps hardly occupies the minds anymore.

Accordingly, in addition to the long-term perspective, the study of moving in and out of Islam would benefit from relativizing the importance of these processes within the overall life stories of individuals. Moreover, scholars should not simply select the clear-cut, outspoken, and obvious cases but include the different shades of salience of the religious transformation in the research. For instance, the reader might think that Peter was perhaps a good example for a portrait of an ex-Muslim but that his conversion was not a "real conversion." He did it mostly in order to marry his wife, so can we call him a real convert? Well, he did convert and declared the profession of faith, he observed some of the rituals, and he believes in God. Besides, in order to become an ex-Muslim he logically needs to have been a Muslim first. Conversely, also as an ex-Muslim he did not come out completely for his disbelief in Islam. He does so online, but not in personal contact with his relatives. Whereas Peter is not the clearest example of a conversion story, it is important to include all the variants of conversion and deconversion in order to reach a nuanced understanding of the multifaceted nature and fuzziness of these processes.

In line with Schielke (2012), who argues that there is too much Islam in the anthropology of Islam, one could argue that there is too much emphasis on religion in the process of moving in and out of Islam. This holds true not only for conversion studies but also, counterintuitively, for studying the process of leaving faith. Of course we should study theological doubts and motivations, but the process of moving in and out entails much more than the religious or doctrinal aspects. In addition, the whole transformation itself can be only a small part of the enfolding life stories of those moving in or out of Islam.

The various strategies of hiding and exposure potentially point to a difference in either moving in or out with regard to the social and legal consequences. Leaving Islam can have potentially life-threatening effects, partly explaining why the strategy of passing as a Muslim is widely deployed. Conversion to Islam can certainly be a difficult social process, including the severing of ties with significant others, but no legal or life-threatening consequences are to be endured. Other possible legal consequences, such as, for instance, the famous case of the late Abu Zayd, who was forced to separate from his wife under the accusation of apostasy, or with regard to inheritance, do not hold in the same fashion for moving in. In both cases stigma and dealing with stigmatization are part of the process, but the severity and extent of condemnation—also in its legal manifestation as state law—is evidently more profound in the process of moving out. Also the content of the stigma might be contrariwise. Whereas converts can be regarded as "extremely prudent," ex-Muslims can be accused of immorality (Van Nieuwkerk, this volume). Yet in both cases dealing with stigma of various sorts and impact are important aspects of the journeys.

This difference in social impact also plays out in methodological access to interlocutors moving in or out of Islam. Whereas converts were generally willing to share the stories, or might even see it as part of *daʿwah* (calling to the faith), locating nonbelievers was much more difficult. The higher level of secrecy around moving out makes studying the various trajectories toward nonbelieving rather challenging. This might further add to the tendency to privilege the clear-cut, outspoken cases.

Yet also this theme of the variant social consequences should be studied in its specific social and political contexts. Within the West these legal consequences for apostates do not hold. Ex-Muslims can even be regarded as champions of enlightened Islam and be widely acclaimed. Yet indifference and disregard for the difficulty of "coming out of the closet" can also befall ex-Muslims from their non-Muslim fellows (see Cottee, this volume). Whereas some Muslim countries apply the death penalty for apostasy, many do not. As long as nonbelief is not actively propagated and not leading to social chaos (*fitna*) it can be condoned both at the state level and the community or family level. The liberal religious scholars promoting total freedom of religion do exist side by side with hardliners. Yet their voice is provided with a less prominent platform (see Larsson, this volume). Accordingly, the social consequences of moving in and out need to be contextualized and related to the various audiences involved. A careful contextualization of the processes and consequences of moving in or out of Islam is what the authors of this volume aim to provide.

INTRODUCTION TO THE CONTRIBUTIONS

In section I, the contributions focus on conceptual issues and critically examine the notions and process of conversion (Barylo, Galonnier) as well as approaches to understand the process of leaving the faith (Enstedt).

Using a theological approach, William Barylo in chapter 1 focuses on the definition of "change in religion" within the three Abrahamic faiths: Christianity, Judaism, and Islam. As Barylo points out, the term "conversion" has been extensively used in a Christian frame of reference, conveying the idea that conversion is a precise turning point with a clear "before" and "after," whereas the experiences of his interlocutors—both "converts" and "born again" Muslims from France, Poland, and the United Kingdom—often show less linear journeys. In Islam, there is no specific term for people who become Muslim. Among the different options, such as *Muallaf* (those whose hearts need softening), Barylo particularly focuses on the concept of *Islah* (reform, amendment) in order to understand the experiences of his interlocutors. He concludes that the notion to "amend," meaning either "to improve, change for the better" or "to correct," can be applied to a wide range of cases such as people who move from a particular religion to another, who did not believe and then started to believe, and people, born and raised within a particular religion, who start practicing at some point in their life.

Juliette Galonnier in chapter 2 examines the recitation of the *shahada*, usually conceived of as the rite of passage that marks the entry into Islam. Under such conceptualization, the conversion moment is expected to be precisely situated in time, with a clear date of record, marking a discontinuity between a "before" and an "after." Among her interlocutors this narrative of discontinuity is often endorsed, and some stories are replete with considerations on radical transformation, purification of self, and erasure of sins. Galonnier argues that such a representation of the *shahada* tends to overlook the lengthy process that is required to incorporate Muslim beliefs and practices into one's life. Relying on in-depth interviewing with eighty Muslim converts in France and the United States, Galonnier proposes to reconceptualize religious conversion as a continuing rather than discontinued event—a progressive transformation rather than a dramatic, terminal change. Accordingly, Galonnier suggests we distinguish between the more abrupt process of "moving in" and the drawn-out process of "moving toward" Islam.

Not only with regard to conversion but also in the study of apostasy, as Daniel Enstedt shows in chapter 3, leaving religion is often conceived of as a more or less linear process, where the apostate is replacing one religion with another or is abandoning religion altogether. Enstedt emphasizes the blurred boundaries not only between the sacred and the secular but also between leaving and keeping a religion like Islam. Leaving religion does not necessarily mean losing religion. Most approaches on leaving the faith focus on the cognitive aspects of religiosity. Enstedt proposes to take into account both the personal and collective apostasy narratives as well as the different kinds of materiality—such as clothing, food, and makeup—that play a part in the process to move out of Islam. Many apostates mark the ex-Muslim position ritually by consuming things that are commonly considered *haram* (forbidden in Islam). Even though ex-Muslims can articulate a severe critique often based on their own life experiences, some habits, norms, and practices that are deeply influenced by Islam still linger on.

The contributions in section II examine issues of race, culture, and ethnicity in the process of conversion (Özyürek, Pirický, and Shanneik) and leaving the faith (Górak-Sosnowska and Łyszczarz).

Esra Özyürek in chapter 4 shows that, even though converting to Islam transforms ethnic Germans' lives dramatically, most German Muslims are invested in opening a space for themselves where they can comfortably embrace their Muslim and German identities at the same time. Consisting as they do almost exclusively of German converts, such communities develop a deep sense of German Islamic identity that is distinct from a Turkish or Arab one. German Muslims claim that as converts they can even be better Muslims than immigrant Muslims. They imply that, by definition, they live a pure Islam not contaminated by cultural practices. Intellectuals among the German converts' communities try to construct an alternative German genealogy that is tolerant and inclusive of Islam. They claim that their contribution to a religiously diverse society makes them better connected to the lost ideals of the German Enlightenment. Özyürek also shows that converts raise their children in ways that are both Islamic and German. These efforts aim to open up legitimate space for Germans who have embraced Islam. At the same time, however, they sometimes end up reproducing antiimmigrant discourses that treat born or immigrant Muslims as not fitting in German society.

Gabriel Pirický's contribution (chapter 5) investigates how converts merge their native Czech and Slovak culture and history with Islam. Whereas for some converts local culture or ethnicity must be separated from Islam, others develop a local Islam that pays attention to Slovak and Czech culture and ethnicity. Pirický particularly examines how some converts reappropriate local history or myth in order to inscribe themselves in the history of Slovakia and Czechia. Slovak and Czech norms often continue to operate after converts' conversion to Islam, which creates a certain degree of particularism in the form of a "Czech" and a "Slovak" Islam. The representational practices of local Muslim converts thus offer a wide variety of options that are usually less known to immigrant Muslims. Converts sometimes disassociate themselves from immigrant Muslims, whom they accuse of practicing "foreign" traditions and cultures instead of Islam. Putting an Islamic frame around local historical narratives helps converts to move toward a cultural orientation that does not conflict with the national interests of the non-Muslim majority.

Yafa Shanneik's contribution (chapter 6) also deals with the born Muslim–convert interaction. Whereas in the previous two case studies converts distance themselves from immigrant born Muslims, this research shows the partial marginalization of converts as an expression of power relations between the two groups as well as a way to secure an "authentic" Shiʿa identity in the diaspora. Within the politically and ethnically diverse Shiʿa communities in London, converts do not share the socioreligious capital needed for leadership positions. Converts oscillate in their relationship with the various Shiʿa communities between a strong feeling of integration and a sense of separation and stigmatization. On one hand, they create a shared repertoire based on the construction of a global unified Muslim *ummah* and on narratives of the marginalization and the suffering of Shiʿas in the Muslim world. On the other, despite converts' religious, linguistic, and cultural competency, they are hardly granted access to leadership positions among Shiʿa communities in London. At certain public events, however, the converts' ethnic and linguistic backgrounds enable them to act as public representatives of the Shiʿa communities in the UK. Yet, this is limited to "talking *about* religion," thereby offering them temporal access to the center of their communities, rather than "talking *within* the religious community."

Chapter 7, the final contribution of section II, deals with the ethnic dimensions of Tatar religiosity that makes it almost impossible for Tatars to move out of Islam. Katarzyna Górak-Sosnowska and Michał Łyszczarz show that, according to their Polish Tatar interlocutors, losing Islam—either by conversion or by leaving religion entirely—means that a Tatar stops being a Tatar and turns into "a person of Tatar origin." Whereas there are several developments that could potentially have propelled Tatars to move out—such as the socialist legacy and its atheization policy, the general secularization in Poland, Polish Islamophobia, and mixed marriages, the authors identify several reasons for Tatars to stay Muslim. On one hand, Tatar religion blended with their ethnicity; that is, Tatar ethnicity and religion are interlinked to the extent that the long-lasting debate about whether they are primarily an ethnic, religious, or regional minority remains unresolved. On the other, adaptation to the Polish majority resulted in a peculiar type of Tatar Islamic religiosity. Tatar Islam has greater cultural significance than strictly religious meaning for the Tatars. Yet, it is Islam in its particular Tatar form that constitutes the core of Tatar identity. Losing faith could mean losing this unique identity and melting completely into mainstream society.

Section III focuses on the transnational movement of people and religious organizations and moving between religious traditions.

Oleg Yarosh in chapter 8 examines the Berlin branches of transnational Sufi orders. He particularly focuses on authority structures and the process of intrareligious conversion, defined as the process of religious learning and gradual adoption of religious norms and practices. Using Donald Taylor's classification of converts into inward, outward, or awkward, Yarosh especially deals with the latter category: those who convert not by ritual but by behavior and retain selective and individualist attitudes toward the Islamic tradition. They attend Sufi meetings and take part in Sufi rituals without formally professing the declaration of faith. Yet there are different discourses and practices among the various Sufi communities in Berlin. The Rabbaniyya community is pluralistic and has a contextualized approach to Islamic norms. The "awkward converts" feel more comfortable within this group because it tolerates their ambiguous attitudes toward the Islamic tradition. Other Sufi communities, such as the Tariqah Burhaniyya, are more *Shari'ah*-oriented, religious authority is more consolidated, and they are ethnically more homogeneous. These Sufi communities are less attractive to converts with a secular or an eclectic religious background. Converts can shop around for different alternatives, allowing them to form a new transcommunal framework of loyalty.

Haifaa Jawad in chapter 9 looks at the deradicalization efforts of the Muslim public intellectual Hamza Yusuf. She examines his role in encouraging people to move from Salafi or politicized Islamic groups into a traditional form of Islam via his project to revive sacred knowledge. His teachings particularly attract converts and born Muslims and enable them to negotiate the complex path between their religious and cultural identity within a Western context. During the 1990s, political-religious groups and Salafis were left relatively undisturbed in the UK, the US, and Canada and gained ground among young born Muslims and converts. Based on interviews with participants of Hamza Yusuf's classes, Jawad particularly highlights how his message of traditional sacred knowledge tried to counteract violence and radicalization. Several interviewees explicated that the teaching of sacred knowledge and the traditional approach of Hamza Yusuf played an important role in moving them from Salafi/politicized Islam into more Sunni/Sufi–oriented forms of Islam.

Martijn de Koning (chapter 10) provides a critical analysis of the securitization around Islam, and particularly Salafism, by analyzing the life story of Abu Bashir, a Dutch convert to Islam who eventually migrated to the UK. Abu Bashir followed the "Salafi path" and preached between 2000 and 2008, a period in which the surveillance of Muslims and converts to Islam increased in the Netherlands and elsewhere. After 9/11, a process of securitization unfolded, and policies on integration shifted almost entirely to Islam and Muslims as a threat to Dutch society. Within this context, "Salafism" emerged as a particularly urgent security matter. The conspicuousness of Salafism encouraged Abu Bashir to migrate to the UK in an attempt to evade the regime of surveillance, also encouraged by the idea that the UK would provide more religious freedom and chance of being able to lead life "the Muslim way." Abu Bashir felt less scrutinized compared to his time in the Netherlands and relatively unmarked in the migrant areas in the UK. The intersection of Islamophobia, secularism, securitization, and counter-radicalization thus produced a hypervisibility of so-called Salafi Muslims that Abu Bashir tried to counter by strategies of opacity and invisibility and by creating a space where he is less affected by the regimes of surveillance.

The contributions in section IV examine the narratives and experiences of people moving out of Islam—born Muslims and converts—in both the Muslim majority context (Van Nieuwkerk, Pauha & Aghaee) and the minority context (Cottee, Alyedreessy).

Mona Alyedreessy in chapter 11 explores the experiences of British converts to Islam who later on decided to leave the faith. By using Rambo's conversion stage model and Ebaugh's framework for understanding the process of exiting, Alyedreessy compares the crises, motives, turning points, differences, and similarities in the conversion and deconversion processes. Through in-depth analysis of five life stories, Alyedreessy shows that certain crisis experiences that encouraged her interlocutors to embrace Islam also compelled them to abandon the faith when it appeared that their crisis worsened or when they were faced with new problems. Instead of finding solutions to their personal crises—belonging to a community or spirituality—they suffered from new crises such as patriarchal relationships, a lack of personal freedom, or racial discrimination. Despite these problems, the continuous process of identity construction through conversion followed by deconversion was believed to make them closer to their "true" identity.

Simon Cottee in chapter 12 discusses the experiences of British and Canadian ex-Muslims, most of whom did not disclose their apostasy. He analyzes their closeted experiences and the strains and stresses of managing secrecy and moral stigma. Building on Stuart A. Wright's suggestion that the process of moving out of a highly committed religious group can be compared to leaving a marriage, Cottee adds a further comparative reference point for capturing crucial aspects of these exits: namely, gay departures from the heterosexual world. Drawing on life-history interviews with thirty-five ex-Muslims in Britain and Canada, Cottee shows that one of the greatest challenges nonreligious ex-Muslims face is adapting to a life *apart*: not only from their former coreligionists but also from non-Muslims who show little understanding of their situation. These experiences of closeted ex-Muslims do not exist in the sociology of religion because the field predominantly defines apostates as outspoken agitators against their former groups. Similar to closeted gays, who are both inside and outside the social world, closeted ex-Muslims must contend with the challenge of living both inside and outside the faith communities from which they have become estranged.

Karin van Nieuwkerk in chapter 13 examines the trajectory of doubt among Muslim skeptics and nonbelievers in Egypt within a highly politicized media debate on "growing numbers" of nonbelievers purportedly due to the one-year rule of the Muslim Brotherhood. Skeptics and atheists have also created their own media, particularly Facebook pages and video channels, and become outspoken. Van Nieuwkerk investigates how nonbelievers are represented by the Egyptian (state) media—that is, not only as deviants, as a secret society, and as a disease but also as ill-guided youths exposed to wrong, extremist ideas about Islam and particularly as immoral beings. Based on interviews and YouTube testimonials, Van Nieuwkerk provides insight into the different experiences and trajectories of doubting and leaving the faith. For most it was invested with deep emotional anguish and pious fear. Whereas some ex-Muslims became vocal activists, most hide their serious doubts and their new convictions. Keeping a low profile makes sense in view of the state and society's condemnation.

In chapter 14, Teemu Pauha and Atefeh Aghaee examine the stories, originally written for an internet discussion group, of around fifty Iranians who left Islam. By identifying common aspects and the general pattern of the stories, they construct four paths out of the faith. They argue that atheism may serve as a form of resistance to a theocratic regime, defined as the path of the rebels, yet there are also other—and possibly more global—types of nonbelieving in Iran, such as the seekers, the rationalists, and the disillusioned. Of the four groups, the seekers were generally the most positive toward God and religion. In contrast to the powerless God of the disillusioned and the despotic God of the rebels, the God of the seekers was a magnificent and positive force, even if beyond human comprehension. Pauha and Aghaee conclude that the stories analyzed and the typology constructed show noteworthy similarities to deconversion stories gathered in other contexts (e.g., Europe and North America). However, this does not mean that context is meaningless. The unique aspects of Islamic theology or Iranian society have a bearing on the details of the deconversion process and the experiences of the ex-Muslims.

Section V deals with debates on apostasy and deconversion from the side of converts (Račius) and Swedish imams (Larsson).

Egdūnas Račius in chapter 15 explores how Lithuanian converts view leaving Islam and how they explain the possible causes, motives, circumstances, and conditions for moving out of Islam, as well as what, if anything, they think should be done with apostates. Račius argues that the terms "disaffiliation" and "apostasy/deconversion" should be treated as denoting different subsequent stages in one's "moving out" of religion. The term "deconversion," which by default is apostasy, should be used only with regard to ex-converts and not applied to those born into tradition. For the Lithuanian converts disaffiliation is barely distinguishable, and they accepted an open declaration of abandoning Islam only as apostasy/deconversion. They contend that Muslims have a right to apostasy and there is no punishment for it. "Closeted apostates" are accordingly treated as Muslims, albeit lapsed ones.

Göran Larsson (chapter 16) focuses on the question of whether it is dangerous for Muslims in Sweden to leave Islam and whether imams condemn those who move out. Several individuals have testified that they have been threatened because they changed their religious belief. Larsson shows that, without denying that individuals can be threatened in connection to moving out of Islam, it is not easy to find police reports of hate crimes on this matter. Even though the available records indicate that a change of religion could result in threats and pressure from peer groups, this problem is not unique to Islam and points to a general problem. In addition, the imams interviewed hold liberal views and contend that there is no compulsion in religion. They perceived faith as a matter of choice and personal conviction. Larsson concludes that there seems to be a gap between public perceptions that it is dangerous to leave Islam and what the imams think about apostasy. It seems to be hard for Muslim theologians to communicate liberal interpretations of Islam to the media, whereas in both public perceptions and media outlets it seems to be easier to convey an image of Islam as a punitive and intolerant religion.

NOTES

1. This edited volume is the result of an international conference organized in Nijmegen by the editor on October 16–17, 2015. This conference was funded by The Netherlands Interuniversity School for Islamic Studies (NISIS), The Royal Dutch Academy of Sciences (KNAW), and the Faculty of Philosophy, Theology, and Religious Studies, Radboud University Nijmegen.

2. His name and some other aspects that could reveal his identity have been changed. Interview with author on September 8, 2013.

3. Also several theses have appeared by Karen Turner, Géraldine Mossière, Iman Lechkar, Vanessa Vroon-Najem, and others.

4. Wafa Sultan's book *A God Who Hates* is acclaimed on the cover, which states: "The courageous woman who inflamed the Muslim world speaks out against the evils of Islam."

REFERENCES

Adang, C., et al., eds. 2016. *Accusations of Unbelief in Islam: A Diachronic Perspective on Takfir*. Leiden: Brill.

Allievi, St. 1998. *Les Converti A L'Islam. Les nouveaux musulmans d'Europe*. Paris: L'Harmattan.

Asad, T. 2003. *Formations of the Secular: Christianity, Islam, Modernity*. Stanford: Stanford University Press.

Berger, M. 2003. "Apostasy and Public Policy in Contemporary Egypt: An Evaluation of Recent Cases from Egypt's Highest Courts." *Human Rights Quarterly* 25, no. 3 (August 2003): 720–740.

Bourque, N. 2006. "How Deborah Became Aisha: The Conversion Process and the Creation of Female Muslim Identity." In *Women Embracing Islam: Gender and Conversion in the West*. K. van Nieuwkerk, ed. Austin: University of Texas Press. 223–250.

Bowen, J. R. 2012. *A New Anthropology of Islam*. Cambridge, UK: Cambridge University Press.

Cottee, S. 2015. *The Apostates: When Muslims Leave Islam*. London: Hurst.

Cragun, R. T., and J. H. Hammer. 2011. "One Person's Apostate Is Another Person's Convert: What Terminology Tells Us about Pro-religious Hegemony in the Sociology of Religion." *Humanity & Society* 35, no. 1–2: 149–175.

Gooren, H. 2010. *Religious Conversion and Disaffiliation: Tracing Patterns of Change in Faith Practices*. New York: Palgrave MacMillan US.

Hafez, Sh. 2003. *An Islam of her Own: Reconsidering Religion and Secularism in Women's Islamic Movements*. New York: New York University Press.

Hirschkind, Ch. 2006. *The Ethical Soundscape: Cassette Sermons and Islamic Counterpublics*. New York: Columbia University Press.

———. 2010. *Is There a Secular Body? The Immanent Frame, Secularism, Religion, and the Public Sphere*. blogs.ssrc.org/tif/2010/11/15/secular-body.

Hirsi Ali, A. 2006. *Caged Virgin*. New York and London: Free Press.

———. 2007. *Infidel*. New York and London: Free Press.

Ibn Warraq. 1995. *Why I Am Not a Muslim*. New York: Prometheus.

———. 2003. *Leaving Islam: Apostates Speak Out*. New York: Prometheus.

Inge, A. 2016. *The Making of a Salafi Muslim Woman: Paths to Conversion*. Oxford: Oxford University Press.

Krämer, G. 2013. "Secularity Contested: Religion, Identity, and the Public Order in the Arab Middle East." In *Multiple Secularities Beyond the West*. M. Burchardt, M. Wohlrab-Sahr, and M. Middell, eds. Boston, Berlin, and Munich: Walter de Gruyter.

Mahmood, S. 2005. *Politics of Piety: The Islamic Revival and the Feminist Subject*. Princeton: Princeton University Press.

———. 2009. "Feminism, Democracy, and Empire: Islam and the War on Terror." In *Gendering Religion and Politics: Untangling Modernities*. H. Herzog and A. Braude, eds. New York: Palgrave MacMillan US.

McGinty, A. Mansson. 2006. *Becoming Muslim: Western Women's Conversions to Islam*. New York: Palgrave MacMillan US.

Olsson, S. 2008. "Apostasy in Egypt: Contemporary Cases of *Hisbah*." *The Muslim World* 98: 95–116.

O'Sullivan, D. 2003. "Egyptian Cases of Blasphemy and Apostasy against Islam: Takfir al-Muslim." *International Journal of Human Rights* 7, no. 2: 97–137.

Özyürek, E. 2015. *Being German Becoming Muslim: Race, Religion, and Conversion in the New Europe*. Princeton and Oxford: Princeton University Press.

Pelkmans, M., ed. 2013. *Ethnographies of Doubt: Faith and Uncertainty in Contemporary Societies*. London and New York: I. B. Tauris.

Peters, R., and G. J. J. De Vries. 1976–1977. "Apostasy in Islam." *Die Welt des Islams* 17, no. 1/4: 1–25.

Rambo, L. L. R. 1993. *Understanding Religious Conversion*. New Haven and London: Yale University Press.

Rambo, L. R., and Ch. E Farhadian. 2014. "Introduction." In *The Oxford Handbook of Religious Conversions*. L. R. Rambo and Ch. E. Farhadian, eds. Oxford: Oxford University Press.

Roald, A. S. 2004. *New Muslims in the European Context: The Experiences of Scandinavian Converts*. Leiden and Boston: Brill.

———. 2006. "The Shaping of a Scandinavian 'Islam': Converts and Gender Equal Opportunity." In *Women Embracing Islam: Gender and Conversion in the West*. K. van Nieuwkerk, ed. Austin: University of Texas Press. 48–71.

Schielke, S. 2009. "Being Good in Ramadan: Ambivalence, Fragmentation, and the Moral Self in the Lives of Young Egyptians." *Journal of the Royal Anthropological Institute* 15, special issue no. 1 (Islam, Politics, Anthropology): 24–40.

———. 2012. "Being a Nonbeliever in a Time of Islamic Revival: Trajectories of Doubt and Certainty in Contemporary Egypt." *International Journal of Middle East Studies* 44, no. 2: 301–320.

———. 2013. "The Islamic World." In *The Oxford Handbook of Atheism*. S. Bullivant and M. Ruse, eds. Oxford: Oxford University Press. 638–651.

Schielke, S., and L. Debevec, 2012. "Introduction." In *Ordinary Lives and Grand Schemes: An Anthropology of Everyday Religion*. S. Schielke and L. Debevec, eds. New York: Berghahn.

Streib, H. 2014. "Deconversion." In *The Oxford Handbook of Religious Conversions*. L. R. Rambo and Ch. E. Farhadian, eds. Oxford: Oxford University Press.

Streib, H., and B. Keller. 2004. "The Variety of Deconversion Experiences: Contours of a Concept in Respect to Empirical Research." *Archive for the Psychology of Religion* 26, no. 1: 181–200.

Sultan, W. 2009. *A God Who Hates*. New York: St. Martin's Press.

Taylor, D. 1999. "Conversion: Inward, Outward, and Awkward." In *Religious Conversion: Contemporary Practices and Controversies*. C. Lamb and M. D. Bryant, eds. London and New York: Cassel. 35–51.

Van Nieuwkerk, K. 2006. "'Islam is your birthright.' Conversion, Reversion, and Alternation: The Case of New Muslimas in the West." In *Conversion in Antiquity and Middle Ages*. W. J. van Bekkum et al., eds. Leuven: Peeters. 151–167.

———. 2013. *Performing Piety: Singers and Actors in Egypt's Islamic Revival*. Austin: University of Texas Press.

———. 2014. "'Conversion' to Islam and the Construction of a Pious Self." In *The Oxford Handbook of Religious Conversions* L. R. Rambo and Ch. E. Farhadian, eds. Oxford: Oxford University Press. 667–687.

Van Nieuwkerk, K., ed. 2006. *Women Embracing Islam: Gender and Conversion in the West*. Austin: University of Texas Press.

Whitaker, B. 2014. *Arabs without God: Atheism and Freedom of Belief in the Middle East*. Create Space Independent Publishing Platform. ebook.

Wohlrab-Sahr, M. 1998. *Konversion zum Islam in Deutschland und den USA*. Frankfurt: Campus Verlag.

———. 2006. "Symbolizing Distance: Conversion to Islam in Germany and the United States." In *Women Embracing Islam: Gender and Conversion in the West*. K. van Nieuwkerk, ed. Austin: University of Texas Press. 71–93.

Zuckerman, P. 2009. "Atheism, Secularity, and Well-Being: How the Findings of Social Science Counter Negative Stereotypes and Assumptions." *Sociology Compass* 3, no. 6: 949–971.

SECTION I

CONCEPTUALIZING RELIGIOUS CHANGE

ONE

PEOPLE DO NOT CONVERT BUT CHANGE

Critical Analysis of Concepts of Spiritual Transitions

WILLIAM BARYLO

When someone comes to the change office and asks for changing British pounds to euros, the change office "converts" the currencies. From a more technical point of view, when one needs to change a jpeg from a gif, one has to "convert" the file. Can the same word that is used for technical or monetary transactions thoroughly fit and describe the social and psychological phenomenon of a spiritual change? Is it relevant, when one changes his or her spiritual orientation—for instance a Christian embracing Judaism, or vice-versa—to call him or her a "convert?"

The legitimacy of calling a person switching to another spiritual matrix a "convert" has therefore to be questioned. In addition, when interviewing practicing Muslims in Europe who describe themselves as having "embraced Islam" at one point in their lives, many indicated that the term "convert" did not suit their subjective perception of self. Thus, there is a need to find more accurate concepts to describe these phenomena in the social sciences. This is the work this chapter tries to achieve. The term "conversion" is rooted in Latin and Greek languages and has been extensively used in a Christian frame of reference. Current widely used concepts convey the idea that conversion is a precise turning point (Nock 1988), with a clear "before" and "after." But from an anthropological perspective, the subjective perception of the idea of conversion has to be taken into account. Social and individual realities and their subjective perception show less linear journeys, without a clear beginning or ending (Lofland and Skonovd 1981; Rambo 1996; Allievi 1998; Suleiman 2013). The idea expressed by my interlocutors is more of a transition, as by its classical Latin etymology of *transire*, which comprises the senses of "to cross, depart, leave, cross over or to be transferred."

Studies on Muslims in Europe such as Suleiman (2013, 2016), Allievi (1998), Valensi (2000), and van Nieuwkerk (2006) show the variety of self-identifications by people who embrace Islam. They show not only that importance has to be given to the subjective perception of converts to Islam about their spiritual journey; they also question the relevance of the idea of conversion itself. Works such as *Method* from the French sociologist Edgar Morin (1986) put forward that when it comes to cultures, spiritualities, and identities it is impossible to put concepts into delineated boxes with sealed borders, as these are the result of numerous cultural and spiritual systems constantly redefined, entangled, and mixing with each other.

In this chapter, I will work from a more theological approach and focus on the definition of "change in religion" within the three Abrahamic faiths: Christianity, Judaism, and Islam. The Hebrew concept of *ger*, which is very different from the Latin Christian *conversio*, is extensively discussed in Judaism (Kellner 1991). In Jewish jurisprudence there is no clear consensus upon who and how one becomes a Jew, and this also varies depending on the different schools of thoughts. Islam, however, does not have a specific term for designating people who become Muslim. Among the different options, such as *Muallaf* (those whose hearts need softening), this chapter will focus on the concept of *Islah* (reform, amendment). I will discuss the relevance of the terminology for "change" within the three Abrahamic traditions[1] in order to understand the experience and self-identifications of Muslim volunteers among whom I conducted fieldwork.

This chapter is based on five years of fieldwork and participant observation among Muslim volunteers in France, Poland, and the United Kingdom between 2009 and 2015. I conducted face-to-face interviews with more than seventy volunteers with an equal proportion of male and females, and ages between 18 and 45 years old. Each interview comprised a set of questions on their perception of faith, relationship with God, and spiritual journey. Among the interviewees were people from native European backgrounds ("converts") as well as people raised in Muslim families who at some point in their lives decided to be more involved in Islam ("born again"). The biographical stories allowed me to define with precision their subjective perception of their faith, identity, and spiritual journey and how they describe themselves at the present time.

The first section below contains a literature review of the different ideas on processes of conversion in the social sciences; the second section highlights my fieldwork with the various self-descriptions of my interlocutors. The third section critically explores the term "conversion" through its English, Latin, and Greek etymologies and compares it to the concept of identity in the social sciences. In the last section, I explore the idea of the change of spiritualities in Christianity, Judaism, and Islam as an attempt to find more accurate alternatives to the current concepts in the social sciences.

SEMANTICS OF CONVERSION

When describing a change in someone's main spiritual or religious frame of reference, the term "conversion" appears as the default option and has been widely used. One of the main definitions of the term in the social sciences has been given by Arthur Nock: "A reorientation of the soul of an individual, the deliberate bifurcation from a state of indifference or from an ancient state of piety to one other, a bifurcation that implies the awareness to be involved in a great change, that the ancient was 'bad' and the new is 'good'" (Nock 1988).

However, some other studies point out a much more complex phenomenon. L. Rambo describes a "multi-faceted process of transformation" (1996: 6–7), which can either be sudden and short or long and progressive, which in any case is not a specific, occasional event. Changing one's religion is not only internalizing symbols but is a constant work of adjusting one's understanding as demands and circumstances change (Hefner 1993). Travisano (1970) writes about "alternation" as a gradual process of transformation of the identity, different from a radical conversion. M. Wieviorka (2000) highlights the social dimension of conversion, describing it as the act of joining a collective identity, and stresses that the process is also built upon new social bonds and not only on a single person. Lofland and Skonovd (1981) put the emphasis on the fact that motives to change one's faith are various and multiple (intellectual, experimental, affectional, mystical, etc.) and that, therefore, journeys of "conversion" are not simple or linear processes. According to Yasir Suleiman's (2013: 21) study on British female Muslims who embraced Islam, "there is no appropriate term in the English language that conveys the idea that a person has decided to embrace Islam." He therefore suggests the use of the term "convert" as a default option for clarity purposes.

Interlocutors who have chosen Islam prefer other terms to describe themselves. Suleiman's study (2013: 21) shows various options preferred by the participants: during the symposia converts referred to themselves as "converts," "reverts," "new Muslims," and "those who had embraced Islam." In van Nieuwkerk's study, subjects employ the expressions "discovering Islam," "I have been a Muslim(a)," "to accept Islam" and "becoming a Muslim(a)," "conversion," "to take *shahada*," "reversion," "to accept Islam," "to embrace Islam" (Van Nieuwkerk 2006: 154–155). Suleiman (2013: 21) points out some lexical matters:

> Other terms such as "New Muslim" have not been used because many of the subjects of this report have been practising Muslims for many years and

> would not, therefore, now consider themselves as new to Islam.... An alternative to the verb "convert" is "revert" which means "to become conscious again, to regain one's senses," or "to recover, to improve in condition." The term "revert" is favoured by some because it is considered to reflect a returning to the natural state of *fitra* (an Arabic concept which denotes a pure and God-given state of being, reflective of the human soul's natural status as submissive to God) which is imprinted upon every individual at birth.

The substantive term "revert," used by the subjects in general, refers to an authentic *hadith* of the Prophet Muhammad stating that "no child is born but upon *Fitra* [the primordial nature of being attracted to God, i.e., as a Muslim]. It is his parents who make him a Jew or a Christian or a Zoroastrian."[2]

However, Van Nieuwkerk (2006: 161–163) also points out the fact that "replacing conversion by reversion as a general analytical concept does not appear to be useful," as it is linked to ideological conception of a perceived "true religion."

The most recent study on male narratives of conversion by Suleiman (2016: 47–48) suggests another Arabic term: *Muallaf*. The term was used by a male who has been advocating the term "revert" at first but thought that the term is "betraying too much of the perspective of an insider." Still, *Muallaf* was deemed not particularly useful by the same persons suggesting it for talking to non-Muslims and non-Arabic speakers and being understood (Suleiman 2016). These terms will be further explored below, but first I will analyze the various self-denominations and how they relate to the subjects' identities.

SELF-IDENTIFICATIONS AND DIASPORIC IDENTITIES

Historically and across cultures, the idea of becoming Muslim was linked to negative stereotypes. Until the early twentieth century in France, people used to qualify new Muslims as people "making themselves Turks." This was a pejorative term linked to the Ottoman enemy, almost a synonym of "becoming a traitor" or "becoming the enemy" (Merle 2003; see also Pirický, this volume). Similar denominations apply in China for new Muslims or people with Arabic names; they are referred to as *maluk melayu*, meaning "they have become Malay" (Ma 2012). Similarly, it was linked to the idea of embracing a foreign culture. For many, choosing Islam means a change in belonging to a community, which involves the learning of a religion and its cultural context, a language, a collective memory, imagination, behaviors, habits, and rituals (Valensi 2000). Moussa, a young journalist in France, testifies, making a retrospective on his life experience: "Back in the days, there was conversion because at the same time as Islam, there was a process of Arabisation [of converts]. Now, people realise it's not accurate, it is more an amendment given that people keep a certain culture" (Moussa, 34, Paris, February 2011). Because of the connotations of the term "convert," volunteers in my study who have chosen Islam do not identify themselves with the "convert" label: "I find it quite stigmatising" (Female, 35, Paris, April 2011); "I am definitely not a convert, although I was not Muslim before, but I don't know other words that can describe my journey" (Male, 24, Saint Denis, 2010). A plethora of self-identifications exists: "embrace Islam," "becoming Muslim," "connected with Islam," or "chose Islam." Through interviews, no consensual definition or expression emerged, but a majority expressed their disapproval of the term "convert." Some argued that, although not perfect, it was the only way to "make people understand." It appears that "convert" is seen as a generic or default term, employed mainly because of its popular use.

The question of the proper term also arises in relation to people who have grown up in a Muslim family but started to practice Islam later in their lives: "I am not a convert, but it is alike, as I was not practising, and at some point in my life, I began to gain interest about Islam" (Male, 35, Paris, 2012). "Meeting my auntie when I came to France at the age of 18 was the beginning of my journey to Islam" (Female, 29, Roissy, 2010). In a discussion about faith, another volunteer from Muslim parents stated that "we are all converts" (Male, 35, Saint Denis, 2010), alluding to the fact that most people in the discussion, although born from Muslim parents, have at one time not been practicing and have experienced a moment in their life when they began to pray or reconnect with the idea of faith and belief.

Myriam François Cerrah, a Muslim public figure in the United Kingdom, wrote a reflection on her blog, urging an end to the use of the word "convert."[3] Her arguments are that "convert" represents an "uncritical approval of Islam" and that the word implies a perpetually "new" dimension of her faith, although she has been practicing for more than ten years. She also reflects on the social—if not political—implications of the concept of conversion in a society and at times when choosing to become Muslim is linked with negative stereotypes of extremism. For her, the word "convert" "delegitimises [my] position by claiming that my adherence to a faith presumed to be regressive in nature necessarily implies my person-hood and views are questionable," and using the word risks "cast[ing] suspicion and doubt over your integrity and respectability." Her argument is that the term "convert" legitimizes the view that choosing Islam is perceived as a form of alienation and is viewed as opposed to modernity, rationality, and to the values of some governments like in France (see also Touraine 1992, Baubérot 2006).

Analyzing personal stories, the narratives on spiritual changes have in common that they are long-term phenomena, ranging from some months to some years, with some yet unfinished: "I started practicing Islam six years ago, and I'm still learning . . . and I think I will never stop until my last breath!" (Male, 26, Paris, February 2010). However, even if they enter a radical and/or extreme form of religiosity aiming to separate themselves from the past, or if they try to erase it, in most cases family bonds cannot be broken and the legacy of the mother culture remains present: "I was born in a French Christian family, I consider my Islam as a continuation of the Christian culture, and I'm planning to open a Halal restaurant serving traditional French meals" (Male, 28, Saint Gratien, 2012). The question of identity becomes crucial, not necessarily for those who embrace Islam, but more for others who don't know in which "box" their friend or children could fit. Some parents talk about their children, saying that they "lost their son/daughter" or that their child "rejects the cultural legacy of the family."[4] This phenomenon is described by Suleiman as a form of "cultural apostasy," a "detrimental expectation that converts needed to give up everything, their culture and their identity, for Allah" (2016: 15). Cultural apostasy is also perceived as the cradle for either religious extremists advocating a complete rejection of Western culture and government policies, as shown by the recurrent public debates around whether it is possible to keep a Muslim identity alongside a "European/French/British identity."

However, many among the Muslim volunteers in this study, whether born from Muslim parents or not, show that Islam is becoming "more of an individual choice rather than an inheritance" (Amiraux 2006). Volunteers interviewed in Poland, even those born to migrant parents, have no problem identifying themselves as "Polish and Muslim at the same time." In the UK, there is a growing trend of a global consciousness, where people, beyond accepting their mixed identities (born in Britain, parents from abroad, fond of a culture mixing European and foreign influences), perceive themselves as "global citizens," "human beings," and "souls" rather than choosing one label over another: "I'm from a working class secular Turkish family. . . . When I got more into religion at the age of 17, it didn't please my family. . . . I don't follow any cults or any *tariqa* [Sufi order], I just consider myself a human being" (Male, 26, London). "I could say I'm British, I'm Bengali, I'm Muslim, I'm a woman, but I would describe my identity as being a bubbly, funny, smiling person" (Female, 29, London). "I'm an earthly being, I only feel at home in my heart" (Female, 30, London). "I'm just a human being loving nature" (Male, 35, London). "I moved from Australia to the Emirates and later to the UK where I embraced Islam. I identify myself as a curious, adventurous, down to earth person" (Female, 35, London). In community hubs such as Rumi's Cave in London, young people from various cultures attend musical events such as hip hop with lyrics inspired by Islam, traditional Arabic *Maqams* or *Qawwalis*, and blues influenced by Sufism played on the guitar (Barylo 2017). Because of the complexity of everyone's identities—some are, for instance, born from Venezuelan parents, African American, Japanese, or Colombian American; some are born from Muslim parents; some are "Muslim since two generations"—their conversations are rarely about who has "embraced Islam" or not. Sometimes, people ask "Were you born Muslim?" or "Are you originally Muslim?" Terms such as "convert" or "heritage Muslims" lose any discursive relevance for the fact that everyone is from a diasporic background: not fitting the mainstream British society, and at the same time not fitting any traditional Muslim community, they are "neither from here, nor from there." If the convert is viewed as a stranger in the mainstream society, it is perhaps also because the very notion of convert actually bears a dimension of otherness or of becoming the other.

CONVERSION: ETYMOLOGY AND CHRISTIAN INFLUENCE

The lexicography and etymology of the term "convert" allude to "transform something in a different thing."[5] To "convert" derivates from the Latin word *conversio*, which means "to turn back." This word derives from the Greek *epistrophê* and/or *metanoïa*. *Epistrophê* means "change of orientation," or "turning back to the origin or to oneself or to the perfect ideal." *Metanoïa* means "change of way of thinking," "to repent," "to be born again," and "to exit a state of perversion and sin" and thus matches the "revert" concept explained above. Focusing on the Christian origin of the term "convert," its first statements are found in the Gospel. The Latin Christian Bible (Vulgate) uses it at some occurrences. For example, in the book of Matthew:

> At that time the disciples came to Jesus and asked, "Who, then, is the greatest in the kingdom of heaven?" He called a little child to him, and placed the child among them. And he said: "Truly I tell you, unless you change [*conversi*] and become like little children, you will never enter the kingdom of heaven. Therefore, whoever takes the lowly position of this child is the greatest in the kingdom of heaven. And whoever welcomes one such child in my name welcomes me" (Matthew 18).

The Latin Vulgate uses the term *conversi,* which has been translated as "change" in verse 3. In the book of Thessalonians, the word expresses the metaphorical abandon of pagan rituals: "They tell how you turned [*conversi*] to God from idols to serve the living and true God" (1 Thessalonians 1:5–9). However, in the Gospel according to Mark, "convert and believe in the Gospel" (Mark 1:15) is a translation of "*paenitemini et credite evangelio.*" Here, *paenitemini* means, literally, "repent." The concept of conversion, in the Christian tradition, denotes a complete change, a turning-back point to the opposite of a previous state, coming along with abandoning the past. This conception may help to understand why families of some people embracing a new faith often react negatively, especially if they hold to the idea that conversion is linked to a "cultural apostasy" as mentioned above. In the Christian Gospel, a particular expression is used in the Gospel according to Luke to describe the spiritual transition of Zaccheus:

> 1 Jesus entered Jericho and was passing through. 2 A man was there by the name of Zacchaeus; he was a chief tax collector and was wealthy. 3 He wanted to see who Jesus was, but because he was short he could not see over the crowd. 4 So he ran ahead and climbed a sycamore-fig tree to see him, since Jesus was coming that way. 5 When Jesus reached the spot, he looked up and said to him, "Zacchaeus, come down immediately. I must stay at your house today." 6 So he came down at once and welcomed him gladly. 7 All the people saw this and began to mutter, "He has gone to be the guest of a sinner." 8 But Zacchaeus stood up and said to the Lord, "Look, Lord! Here and now I give half of my possessions to the poor, and if I have cheated anybody out of anything, I will pay back four times the amount." 9 Jesus said to him, "Today salvation has come to this house, because this man, too, is a son of Abraham. 10 For the Son of Man came to seek and to save the lost" (Luke 19:1–10).

Jesus stated that "this man, too, is a son of Abraham" when Zaccheus started to believe in God, referring to Zaccheus neither as a "former unbeliever," nor as a "new believer," but simply as a status ("son of Abraham"), alluding to one of the common roots shared with Jewish scriptures.

The reference to Abraham leads to an exploration of the concept of spiritual transitions in Judaism. A particular occurrence is found in the book of Ezekiel:

> 30 "Therefore, you Israelites, I will judge each of you according to your own ways, declares the Sovereign Lord. Repent! Turn away from all your

> offences; then sin will not be your downfall. 31 Rid yourselves of all the
> offences you have committed, and get a new heart and a new spirit. Why
> will you die, people of Israel? 32 For I take no pleasure in the death of any-
> one, declares the Sovereign Lord. Repent and live!" (Ezekiel 18: 30–32).

In the Latin Vulgate, the last sentence is translated as: *revertimini et vivite.* How does one call a nonpracticing person who starts attending religious duties at a certain point of his life? The idea explicitly refers to the subjects of Grace Davie's *Belonging without Believing* (2001). Some have suggested the idiom "convert from the inside" as opposed to "convert from the outside" (Hervieu-Léger 2001), but is it possible to "convert" while being already part of a certain tradition or religion? A similar conceptual problem arises when describing an atheist starting to believe in God. The term "convert" appears limited in these regards. Describing conversion as a "half-turn" (Nock 1988) doesn't fit the concept of human identity, which is rather fluid: "Identity is from a sociological point of view just a relative and floating state of things" (Weber 1965: 360). Identity is a process perpetually adjusted according to people's life experiences, as observes S. Vermeersch with volunteers in charities: "Identity is not given once and for all, but is in perpetual construction and renewal" (Vermeersch 2004: 685). Therefore, labeling people as "converts" is either valid for a short amount of time, or has to find an alternative, as per Edgard Morin's definition of identity: "A living being does not have a substantial identity as its substance modifies and transforms itself always" (Morin 1986: 296).

Embracing a new faith is a long-term process. One does and cannot completely leave his or her past behind: No one knows when the transition starts, nor when it finishes; the phenomenon can be described as a *continuum* (Allievi 1998). Thus, it is not a radical process of interior change but an initial event, inducting the process of change that defines the conversion as the creation of an interval (Valensi 2000).

Back to the etymologic roots of "conversion": *conversio*, *metanoia*, and *epistrophê* each express the idea of a radical change with a time "before" and a time "after" the transition, with a sealed boundary between. As explained above, the reality of spiritual changes among the volunteers is not black and white but is rather a long process, full of gray zones defining a long and thorough work of the subject. Moreover, it is a perpetual reconstruction of the mind: new values are acquired as some other values are abandoned. This is a time for self-introspection and intense self-questioning. This process defines new social, personal, moral, and ethical references to achieve a state of equilibrium. As I have shown, Christian literature may reflect some conceptual limitations to capture these processes. Hebrew texts from the *Tanakh* (Old Testament) and Islamic scriptures, however, show a very different perspective on religious change.

GER, *MUALLAF*, AND *ISLAH*

When the Latin Vulgate is translated in the Hebrew language, the term used for "change," "repent," or "convert" is *Hashiv*, which means, literally, "to turn/ to return."[6] Except from prophets who have experienced direct revelation from God, the Jewish scriptures, the *Tanakh*, hardly mention people experiencing spiritual transitions. For example, Genesis mentions "the people that [Abraham and Sarah] had acquired in Harran" (Genesis/Bereshit 12:5), meaning people that have accepted faith. Jethro, Moses's father-in-law, said after leaving Egypt: "Now I know that the Lord is greater than all other gods" (Exodus/Shemot 18:11). Ruth said to Naomi: "Your people will be my people and your God my God" (Ruth 1:16). There is no word qualifying precisely the person who experienced the spiritual transition in the Hebrew *Tanakh* except *ger* (plural: *gerim*), according to commentaries, and specifically with its form *Ger Tsedek*, meaning "the righteous *ger*." *Ger* is an ambivalent word sometimes translated as "stranger." In fact, *ger* derivates from the root *gur*, meaning "to inhabit," "to reside," "to sojourn." The concept of stranger already has a word in Hebrew language: *nokhri*. The Jewish scriptures state that Hebrews were all *gerim* in the land of current Israel: "You will love the *ger* for you have been *gerims* in the Land of Egypt" (Devarim/Deuteronomy 10:19). "A *ger* shalt thou not oppress; for ye know the heart of a *ger*, seeing ye were *gerims* in the land of Egypt" (Exodus/Shemot 23:9). And: "The Lord preserveth the *gerims*" (Psalms 146:9).

The *ger* is the one who moves to settle somewhere else. He is the one who settles in a new home; he is a traveler who does not change himself but changes his homeland, the place of his home. In Judaism, the word does not connote the idea of return but rather the idea of traveling or emigrating. However, the *ger* is anyone who is already part of the land and the society he or she has settled in. Therefore, those who have embraced faith in God are not strangers in Judaism. They are already members of the community of believers. The idea of *ger* has been put forward to get rid of the doubts concerning the legitimacy of new Jews, arising from the *gerim*'s past—if they were polytheists, for instance (Kellner 1991). A newcomer to Judaism (in that case) is not primarily regarded as a "former Christian/Muslim/atheist" but simply as a Jew. However, there is no consensus about who becomes a Jew and how.

Ger may be used to describe "gentiles" or people "friendly" toward Judaism. According to Kellner (1991: 44), a *ger toshav* (or Noahide or "semi-convert") could be a transitional stage on the way to becoming a *ger tzedek* (Hebrew: גר צדק) or "righteous alien," a convert to Judaism. He conjectures that only a full *ger tzedek* would be found at the time of the Messiah. According to some jurisprudence, a *ger toshav* has to accept the Seven Mitzvot (Seven laws of Noah) but is not required to appear before a rabbinical court to become a *ger toshav*. Talking about *gerims* is about moving from a certain point (geographical but on a comprehensive scale also cultural and spiritual) to another location. But the question remains whether the concept of *ger* is relevant for individuals who have grown up in a monotheistic (Jewish) tradition without believing in it. Within Judaism, belief does not necessarily define Jews, but more the lineage (Kellner 1991). However, the concept of *ger* focuses on the current state of the former migrant, who is considered a plain "resident" and thus can be applied to people—whether they were atheists or following other traditions—who choose Judaism. Although people may have moved from a certain belief (or unbelief), the *ger* is considered what they are at the current time. They would say: "My faith resides now in the Jewish/Christian/Islamic, etc. . . . faith" or "My home is the one of the community of believers" or "I reside in Judaism" or etc.

Whereas in Judaism the idea of *ger* is linked to movement and emigration, the idea of choosing Islam in the Qur'an and the *hadiths* belong to the semantics of inner and personal change. In Islam, a substantive term for an individual embracing faith does not exist. In Arabic usage, people adopting the Islamic faith may be understood to enter (*yadkhul*) or embrace (*ya'taniq*) Islam (Suleiman 2013: 21). The substantive "revert" used by the subjects in the fieldwork refers to the concept of *fitra* (the primordial nature of being attracted to God, i.e., as a Muslim). Embracing Islam is thus perceived as going back to this primordial nature. Some Islamic scholars prefer to use the word *Muallaf* from the Arabic *Al-Muallafa Qulūbuhum*, which means "those whose hearts are won over" or "those hearts that need softening" (Bosworth et al. 1993: 254). The term comes from the root وَلَفَ (W-L-F) meaning "to associate," "to combine," "join together," "friend," or "companion." It appears in a verse of the Qur'an about the *zakat* (almsgiving): "Zakāt is for: the poor, the destitute, those who collect it, reconciling people's hearts (*Muallaf*), frees slaves, spending in the way of Allah, and travellers. It is a legal obligation from Allah. Allah is all knowing, all wise" (Qur'an 9:60). However, as the term is not clear, Islamic scholars such as Sheikh al-Qaradawi suggest it can be used for non-Muslims about to embrace Islam (see Ma 2012).

Looking at the etymology of the word "Muslim" may help us understand the concept of embracing Islam in the scriptures. "Muslim" derivates from the word "Islam" itself. Literally, it means "those of Islam." Islam comes from the Arabic root سلم (S-L-M). This root is found in the word سلام *Salaam* (peace). But Islam is different from *Salaam*, so it does not (only) mean peace. Islam does not come from the verb *Istaslama*, إستَسْلَمَ (to surrender), because this comes from a different root. *Islam* is usually translated by "submission" (Lewis and Churchill 2009), but the Arabic language already has a word for submission, which is *Khada'a* خضع in Arabic. A similar word to *Salaam* can be found in Hebrew: *Shalom*. The Hebrew language may shed some light on the meaning of Islam, as *Shalom* (שָׁלוֹם) shares the same linguistic root with سلام *Salaam*. Although also usually translated as "peace," the meaning of the term *Shalom* is not limited to this. The book of Isaiah gives a relevant example: "I form the light, and create darkness; I make [*Shalom*, שָׁלוֹם], and create [*Ra*, the chaos, disorder]; I am the LORD, that doeth all these things" (Isaiah 45: 7).

According to Neil Gillman's (2008: 41) analysis of the verse, it suggests that not only God makes the *Shalom* and the *Ra* as two opposite and distinct entities, but, moreover, he creates them between Light and Darkness. Thus, as peace cannot be made between unanimated entities, there is a deeper meaning, as Gillman explains: "This enables us to translate *shalom* not as the conventional 'peace,' but rather 'completeness,' 'harmony,' or simply 'cosmos,' and *ra* as its opposite, 'chaos.'" In Islamic scriptures, Islam does not refer to an organized religion or belief but as a concept present since the creation of the universe. In the Qur'an, animated and unanimated creatures do follow originally Islam:

> Do they seek for other than the Religion of God?-while all creatures in the heavens and on earth have, willing or unwilling, bowed [*aslama* in Arabic] to His Will (Accepted Islam), and to Him shall they all be brought back (Qur'an 3:83).

Also, in the Qur'an Abraham is described as a Muslim (Qur'an 2: 131) in the sense that he "has surrendered [*Aslama*] to the Lord of the Worlds." Here, *aslama* is rather the equivalent of being "subordinate" as from the Latin *sub+ordinare*, "set in order." By extension, the whole creation is perceived as subordinated, willing or not, by default to universal laws God has set the world with, like the laws of physics or chemistry. The creation thus belongs to a certain order, a symbiosis, a balance, or a harmony, referring to the terms of Gillman's analysis. Therefore, there is no idea of submission. Submission means literally "to yield or surrender (oneself) to the will or authority of another"[7] with the idea of a superior will or force,[8] and denotes the idea of violence. Moreover, the idea of submission would be opposed to one fundamental principle of Islam that there is "no compulsion in religion" (Qur'an 2: 256). Therefore, embracing Islam consciously would be to make oneself willingly part of the fundamental harmony of the world set originally by God, as defined by the Abrahamic religions, and thus trying to safeguard the fragile balance of forces. This is an idea found in the Qur'an where the human being is called the *Khalifat* of God on earth (Qur'an 2: 30), meaning the bailee, the agent, the delegate, the entrusted of God on earth—and thus in the duty of safekeeping the creation. Accordingly, defining a "Muslim," literally *Mu-Slimûn*, the following translation can be suggested as "those of the harmony," or "those responsible for harmony."

Looking more closely into the Qur'an, one can find a word that may describe a spiritual transition. Its transliteration *Islah* is usually translated as "amendment" or "betterment." Below are some occurrences of the word *Islah* and its derivates, as translated in English: "But if the thief repents after his crime, and amends his conduct, Allah turneth to him in forgiveness; for Allah is Oft-forgiving, Most Merciful" (Qur'an 5: 39). "Unless they repent thereafter and mend (their conduct); for God is Oft-Forgiving, Most Merciful" (Qur'an 24: 5). "He [God] said: 'O my people! See ye whether I have a Clear (Sign) from my Lord, and He hath given me sustenance (pure and) good as from Himself? I wish not, in opposition to you, to do that which I forbid you to do. I only desire (your) *betterment* to the best of my power; and my success (in my task) can only come from God. In Him I trust, and unto Him I look'" (Qur'an 11: 88).

To "amend" something means either "to improve; change for the better" or "to remove faults from; or to correct."[9] Because it is free from any time frame, and does not refer to any particular belief, the concept of amendment can be applied to a wide range of cases. The concept fits well for describing people who move from a particular religion to another; people who did not believe and then started to believe; and people born and raised within a particular religion who start practicing at some point in their life. The English word "amendment" is not linked to any spiritual frame of reference and thus shows an interesting flexibility for describing changes in beliefs, culture, or behaviors, especially at times when more people don't identify themselves with precise religious or spiritual movements (Davie 2001). Along with the idea of *ger*, these concepts avoid any time scale and landmarks such as "before," "after," "beginning," and "end," as it has simply no precise beginning and no end, making it a potential alternative to the previously analyzed concepts revolving around the idea of "conversion" or "reversion."

However, they pose other limitations: On a linguistic level, is it possible to adapt *ger* or *Islah* to Latin languages or others, as they cannot be translated faithfully with only one word? On a functional level, is it possible to replace the old concept of "conversion" in popular culture and the social sciences? Although the question of individual religion and spirituality is becoming more and more complex, the term "convert" remains a simple but efficient way for expressing the change of religious affiliation that is understood by most. How is it possible to find an effective all-around substantive term for "people who have changed their religion," "people who started to believe" or people who "reconnected with their tradition"? These questions remain open, but in the meantime, perhaps the best alternative remains to clearly define the terms used to describe persons and their spiritual orientation or journey.

CONCLUSION

My research among volunteers in France, Poland, and the UK showed that the term "convert" is not a consensual word with which they would choose to define themselves. The term is mainly used as a generic or default word because of the popular usage. However, looking at its etymology, and how the concept has been coined and defined by its Latin Christian legacy, it does not fit accurately in the social and psychological reality experienced by the interlocutors.

Their journey is more of a transit between spiritual and cultural frames of references, as per the Latin word *transire*, meaning "to cross," "to depart," "to leave," or "to be transferred." One does not simply abandon a previous tradition or belief, but only parts of it, and one also acquires new elements of references. There is no clear distinction between "before" and "after," and there is no absolute rejection of a past identity (even if rejected, it is not total) but rather the construction of a new one. Even settled in a particular frame of reference or religion, people are pursuing their journey and are continuously evolving. Whatever the background of the person, one has the ability to change in one direction or another or even to reverse the change. These ideas are intimately connected to one's identities—how they define themselves and, at the same time, how others define them. Therefore, they are traveling between multiple and complex sets of identities. Edgar Morin's theory (1986) understands cultures and identities as complex systems perpetually mixing with each other and building each other from one another. Likewise, humanity is continuously amending itself (in a certain way) and perpetually settling into new spiritual or philosophical, cultural, and spiritual realms. In that sense, the concepts of *ger* (the settled stranger) and *Islah* (amendment) both offer original and perhaps better alternatives to describe these transitions, going beyond the limited semantics of Latin languages and avoiding ethnocentric biases when analyzing social or psychological phenomena belonging to other cultural areas.

This chapter does not suggest using one word instead of another but rather offers an overview and a discussion of the concepts currently in use. First, the idea of "conversion" appears too limited to describe the array of various spiritual journeys, such as people who were not believing and start to believe, or people reconnecting to the religious tradition of their parents. Second, this same term does not describe accurately the progressive process of change, in which people do not necessarily do a U-turn from one tradition to another. Third, alternative terms such as "revert" or *Muallaf*, which stem from the Muslim subjects, pose either problems of subjectivity or translation, which makes them difficult to use outside of their context. Finally, exploring the idea of religious change in Judaism and Islam offers the terms of *ger* and *Islah*, which are free from any time or space frame and translate the idea of transition efficiently.

Still, these findings show some limitations. How is it possible to translate *ger* or *Islah* or to find an adjective or a noun from these terms? Would an expression as "amended to Islam" replace the old term of "converted"? Using the concept of amendment, is it possible to simply not label the subjects and consider them in a transitional state? An alternate option would be—pursuing the idea of *ger*—perhaps to consider every subject according to one's own current subjective perception. Myriam François Cerrah ends her article with: "Today? I'm just Muslim thanks." Then, perhaps a consensual option would be to say that people do not "convert" but "amend" themselves, becoming a Muslim, a Christian, a Jew, a Sikh, a Hindu, or an atheist, coming from a certain background and moving on a particular spiritual journey.

NOTES

1. The choice for a particular translation of the sacred texts is a difficult one, especially regarding the Qur'anic text. This chapter focuses mainly on the etymology of very specific words in a translingual perspective but always starts from the original language of the texts. The purpose of this chapter is to discuss the analysis of the meanings of these specific terms around the concept of conversion and spiritual transitions, which are generally similar across the different translations. The translation I have chosen, the Abdullah Yusuf Ali version, is the most popular translation across the world and considered a "safe" option by most contemporary religious scholars. However, it serves only as a tool to put these terms in the context of a whole verse, and this work does not hold the

translation as a reference point; the same principle goes for the translations of the other scriptures. For further discussion, I invite the reader to read Khaleel Mohammed's objective comparison of the main existing translations available at www.meforum.org/717/assessing-english-translations-of-the-quran.

2. Sahih Bukhari: vol. 2, bk. 23, no. 441.

3. myriamfrancoiscerrah.wordpress.com/2013/06/15/dont-call-me-a-convertrevert.

4. Author interviews with parents, 2009–2013.

5. *Collins English Dictionary—Complete and Unabridged.* © HarperCollins Publishers 1991, 1994, 1998, 2000, 2003.

6. See *Amplified Bible*, online edition, www.biblegateway.com.

7. *The American Heritage Dictionary of the English Language*, 4th ed. Boston: Houghton Mifflin. Updated 2009.

8. *Collins English Dictionary.*

9. *Collins English Dictionary.*

REFERENCES

A Hebrew-English Bible, according to the Masoteric text, and the 1917 JPS edition.

Amiraux, V. 2006. "Speaking as a Muslim: Avoiding Religion in French Public Space." In *Politics of Visibility. Young Muslims in European Public Spaces.* Gerdien Jonker and Valérie Amiraux, eds. Bielefeld: Transcript Verlag.

Amplified Bible. Amplified and New International version, online version. www.biblegateway.com.

Allievi, S. 1998. *Les convertis à L'Islam: les nouveaux musulmans d'Europe.* Paris: L'Harmattan.

Barylo, W. 2017. *Young Muslim Change-Makers.* London: Routledge.

Baubérot, J. 2006. *L'intégrisme républicain contre la laïcité.* Paris: Éditions de l'Aube.

Bosworth, C. E., et al., eds. 1993. *The Encyclopaedia of Islam: Mughais-Muhammad/Fascicule* (Encyclopaedia of Islam New Edition), vol. 7. Leiden: Brill Academic.

Davie, G. 2002. *Europe—The Exceptional Case: Parameters of Faith in the Modern World.* Sarum Theological Lectures. London: Darton, Longman & Todd.

Gillman, N. 2008. *Doing Jewish Theology: God, Torah, and Israel in Modern Judaism.* Woodstock, VT: Jewish Lights Publishing.

Hefner, R. 1993. *Conversion to Christianity.* Berkeley: University of California Press.

Hervieu-Léger, D. 2001. *Le Pèlerin et le converti, la religion en mouvement.* Paris: Flammarion.

Kellner, M. 1991. *Maimonides on Judaism and the Jewish people.* Menachem, SUNY Series in Jewish Philosophy. Albany: State University of New York Press.

Lewis, B. E., and B. E. Churchill. 2009. *Islam: The Religion and the People.* Philadelphia: Wharton School Publishing.

Lofland J., and N. Skonovd 1981. "Conversion Motifs." *Journal for the Scientific Study of Religion* 20, no. 4 (December 1981): 373–385.

Ma, R. 2012. "Being Chinese in Malaysia." In *Malaysian Chinese: Recent Developments and Prospects*. Lee Hock Guan and Leo Suryadinata, eds. Singapore: ISEAS Publishing. 26–44.

Merle, A. 2003. *Le miroir Ottoman: Une image politique des hommes dans la littérature géographique espagnole et française (XVIe–XVIIe Siècles)*. Paris: Presses de l'Université de Paris-Sorbonne.

Morin, E. 1986. *La méthode: La vie de la Vie*. Paris: Seuil.

Nock, A. D. 1988. *Conversion: The Old and the New in Religion from Alexander the Great to Augustine of Hippo*. Baltimore: Johns Hopkins University Press.

Qur'an. Trans. Abdullah Yusuf Ali, online edition: www.altafsir.com.

Rambo, L. 1996. *Understanding Religious Conversion*. New Haven: Yale University Press.

Suleiman, Y. 2013. *Narratives of Conversion to Islam—Female Perspectives*. Cambridge: Prince Alwaleed Bin Talal Centre of Islamic Studies.

Suleiman, Y. 2016. *Narratives of Conversion to Islam—Male Perspectives*. Cambridge: Prince Alwaleed Bin Talal Centre of Islamic Studies.

Touraine, A. 1992. *Critique de la Modernité*. Paris: Fayard.

Travisano, R. V. 1970. "Alternation and Conversion as Qualitatively Different Transformations." In *Social Psychology Through Symbolic Interaction*. G. P. Stone and H. A. Farberman, eds. Waltham, MA: Ginn-Blaisdell. 594–606.

Valensi, L. 2000. *Paroles d'islam, Relations intercommunautaires et changements d'affiliation religieuse au Moyen-Orient au XVIIIè et XIXè siècles*. Paris: Maisonneuve & Larose.

Van Nieuwkerk, K. 2006. "'Islam Is Your Birthright.' Conversion, Reversion, and Alternation: The Case of New Muslimas in the West." In *Cultures of Conversion*. J. Bremmer, W. Van Bekkum, and A. Molendik, eds. Leuven: Peeters.

Vermeersch S. 2004. *Entre individualisation et participation: l'engagement associatif bénévole. Revue Française de Sociologie* 45, no. 4: 681–710.

Wieviorka, M. 2000. *La différence*. Paris: Balland.

TWO

MOVING IN OR MOVING TOWARD?

Reconceptualizing Conversion to Islam as a Liminal Process[1]

JULIETTE GALONNIER

The ceremony of conversion to Islam is well established and codified. It entails reciting three times in a row the profession of faith (or *shahada*)[2] in front of Muslim witnesses. This parsimonious ceremonial can be preceded by a ritual bath (*ghusl*), which involves a full body-washing and the performing of *wudu'* (ritual ablution required before prayer). As it is framed by the Islamic tradition, the *shahada* constitutes a rite of passage: it marks out the entry of an individual into Islam and delineates the state of non-Muslimness from that of Muslimness.

This is at least the role it is expected to perform in theory. What happens in practice and in the minds of individuals seems much more complex and ambiguous, as exemplified by Boran's story.

Boran is a 35-year-old American man of Cambodian descent. He came to the US as a child in the early 1980s after surviving the Cambodian killing fields and grew up in a disadvantaged neighborhood of New York. As a teenager, Boran was heavily involved in hip hop music and deejayed at various parties. At age 17, weary of that lifestyle, he started looking for religion. First acquainted with the teachings of the Nation of Islam and the Five Percenters[3] through hip-hop lyrics, he discovered Sunni Islam through a Muslim storeowner who lived a couple of blocks away from his high school. After being initiated to the fundamentals of Islam, Boran decided to become Muslim. Yet, he is confused about the exact moment he did so:

> [The storeowner] started teaching me *Al-Fatiha* [first chapter of the Qur'an]. We read the Qur'an together. He would teach me bits of the alphabet. He would tell me stories from the *hadith*. And then, there were times when he would just close the store and say "let's pray together. Let me teach you how to make *wudu'*." So we did all these things and I took my *shahada* technically with him first. And then one day he said "you know we need to go to the *masjid* [mosque] for *jum'a* [Friday congregational prayer]." I went with

> him and then, I took my *shahada* again there. But I didn't know that day that I was already Muslim at that point. You know I didn't know by taking my *shahada* with him, that I had already become Muslim. I was already praying, we made *wudu'*, I thought I was still learning about it. I thought it was only official when you took *shahada* in a public forum with the imam.

Boran does not know for sure the exact date he became formally Muslim. His story raises questions for the study of conversion to Islam: What constitutes conversion? What exactly marks the entry into Islam? Is it when one reaches the inner conviction that Islam is the truth? Is it when one utters the words of the profession of faith? Is it when one performs the conversion ceremony in front of a Muslim audience and is recognized as Muslim by fellow coreligionists? Is it when one starts practicing Islam?

The purpose of this chapter is certainly not to provide definite answers to these questions. These are highly complex issues that belong more to the theological realm than to social sciences and raise a number of normative implications that largely supersede the scope of this contribution. What I intend to do is rather to examine the range of answers Muslim converts themselves give to these questions. More specifically, I explore in this chapter how converts relate to the rite of passage that is the *shahada*. Relying on in-depth interviewing with eighty-two converts to Islam in France and the United States as

FIGURE 2.1.
A typical conversion ceremony.
Credit: Abd al Malik (2014). Screenshot from the movie Qu'Allah bénisse la France *(2014), which describes the spiritual journey of the French rapper of Congolese descent Abd Al Malik. In this picture, he recites his* shahada *in a small prayer room, in front of two Muslim witnesses.*

well as ethnographic observations in convert associations, I investigate how converts determine and make sense of the moment they entered Islam. By shedding light on the variety of meanings they ascribe to the act of "moving in," I demonstrate that the entry into Islam is blurrier and fuzzier than what the ritual of the *shahada* suggests.

MOVING IN AND MOVING TOWARD

In order to investigate the meanings that converts ascribe to the *shahada* in their religious journey, I contrast two strands of the literature: scholarship that focuses on the social meaning of "rites of passage" (or "rites of institution") and scholarship that conceptualizes conversion as a gradual process rather than a dramatic change.

Moving in

Unlike Christian understandings of conversion, the *shahada* is not considered "the terminal point where one may say 'I am saved'" (Woodberry 1992: 34). Becoming nominally Muslim through the act of conversion does not ensure redemption and deliverance, which, in line with the orthoprax nature of Islam, can be attained only through devout practice and good deeds. Reciting the *shahada* is merely the outward and formal means through which one enters Islam and joins the *ummah*, or the global community of Muslims. As understood by the Islamic tradition, therefore, the *shahada* is not a ritual of salvation but rather a change in one's social identity (Mossière 2007). It is a procedure of public recognition whereby the individual is accepted as Muslim by coreligionists.

As such, it is best characterized as a rite of passage (Van Gennep 1960 [1909]) or a rite of institution (Bourdieu 1982), that is, a rite during which the individual moves from one specific social position to another. Van Gennep defines rites of passage as "rites which accompany every change of place, state, social position and age" (cited in Turner 1967: 94). Ceremonies that he identifies as similar in nature escort individuals as they move across various life thresholds (birth, puberty, marriage, death, travel, entry into a profession, etc.). Van Gennep is particularly interested in the sequencing of those rites, which are systematically divided into three distinct phases: *a phase of separation* whereby individuals detach themselves from their earlier social position; *an intervening liminal phase* during which individuals pass through an in-between, ambiguous cultural realm; and *a phase of reincorporation* during

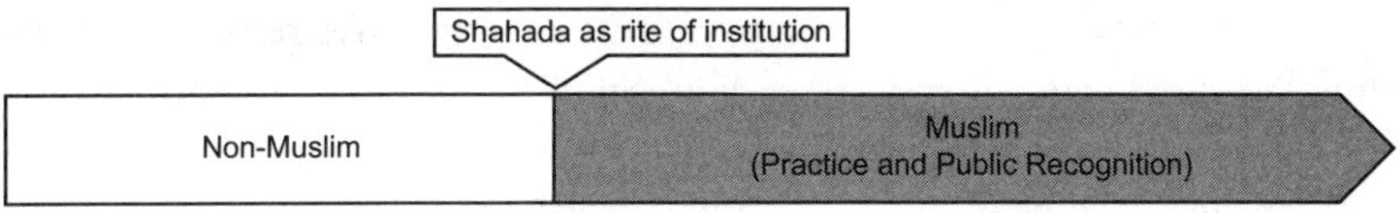

FIGURE 2.2.
The shahada *as rite of institution.*

which the passage is fully enacted. By embracing a new religion, converts cross a threshold. They leave their earlier social positions and become ex-Christians, ex-Jews, ex-Hindus, or ex-atheists (Ebaugh 1988). This exit puts them into a liminal phase, which lasts until they are fully recognized as Muslims.

Bourdieu extended Van Gennep's theory by shifting attention from the description of rites to their actual social function. In doing so, Bourdieu renamed rites of passage "rites of institution," highlighting the fact that they consecrate and institute a new status for the individual. According to Bourdieu, rites of institution, such as circumcision or the attribution of titles, separate a "before" and an "after." They consist of "sanctioning and sanctifying a difference by making it exist as a social difference, known and recognized as such by the agent invested and everyone else" (Bourdieu 1982: 59). For Bourdieu, rites of institution are acts of "social magic" in the sense that they produce difference ex nihilo. They possess symbolic efficacy by "signify[ing] to someone what he is and how he should conduct himself as a consequence" (Bourdieu 1982: 60). This consideration is in line with theories on the power of rituals (Bell 1992; Douglas 2009 [1966]). In his study of conversion rituals across the Mediterranean during antiquity, Finn (1990) also states that, after going through the conversion ritual, "one's values and conduct had to change."

As described in the Islamic tradition, the *shahada* can therefore be characterized as a rite of institution. By instituting the individual as a Muslim, it modifies the social perception that fellow Muslims have of them. It also encourages the individual to act as per their new status by practicing Islam seriously. The ritual of the *shahada* is alleged to produce discontinuity: it separates Muslims from non-Muslims and delineates practice from nonpractice.

Moving toward

Contrasting with this narrative of discontinuity, sociological and anthropological accounts of conversion have tended to emphasize the continuous nature of religious change. Several scholars have proposed to conceptualize conversion as a *process* (Straus 1979; Greil and Rudy 1983) and even as a *career*

(Richardson 1978; Gooren 2010: 43–52) that stretches over time and largely supersedes the ceremony of conversion. Straus argues that "the act of conversion is not a terminal act" (1979: 163). Rambo and Farhadian also write that "authentic conversion is an ongoing process of transformation. The initial change, while crucial, is a first step in a long trajectory of transformation" (1999: 32). In short, what matters for these scholars is not so much the decision to convert or the conversion ceremony itself but rather how converts progressively solidify religious dispositions. Conversion is portrayed as a process of accomplishment, rather than a fait accompli.

Scholars working on conversion to Islam specifically have come to similar conclusions. Jensen explores how converts learn to become Muslim, emphasizing that conversion to Islam is "a gradual process of change and transformation" (2006: 645). Galonnier and De los Rios (2016) also propose to reconceptualize religious conversion as a time-consuming learning process. As for McGinty, she writes that "the process of becoming Muslim, is neither final nor predictable. When the self is becoming, there are no sudden breaks or absolute changes; it is gradual" (2006: 188). Van Nieuwkerk (2014) equates conversion to Islam with the "construction of a pious Muslim self" and writes that "conversion does not stop at the moment of embracing Islam .... It requires the embodiment of new social and religious practices" (Van Nieuwkerk 2014: 681). Similarly, in his ethnography of Muslim converts in Missouri, Daniel Winchester finds that "converts understood practices such as prayer and fasting as central to the ongoing development of their new moral selves" (2008: 1755).

In understanding the process of conversion, therefore, these scholars do not limit themselves to the act of converting but also focus on the conversion career initiated by this very act. They relativize the significance of the instituting rite of conversion, which is merely a labeling moment, and put the emphasis on embodied, daily religious practices as the true locus of self-transformation. They talk of "converting persons" rather than "converts," for the learning of a new religion is a drawn-out process that starts (rather than ends) with the conversion ceremony.

There is therefore a marked difference between the literature on rites of institution that emphasizes the radical transformative power of conversion rituals and the literature on religious conversion that promotes a more gradual and processual understanding of change. The contrast between these two approaches is best illustrated by the expressions "moving in" and "moving toward." Whereas the former implies a marked separation between a "before" and an "after" symbolizing the entry into Islam, the latter suggests that converting to Islam is a convoluted process that does not boil down to a discontinuous rite of passage. Both approaches are important and interesting. This chapter combines them in order to investigate Muslim converts' relationships to time and change. What significance do converts assign to the specific moment of the *shahada* within their larger religious trajectory? Does the ritual bring about the conversion it signifies? In other words, do converts conceptualize their conversion as an *act* of "moving in" or as a *process* of "moving toward"? Upon talking to my interviewees, I realized that the *shahada* was endowed with a wide range of forms, contents, senses, and textures. After presenting my research methods, I explore the diversity of styles that the ritual of conversion can take. I then examine the variety of meanings embedded in that ritual and whether it constitutes a significant temporal landmark for converts. Finally, I investigate the aftermath of the *shahada* and whether it induced significant status changes for converts. I conclude with a reflection on the centrality of the concept of "liminality" to account for the conversion experience.

METHODS

My research relies on a qualitative strategy and builds on multiple sources. The data for this chapter comes from an ethnographic and interview study conducted in the United States from January 2013 to April 2014 and in France from April 2014 to January 2016.[4]

I conducted forty semistructured interviews with Muslim converts in the United States and forty-two in France. I recruited informants through snowball sampling, but the absence of reliable statistics on Muslim converts makes it difficult to assess the representativeness of my sample. My interviewees were between 19 and 74 years old, with a mean of 30 years old. I interviewed men and women in equal numbers. Even though most of my respondents can be classified as white (n=19 in the US, n=34 in France), I also interviewed converts from other ethnoracial backgrounds.[5] I sought interviewees from various communities, following different theological orientations (Sunnis and Shiʿas; conservatives and liberals; Sufis, Salafis, and mainstream Muslims), but Sunni mainstream Muslims largely predominate in my sample. I diversified my field inquiry by conducting research in several cities: Chicago (n=26), St. Louis (n=6), and Detroit (n=8) in the United States; Paris (n=24), Lille (n=11), and Marseille (n=7) in France. Contrary to dominant media and cultural representations, which tend to portray Muslim converts as extremist/unstable individuals, my respondents work stable jobs: there are a lot of students, engineers, nurses, academics, and accountants in my sample. In terms of conversion motives, my sample features both the "rational" and "relational" ideal-types identified by Stefano Allievi (1998: 94),[6] although "rational" itineraries of conversion tend to predominate. Interviews lasted between one and four hours and were audio-recorded and transcribed.

I supplemented this interview data with ethnographic observations among convert support groups in both countries. In the United States, I worked with an organization called American Daʿwah,[7] which caters to the needs of American converts who express a need for guidance and feel spiritually disoriented or socially "out of place" in conventional Muslim religious spaces. Born Muslims wishing to recommit to their religion after a period of disengagement are also welcome. There, I attended monthly discussion groups (covering a wide range of topics such as "how to tell your family about your conversion," "how to practice Islam in the workplace," and "finding your place in the community") as well as the weekly "New Muslim" class, which was taught by John, a white convert in his thirties. The class was aimed at teaching converts strong fundamentals about Islam as well as offering a safe space in which they could share their struggles. Most students were new Muslims who had converted a couple of months or years before. They were young, in their twenties or thirties, and were also educated for the most part.

In France, I worked with an association called Bienvenue en Islam, which provides help, support, and a community network to new Muslims. Less endowed financially than its American counterpart, the association organized "monthly chats" with the president of the association, an older French woman who converted to Islam several decades ago. Converts went there to discuss their journey, share their doubts, and meet new people. The association also organized women's gatherings, monthly conferences, and small parties to celebrate Muslim religious festivals. Most attendees were recent converts and came from various social backgrounds.

SHAHADA STYLES

In the following lines, I describe the diversity of "*shahada* styles" and demonstrate that conversion ceremonies form a continuum ranging from the most codified and community-oriented ones to the most individualistic and personalized. I classify these styles of *shahada* into two broad categories, taken from David Riesman's classical study (1950: 23–25):

- Other-directed types are characterized by a "need for approval and direction from others." The *shahada* is performed in front of people whose validation matters.

- Inner-directed types, by contrast, rely on converts' "internal gyroscope and piloting." Converts accomplish the *shahada* on their own, in the solitude of their soul: loneliness is embraced as the true locus of religious authenticity, without regard to the social character of instituting rites.

Other-directed shahadas

Community-oriented. Several respondents took their *shahada* in the classical sense of the term. They decided to go to a mosque or religious organization and pronounced the testimony of faith in front of an imam and lay members of the congregation. Adèle, a 29-year-old white woman working as a banker in Marseille, went to the mosque with her close Muslim friend and pronounced the *shahada* in front of the imam after a short conversation on the basic tenets of Islam. He invited her to recite it again the following Friday, in front of the entire congregation, and explained: "This is not mandatory. That won't make you more Muslim than you are right now but it is just a way to introduce you to the community, to help you meet people." Adèle, therefore, took her *shahada* twice. The second time, she recalled that "it was really moving in the sense that everybody was there. There were hundreds of people and they all congratulated me." Some interviewees remembered their entry into Islam as exhilarating. Pablo, a 22-year-old black and Latino student from Chicago, decided to take his *shahada* during *laylat-al-qadr*, a particularly intense Ramadan night of worship during which mosques typically register the largest attendance: "I told the *sheikh*: 'I want to convert to Islam.' He said 'are you serious? Right now?' He was so excited! And he is like 'oh my God, people are going to go crazy tonight!' . . . And the whole mosque went crazy. . . . People were crying, I was crying! It was one of the most emotional moments in my life." In some instances, the conversion ceremony is also used to strengthen the bonds of the group. One evening after a discussion group at American Da'wah, Debora, a young white woman, expressed the desire to take her *shahada*. John, the main organizer, enthusiastically fulfilled her demand but added a collective dimension to the ritual by asking everybody to repeat the words along with her. Sitting in the center of the room and surrounded by the group, Debora was pronouncing the Arabic words quietly. Her voice, however, was almost inaudible, covered by the exclamations of the group, which repeated the sentence three times, in perfect unison. John managed to transform Debora's personal rite of passage into a moment of collective effervescence. The objective here is to remind Muslims of their duties toward new converts and to show converts that a whole community is standing behind them. The emphasis is placed on the institutional and collective dimension of the *shahada*, which performs its social role as a rite of institution.

Friends and family-oriented. Yet some converts opted for a more relaxed and intimate conversion ceremony. Many organized a party and turned the event into a friendly gathering. Sonam, a young American medical student of Indian descent who used to come very often to the activities organized by American Daʿwah, created a Facebook event and invited many of her friends. Her friend Lisa, a convert too, brought what she called a "*shahada* cake" with *happy shahada* written on it. Before Sonam pronounced the testimony of faith, each of the attendees said a couple of nice words about her personality. After the ceremony, all her friends hugged her and ate food together. In this type of ceremony, the emphasis is put on sharing a nice moment with loved ones in order to mark the occasion. The main objective is for friends and family to acknowledge a significant biographical change in the convert's life. In fact, as mentioned by Noémie, a 27-year-old Parisian housewife, "ceremony" is a big word to describe the small gathering that she put together to make her religious change public. The ceremony is neither institutional nor intimidating. It rather feels like a housewarming party or a baby shower.

Witness-oriented. By contrast, some respondents simply fulfilled the basic conditions required for conversion to be valid and did not strive to make the event friendly or memorable. Caroline, a 28-year-old PhD student of mixed descent living in Marseille, embraced Islam when she was in high school. This is how she describes the moment she converted:

> I told my female friends: "Tomorrow morning, you will come with your ablutions and me too, and I will recite in front of you right before the history class." And this is how we planned it! But one of them didn't arrive on time and the history class was about to start so I told another girl who was sitting there: "what about you, don't you want to be my witness? Do you still have your ablutions?" She said "yes." I told her "OK, good, you are going to stand here and listen to me." And here you go. I recited the sentence and that was it.

Caroline performed her *shahada* quickly, in the hallway of her high school, between her mathematics and history classes. She just wanted to get it done. Emiliano, a 28-year-old student of South American descent living in Paris, also reported that his *shahada* was really odd: during the period when he was still learning about Islam, he went to the hairdresser. As he was getting his hair cut while reading a book about Islam, one of the hairdresser's Muslim friends showed up. Amused, he asked Emiliano to repeat after him the testimony of faith in Arabic, thinking Emiliano did not know the actual meaning of the words. Emiliano, perfectly aware of what was going on, went along and effectively recited the *shahada* in front of two witnesses: "So yeah, that's when I did it. It is a bit quirky." Emiliano's *shahada*, in sum, was based on both a joke and a misunderstanding. There was nothing majestic or emotionally powerful about it, but it can be considered as "valid" from a strictly formal standpoint. Several converts in my sample also recited their *shahada* over the phone with an imam. When they hung up, they found themselves alone in their apartment, aware that they had just done something important but disconcerted by the dryness and simplicity of the ritual. In those examples, converts performed the ceremony's very basic requirements. They were preoccupied only with becoming Muslim in the strict sense of the term. Many ended the description with a simple "You know, that was it," emphasizing the short and modest character of the event.

Inner-directed shahadas *and autonomous conversions*

In each of the three ceremonial styles exposed above, the minimum conditions were met for the *shahada* to be effective in the orthodox acceptance of the term. Yet some converts did things differently and created a ritual on their own. A significant number performed the *shahada* without any witness. These converts do not consider the *shahada* as a rite of institution but rather as a private commitment to God. The collective dimension of conversion is bypassed, and the covenant takes place only between the individual and the divine. Public recognition is perceived as superfluous and embarrassing, as expressed by Melissa, a 27-year-old Parisian white woman working in a Muslim organization:

> My conversion was a bit special. I didn't convert at the mosque. For me, that was out of the question. The idea of finding myself in front of all these people whom I don't know, red-faced in front of everybody. Really, that was beyond me. I said to myself, "If I convert, it will be at home, chilling. It is between *me and God and no one else*."

No one was invited to witness and vouch for Melissa's religious transformation. Like her, a sizeable part of my sample (fifteen people, or 20 percent) performed the *shahada* by themselves. Conversion to Islam is understood here as a reorientation of the soul (Nock 1933), or a change of heart (Heirich 1977), but not a change in social identity. What matters is that the ritual of conversion makes sense to the individual and aligns with their inner feelings and convictions. This is best exemplified by the story of Blandine, a 25-year-old Parisian white woman working as a music teacher, who embraced Islam after a first conversion to evangelical Christianity. Emphasizing the continuity between the Christian and Muslim faith traditions, Blandine crafted her own conversion ritual, mixing elements from both religions:

> When I was told that [the *shahada*] was "there is no god but God and Muhammad is His Prophet," I was like "huh … yeah … it is a bit too obvious! Can't we do a bit more than that?" [laughs] . . . So I told to myself: "I am going to do a Muslim baptism!" [laughs] I did not want to just pronounce the *shahada*, it was too simple. I wanted to say it but I wanted to add other things to emphasize the link between the Bible and the Qur'an. So I took a verse from the Qur'an that cites all prophets and I added that. I also added a prayer where I talk about the meaning of purification through water, how it washes your sins away. So I made something up for myself and then I said to myself, "I can't bring all this to an imam! He is not going to understand a thing! So forget about the imam, I will do it on my own." Then I could have done it with witnesses. I could have found friends to do it; it wouldn't have been a problem. But I just wanted it to be between me and God. So I did that in my bathroom, alone. I used the bathtub for the purification through water, I recited my stuff with the *shahada* in it, and there you go, I was converted.

The converts described above consider the traditional, standardized *shahada* ritual unsatisfactory and displayed a great sense of inventiveness in crafting their own conversion ceremony. Although their do-it-yourself rituals significantly departed from orthodox acceptance of the testimony of faith, they saw themselves as Muslim after performing them. In some cases, the choice for an individual conversion took almost militant overtones and strongly aligned with a rhetoric of religious individualism. For instance, Mark, a 31-year-old unemployed white man living in Chicago, told me: "People say, 'You've got to publicly profess it.' But I mean you can publicly profess anything, and not be sincere about it. I mean you can do it just for the looks. . . . I was by myself, it made sense to me. It wasn't like I needed this huge ceremony and the 5 minutes of popularity! Because I know what I am, I know what I believe." Inner-directed converts see themselves as self-sufficient regarding religious matters. To use the words of the French sociologist Danièle Hervieu-Léger (1999: 181), the regime of mutual or community validation of belief gives way to a regime of self-validation. Their entry into the sacred is personal and intimate; the authenticity and legitimacy of their conversion relies exclusively on their own subjectivity.[8] This clearly goes against accepted understandings of rites of passage, which need to be sanctioned by the group.

SHAHADA MEANINGS

The variety of *shahada* styles outlined above matches the equally great variety of meanings that converts ascribe to their conversion ceremony. While, for some, it represented a clear temporal rupture from their previous life as non-Muslims, for others it was an insignificant formality that did not correspond to the actual moment they became Muslim. I find that other-directed ceremonial styles usually embody a relationship to time and change that is discontinuous, whereas inner-directed ones intersect with more continuous and progressive experiences of religious time.

The shahada *as ritual climax*

December 27, 2013, 1:15 a.m. A 23-year-old MBA student living in Paris, Jean remembers exactly the moment he recited his *shahada*. During our interview, he recalled the steps leading up to it, explaining that he used to be a devout Catholic who would often participate in heated theological debates with his Muslim friends. After losing a number of arguments, he started questioning his faith and decided to investigate Islam in further depth. For a long time, however, he retained doubts and hesitations and refused to convert. Until that night of December 27:

> I was in the bus and started reading the Qur'an. And I reached a passage that talked about hypocrites . . . and their punishment. These people are going to catch hell! And I told to myself, "But this is me right here! If I die now, I will be on the wrong side!" So I read the entire verse. . . . I closed the Qur'an, I went home, and took my *shahada*.

Jean retains clear memories of the instant he uttered the profession of faith. He remembers it as the moment he stopped being a hypocrite destined for hell and started being a sincere believer. For Jean, December 27, 2013, 1:15 a.m. marks a milestone, a rupture between a "before" and an "after." Like

Jean, most converts know the exact date of their conversion, and some even celebrate every year their "Shahadaversary" or "Muslimversary." For some, the date of the conversion ceremony operates as a landmark that granted them a fresh start in life. Denyse, a 58-year-old African American IT services employee in Chicago, struggled with smoking addiction, severe weight issues, loneliness, and depression before embracing Islam, and she talked at length about the all transforming power of her conversion ceremony. After reciting the testimony of faith in front of two Muslim witnesses in a small room at the mosque, she said: "I felt this weight just lift off of me.... Like it was being pulled from the inside out and I felt all of my bad sins and stuff being pulled out of me and making me anew. And for the longest time afterwards, people kept saying 'You are glowing! Can you turn it down? You are glowing!' [laughs]." Denyse was not the same person before and after pronouncing the *shahada*. She marveled at the power of the profession of faith and highlighted its symbolic meaning, its "social magic." After coming back from the mosque, she quit smoking, opened up all the windows of her apartment, and repainted it entirely. She put on a *hijab* and started losing weight drastically. For Denyse, the *shahada* fully performed its role as a rite of institution: it projected her into a new life and a new persona.

The might of the ritual is such that many of my interviewees reported being really scared and stressed out beforehand. Elizabeth, a 30-year-old white woman working as a nurse in Chicago, had been researching Islam for six years prior to reciting her *shahada*. Throughout that period, she would pray several times a day in Arabic and recite various *surah* (chapters) of the Qur'an. Yet she would never allow herself to utter the words of the profession of faith (which is to be pronounced at the end of each prayer unit): "Even when I was saying prayers before, I would never say the *shahada* because I thought that was something special." Like Denyse, Elizabeth invested the *shahada* with an almost magical meaning. Once the words were pronounced, there would be no going back. She perceived the conversion ritual as a meaningful act that would "make" her a Muslim and force her to take public responsibility for her religious beliefs.

The shahada *as an anticlimactic moment*

While the above testimonies ascribe significant meaning to the conversion ceremony, several respondents in my sample experienced their *shahada* as an anticlimactic, almost insignificant moment. James, a 48-year-old white man living in Detroit working as an English teacher, describes his conversion as such:

> You know the most powerful moments to me were the moments leading up to it.... The *shahada* was beautiful and that was meaningful but it was also anticlimactic because it was the moving of the heart beforehand, I think, that really felt like the moment when I became Muslim. The rest was formalizing it.

In comparison to James's first mystical and spiritual moments, his *shahada* felt formal and insipid. Romain, a 30-year-old unemployed white man living in Paris, expressed a similar feeling when he compared the *shahada* to "quote-unquote 'registering for school,'" a rather flavorless event in comparison to his first prayer in congregation. These converts relativize the significance of the *shahada* in their journey. In fact, many of them were already practicing the religion before their conversion ceremony, praying, fasting in Ramadan, eating *halal* food and avoiding illicit things such as pork, alcohol, and dating. This, for instance, is how Melissa describes the process through which she became Muslim:

> I didn't take my *shahada* overnight. My faith was becoming stronger and stronger but I couldn't content myself with simply believing.... I had to pray, I had to comply with the rules.... It was out of the question for me to be a piecemeal Muslim. So I felt the need to start practicing. I stopped smoking, I stopped eating pork.... And then I started eating *halal* food. ... And little by little, I set about praying.... And then I told to myself "OK, next Ramadan, I will take my *shahada*." ... But I had already been practicing for a year before that.

Starting her practice enabled Melissa to strengthen her faith and consolidate her belief. Immersing herself into some of the norms and rules of Islam was a way for her to achieve certainty, before formally entering the fold. This certainty was not intellectual but rather practical and embodied, which ensured its viability and authenticity. Melissa's experiences go against the straightforward schematization of conversion as *belief* => *shahada* => *practice*. In her case, it is replaced by a more complex model whereby beliefs and practices fuel one another before culminating in the decision to convert. One can therefore be a practicing Muslim for several months or years before becoming officially Muslim through the act of taking *shahada*.[9] In this model, the practice unfolds in a continuous way from the moment the individual expresses interest in Islam and starts incorporating some basic precepts into their life. The *shahada* simply punctuates this trajectory of transformation, without constituting a major landmark that demarcates practice from nonpractice.

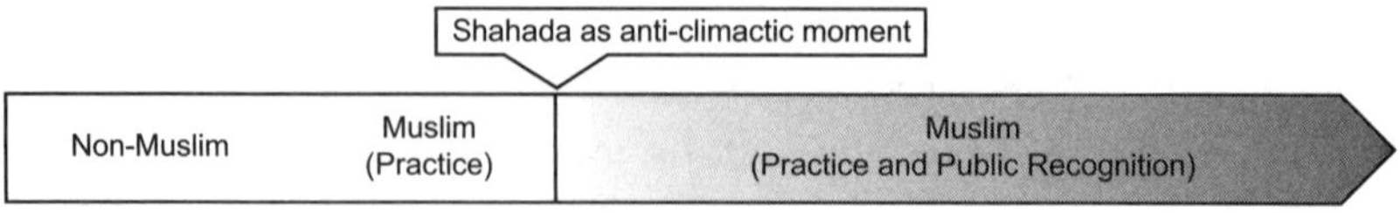

FIGURE 2.3.
The shahada *as anticlimactic.*

The reluctance to consider the *shahada* as a significant milestone is best exemplified by the case of Brian, a 23-year-old white student from Chicago, who describes himself as a "naysayer" critical of organized religion. Brian explained that he "had committed himself to Islam a long time before he took the *shahada*" and described his ceremony of conversion as "very random." He said he contacted two of his Muslim friends and told them: "'All right, I am just going to say my *shahada*, you guys are going to witness, just stay here for like 3 minutes.' And they were like '*Mash'Allah! Mash'Allah! Mash'Allah!*' I was like 'Would you guys cut the bullshit? Seriously. All right? Stop this shit.'" Brian emphasized that he did not want his *shahada* to be fetishized: "It is nasty when it becomes fetishized. That has no real significance. I mean, it does, if you commit to it. But no convert commits fully! You only commit fully in time. So for me, the *shahada* was much more about not drinking anymore, than saying seven words." Like several scholars of religion, Brian advocates an understanding of conversion as gradual, emphasizing the progressive consolidation of religious practice throughout one's life.

Some converts also remembered their *shahada* as a complete disaster. Such was the case of Sophie, a 27-year-old white woman living in Marseille working as a caseworker. Sophie discovered Islam during a trip to Morocco, where she stayed with a Muslim family. She progressively tried to incorporate Islamic teachings and practices into her life and gradually renounced her former lifestyle, which involved rapping, doing graffiti, drinking, and being surrounded by male friends. She did not change overnight, however, and her *shahada* took place at an inappropriate moment:

> One day I went to visit my Muslim neighbor and she told me "Oh it is amazing, you are praying! Come with me to the mosque, we are going to give you your *shahada*!" I said "OK, I am coming." But it was so strange because I didn't decide on doing it.... I just went to say hi to my neighbor and I ended up at the mosque! So I took my *shahada* but I hadn't realized that the night before I had drunk alcohol. I hadn't showered beforehand, because I didn't know you are supposed to follow that protocol before converting. So I found myself in the middle of this thing.... I wasn't firm

> about it. . . . I mean I was completely convinced, I was testifying that *Allah subhanahu wa ta'ala* is unique and that *Muhammad sallallahu 'alayhi wa salaam* is His messenger but . . . I was just following the movement [and] I don't know how to express it. . . . May God forgive me because it was clumsy and inappropriate. That moment which is supposed to be sacred, I did it without purifying myself. . . . I was just testifying. But in fact I am testifying every day when I am praying you know. And now retrospectively, that moment in the mosque, I don't think that is the moment when I actually converted. The moment when I converted was before that.

For Sophie, the ritual of the *shahada* at the mosque did not feel like a rite of passage. It was also dispossessing because she was not adequately prepared for it.

Finally, it is important to note that some converts did not even take their *shahada*. They simply drifted progressively toward being Muslims, without any significant milestone or starting point. When I asked Fabien, a 21-year-old white man living in Paris studying journalism, what his conversion ceremony was like, he could not really answer my question:

> I became Muslim through my interactions with brothers and everything, I don't really know. There would be evenings where I would go to the mosque, I didn't even have my ablutions done, I would go pray. . . . Whatever! Nonsense!. . . I am telling you, I feel like it really came down to me. I am incapable of telling you how it came. . . . Even to count up all the prayers I have to make up, I don't know! So I decided on a fictional date, hoping it is the actual date, but I have no idea, no way to keep track. . . . I never took my *shahada* in public, I don't know if I ever really took it you know.

Contrary to his friend Jean, who clearly remembered his conversion date (see above), Fabien was at a loss of words to determine the moment he became Muslim. While he considers himself a Muslim and lives his life as a Muslim, he never really took his *shahada* and was never formally instituted as a Muslim.

SHAHADA AFTERMATHS

The ritual of the *shahada* is therefore endowed with different meanings and significations—decisive for some, insignificant for others. While it is supposed to be well institutionalized and codified, there is considerable leeway and room for interpretation around it. I now turn to what happens in the aftermath of that ritual. Do converts start living their lives as Muslims upon taking the *shahada*? In other words, does the rite bring about the conversion it signifies?

Islam as a sprint or a marathon

Some converts drastically changed their behavior after the instituting rite of the *shahada*. Hasan, a 35-year-old white male who grew up in a poor household and converted to Islam at age 17 after suffering from drug addiction, explained how he joined the Salafi movement and forsook his former lifestyle overnight. Thus, when some coreligionists told him music was *haram* (forbidden in Islam), he gave away his entire music collection to a friend. This sudden, abrupt renunciation stems from the power of the *shahada* as a rite of institution, as converts feel the need to undergo radical life changes in order to validate their religious transformation. This "absolutist" behavior is jokingly referred to as "convertitis" by the British convert Tim Winter (also see Jensen 2006; Turner 2016). During the interview, however, Hasan recognized that his stringent approach could not suit everybody:

> At some point, you have to feed a baby with baby food. You have to bring them up to toddler. You have to bring them up to speed. With me, when I took *shahada*, we were babies eating steak! Right then! . . . And I could take the steak. I was OK. I had the teeth to eat the steak. . . . But I have seen people run away. . . . And I think that they needed maybe baby food at that time.

Contrary to Hasan, most of the converts in my sample did not "eat steak" right away, and their conversion ceremony did not entail a complete refashioning of self overnight. It was rather the first step of a long and gradual transformational process. As put by Fred, a 28-year-old student from Chicago, "Nothing happened at once, you know, I still was living the same life that I was living before." Sometimes it took months or years before converts reached the level of practice they deemed sufficient. Converted at age 17, Romain compared his practice of Islam in the first few years to that of a "born Muslim." In his conceptualization, a born Muslim is someone who was born into the faith and is therefore nominally Muslim but does not practice seriously.

> So let's say that from age 17 to age 22, I converted but in fact I almost acted like a born Muslim, meaning that. . . when you are a born Muslim, you

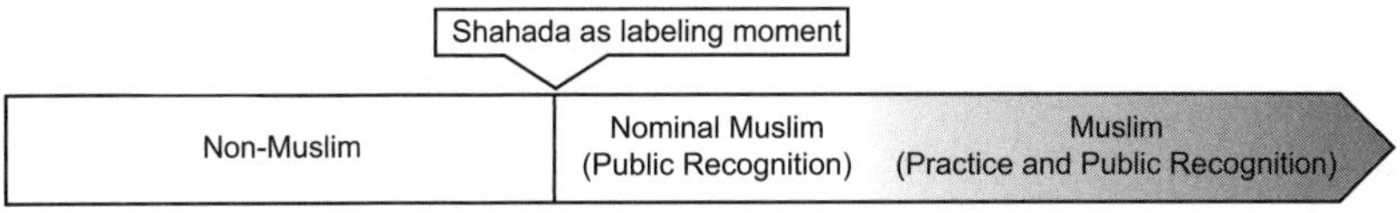

FIGURE 2.4.
Nominal shahadas.

> don't think much. . . . Me I was a little bit like a born Muslim, in the sense that OK, I wouldn't eat pork, I would fast in Ramadan, but yeah, that was it. I wouldn't drink alcohol, but you know this is just the basic stuff that everyone does to be able to say "Yeah, I am Muslim." . . . It is only after, at age 22–23, that I really started getting into it. I started praying, going to the mosque, reading books, learning Arabic and everything. Let's say that *I got into it little by little.*

In his view, Romain started as a piecemeal, thoughtless practitioner. He incorporated Muslim practices into his life "little by little" and progressively substantiated his nominal Muslim identity with actual spiritual content and practice. What he considers his "real" entry into Islam took place five years after his *shahada*. In this case, the *shahada* appears as a ritual that simply turns the individual into a nominal Muslim but that does not necessarily delineate practice from nonpractice.

The two convert associations I studied were very much aware of the obstacles and difficulties that converts faced in coming to terms with their conversion and stabilizing their religious shift. The French association constantly warned recent converts against abrupt and sudden changes, reminding them of the risk of religious "burnout." It enjoined them to pursue a progressive path of religious transformation, by constantly repeating the same mantra: "slowly, slowly, slowly." The American association promoted a similar, gradual approach to spiritual growth. In the "New Muslim" class, John repeatedly emphasized the importance of time, moderation, and step-by-step progress: "Islam is a marathon, not a sprint. Don't start too fast. You have to pace yourself because the journey is long. And if you start too quickly, you won't make it till the end." These excerpts reveal that converting to Islam is not a black-and-white, clear-cut transformation that materializes with the *shahada*. It is rather a long process that stretches over time, sometimes way beyond the *shahada*.[10] This drawn-out process has many shades and textures. It involves trials and errors, false starts, doubts, hesitations, and gradual improvements. As evidenced by the "baby food" and "marathon" metaphors, it takes time before some converts reach a comfortable "cruising speed" in their religious practice.

The longest shahada *ever*

As put by Viswanathan (1998: 89), "A change of religion is less a change of beliefs than a change of community." To be complete and successful, the religious transformation has to be acknowledged and accepted by one's coreligionists. Yet many converts in my sample expressed their frustration and disillusions concerning their interactions with other Muslims. As new Muslims involved in a process of learning, they sometimes felt treated like small children or despised as inauthentic and disingenuous. In many instances, converts explained that they remained perceived as "converts" rather than full-fledged Muslims. Suhaib Webb, who is currently the imam of the Islamic Society of Boston Cultural Center and was named one of the world's 500 most influential Muslims by the Royal Islamic Strategic Studies Centre in 2010, recently expressed his discontent during a talk: "I converted over 20 years ago. Conversion was an event. Islam was a process. But still now I am called a convert. Now, I converted in November 1992. This has been like the longest *shahada* ever! [laughs]."[11] Suhaib Webb indicated that his rite of passage was incomplete. He remained stuck in the limbo of the liminal phase, as if his *shahada* was still lasting. His comment is in line with Finn's observations, according to which converts are "neither insiders nor outsiders but people in between. In transition, they stand on the no-man's land between the world which they seek to leave and the church which they seek to enter" (1990: 600). As put by Le Pape (2015: 84), "a successful conversion is one that is made forgotten." Yet the idea that an enduring stigma was attached to their conversion pervaded several converts' narratives. In the following excerpt, Adèle recalls how a Muslim woman made her redo the *shahada* after expressing doubts about its validity:

> There was an association doing Islamic charity work, something like that, but it was a bit … special!… The first time I went, the lady who welcomed us told me "How did you convert?" And I told her how it happened: it had been two or three weeks already. And she said "But how did you pronounce it?"… So I repeated in Arabic. And she said, "But you are not Muslim!!! You are not converted, you are mispronouncing! And if you don't know how to say it properly, you are not Muslim!"… When she told me that, I was like, "Well, that's strange," but I didn't know so I tried to say it again, even if it was difficult. I succeeded and then she said, "OK, now it is good, *now you are Muslim!*" [laughs].

As Leon Moosavi (2012) explains in his study of British Muslim converts, practicing a religion is not only about doing something that would impress

God; it is also about doing something that would impress other coreligionists. As the previous testimonies demonstrate, being accepted as an authentic member of the Muslim community is a process that is never completely over and done with. Complete religious change—and thus full membership in the new religious community—are not necessarily acquired through the mere recitation of the *shahada*.

CONCLUSION

The *shahada* is the "outward" and "vocalized" expression of Islam (Woodberry 1992: 34). Its recitation in front of witnesses is commonly understood as the rite of institution that marks the entry into Islam. In this chapter, I have investigated what that moment meant for Muslim converts themselves and what significance they ascribed to it within their longer religious journey. The accounts varied markedly. In fact, the diversity of personal trajectories is such that the social scientist has a hard job coming to grips with it. For some, the *shahada* fully performed its role as a rite of institution, marking a clear temporal rupture between a "before" and an "after." For most converts, however, the relationship to time and change proved more multilayered. Some found the ritual of the *shahada* unsatisfactory and crafted their own ceremony, in line with their inner spiritual feelings. Others were already devout and practicing Muslims before performing the *shahada*, which as a result was not remembered as *the* moment they became Muslim. Others felt that the *shahada* made them only nominally Muslim, but it took years before they reached the level of practice and sincerity they deemed sufficient to "feel Muslim." Their conversion was a partial and ongoing process that both preceded and lasted beyond the ceremony of conversion. It did not fit into a simple narrative of discontinuity: situated both upstream and downstream, it could not be circumscribed within clear temporal boundaries. Finally, some converts confessed that their rite of passage was incomplete, as they remained seen as "converts" and never as full-fledged Muslims. In their cases, the ritual of conversion did not bring about the public recognition it was supposed to fulfill. Therefore, I argue that the conceptualization of the *shahada* as a clear and definite rite of institution tends to obscure the complexities of the workings of faith and to overlook the lengthy process that is required to incorporate Muslim beliefs and practices into one's life and be accepted by the Muslim community. In light of my respondents' testimonies, I suggest that conversion is best characterized as a process of "moving toward" Islam rather than an act of "moving in."

Yet the notions of rites of passage and rites of institution remain crucial to understanding conversion. Even if they do not encompass all converts' experiences, they resonate with some and retain a heuristic value to describe temporal changes. In order to reconcile the conceptualizations of conversion as either a "rite of passage" or as a "gradual process," I propose the concept of *liminality*, as elaborated by Victor Turner (1969) on the basis of Van Gennep's work stated above. In his study of Ndembu rituals in Central Africa, Turner paid particular attention to the intermediate, liminal phase that comes after the phase of separation and that precedes the phase of reincorporation (*limen* is a Latin word meaning "boundary" or "threshold"): "*The attributes of liminality or liminal personae are necessarily ambiguous . . . Liminal entities are neither here nor there; they are betwixt and between the positions assigned and arrayed by law, custom, convention and ceremonial*" (1969: 95). I argue that the concept of liminality is particularly relevant to understand converts' experiences. By reciting the *shahada*, converts crossed a threshold and entered a liminal phase, which, as evidenced by Suhaib Webb's comment, can last for a while. In some instances, converts do not really ever quit this liminal phase, since the stigma of conversion prevents them from successfully completing their rite of passage. They remain "threshold people," whose relationship to time is both continuous and discontinuous, caught between moving in and moving toward.

NOTES

1. I would like to thank Judith Ijtihad Lefebvre, Karin van Nieuwkerk, and all the participants in the "Moving In and Out of Islam" conference (Radboud University Nijmegen, October 16–17, 2015) for their comments on this chapter.

2. *Ashadu an la ilaha ill-Allah, wa ashadu anna muhammadan rasul ullah* ("I testify that there is no god but God, and Muhammad is His Prophet").

3. The Nation of Islam and the Five Percenters are African American movements that use Islamic referents to promote black dignity.

4. I chose to compare France and the United States because these are two Western democracies that currently entertain a troubled relationship to Islam and are both witnessing an upsurge in the number of their citizens who embrace Islam. Historically, these two countries have also been characterized by different understandings of religion and secularism. They have also had contrasting historical encounters with Islam and the Muslim world. Although I do not have room in this chapter to develop a comparative analysis of French and American converts, I redirect readers interested in the comparative dimension of my research to Galonnier (2015)f.

5. I interviewed African Americans (n=11), Latinos (n=4), Asians (n=3), and individuals of mixed descent (n=3) in the United States and people of West Indian (n=4), South-American (n=1), and mixed descent (n=3) in France.

6. According to Allievi, relational conversions stem from interactions with Muslims, while rational conversions are the result of intense quests for meaning. In sum, relational

converts are people who met Muslims before Islam, while rational converts met Islam as a religion before interacting with Muslims. These, obviously, are ideal types. In most cases, the various motives are closely intertwined.

7. For the sake of anonymity, the name of all respondents and associations have been modified.

8. These "autonomous conversions" were also encountered by Loic Le Pape (2015: 38–40) in his study of conversions in France.

9. In her study of Dutch converts to Islam, Vanessa Vroon (2014: 74) also found that "the practice of Islam often predates the threshold moment of conversion."

10. For this reason, scholars and converts themselves tend to reject the term "conversion" to describe their trajectory. They employ a variety of words that convey the more continuous and processual nature of their spiritual transformation, such as "transition," (Wadud 2007: 5), "continuation" (Shanneik 2011), or "existential reorientation" (Vroon 2014: 71). For an analysis of conversion concepts, see Barylo (this volume).

11. The talk was organized by the Northwestern Muslim Students Association (MSA) on November 21, 2013: www.youtube.com/watch?v=xczL8kxv6u4.

REFERENCES

Allievi, S. 1998. *Les Convertis à l'islam: les Nouveaux Musulmans d'Europe*. Paris: L'Harmattan.

Bell, C. 1992. *Ritual Theory, Ritual Practice*. Oxford: Oxford University Press.

Bourdieu, P. 1982. "Les rites comme actes d'institution." *Actes de la recherche en sciences sociales* 43: 58–63.

Douglas, M. 2009 [1966]. *Purity and Danger: An Analysis of Concept of Pollution and Taboo*. New York: Routledge.

Ebaugh, H. R. F. 1988. *Becoming an Ex: The Process of Role Exit*. Chicago: University of Chicago Press.

Finn, T. M. 1990. "It Happened One Saturday Night: Ritual and Conversion in Augustine's North Africa." *Journal of the American Academy of Religion* 58, no. 4: 589–616.

Galonnier, J. 2015. "The Racialization of Muslims in France and the United States: Some Insights from White Converts to Islam." *Social Compass* 62, no. 4: 570–583.

Galonnier, J., and D. De Los Rios. 2016. "Teaching and Learning to Be Religious: Pedagogies of Conversion to Islam and Christianity." *Sociology of Religion* 77, no. 1: 59–81.

Gooren, H. 2010. *Religious Conversion and Disaffiliation: Tracing Patterns of Change in Faith Practices*. New York: Palgrave MacMillan US.

Greil, A. L. and D. R. Rudy. 1983. "Conversion to the World View of Alcoholics Anonymous: A Refinement of Conversion Theory." *Qualitative Sociology* 6, no. 1: 5–28.

Heirich, M. 1977. "Change of Heart: A Test of Some Widely Held Theories about Religious Conversion." *American Journal of Sociology* 83, no. 3: 653–680.

Hervieu-Léger, D. 1999. *Le pèlerin et le converti: la religion en mouvement*. Paris: Flammarion.

Jensen, T. G. 2006. "Religious Authority and Autonomy Intertwined: The Case of Converts to Islam in Denmark." *The Muslim World* 96, no. 4: 643–660.

Le Pape, L. 2015. *Une autre foi: Itinéraires de conversions en France. Juifs, chrétiens, musulmans.* Aix-en-Provence: Presses Universitaires de Provence.

McGinty, A. M. 2006. *Becoming Muslim: Western Women's Conversions to Islam.* New York: Palgrave Macmillan.

Moosavi, L. 2012. "British Muslim Converts Performing Authentic Muslimness." *Performing Islam* 1, no. 1: 103–128.

Mossière, G. 2007. *La conversion religieuse: approches épistémologiques et polysémie d'un concept.* Montréal: Groupe de recherche diversité urbaine: Centre d'études ethniques des universités montréalaises, Université de Montréal.

Nock, A. D. 1933. *Conversion.* New York: New York University Press.

Rambo, L. R. and C. E. Farhadian. 1999. "Converting: Stages of Religious Change." In *Religious Conversion: Contemporary Practices and Controversies.* C. Lamb and D. M. Bryant, eds. New York: Cassell. 23–34.

Richardson, J. 1978. *Conversion Careers: In and Out of the New Religions.* Beverly Hills, CA: Sage.

Riesman, D. 1950. *The Lonely Crowd: A Study of the Changing American Character.* New Haven: Yale University Press.

Shanneik, Y. 2011. "Conversion and Religious Habitus: The Experiences of Irish Women Converts to Islam in the Pre-Celtic Tiger Era." *Journal of Muslim Minority Affairs* 31, no. 4: 503–517.

Straus, R. A. 1979. "Religious Conversion as a Personal and Collective Accomplishment." *Sociological Analysis* 40, no. 2: 158–165.

Turner, K. 2016. *Pork, Pop Music, and Purity: Convertitis, Pollutants, and the Struggle with Liminality.* Paper presented at the conference "Investigating Conversions to Islam: Which Approaches in Social Sciences?" February 15–16, 2016. Sciences Po Paris, Paris.

Turner, V. 1967. *The Forest of Symbols: Aspects of Ndembu Ritual.* Ithaca: Cornell University Press.

Turner, V. W. 1969. *The Ritual Process: Structure and Anti-Structure.* Chicago: Aldine.

Van Gennep, A. 1960 [1909]. *The Rites of Passage.* Chicago: University of Chicago Press.

Van Nieuwkerk, K. 2014. "Conversion to Islam and the Construction of a Pious Self." In *The Oxford Handbook of Religious Conversion.* L. R. Rambo and C. E. Farhadian, eds. Oxford: Oxford University Press, 667–686.

Viswanathan, G. 1998. *Outside the Fold: Conversion, Modernity, and Belief.* Princeton: Princeton University Press.

Vroon, V. 2014. *Sisters in Islam: Women's Conversion and the Politics of Belonging. A Dutch Case Study.* Diss. in Social Sciences, University of Amsterdam, Amsterdam.

Wadud, A. 2007. *Inside the Gender Jihad: Women's Reform in Islam.* Oxford: One World Publications.

Winchester, D. 2008. "Embodying the Faith: Religious Practice and the Making of a Muslim Moral Habitus." *Social Forces* 86, no. 4: 1753–1780.

Woodberry, J. D. 1992. "Conversion in Islam." In *Handbook of Religious Conversion.* N. H. Malony and S. Southard, eds. Birmingham, AL: Religious Education Press, 22–40.

THREE

UNDERSTANDING RELIGIOUS APOSTASY, DISAFFILIATION, AND ISLAM IN CONTEMPORARY SWEDEN

DANIEL ENSTEDT

When the recording equipment was turned off, after a long interview with Arsalan, a homosexual ex-Muslim man living in Sweden, he turned to me and said: "You know, Muhammad was a pedophile." I quickly turned the recorder back on, as he continued to talk about Mohammad's relationship to Aisha. "She was a child, she was abused. . . . When I hear [about] a 46-year-old man married with a 9-year-old [girl] . . . I think that he was sick, really sick." Arsalan continued to talk about the Qur'an and the formative years of Islam, and he retold a discussion that he had with a Muslim: "'Do you believe this religion come from god? Please open your eyes.'"

Laila, another ex-Muslim, reacts very negatively when she sees women wearing *hijabs* in Sweden. She associates the veil with religious oppression. For her, as well as for Arsalan, Islam stands for ignorance, deception, and oppression. But when I asked her about her parents' religion, another version of Islam emerged:

> My father was a believing Muslim, I mean really believing. . . . There is a difference between my father and other Muslims. My father kept his religion for himself and didn't want to bother anyone else. He didn't drink alcohol or eat *haram* meat, but he never told me that "you shouldn't do this or that." I was free.

During my fieldwork among ex-Muslims in Sweden it became clear that there are a couple of recurring themes in the narratives about Islam. While interviewees, like Laila, denounced Islam altogether, they could also, at the same time, tell a different story in which Islam was portrayed in a more positive light. Some of the interviewees even keep part of the religious tradition, practices, and beliefs intact. This kind of ambiguity is also evident in the narrative of Yusuf, a disaffiliated, homosexual Muslim. While still observing some rules, norms, and practices that are associated with Islam—Yusuf drank alcohol but didn't eat pork; he sometime prayed at home but not in a mosque—he said that gays are not welcomed in Muslim communities and societies: "If someone finds out I can be killed in my apartment." Since he still sees himself as a Muslim, even though he had left the Muslim community, he now lives with a sort of internalized homophobia: "It is difficult for me to accept me for what I am. It's like having a nightmare. It is quite difficult for me to accept homosexuality."

The examples above raise several questions that revolve around religious apostasy. The phenomenon is highlighted and given new meanings when Islam is growing in what used to be a mainly Christian country like Sweden. The focus in this chapter is not, however, on the ex-Muslim situation in Sweden per se but rather on predominant theories about apostasy, deconversion, and religious disaffiliation. The question is how to theoretically understand leaving Islam in contemporary Sweden. This focus relates to how apostates describe and narrate their experiences as former Muslims, as well as the problems associated with the apostasy process in present-day Sweden. I will examine how different kinds of materiality—such as clothing, food, and makeup—play a part in the critique of Islam and the role of personal and collective apostasy narratives. The aim is to outline new theoretical perspectives that enable a more nuanced understanding of individual religious change of which religious apostasy and disaffiliation is a part.

I will proceed from Linda Woodhead's sociologically informed discussion of the shortcomings of the prevailing concepts of religiosity in religious studies when discussing previous research on apostasy, disaffiliation, and deconversion. Instead of understanding religion solely as a mind-set, a cognitive script or a worldview, as many studies on apostasy have done, Woodhead (2011) discusses concepts such as religion as culture, identity, relationship, practice, and power.[1] While some dominant trends in the recent social scientific study of religion have put the emphasis on religion as belief in a system of meaning or a supernatural power or force (i.e., the *sola fide* aspect of religion), Woodhead underlines the importance of other aspects, especially religion as *power*, that is "recessive in sociology, but in urgent need of revival" (Woodhead 2011: 123). Following Woodhead's suggestions I will discuss theories about apostates' life-story narratives and truth claims, as well as materiality and embodiment, with the emphasis on food, clothing, gestures, and other bodily behaviors. Furthermore, a heightened focus on the blurred boundaries not only between the sacred and the secular, but also between leaving and keeping a religion like Islam, situates this article in the broader field of *lived religion* (see McGuire 2008; Ammerman 2007; Ammerman 2013). I will take these aspects into account when discussing leaving Islam in present-day Sweden, even though I cannot address them all in great detail.

ISLAM AND APOSTASY IN SWEDEN

The prohibition against apostasy, or abandoning one's religion, is nothing new in Islam, and it is not only interpretations of Islam that take a negative stance on apostasy. However, it is Islam that is usually portrayed as the most extreme religion when it comes to defections (Enstedt and Larsson 2013; Larsson, this volume). In Islam, apostasy (*irtidād, ridda*) has frequently been linked to other negatively charged terms, for example, unbelief, blasphemy, heresy, and hypocrisy (Griffel 2016). In *Freedom of Religion, Apostasy, and Islam* (2003), Abdullah Saeed and Hassan Saeed examine the contradiction between freedom of religion and interpretations of Islam implying that apostasy should be punished with death. They point out that this decree is contrary to other fundamental texts and beliefs in Islam and emphasize the often contradictory statements about apostasy that have been made throughout history. Paul Marshall and Nina Shea's *Silenced: How Apostasy and Blasphemy Codes Are Choking Freedom Worldwide* (2011) should also be mentioned in this context. Marshall and Shea survey how restrictions on apostasy and blasphemy are applied in Muslim-majority countries, as well as the contemporary debates on apostasy and blasphemy in non-Muslim–majority countries. Even though Marshall and Shea's main focus is on freedom of religion, international law, and politics, they demonstrate, at least indirectly, how the process of leaving Islam, and legal responses to apostasy, differ between Muslim-majority countries and non-Muslim–majority countries. Only a few studies about Islam and apostasy have been conducted in recent years (Cottee 2015; Adang et al. 2015; Kefeli 2014), and no study has yet focused on the situation in Sweden.

Islam's presence in what now is a multireligious Sweden has taken place through migration from countries and regions that have long been influenced by Islam, such as Turkey, the Middle East, the Horn of Africa, and the Balkans. From being a minority religion that has been associated mainly with labor migration, Islam has come to be Sweden's second largest religion. The Muslim community is heterogeneous in terms of cultural, religious, and socioeconomic factors, and there is not a uniform view of religion and religiosity (Sedgwick 2015; Otterbeck 2010; Larsson and Sander 2007). The increased Muslim visibility, in the form of mosques and Islamic institutions, has vitalized the public discussion about religion and the place of religion and religiosity in the public sphere. Even though questions about clothing (i.e., the veil), methods of slaughter, and the building of mosques cannot be automatically linked to a discussion of apostasy, it is clear that public speech about Islam and increased anti-Muslim—or Islamophobic (Gardell 2011; Allen 2010)—rhetoric in society has important implications for the debate about people who leave Islam.

Sweden is, from time to time, portrayed as one of the world's most secular countries (Norris and Inglehart 2011: 60, 277–278). "In terms of religion," as Peter Berger, Grace Davie, and Effie Fokas symptomatically put it, "India and Sweden can serve to mark the antipodes of religiousness and secularity" (Berger, Davie, and Fokas 2008: 12). Data from the *World Values Survey* shows that Sweden, from a global perspective, scores high when it comes to the variables Self-Expression Values and Secular-Rational Values, which distinguish Sweden from countries with more traditional values (Inglehart and Welzel 2010: 554). From this perspective, religious involvement is reduced and Swedish citizens have lost their religious faith in favor of secular ideas, values, and perspectives. Leaving Islam in contemporary Sweden can thus be understood as part of a more general, societal trend, signified by the term "secularization."

In *Habits of the Heart* (1985), the sociologist Robert Bellah coined the often cited term "Sheilaism." The type of religion, or rather spirituality, that Sheilaism expresses is emblematic for post-1960s America, and several aspects of it have been addressed at length in religious studies since then.[2] It is about individualism, antiauthoritarianism, religious bricolage, religious experiences and emotions, self-centeredness, and, not least, disaffiliation from religious groups, established religious organizations, and structures (see Bellah 1985: 221). The decline of religious members (i.e., "churchgoers") and the increasing number of disaffiliates, deconverts, and apostates around the world seems, on one hand, to suggest that religiosity is declining, or at least losing the impact that it previously had on society; on the other hand, Sheilaism points at the direct opposite: religion is not vanishing but rather changing characteristics, even in ways that sometimes would be difficult—even for scholars in the field of religious studies—to recognize as religion.

Islam's visibility in present-day Sweden has not only generated a Swedish Islam but also given rise to prejudices about Islam and Muslims. The cultural geographer Lily Kong argues that such a public Islamophobia can "construct Islam as antithetical to 'Western' culture and Muslim women as the embodiment of a 'fundamentalist' and repressive religion" (Kong 2010: 758). The emphasis on religious belonging and affiliation, which is at issue here, has had the result, Kong continues, that "young Muslim people are increasingly defining their identities in terms of their religion, as opposed, for example, to their parental country of origin" (Kong 2010: 758). That correlates well with what Synnøve Bendixsen has pointed out in her study of young female Muslims in Berlin, where the second and third generations of migrants actually turn to Islam "in a quest for authenticity, an individual identity, and as part of their group orientation" (Bendixsen 2010: 95). Interestingly, the young female Muslims are on a quest for a *purer* form of Islam than the "traditional" culture-based Islam that they ascribed to their parents (Bendixsen 2010: 99). This indicates that "Islam" is not simply passed on from one generation to another, as a solid entity, but rather (re)created and reformulated more or less eclectically by the next generation. The embodiment of the *true* Islam in a society such as Germany also includes wearing religious symbols, clothes, and other attributes. As Nilüfer Göle has pointed out: "Islamism as a collective social movement enables Muslim actors to adopt voluntarily the religious attributes that are considered potentially discrediting from the point of view of the normative framework of a modern [secularist] culture" (Göle 2003: 811). Interestingly, the second- or third-generation immigrants that "turn to Islam" confirm the same image when joining the Islamic State and criticizing mainstream Islam. By military action, guerrilla wars, and a certain kind of masculinity these young men are embodying the images of Islam that are produced in Western cultures' anti-Muslim discourse. Such an understanding of Islam also plays a crucial part in their narratives about leaving Islam. Even though my interest in this chapter is about the *turn from*, rather than the *turn to*, Islam it is important to point out that, when it comes to migration and religious change, the effects are multidirectional.

One aspect of the exit process that Helen Ebaugh discusses in *Becoming an Ex* (1988), which is directly related to leaving Islam in contemporary Sweden, is the social desirability of the exit. While some exit roles entail a social stigma, other exit roles are desirable and socially approved (Ebaugh 1988: 196). The hegemonic public view of Islam in contemporary Sweden has been negative since the 1990s; Islam has been associated with ignorance, oppression of women, and terror. Such a setting makes the ex-Muslim role more socially desirable in Sweden than in, for example, Somalia. But, as Eliza F. Kent writes:

> In a historical moment of heightened Islamophobia in the West due to the September 11th terrorist attacks and the ensuing so-called War on Terror, many find it surprising that any European or American would convert to Islam. Given the widespread perception of Islam as oppressive toward women, the evidence suggesting that more women than men are embracing Islam may be even more startling (Kent 2014: 307).

Another important factor to take into account is how the cultural understanding and image of Islam is framed in contemporary Sweden and how that picture is related to the alternatives in society—for instance, various forms of Christianity or nonreligion. If Swedish Muslims and immigrating Muslims perceive their own religion as "antimodern," repressive, and ignorant, and the alternatives as liberating, they have to deal with that predicament and antagonism either by (1) simply accepting it, or by (2) reformulating or motivating Islam in the Swedish context, or by (3) abandoning Islam in favor of another religion or nonreligion (cf. O'Brien 2004). One incentive to leave Islam in Sweden is that the religion is aligned with Western stereotypes and prejudices that can include a social stigma that Muslims have to deal with (Göle 2003).

Immigration being the main cause of the increased number of Muslims in Sweden does not rule out other factors such as converts or births. One way to describe religious change from a macro-sociological perspective is to take both *positive* factors (births, converts, and immigrants) and *negative* factors (deaths, defectors, and emigrants) into account. The relation between these six factors will contribute to a more nuanced picture of religious change in Sweden (Johnson 2014: 62–63). The scope of this chapter is, however, on the negative factors that contribute to the *decrease* of Islam in Sweden. Another aspect of apostasy and migration is related to the second-generation immigrant's failure or success when it comes to giving the children a religious upbringing. If the parents' religiosity and the family's religious and social base are weak, the children are more likely to be nonreligious (see Altemeyer and Hunsberger 1997). When migrating from one country to another, one key factor in the process of religious change is, as Lily Kong and Seeta Nair point out, a personal contact with persons from the group one is joining (Kong and Nair 2014: 72). That is the case when converting to a new religion but also when leaving religion; if there is no relevant social base for the migrant, leaving religion altogether can be the only rational way to go.

I have examined three different apostasy groups during my fieldwork among ex-Muslims in present-day Sweden. (1) Ex-Muslims who are aligned with the Central Council for ex-Muslims in Scandinavia. This group consists mainly, but not only, of immigrants from Iran and is part of a global network of ex-Muslims. Notably, they express a severe critique of Islam from a nonreligious viewpoint that they share with other groups in Sweden, such as the Swedish Humanist Association, which takes a critical stance against religion in general. (2) Neo-Pentecostal and "Free Church" Christian missions among immigrants from Muslim countries, mainly Somalia, have convinced former Muslims to convert to Christianity. This group differs from the first ex-Muslim group since they still argue from a religious position and compare Christianity and Islam, and Jesus with Muhammad. (3) Nonorganized religious disaffiliates who still, in some sense, believe and/or practice religion without belonging to any Muslim community. There are, for instance, gay Muslims in Sweden who say that they have to *leave* religion to *keep* their faith, that is to say, "non-denominational Muslims" (cf. Yip 1997: 112). The critique of Islam in this group of disaffiliates, on the one hand, focuses on what they see as the Muslim community's narrow and traditional understanding of (homo)sexuality, and, on the other hand, expresses their own internalized homophobia. Besides archive material and online, print, and other media material, I have examined life stories, memories, relation to food, religious practices, artifacts, norms, and values in relation to the above-mentioned groups. Setting aside a calculation of the number of Muslims who are leaving Islam in present-day Sweden, I will discuss the logic behind religious defection, primarily on a theoretical level. The overall aim is to enable a more nuanced understanding of the religious *change* that leaving religion is, or can be, a part of.

Most studies on apostasy have been conducted in a Christian context or in relation to New Religious movements. I cannot mention all of these studies here, but I will point out the general trends in previous research that are relevant to the discussion.

PERSPECTIVES ON APOSTASY AND RELIGIOUS DISAFFILIATION

In *The Religious Drop-outs*, published in 1977, David Caplovitz and Fred Sherrow aim to identify the causes of religious apostasy among Jewish, Catholic, and Protestant college students in the US. They suggest that a wider range of various causes, or traits, is to "be seen as questioning either religiosity or the commitment to social groups" (Caplovitz and Sherrow 1977: 182). These conclusions from the 1970s can actually be seen as a symptom of how religious apostasy has been explained and understood in the sociology of religion (and elsewhere); it is all about religious *beliefs* ("religiosity") and religious *belonging* ("commitment to social groups"). With such emphasis on religious *belief*, their conclusion is indeed not surprising: "Of all the factors related to apostasy, the most significant, not surprisingly, was religious belief" (Caplovitz and Sherrow 1977: 182). Furthermore, it is mostly "intellectual students" who put religious articles of faith into question. Thus, when religious beliefs collide with rational arguments religion is abandoned by such students. The "rationality argument" is not frequently used in contemporary studies, but it has had a major impact in apostasy circles as well as in the New Atheist movement (see Enstedt and Larsson 2013). Such an understanding of religion as believing and belonging has had a vast impact on the study of religious apostasy.

A closely related perspective on religious apostasy that has gained much attention is connected to the brainwashing hypothesis, which is noticeable when dealing with so-called cults. But as Stuart A. Wright has already noted in *Leaving Cults* (1987), the image of the brainwashed cult member is based on popular "misconceptions [that] derive, in part, from accounts perpetuated by ex-members, anticult organizations, and the resulting images often perpetuated by the media" (Wright 1987: 93). The narrated experiences from critical ex-members have become characteristic not only for the general understanding of cults but also for "religion" per se, or as Wright (1987: 94) puts it, quoting an anticult organization: "All religion is brainwashing." A similar kind of general critique of "religion" is also articulated from several different positions associated with apostasy and leaving religion in contemporary Western countries. Even though this antireligious rhetoric can be formulated from a wide range of positions, a shared rationale, or *doxa*, binds them together, at least discursively. Anti-Muslim rhetoric on internet sites such as WikiIslam.net, apostatesofislam.com, and faithfreedom.org, as well as the New Atheist writings of Dawkins, Dennett, Hitchens, and Harris (the "four horsemen"), reproduce a negative image of religion that is associated with Islam. Such an image is also nurtured by a growing number of political groups in Europe where the critique of Islam is an essential and constitutive part of the groups' politics.[3] Even though such negatively charged images of Islam are also common in apostasy narratives, I am not suggesting that apostates share other views of the diverse political groups mentioned.

If you have a religious upbringing but at one point decide to leave your religion "of origin," it will, Caplovitz and Sherrow argue, "represent a break with the family of origin" (Caplovitz and Sherrow 1977: 49–50). In their *Amazing Conversions*, Bob Altemeyer and Bruce Hunsberger ask questions about what happens when the predictions made by the socialization theory fail, that is, when a *strong* emphasis on religion during childhood leads to apostasy and vice versa, when a nonreligious upbringing results in religiosity (Altemeyer and Hunsberger 1997: 12).[4] Their focus is thus on the exceptional cases that contradict the socialization theory's more deterministic predictions. Furthermore, when measuring *attitudes* toward and *thinking* about religion in the way that Altemeyer and Hunsberger do when using questionnaires, they are examining the cognitive aspects of religiosity, setting aside other crucial aspects of religiosity in relation to religious apostasy and conversion (see argument below). However, the Religious Emphasis Scale does ask questions about religious practices as well, and the qualitative interviews contain more dynamic life narratives and examples. One of the results of Altemeyer and Hunsberger's study is that the amazing apostates became apostates "because they felt intellectually compelled to do so" and that "*reason* gave them no choice" (Altemeyer and Hunsberger 1997: 212, emphasis added). It is thus all about rationality, an intellectual journey from religious belief to a clear rejection of that religious faith. After a thorough investigation of the religion's tenets, the apostate comes to the conclusion that the religion's veracity is flawed. In their study, Altemeyer and Hunsberger thus focus on the cognitive aspects of religious beliefs and nonbeliefs. Interestingly, their findings also suggest that, even though the apostates have abandoned their childhood religion, they would not advise young religious people and seekers to follow their path. Even more surprisingly, they would not even keep their future children from a religious upbringing, even though they would not engage in it themselves; instead they let the children's grandparents or a church take the responsibility to educate the children in religion (Altemeyer and Hunsberger 1997: 217–219).

In Ebaugh's influential study *Becoming an Ex*, the shifting between different roles is described as characteristic of modern society. Through an analysis of a wide range of different exit roles, the ex-nun Ebaugh extracts an exit process that passes through a common pattern, a defined set of stages, before the exit role is finally internalized. That process differs significantly from socialization into a role, even if the process also differs depending on whether or not it leads to another major role, as it does when converting from one religion to another, or if the process solely leads to the antithetical exit role. What characterizes the exit role in the second case is that the "identity as an ex rests not on one's current role but on who one was in the past" (Ebaugh 1988: 180). While studies of conversion have focused on the process that leads to the new role, the studies on deconversion and apostasy focus on the process of leaving a position. Ebaugh: "In the process of role exit, there tends to be mutual disengagement in that the individual moves away from the group while the former group simultaneously withdraws from the individual with regard to expectations and social obligations" (Ebaugh 1988: 181–182). The role exit process's stages are (1) doubts that usually are a consequence of change in life situation (i.e., unemployment, migration, change in organization or relations, etc.); (2) seeking alternatives that also work to reinforce the initial doubts; and (3) the turning point and its three functions: "the reduction of cognitive dissonance, the opportunity to announce the decision to others, and the mobilization of the resources needed to exit" (Ebaugh 1988: 184; see also Alyedreessy, this volume). After the significant turning point, the fourth and last stage consists of creating the exit role that includes a new self-presentation. A model of the apostasy process is found in *Deconversion* (Streib et al. 2009). The authors use the term "deconversion" instead of apostasy when they point out five characteristics of deconversion: "1. Loss of specific religious experiences; 2. intellectual doubt, denial or disagreement with specific beliefs; 3. moral criticism; 4. emotional suffering; 5. disaffiliation from the community" (Streib et al. 2009: 22). Besides these aspects they also list a range of possible "deconversion avenues," or possible outcomes of the deconversion process, such as (1) leaving religion, (2) finding a new religion, or (3) leaving the religious group while keeping some aspects of the religious faith (Streib et al. 2009: 26–28; see also Pauha and Aghaee, this volume).

The results of Streib's study indicate that deconverts are characterized by a *quest*-oriented religiosity (i.e., a tentative ongoing religious search), as well as what Streib describes as "multiple deconversions."[5] Even though Streib's typology of deconversion can be an interesting point of departure when talking about apostasy narratives, I find his choice of theory and method problematic when it comes to explaining deconversion from personality psychology and theories about religious orientation. It does not, for instance, seem surprising that deconverts score higher on the *quest*-variable and *openness to experience*–variable when answering questionnaires *after* the deconversion process. The question is, then, whether Streib's results explain anything at all when it comes to *why* some former religious persons leave religion.

To sum up, the overall emphasis in the previous research about apostasy has been on religious faith/belief, the cognitive faith development, and the process from one (religious) position to another (religious or nonreligious). Let me now turn to approaches to understand the apostasy narratives.

NARRATIVES, MEMORIES, AND BIOGRAPHICAL PERSPECTIVES

One of the previously and perhaps most commonly held views on religious conversion was that it is about a sudden, radical, and usually individual change of perspective. Even though that view has been criticized by several scholars in the field, at least since Rambo's *Understanding Religious Conversion* (1993), where conversion is understood as a process, it still lingers on even in scholarly literature. In the preface to *The Anthropology of Religious Conversion* (2003), the editors Andrew Buckser and Stephen D. Glazier express such a point of view: "To change one's religion is to change one's world, to voluntarily shift the basic presuppositions upon which both self and others are understood. . . . What can prompt such an abrupt and total transformation?" (Buckser and Glazier 2003: xi). It is, of course, easy to challenge these presumptions by giving examples of when a change of religion does not imply a change in worldview or other kinds of transformation.

Furthermore, one needs to make a clear distinction between *narratives* about religious conversion that indeed can describe it as an abrupt, total transformation, on the one hand, and an empirical understanding of the process that underlies the conversion, on the other hand. When it comes to religious disaffiliation it is more common that the narratives are about a period of time that is characterized by religious doubts of different kinds that lead up to the disaffiliation. In autobiographical writing about conversion to Islam, the Jewish-born Muhammad Asad's *Road to Mecca* (1954) is one of the most influential in the twentieth century.[6] Another important spiritual autobiography is *The Autobiography of Malcolm X* (1965), which follows the conversion narrative that has been hegemonic since Augustine wrote his *Confessions* (397). In other words, the apostasy narrative follows a similar pattern but changes the place of religion that the narrator has left (Barbour 1994: 4). But *leaving* religion does not necessarily mean *losing* religion. A change of religion can also imply yet another conversion; another religion is found and replaces the former one, which is also the case in some of my material.

The apostasy narrative is characterized by a severe critique of the religion one has left. However, that does not imply that the narrative gives a "correct," "corresponding" description of the past, and even if it did, "the analyst," as Peter G. Stromberg writes, "has no access to the original conversion event, and whatever it was that happened there, it cannot be observed" (Stromberg 2014: 130). The language of a deconversion or apostasy narrative is shaped by the culture in which it is expressed—the question is whether even the apostasy process itself can be said to be shaped by culture (Stromberg 2014: 120). The ordering of events in the past into a causal and meaningful order in the present in the form of a deconversion narrative indicates that such a narrative is informed by and indeed embedded in culture and its norms, values, and ideologies. The transformation aspect of religious conversion and disaffiliation is, as Stromberg puts it, "best understood as accomplished not in the original conversion event but rather in the ritual recounting of that event, the conversion narrative" (Stromberg 2014: 130).

Furthermore, the distinction between "conversion as lived experience and conversion as narrated in words" is essential (Hindmarsh 2014: 345). The same is true for apostasy. Bruce Hindmarsh continues: "The experience [raw data] of religious conversion has led, that is, to creative re-reading of one's own life in these new terms, as a second conversion of life into text" (Hindmarsh 2014:

349). From a narratological perspective an apostasy narrative is always also a "conversion of life into text" (Hindmarsh 2014: 349). That implies a discrepancy between "life" and "narrative," a commonly held presumption within the field of autobiographical studies, that does not primarily understand the narrator's retelling and memory of the conversion as simply "raw data" but as a narrative (Smith and Watson 2010: 15–16). The narratological perspective on the apostasy narratives understands it as belonging to a specific genre, with explicit or implicit codes, values, and syntax. Even if these codes can be similar across cultures and religions, there are certain elements that are time-bound and more context-specific than others. I have observed a couple of themes after going through a wide range of contemporary apostasy narratives.

From the narratives that I have examined it is clear that Islam is presented in a negative way and can be summed up as follows: "(1) Islam is an irrational, illogical way of thought and the beliefs that Muslims hold to be true are actually false... (2) Islam is not about peace, high standards and God; Islam is an evil, self-centered and morally corrupt religion, and Muslims are hypocrites... (3) Islam is an oppressive, misogynist and violent religion, and it is negative for its followers, especially women, even if they don't know it themselves" (Enstedt and Larsson 2013).[7] The recurring phrases characterizing the apostasy narratives are words that seem to be impossible to combine with Islam: "rationality, logic and truth; peacefulness, happiness; freedom, equality and autonomy" (Enstedt and Larsson 2013). This way of describing Islam has been frequent in Western culture. Islam is described as a more or less fundamentalist religion, far from the peace-loving and democratic image of Islam sometimes given by Muslim advocates. The apostates confirm these stereotypes about Islam by referring to their own experiences as Muslims, giving their image of Islam an air of authenticity. Such an image of Islam plays a crucial part in their narratives about leaving Islam.

A key aspect of the apostasy narratives' truth claim is that they are based on the narrators' memory and experience. That does not mean that the narrative is personal in the sense of being private. The narrator rather uses and reproduces a conventional, hegemonic narrative about what it means to leave Islam. From a theoretical stance, memory is not only about a personal and private experience but also exists *outside* the individual, as a constitutive element of the social world. And as such, the collective, cultural memory is always related to the specific space where memory takes place. A conceptual tool that Steve Stern, among others, uses when analyzing memories and narratives is "the idea of 'emblematic memory' and its unfolding interaction with the lore of 'loose memory'" (Stern 2010: 10). While the "loose memory" is understood as personal, socially unanchored, the "emblematic memory" is always embedded in a specific social framework of meaning and drawn from experience. According to Stern, the "'loose memory' provides a rich lore of raw material, the authenticity of stories and symbols grounded in particular lives and useful for the making of emblematic memory" (Stern 2010: 10). I do find this distinction useful, even if I don't agree with Stern's understanding of loose memories as strictly personal. Theories about emblematic memories do, however, emphasize the concept of power, especially when focusing on how hegemonic memories are at work in the formation of religious and nonreligious groups and, at the same time, exclude—erase or silence—nonhegemonic memories about, for instance, experiences of apostasy.

When narrated, the memories about the time as a Muslim and the apostasy process that leads to leaving Islam are, to different degrees, embedded in a contemporary and widespread Islamophobic discourse about Islam, and some of my interviewees use several arguments that also can be found in the New Atheism movement. The new emblematic memories about leaving Islam are first and foremost emerging in Western countries, and when these memories are shared by people from other parts of the world they are also arguing in similar ways. I would like to reverse Stern's use of emblematic and loose memories and say that the emblematic memories are, at least, as much "raw material" as the loose memories when memories are produced. Furthermore, the new groups of apostates that I have studied share similar emblematic memories about Islam, as I already have pointed out in the introduction to this chapter. My point is that the emblematic memories of Islam and of being an ex-Muslim constitute the apostasy groups. And to be a part of the apostasy communities that are emerging in Sweden and elsewhere, the apostates have to use the now hegemonic and emblematic memories when narrating about their experiences as former Muslims.

MATERIALITY, EMOTIONS, AND VALUES

In addition to narratological perspectives and the embodiment of Western Islamophobic discourse—where Islam still plays an important role as "the other," as the mirror image of the apostates' identification as former Muslims—there are still other perspectives on apostasy that need to be discussed. Even though the apostates have left Islam, at least in one sense, and articulate a severe critique often based on their own life experiences, some of them still linger on as habits, practices, norms, and values that are deeply influenced by Islam (cf. Yang and Abel 2015). Some apostates, in fact, keep parts of the religious tradition intact, while, and on another level, renouncing Islam. A real change of these habits would demand a (re)habituation that leads to another habitus (Mahmood 2005: 136–139; Bourdieu 1977).

Many apostates mark the ex-Muslim position ritually by eating or drinking things that are commonly considered *haram* (forbidden in Islam).[8] Some eat pork and drink alcohol; others change their clothing by, for instance, removing the *hijab*. One recent expression of the latter is the website My Stealthy Freedom, where mostly Iranian women post pictures of themselves without the *hijab*, or with the *hijab* as a piece of cloth, in the wind above their head, as an expression of freedom and as a critique of the Iranian regime.[9] Apostasy is demonstrated when central symbols and identity markers of Islam are blasphemed. Even though some of the apostates who I have interviewed had tried pork and alcohol before becoming an ex-Muslim—not least those who had migrated from Iran who bought pork meat from the Assyrian population and drank locally produced wine—apostasy was, for some of them, marked symbolically by eating non-*halal* meat. Simon Cottee has also noticed this in his recent study about ex-Muslims in the UK and Canada. These are the words of one of his interviewees:

> A lot of Muslims have sex, drink alcohol and eat non-*halal* meat, but the ultimate thing for them is the bacon, is the pork. So for me it was symbolic. It was the last bit of Islam (Cottee 2015: 76).

Eating bacon is for some of the ex-Muslims the final step to becoming an apostate. Bacon is also discussed in the interviews that I have conducted. One of the interviewees mentioned that he orders bacon every time he eats hamburgers, even though he thinks bacon is repulsive. For him, it is a way to show others around him—people who he thinks see him as a Muslim due to his appearance—that he is not a Muslim. Another interviewee, Yusuf—a gay disaffiliated "non-denominational" (cf. Yip 1997: 112) Muslim—describes how his throat started to itch when he accidentally ate bacon. The bacon made him feel "sick" and caused him to spit out the food.

Another interviewee mentioned the strategies she and her friends used to criticize the Iranian regime. They wore the veil at the limits of what was allowed and expressed their political position by showing their hair in public. They also opposed the regime by using a similar strategy by applying makeup in an exaggerated way, according to the interviewee. Even after becoming a Swedish citizen she put on makeup in the same manner, since it defined who she was, even though the Iranian regime was, at least in a geographical sense, distant.

The position of these symbols—the bacon (food), veil (clothing), and

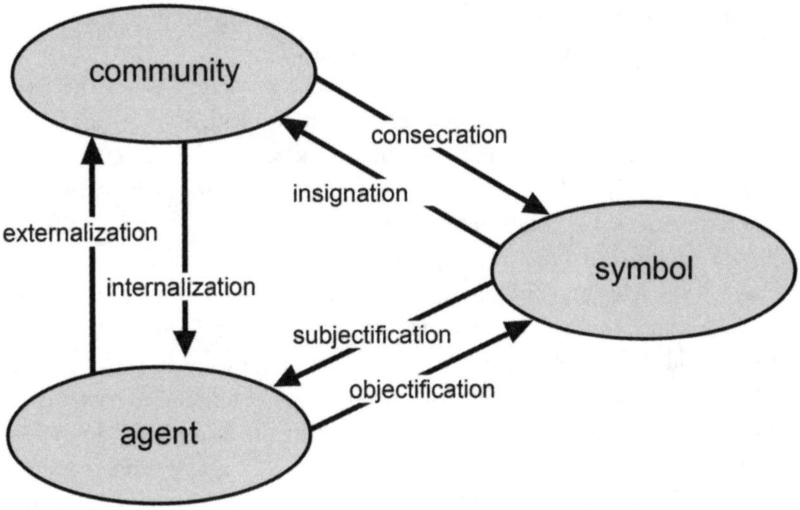

FIGURE 3.1.
Dialectical relations.

makeup (bodily practices)—in relation to the apostasy narrative can be better understood through Linda Woodhead and Ole Riis's (2010: 118) dialectical model of the relation between agent, symbol, and community (see figure 3.1). The model illustrates a well-functioning relation between the agent, community, and symbol, what Woodhead and Riis call a "balanced religious emotional regime" where:

> an agent's emotions are shaped by internalizing norms enacted by a community, and by subjectifying emotions related to sacred symbols. The agent may objectify religious emotion by creating or appropriating symbols that are emotionally meaningful to him or her. Feelings relating to such symbols are shared with others in the process of insignation, and insignation is disciplined by consecration (Woodhead and Riis 2010: 118).

The symbols that are consecrated in, for instance, a Muslim community work as a signifier for the same community. The agent that is part of the community shares the consecrated, or sacred, meaning of the symbols and manifests it through bodily and emotional expressions. Leaving the Muslim community could accordingly also mean that the values that the community has ascribed to the symbol is, to use Woodhead and Riis's vocabulary, "disconnected" (2010: 123–146). Interestingly, as the example above shows, even if the apostate denounces Islam and withdraws from the Muslim community, parts of the religion's values and norms that the apostate has cultivated for a long time can still remain as part of the apostate's habitus.

The symbolic act of eating bacon makes the apostate part of the non-Muslim community, and the emotional reaction on accidentally eating bacon and spitting it out can accordingly be understood as norms, values, and practice that are deeply embedded in Islam still playing an important part for the nondenominational apostate. In practice, emotionally, he is still a Muslim, even though his sexuality is considered *haram*, even by himself. Even though he has left the Muslim community, he still observes some of its central symbols, such as not eating or drinking anything *haram*. Religious practices concerning food and beverages, norms, and values and, in some cases, religious holidays can still be observed by ex-Muslims who have renounced Islam. Even in cases where Islam has been left for another religion, Islam is still an important part of the identification as a non-Muslim. There is a continuing preoccupation with Islam that constitutes the new identification as an ex-Muslim, as well as, in some cases, continued practice, values, and emotions that are linked to the religion that has been abandoned. This makes the apostasy process more ambiguous, since the boundaries between the religious and the secular, or between two religions, become blurred (cf. Knott 2013: 145–160). The question that arises is then about *what* has actually changed during a process of religious disaffiliation, deconversion, and apostasy.

Furthermore, as Simon Cottee points out, there is no reliable "ex-Muslim post-apostasy script" (2015: 173). Islam is still present through old habits, values, and emotions. The apostates also tell about a struggle with the "*halal* voice" and their "inner Muslim," which they do not completely succeed in getting rid of, or, as Cottee concludes: the apostates may have left Islam but Islam has not left them (Cottee 2015: 203; see also Cottee, this volume).

Studies about leaving new religious movements—so-called cults—have, at least since the 1980s, influenced the general study about leaving religion (Wessinger 2000: 6; Richardson and Introvigne 2001: 163). In more recent times, new theoretical and methodological approaches have been developed, and many of them seem to linger on in an idea about apostasy where leaving religion is a more or less linear process, where the apostate is replacing one religion with another or abandoning religion altogether. In apostasy narratives such a process is often described metaphorically as a journey from one relatively stable religious position to another (Smith and Watson 2010: 266). Furthermore, different religious positions (i.e., Muslim, Christian, or Jew) are often portrayed as incompatible in these narratives. However, leaving religion should not be understood merely as a change from one position to another but instead as a multidirectional process where some aspects of religion—in this case of Islam—are kept intact, while other aspects are renegotiated, are reformulated, and acquire another relevance and function in an apostate's life and narrative. In analyzing an apostasy narrative one also has to take into account the cultural narrative(s) about Islam and how such anti-Muslim narratives are embodied by the apostates. While a person may tell an apostasy narrative according to the cultural script where Islam is denounced altogether, he or she may also—at the same time—have other views on Islam where the religion is understood in more positive terms; their parents' or grandparents' Islam may, for instance, differ significantly from the regime in Iran or in Somalia before Al-Shabaab. What a closer analysis of the apostasy narratives shows is that they are multivocal, polyphonic, or, as Mikhail Bakhtin would have phrased it, characterized by heteroglossia, that is, each narrative contains different, sometimes incoherent voices (Bakhtin 1984; Holstein and Gubrium 2003: 22). In addition, by focusing on other types of material than the narratives, such as materiality, symbols, and bodily and gendered practices, one might find that leaving Islam is not about a linear process from one position to another but is rather multidimensional. It may also be multidirectional where apostasy is part of an ongoing personal, cultural, and societal change, not least in a migration context where the coordinates that define the person have changed. Still, that change does not necessarily indicate a more radical change of that person's habitus.

CONCLUDING REMARKS

The previous studies on religious apostasy have, as I have shown above, focused on the *belief* and *belonging* aspects of religion. In this chapter I have examined other aspects that can challenge and contribute to the understanding of religious apostasy. I have questioned a one-sided "cognitive" understanding of religion, where religion is commonly understood as ideas, perspectives on life, or cognitive schemas. There is a continuing preoccupation with Islam that constitutes the new role as ex-Muslim and, in some cases, continued practice that is linked to the religion that has been abandoned.

To conclude, while religious *commitment* tends to vary, not least in a migration situation, "one's basic religious orientation" does not have to change (Yang and Abel 2014: 143). And while one's religious *beliefs* can be abandoned, or denounced as in an apostasy narrative, the faith can be intact and so can habits and practices, norms, and values that are deeply connected with, in this case, Islam. One can therefore leave the social and belief aspects of religion but still be religious in a range of other aspects. The apostasy narratives are aligned with a hegemonic Western anti-Muslim discourse. Seemingly as an oxymoron, parts of Islam—such as certain norms, values, and habits—can still be observed, to different degrees, by some apostates, but these practices are primarily carried out at home, in the private sphere, where "religion" can be practiced without being put into question in contemporary Sweden. The former Muslims' habitus does not change as dramatically as the narratives sometime indicate. The apostates are, in a way, assimilated into mainstream Swedish culture, where religion is usually understood as differentiated and separated from other spheres of society or can be practiced at home.

NOTES

1. Woodhead (2011) discusses concepts of religion such as religion as (1) *culture*, where meaning, belief, and values are included; (2) *identity*, with the focus on religious groups, boundaries, and belonging; (3) *relationship*, including experiences, emotions, and social and super-social relations; (4) *practice*, that is embodiment, rituals, and "lived religion"; and (5) *power*, on macro-, meso-, and micro-levels.

2. Twenty years after Bellah's and Madsen's publication, Linda Woodhead and Paul Heelas et al. published *The Spiritual Revolution* (2005). Heelas and Woodhead suggest that a spiritual revolution is about to happen and that there already is evidence that it has started, as they found Sheilaism in Kendal.

3. Including Front National (France), EDP (Great Britain), Jobbik (Hungary), Sverigedemokraterna (Sweden), Fremskrittspartiet (Norway), to name a few.

4. Altemeyer and Hunsberger (1997: 21) define apostates as "persons who have abandoned a religion they once believed in." The *amazing* apostates are those relatively few who had have an intensive religious upbringing and yet left their parents' or primary caregivers' religion. According to Altemeyer and Hunsberger's findings, males "demonstrated a greater tendency to become Amazing Apostates," which also confirms the more general findings in the study of religion, that is, that men are less religious than women (Altemeyer and Hunsberger 1997: 107–108).

5. The deconverts also score higher than in-tradition members on the Big Five's openness to the experience variable (and lower on variables such as religious fundamentalism and right-wing authoritarianism) and share, according to the study, a common personality trait.

6. A film called *A Road to Mecca—The Journey of Muhammad Asad* (2008), directed by Georg Misch, was based on that book.

7. The quote is taken from the online journal *CyberOrient* 7, no. 1 (2013) (www.cyber orient.net); no page numbers.

8. However, there is not a single, unified understanding of what *haram* is in Islam (see Svensson 2015: 31–33).

9. mystealthyfreedom.net/en.

REFERENCES

Adang, Camilla, et al., eds. 2015. *Accusations of Unbelief in Islam: A Diachronic Perspective on Takfīr*. Leiden: Brill.

Allen, Christopher 2010. *Islamophobia*. Farnham, Surrey: Ashgate.

Altemeyer, Bob and Bruce Hunsberger. 1997. *Amazing Conversions: Why Some Turn to Faith and Others Abandon Religion*. Amherst, NY: Prometheus.

Ammerman, Nancy T., ed. 2007. *Everyday Religion: Observing Modern Religious Lives*. Oxford and New York: Oxford University Press.

Ammerman, Nancy Tatom 2013. *Sacred Stories, Spiritual Tribes: Finding Religion in Everyday Life*. New York: Oxford University Press.

Asad, Muhammad. 1954. *The Road to Mecca*. New York: Simon and Schuster.

Bakhtin, Mikhail. 1984. *Problems of Dostoevsky's Poetics*. Manchester: Manchester University Press.

Barbour, John D. 1994. *Versions of Deconversion: Autobiography and the Loss of Faith*. Charlottesville: University Press of Virginia.

Bellah, Robert Neelly, ed. 1985. *Habits of the Heart: Individualism and Commitment in American Life*. Berkeley: University of California Press.

Bendixsen, Synnøve. 2010. "Islam as a New Urban Identity? Young Female Muslims Creating a Religious Youth Culture in Berlin." In *Gender, Religion, and Migration Pathways of Integration*. Glenda Tibe Bonifacio and Vivienne S. M. Angeles. Lanham, MD: Lexington Books. 95–114.

Berger, Peter L., Grace Davie, and Effie Fokas. 2008. *Religious America, Secular Europe: A Theme and Variations*. Aldershot, UK: Ashgate.

Bourdieu, Pierre. 1977. *Outline of a Theory of Practice*. Cambridge: Cambridge University Press.

Caplovitz, David, and Fred Sherrow. 1977. *The Religious Drop-Outs: Apostasy among College Graduates*. Beverly Hills, CA: SAGE.

Cottee, Simon. 2015. *The Apostates: When Muslims Leave Islam*. London: C. Hurst.

Ebaugh, Helen Rose Fuchs. 1988. *Becoming an Ex: The Process of Role Exit*. Chicago: University of Chicago Press.

Enstedt, Daniel, and Göran Larsson. 2013. "Telling the Truth about Islam? Apostasy Narratives and Representations of Islam on WikiIslam.net." *CyberOrient* 7, no 1.

Gardell, Mattias. 2011. *Islamofobi*. 2. uppl. Stockholm: Leopard.

Göle, Nilüfer. 2003. "The Voluntary Adoption of Islamic Stigma Symbols." *Social Research* 70, no. 3: 809–828.

Griffel, Frank. 2016. "Apostasy." *Encyclopaedia of Islam, THREE*. Kate Fleet et al., eds. Brill Online. referenceworks.brillonline.com.ezproxy.ub.gu.se/entries/encyclopaedia-of-islam-3/apostasy-SIM_0044.

Heelas, Paul, and Linda Woodhead. 2005. *The Spiritual Revolution: Why Religion Is Giving Way to Spirituality*. Malden, MA: Blackwell.

Hervieu-Léger, Danièle. 1998. "The Transmission and Formation of Socioreligious Identities in Modernity: An Analytical Essay on the Trajectories of Identification." *International Sociology* 13, no. 2: 213.

Hindmarsh, Bruce. 2014. "Religious Conversion as Narrative and Autobiography." In *The Oxford Handbook of Religious Conversion*. Lewis R. Rambo and Charles E. Farhadian, eds. Oxford and New York: Oxford University Press. 343–368.

Holstein, James A., and Jaber F. Gubrium. 2003. "Inside Interviewing: New Lenses, New Concern." In *Inside Interviewing: New Lenses, New Concerns*. James A. Holstein and Jaber F. Gubrium, eds. Thousand Oaks, CA; London; and New Delhi: SAGE. 3–30.

Inglehart, Ronald, and Christian Welzel. 2010. "Changing Mass Priorities: The Link between Modernization and Democracy." *Perspectives on Politics* 8, no. 2 (June): 551–567.

Johnson, Todd M. 2014. "Demographics of Religious Conversion." In *The Oxford Handbook of Religious Conversion*. Lewis R. Rambo and Charles E. Farhadian, eds. Oxford and New York: Oxford University Press. 48–64.

Kefeli, Agnès Nilüfer. 2014. *Becoming Muslim in Imperial Russia: Conversion, Apostasy, and Literacy*. Ithaca: Cornell University Press.

Kent, Eliza F. 2014, "Feminist Approaches to the Study of Religious Conversion." In *The Oxford Handbook of Religious Conversion*. Lewis R. Rambo & Charles E. Farhadian, eds. Oxford and New York: Oxford University Press. 297–326.

Knott, Kim. 2013, "The Secular Sacred: In-between or Both/And?" In *Social Identities Between the Sacred and the Secular*. Abby Day et al., eds. Farnham, Surrey: Ashgate. 145–160.

Kong, Lily. 2010. "Global Shifts, Theoretical Shifts: Changing Geographies of Religion." *Progress in Human Geography* 34, no. 6: 758.

Kong, Lily, and Nair Seeta. 2014. "Geographies of Religious Conversion," In *The Oxford Handbook of Religious Conversion*. Lewis R. Rambo and Charles E. Farhadian, eds. Oxford and New York: Oxford University Press. 65–83.

Larsson, Göran and Åke Sander. 2007. *Islam and Muslims in Sweden: Integration or Fragmentation? A Contextual Study*. Berlin: Lit.

Larsson, Göran. 2015. "Apostasy in the West: A Swedish Case Study." In *Accusations of Unbelief in Islam: A Diachronic Perspective on Takfir*. Camilla Adang et al., eds. Leiden and Boston: Brill. 381–392.

Mahmood, Saba. 2005. *Politics of Piety: The Islamic Revival and the Feminist Subject*. Princeton: Princeton University Press.

Marshall, Paul A., and Nina Shea. 2011. *Silenced: How Apostasy and Blasphemy Codes Are Choking Freedom Worldwide*. New York: Oxford University Press.

McGuire, Meredith B. 2008. *Lived Religion: Faith and Practice in Everyday Life*. New York: Oxford University Press.

Norris, Pippa, and Ronald Inglehart. 2011. *Sacred and Secular: Religion and Politics Worldwide*. 2nd ed. Cambridge: Cambridge University Press.

O'Brien, Jodi. 2004. "Wrestling the Angel of Contradiction: Queer Christian Identities." *Culture and Religion* 5, no. 2: 179–201.

Otterbeck, Jonas. 2010. *Samtidsislam: unga muslimer i Malmö och Köpenhamn*. Stockholm: Carlsson.

Rambo, Lewis R., and Charles E. Farhadian, eds. 2014. *The Oxford Handbook of Religious Conversion*. Oxford and New York: Oxford University Press.

Rambo, Lewis Ray. 1993. *Understanding Religious Conversion*. New Haven: Yale University Press.

Richardson, James T., and Massimo Introvigne. 2001. "'Brainwashing' Theories in European Parliamentary and Administrative Reports on 'Cults' and 'Sects.'" *Journal for the Scientific Study of Religion* 40, no. 2: 143–168.

Riis, Ole, and Linda Woodhead. 2010. *A Sociology of Religious Emotion*. Oxford: Oxford University Press.

Saeed, Abdullah, and Hassan Saeed. 2003. *Freedom of Religion, Apostasy, and Islam*. Aldershot: Ashgate.

Sedgwick, Mark J., ed. 2015. *Making European Muslims: Religious Socialization among Young Muslims in Scandinavia and Western Europe*. New York: Routledge.

Smith, Sidonie, and Julia Watson. 2010. *Reading Autobiography: A Guide for Interpreting Life Narratives*. 2nd ed. Minneapolis: University of Minnesota Press.

Stern, Steve J. 2010. *Reckoning with Pinochet: The Memory Question in Democratic Chile, 1989–2006*. Durham: Duke University Press.

Streib, Heinz. 2014. "Deconversion." In *The Oxford Handbook of Religious Conversion*. Lewis R. Rambo and Charles E. Farhadian, eds. Oxford and New York: Oxford University Press. 271–296.

Streib, Heinz, et al. 2009. *Deconversion: Qualitative and Quantitative Results from Cross-Cultural Research in Germany and the United States of America*. Göttingen: Vandenhoeck & Ruprecht.

Stromberg, Peter G. 2014. "The Role of Language in Religious Conversion." In *The Oxford Handbook of Religious Conversion*. Lewis R. Rambo and Charles E. Farhadian, eds. Oxford and New York: Oxford University Press. 117–139.

Svensson, Jonas. 2015. *Människans Muhammed*. Farsta: Molin & Sorgenfrei. 31–33.

Wessinger, Catherine Lowman. 2000. *How the Millennium Comes Violently: From Jonestown to Heaven's Gate*. New York: Seven Bridges Press.

Woodhead, Linda. 2011. "Five Concepts of Religion." *International Review of Sociology: Revue Internationale de Sociologie* 21, no. 1: 121–143.

Wright, Stuart A. 1987. *Leaving Cults: The Dynamics of Defection*. Washington, DC: Society for the Scientific Study of Religion.

X, Malcolm. 1965. *The Autobiography of Malcolm X*. Harmondsworth: Penguin.

Yang, Fenggang, and Andrew Abel. 2014. "Sociology of Religious Conversion." In *The Oxford Handbook of Religious Conversion*. Lewis R. Rambo and Charles E. Farhadian, eds. Oxford and New York: Oxford University Press. 140–163.

Yip, Andrew K. T. 2000. "Leaving the Church to Keep My Faith: The Lived Experiences of Non-heterosexual Christians." In *Joining and Leaving Religion: Research Perspectives*. Leslie J. Francis and Yaacov Julian Katz, eds. Leominster: Gracewing. 129–145.

SECTION II

(DE)CONVERSION, RACE, CULTURE, AND ETHNICITY

FOUR

GIVING ISLAM A GERMAN FACE

ESRA ÖZYÜREK

Afeefa looked flustered at the weekly breakfast for women at the DMK (Deutschsprachiger Muslimkreis, or German-Speaking Muslim Circle), which meets at the Bilal mosque in Wedding, a poor neighborhood with many immigrant residents.[1] About ten to fifteen women, all converts to Islam, attend these breakfasts every Wednesday at 10:00 a.m., right after they drop off their kids at school and perhaps run a few errands. They say it is a great place to catch up with friends and have a few hours to oneself. It also offers a unique opportunity for converted German Muslim women to be among people like themselves and feel comfortable. Because regulars at this breakfast feel it is important to find German Muslim women when they first convert, they make an effort to ensure that the breakfasts are regularly held to welcome potential newcomers to the group. Women who call up to say they have converted to Islam or are thinking about it, and even sometimes those who are worried about their daughters or sisters converting, are heartily invited to this breakfast so that they can meet indigenous German Muslims. As one of the people responsible for this particular Wednesday breakfast, Afeefa brought along about forty freshly baked white rolls (*schrippe*) and a dozen organic eggs that she planned to soft-boil. She took several sticks of butter, a couple of berry jams, Nutella, *halal* cold cuts and sausages, and tubes of cheesy spreads from the well-stocked fridge, and prepared the double coffeemaker with many scoops of coffee.

After we sat down and a few of the women took off their headscarves in the intimate company of their Muslim sisters, Afeefa said that she had had it with her non-Muslim cousin, who had been visiting her family for a week. The entire time, the cousin had accused Afeefa of not being a German anymore. She told her, "Look, you dress differently, you eat differently, you say these strange Arabic words to your friends, you have nothing German about you anymore." Afeefa was angry with her. She kept saying, "Of course I am German." She compared herself to another cousin in the family. "Katarina is vegetarian. She also does not drink alcohol. Somehow she can still be German, but I cannot be because I do not eat pork or drink alcohol!" She was especially annoyed at her cousin for sitting at the breakfast table every morning in low-cut shirts: "Why did my husband have to look at her breasts all morning?"

German scholars—and most of mainstream German society—tend to think of German converts to Islam as people who are fleeing their German identity—something still an embarrassment to many Germans more than sixty years after the end of World War II—and symbolically emigrating elsewhere (Wohlrab-Sahr 2002). My research shows that even though converting to Islam transforms ethnic Germans' lives dramatically, and usually in ways that they did not prepare themselves for, most German Muslims are invested in opening a space for themselves where they can comfortably embrace their Muslim and German identities at the same time. The Swedish scholar Anne Sofie Roald (2006), who is also a convert to Islam, states that, since the 2000s, a good number of Scandinavian converts have tried to integrate what they see as Scandinavian values into their understanding of Islam as well. A golden mean that brings German and Muslim identities perfectly together is not always easy to find—and definitely not something shared by all members of the German Muslim community. Most German Muslims, especially those who socialize with other German Muslims in contexts such as the DMK, strongly believe that it is possible to be a good Muslim without sacrificing one's German identity. German Muslims claim that, as converts, they can even be better Muslims than immigrant Muslims.[2] They imply that, by definition, they live a pure Islam not contaminated by cultural practices and urge native-born Muslims also to purify their Islamic practice of the stigmatized cultural traditions.[3] Furthermore, some suggest, their commitment and contribution to a religiously diverse society makes them more tolerant as well as better connected to the lost ideals of the German Enlightenment, best represented in the writings of Johann Wolfgang von Goethe (1749–1832) and Gotthold Ephraim Lessing (1729–1781). Thus, many German Muslims promote the idea that their stance is closer not only to the true nature of Islam but also to the best of German and European ideals.

THE GERMAN-SPEAKING MUSLIM CIRCLE

As one of the first German-speaking Muslim associations in postwar Germany, the DMK, founded in Berlin in the 1990s, has a special role in Muslim Germany. The DMK was originally established not by German converts to Islam but rather by non-Turkish and non-Arab Muslim students who came to Germany to study and could not find a religious community for themselves. These students thought that a German-language Muslim community would be able to bring together Muslims who do not speak the languages that are used in mosques in Germany. Once it was founded as the only German-speaking Islamic forum in Berlin, the DMK quickly united the diverse German converts to Islam and brought them together as a community, becoming a popular address. The DMK community consists of a few hundred registered members and an approximately equal number of others who attend the mosque without being members. Of its congregation, about half of the people are German, Russian, French, Argentinean, and Polish converts to Islam, and the other half consists of Muslims with roots in different Muslim-majority countries around the world.

Being able to provide a German-speaking Muslim space where no Islamic tradition is preferred over others, and Muslims of different backgrounds thus feel themselves at home, is crucial. The DMK's web page emphasizes that it bases itself only on the Qur'an and *hadith* and does not prioritize any Islamic legal school or tradition above others. It states: "We follow Allah's word in Sura 2, verse 256 'There is no compulsion in religion!' and we respect different interpretations and legal schools." It defines itself as a community where "Muslims with different mother tongues and cultures get together under the common banner of Islam and the German language. That is why, when a visitor comes to the DMK we do not ask them to which legal school they belong to. Rather we offer all Muslims the possibility to encounter each other with an equal footing."[4]

In addition to its stress on the German language and commitment to a nonsectarian approach to Islam, the DMK differs from other mosques in Germany in that a high proportion of its members have BAs or even PhDs. Most likely because it was first established by foreign Muslim students who came to study in German universities, the mosque continues to be a gathering place for foreign, native-born Muslims along with converted Muslims pursuing graduate or postgraduate studies. The DMK is also unique in Germany for the high number of women among its membership and also at the Shura, a democratically elected consultation board. Women participate to such an extent that the DMK's Shura had to institute a bylaw ensuring that neither gender is represented by more than 60 percent on this board. In 2013, the mosque's *amir* (leader) was a woman. The active involvement of women in this mosque is readily apparent from their presence at any event or discussion that takes place there. In its respect for diversity in Islam, commitment to democracy and women's representation, and emphasis on the German language, the DMK promotes itself as both a model democratic German community and an Islamic community that puts the best possible German face on an Islamic practice that its members see as true to its founding principles.

BECOMING MUSLIM WHILE REMAINING GERMAN

German Muslims who convert to Islam share common experiences with immigrant Muslims when it comes to living their religion in a non-Muslim society that is not accommodating to the Islamic lifestyle. Much of the everyday experience of converts is unique to them, however, in that they do not fit in either the German mainstream or Muslim immigrant communities. Zeynep, a 43-year-old convert who embraced Islam around twenty years ago, told me that the most distinctive feeling she has about being a German Muslim is not fitting in coupled with the consequent loneliness. A sensitive and reflective person, Zeynep observed:

> I feel that as German Muslims, we are doubly marginalized. First Germans push us aside, and then Turks and Arabs turn their backs on us. That makes one feel very lonely. No one thinks about us when people talk about Muslims in Germany. We are totally invisible. Germans most often think we are crazy. Once a politician even said we are dangerous. Others think we converted because we got taken by a macho man. They call us traitors, people who left their culture behind and took someone else's. This is when they realize that I am a convert. Other times, it does not even occur to them that I might be a German. They treat me like an ignorant immigrant who does not speak German, who cannot be an intellectual, who cannot raise her children properly.

The reaction that converts received from born Muslims was not all that different. As Zeynep recounted:

> And Turks do not accept us either. In my son's class, there are some Turks. They tell him that "your mother is a German so she does not need to cover her hair." It is not possible for them to accept that I am also a Muslim. Older Turkish women tell me that I cannot be a Muslim. They think Islam is only for Turks. It is hard even when people have the best intentions. When I first converted, a Turkish family took me in and treated me like their daughter. But even there I felt very lonely, because I was very different from them. They were very nice but very simple people. I couldn't relate

> to them at an intellectual level. In the end, I feel as though no one understands who I am. And I always feel in the wrong category.

Many German converts to Islam told me that as time passed they felt more and more strongly that they did not fit in any category. As the intensity of the conversion experience mellows, converts become aware of the new social role they find themselves in and realize the new walls that surround them. What has been most appalling to converts to Islam, especially women who don the headscarf, has been being taken as a foreigner in the society they grew up in comfortably and thereby losing the feeling that they totally belonged to it. During a conversation with Miriam about her early experiences of becoming a Muslim, the most outrageous thing for her was what she called "becoming a third-class citizen." In the women's section of a mosque cafeteria, Miriam told me that her life changed not when she converted to Islam but instead when she put on the headscarf. "I was outraged," she told me. "Overnight everyone on the street lost all the respect they paid me as a regular German woman, with nothing special about her." No one would make eye contact with her, salespeople were rude, and government officials did not listen to her carefully or let her talk.

According to Miriam, this all happens because they think she is a foreigner. Miriam wears long black or dark brown overcoats, large headscarves, and big, brown-tinted glasses. Something about her round face or relatively short, plump body actually does make her look more like a Turkish grandmother than most other converts I met. So when she tells people that she is German, they still do not believe her:

> They think I mean I am an immigrant with a German passport. I have often been told patronizingly that I should not assume I am a German just because I hold a German passport. To them, there is no such thing as a German Muslim. One has to be a foreigner. Then if I feel like continuing the conversation at all, I say, "My grandparents were Prussians. Is that German enough for you?"

When it is revealed that she has a German name, the change of reaction is impossible to miss. "When I am waiting for my turn at the government office, everyone would be ignoring me as usual. But when I hand in my papers with my German name, everyone looks horrified. They look at me as if I am a traitor. I know they are thinking that I converted because a man treated me so well in bed. But I used to notice such things only during the early years of my conversion." She laughed bitterly and confessed that, after fifteen years of it, she had become pretty insensitive to such treatment. "I do not expect anything different, and at least I do not get disappointed." She stopped and reflected. "Maybe," she said, "as I become older, I care less about others. Or maybe things have changed in Germany in the past fifteen years. I must say, I no longer come home outraged every time I go out, as I used to."

My conversations with more-recent converts tell me that Miriam's speculation about things changing in German society and making German Muslim existence easier is not completely true. It is, I suspect, the increase in the number of German converts that has helped Miriam, especially the creation of German Muslim circles where they can learn about Islam, practice their religion, and, most important, socialize with one another. As she became more active in such milieus, Miriam established many meaningful friendships with like-minded people. In the process, she also changed herself, and now that she is closely affiliated with a more or less isolationist Muslim community with tight in-group relations, she does not have to rely on mainstream society—or immigrant Muslims, for that matter—for emotional or intellectual support. Most likely, she has learned not to care about or expect much from her obligatory interactions with non-Muslims. She feels good about herself among her German Muslim friends, where she is a well-known and respected woman.

Consisting as they do almost exclusively of German converts, such growing communities develop a deep sense of German Islamic identity that is distinct from a Turkish or Arab one. In fact, some native German Muslims seek to create a German Islamic practice by stripping away Turkish and Arab cultural influences. Intellectuals among them go further and try to construct an alternative German genealogy that is inclusive of Islam based on the history of the German Enlightenment. Converts find ways to raise their children that are undoubtedly both Islamic and German. These efforts aim to open up legitimate space for Germans who have embraced Islam. At the same time, however, they sometimes end up reproducing anti-immigrant discourses that treat born or immigrant Muslims as not fitting in German society.

EUROPEANIZING ISLAM THROUGH PURIFICATION

"What is special about being a German Muslim?" I asked Hadi, a German convert and active member of the DMK, when we met over coffee and cookies at the organization's humble main office. What German-speaking Muslims practice is "do-it-yourself Islam," he said. "You try to acquire knowledge from totally different sources. There is no religious body and no full-fledged structure. There are no traditions you feel obliged to follow. As a result, you can decide on your own." Hadi did not think this was a bad thing. Rather, he saw it as an opportunity. "As a result, you can approach Islam more critically than you could in an Islamic country," Hadi explained:

> In general, Germans who embrace Islam have to be more critical. They have to be able to differentiate between Islam and culture. Some people like the culture, the music, the people, the style, and take the religion along with it. But most converts try to differentiate between what is Islamic and what is traditional. Also some rules that are taken for granted in Turkey may not fit in Germany. Then converts raise the question of why I have to do things this way, and see if it really has an Islamic basis. Because converts have no roots in any Islamic tradition, they can practice an Islam that is purified of traditions.

All Muslim residents of Germany (or any non-Muslim country, for that matter) have to struggle with the challenge of adapting Islam—or, more precisely, a Muslim lifestyle—to the local living conditions. Converts are, of course, those most invested in this project. The dominant approach, especially among them, is to strip Islam of its cultural baggage so as to make it fit a German/European lifestyle.

A lecture at the DMK by Imam Muhammad Salama of the Wolfsburg Islamic Center titled "Islam in Europe—European Islam?" explored the issue of experiencing Islam in Europe as European Muslims. It was attended by over forty members—mostly German converts. The concerns raised by the lecture were discussed intensely over five hours on the first day of spring, a Sunday, after a long winter.

The lecture began with a look at whether we can talk about a European Islam or not. Salama, whose background is Arab, made his position clear by making extensive references to the Swiss Muslim Tariq Ramadan, who promotes the view that one can be a good Muslim and good European through a rereading of the foundational texts of the Qur'an in their European context. According to Ramadan (1999, 2004), it is the cultural traditions that immigrant Muslims bring to Europe, and not Islam, that gets in the way of their being engaged European citizens. Like Ramadan, Salama saw the European experience of Islam as an opportunity for Muslims in general to free themselves of detrimental accretions and to accept the best aspects of Islam, which lie in its foundations.

A good portion of the participants were favorable to Ramadan's approach, and when Salama asked if they had either read his work or attended his recent talk in Berlin, most raised their hands.[5] In this interactive lecture, most participants shared the opinion that a part of what we commonly call "religion" is actually culture, and also that we can talk about an Arab, Indonesian, or Chinese Islam. They agreed that this conversation opened the doors for speaking about a European or German Islam—but what exactly that meant was not clear to anyone present. A number of participants raised their hands to warn that the term "European" Islam is usually used to promote a "liberal" Islam stripped of its essential features. A middle-aged German male listener raised his hand to observe:

> There is a difference between saying Islam in Europe or European Islam. When people promote the second, they usually mean a relaxed approach to religion—for example, one where the headscarf is not necessary. An Islam that is open to prostitution or gambling. That is why when I see the words European Islam, my stomach turns. As for myself, I want to say first I am a Muslim and then I am a German. When I say European Islam, I have the sense that it prioritizes the nationality rather than the religion.

Salama suggested that one could talk about an Islam that is influenced by European traditions. For instance, he said, "Arabs bring their own character traits to Islam. But because Europeans have calmer personalities, that will inevitably influence the way they live Islam. Experiences since the French Revolution will of course have an influence on Islam." He added, "God willing, the Islamic developments here are positive influences. For example, in the Middle East men have a patriarchal culture. But as Middle Eastern immigrants eventually become European Muslims, such traditions that are not part of Islam will be left behind. And we will be able to experience an Islam that is truer to itself."

At this point, the conference took a break for the noon prayer and lunch. During the lunch break, women in smaller groups continued discussing what it means to be a European Muslim. A German Muslim woman said, "We also need to question the concept of a European tradition to begin with. Now there is this big talk about Judeo-Christian tradition, and the Jews approach this discourse skeptically. Maybe there is no one big European tradition we need to adhere to. Maybe it already consists of many different segments. Then Islam is definitely one part of Europe." Another German convert to Islam brought a more concrete illustration to the conversation:

> I don't think our lifestyle as German Muslims is entirely different from all other Germans. My mother, for example, is not a Muslim, but her life is

> not so different from mine. Once in a while she drinks beer, but I cannot see anything that is really different between her life and my life. It is wrong to think that all Germans are always dancing away at a disco or that they are all gamblers. So maybe we Muslims are not all that different after all.

When the conference reconvened, Salama wanted to talk about the specific everyday challenges Muslims face in Germany and the solutions they can find. The problems that listeners listed consisted of a life that does not always respect the prayer times, employers who do not allow them to wear a headscarf, working situations that might require a man and woman to be alone together in a room, and having to be in social contexts where alcohol is consumed. In terms of finding solutions, the imam recommended that everyone decide for themselves and make a choice that allows them to feel comfortable facing God. "Only the person can decide on their own whether they have exhausted all the possible options or not," he said. "Religion isn't like mathematics; there are no firm answers valid for everyone and every situation."

This individualized solution-finding approach made some of the listeners uncomfortable. An older and much more vocal member of the community, who is sympathetic to the Salafi interpretation and regime in Saudi Arabia, accused the imam of giving a covert fatwa allowing for the removal of the headscarf. Salama objected, asserting that religious leaders have the responsibility to take the lives of people into consideration, and also that every single individual can decide what to do on their own. He stated, "Naturally, I see the headscarf as a duty, but also as a freedom. But in the end, women can decide if they want to fulfill this duty or not. No woman should be forced to wear or take off a headscarf."

In addition to an Islam that leaves decision making to the individual, the imam also promoted the idea of tolerance. He noted that people prejudge Islam as intolerant, especially of other religions. To counter such a belief, he said, we need to be particularly careful about which translations of the Qur'an we use. Salama recommended to the audience that they use the German Jewish convert Weiss/Asad's translation and try to focus on pieces of the text that emphasize tolerance and openness. "In three places in the Qur'an it says that those who believe in God—here meaning Jews and Christians—will also be rewarded after death. But then," the imam remarked, "here we are talking about how to live together in this world. It is another thing to say things will be such and such in the other world. Every religion has its own particular approach to this matter, and we are free to say what we like."

It is not only converted Muslims who promote a European Islam stripped of seemingly patriarchal, intolerant, and undemocratic cultural traditions attributed to immigrant Muslims. There are also a good number of born Muslims who promote the idea of a purified Islam that is both truer to itself and true to the European values of equality, freedom, and democracy. These concepts are not new but instead are inspired by earlier Islamic reformers as well as Enlightenment thinkers. Some of the same ideas that were originally promoted by Asad, a European convert to Islam, are now embraced by a number of Muslims with immigrant backgrounds. Still, indigenous European and converted Muslims are much more invested in stripping Islam of its cultural and national baggage so as to legitimate and normalize their position not only in mainstream German society but also in the Islamic *ummah*.

RAISING CHILDREN AS GERMAN AND MUSLIM

The complexities of being German and Muslim, along with the converts' desire to bring these identities together, are strongly reflected in how they raise their children. Many German Muslims I met spent most of their emotional and intellectual energy raising their children to feel comfortable as Germans and to be good Muslims. They are often frustrated, however, when teachers, neighbors, or other acquaintances accuse them of raising their children with another culture and even language. Zeynep, a 43-year-old convert who is a mother of four children, said: "For me, religion is a way, not a culture. I cannot teach my children a culture I do not know. So I teach them the German culture that I know. They sing German songs, they eat German food. I teach them what I know. Many times people ask me if I speak German to my children. Yes, I speak German because I am a German." Zeynep gets annoyed when people claim that she cannot raise her son properly because of her beliefs:

> My five-year-old son is a little bit naughty. At his preschool, his teachers told me that because he is being raised by Muslims, he has behavior problems. I was very angry. I told them that I am German, not an Arab, so he is not being raised by people who are different from them. Then they tell me that because his father does not respect women's rights, my son does not learn how to respect me, and that is why he does not listen to me or his other women teachers! I get furious when I hear such accusations. I am an educated woman and I am German. They always think I am a stupid immigrant. That makes me very angry. And what they say is not true at all. My husband always tells my children that they should respect their mother, that they should not make me upset. That is the most important thing, he

keeps telling them. Plus, my other children had a very easy time at school. It is just my son's personality; he is a little bit hyperactive. It is not a religious or cultural issue.

The issue of raising German Muslim children is frequently discussed in the DMK. Amina, who gives weekly Saturday lectures to women and works at an Islamic preschool, reminded everyone one Saturday afternoon of the difficulties they face as German Muslim mothers. "Our children are in a different position than children who grow up in Muslim majority countries," she said. "In such places, the fact that God exists and he is all powerful is an unquestioned reality of life. The questions our children ask us here, like if God is really big, where he sits, whether he eats or drinks, are questions asked to us because we live in a non-Muslim country." Amina added: "And that is why we have to be especially clear about the answers we give to our children. More important, we have to be very clear about these answers in our mind before we talk about them, so that we can pass this clarity to our children. We have to be especially good role models if we want to raise them as good Muslims in this non-Muslim society."

All Muslims who live in Germany confront the same challenge of raising their children in a Muslim-minority land. But converts to Islam have other hurdles too. For example, they need to negotiate the ways their non-Muslim parents relate to their children without questioning their beliefs. They also need to invent traditions for their German children in celebrating Muslim holidays. Jolanda, who is accepted as a Muslim by her German family, started to feel some tension building up after she had children. Her parents wanted her to join them along with her other siblings, nieces, and nephews for Christmas. She decided that she did not want to miss the opportunity of being part of a nice family gathering. Her compromise was to go there for Christmas dinner, but not for the service at the church. Jolanda also told her mother that they would not be there when Santa Claus came to bring children gifts. When her son reached the age of four, though, she realized how upset he would be when all the children but him received nice gifts. In the end, she and her mother reached the agreement that for Christmas, Jolanda's son, Ibrahim, would receive a small gift from his grandparents so that he would not feel left out. Jolanda's mother agreed to give him a big gift on Islamic holidays.

As her kids began to grow, Jolanda discovered that negotiating Christmas was not the only problem for a German Muslim mother; she had to figure out how to celebrate the Islamic holidays as well. She told me that she would not mind if her Algerian husband took the initiative and organized an Algerian-style celebration for the family, but he did not seem too invested in that. Jolanda explained that she realized that many of the things they do for holidays in Algeria did not make sense in the German context anyway. During Eid, for instance, Algerian children receive a set of new clothes. "But," she told me, "I felt as though this would be too little for my son. He gets new clothes all the time! So I had to buy him something more significant, something like a train set."

Jolanda then found the solution in bringing what she once did to celebrate German holidays into her Islamic practice. For Ramadan, say, she prepares a calendar for her son just like the advent calendar that is popular among Christian Germans. She told me that she made one herself, with a small gift for every day, so Ibrahim could open it up and find a surprise. She decorated her Ramadan calendar with moons, camels, and minarets, instead of the snowflakes and Santa Clauses that embellish advent calendars. Jolanda does not believe that she has to give up everything. She is a German and can celebrate her Islamic holidays only in the German way.

It gave Jolanda great comfort to send her son to an Islamic preschool run by converted women and attended mostly by children of converts. These preschools are not openly Islamic. Rather they are registered as bilingual: Arabic and German or Turkish and German. Even though there are many Protestant, Catholic, and even a Jewish preschool in Berlin, Islamic preschools are not allowed, because Islam does not have the status of a publicly recognized religion. Because there are many more converts married to Arabs than to Turks, and because Arabic is the holy language of Islam, converts and their children are commonly found in Arabic German schools and not so much in Turkish German schools. In these preschools, converted German women are active as both parents and teachers.

I visited one such preschool in Wedding several times and interviewed a converted German teacher about her philosophy in educating children as German and Muslim. Ayat told me that many of their aims are no different from those of other German preschools: they want to have children who can follow the rules, are able to establish social contact, can understand if someone needs help, and so on. In terms of identity, she continued, their aim is for children to recognize themselves as Muslim Berliners regardless of the background of their families. Ayat thinks it is crucial that the children see themselves and their future in Berlin as opposed to being fixated on the background of their parents, be it Arab or German. This sentiment resonates well with a recent survey conducted among Muslims living in the Kreuzberg neighborhood of Berlin (Mühe 2010). Muslim Kreuzbergers did not see themselves as German but instead felt themselves to be Berliners and were especially emotionally attached to their neighborhood. This survey was quoted in the newspaper as a failure, since most immigrant families did not feel themselves to be German. Along with a few others, I nevertheless saw it as a positive indicator that most people I interviewed felt attached to their city and particularly their neighborhood. This Islamic preschool in Wedding also wanted to foster this sense for a new generation of Muslims without making any reference to the thorny issue of ethnic identity.

As a teacher, Ayat explained, she wanted the children at the school to have an idea about why they do things as Muslims. "For example," she said, "we say a prayer before dinner." She did not find it essential if the children made fun of praying or any other Islamic practice. "Children cannot sin," she told me. "But when I ask them why they think they pray, I want them to have some answer as to why they are praying to God. That is what is important at this stage. As a principle," she told me, "we motivate them positively, and never scare them by saying if you do so and so you will go to hell." What was most critical, in her view, was that the children see people living their religion naturally. "They see that their teacher wears a headscarf and that during the flow of the day she prays. During prayers, the children stay quiet, and older kids take responsibility for that short period of time. They observe Islam as a normal thing, as a part of the flow of the day."

Ayat believes that Islamic preschools fulfill a key function not only for Muslim children but also for the mainstream society. It is important to her that they take Muslim children on field trips to visit places such as museums, art exhibits, theaters, concerts, and so forth, as is common with other Berlin preschools. The difference is that the teachers wear headscarves. Ayat mentioned that they get noticed quickly, especially when they are at places that are not usually frequented by Muslims. She thinks it is essential for both mainstream society and the Muslim children to realize that Muslims have a natural place in all parts of the city, that Muslims go everywhere and enjoy art, history, music, and architecture like all other Germans. They realize that Muslims do not need to be confined to certain neighborhoods, certain parks, and their homes. These kinds of gestures seem daring to born Muslims, or most likely never occur to them, because they grow up internalizing their exclusion from the mainstream society. Converted Muslims, who experience this self-inflicted and externally imposed exclusion at a later stage in their lives, are most invested in changing the landscape and going beyond the segregation of Muslims from mainstream German society.

In my research, I observed that the children of the most active converts turned out to be the most devotedly practicing as well as most active members of German-speaking youth organizations such as the DMK and Muslim Youth. They would participate in activities that are common for mainstream

German youths, such as camping trips, sports activities, and outings in the city, but in ways appropriate to orthodox definitions of Islam, such as gender segregation, *halal* food, and allotted times for prayers. These groups are often ethnically better mixed than most Islamic groups, which frequently cluster around one ethnic group. Children of converts are often ethnically mixed. When I asked teenage children of converted Germans if ethnic background was an issue in their groups, they repeatedly replied that it never comes up. The generation now growing up unambiguously German and Muslim will most likely be able to go beyond the dichotomy of German and Muslim.

CONCLUSION

Many experiences of converted German Muslims are similar to those of immigrant Muslims in Germany. They need to live their lives and fulfill their Islamic obligations in a society not organized for it, and they face resistance when they demand the right to do so. Both converted and born Muslims live in a society where Islam and especially headscarves are seen as a symbol of an inherently foreign culture as well as a mark of oppression. Despite these commonalities, many experiences are unique to converted German Muslims. When they convert, they have to deal with a dramatic loss of status in society—something for which they were not prepared. Born Muslims grew up learning the limits that society set for them. Even if they struggle against and challenge them, the marginalization they experience is a routine phenomenon. After being marginalized in the mainstream society to which they once unproblematically belonged, German Muslims face another unwelcome surprise when they realize that they do not fit in or are not welcomed by the existing Muslim communities in Germany, predominantly made up of Turkish and Arab communities that constitute the poorest, least educated segments of German society.

German converts to Islam resist their exclusion from the German national body and their dramatic fall in the symbolic social system by defending an Islam that is culturally compatible with Germanness. Like the African Americans that Du Bois (2013 [1903]) discusses, German converts to Islam develop a double consciousness, a peculiar sensation about being Muslim in Europe. In their efforts to easily and simply be both German and Muslim, they find themselves in a position to play a double role in transforming both mainstream German society and the immigrant-majority Muslim community. To Germans, they try to convey the message that there is a place for Islam in Germany, both historically and culturally. They remind them that the most prized intellectuals of German history were tolerant of and open-minded about Islam. They try to be model Muslims who do not carry the immigrant Muslims' stigmas and hence put a better face on Islam for German society. Then they turn to Muslim communities to show them what they consider their mistakes as well as encourage them to purify their lives of their un-Islamic and detrimental traditions. German converts to Islam demonstrate that being a German Muslim involves embodying the very best qualities of both German society and the Islamic community.

Many ideas that German Muslims promote to open up legitimate space for Islam in Germany are inspired by Enlightenment ideas of human reason and religion. First, they are based on the notion that fully free, unprejudiced humans (here meaning Germans) will judge for the best and be open-minded about Islam. Second, once stripped of its traditional interpretations, it will be obvious (again to Germans) that Islam is closest to the Enlightenment idea of a "natural religion," which is based on the concept that God simply reveals himself to the rational individual.[6] Needless to say, the particulars of deism are irrelevant for Muslims, yet the repeated emphases on the naturalness and rationality of Islam are clear references to an understanding of religion seen through the lens of Enlightenment values. In practice, the pure German or European Islam that is being promoted comes across as best suited to the rational European mind and unsuited to Oriental minds muddled by oppressive cultures and traditions. It thus often ends up being Europeanist and Eurocentrist.

NOTES

1. All the names used in this book are pseudonyms, unless referencing public figures. While choosing pseudonyms, I made sure that the names reflected the choice of individuals in using German, Arabic, or Turkish names. Some German converts use their original German names, and others adopted Arabic or Turkish names.

2. It is important to note that a number of Muslims in Europe with second- or third-generation immigrant backgrounds also embrace a similar stance (Bowen 2010). This spirit is best expressed in the work of the Swiss Muslim Tariq Ramadan (2004).

3. Mikaela Rogozen-Soltar (2012: 612) refers to a similar sentiment expressed by Spanish converts to Islam: "Converts often claim to practice a 'culture-free' Islam, which they contrast to Moroccans' 'traditions,' using a discourse that cloaks convert religiosity within an unmarked category of 'European' and marks migrant Muslims as outsiders."

4. See www.dmk-berlin.de.

5. It is important to note that Ramadan's view would not be approved of in some other settings frequented by converted German Muslims, such as Sufi lodges or Salafi-oriented

Sunni mosques. Sufis would find him too politically oriented, and Salafis would argue that he is making new and hence undesirable innovations.

6. The idea of natural religion first developed in England and spread to continental Europe and the United States. The deism that developed out of this thinking has different ideas about creation, God's involvement, afterlife, miracles, and so on. It is mainly the basic ideas regarding the rational individual and simple religion that are relevant to the above discussion. For the history of natural religion and deism, see Gay (1968).

REFERENCES

Bowen, John. 2010. *Can Islam Be French? Pluralism and Pragmatism in a Secularist State.* Princeton: Princeton University Press.

Du Bois, W. E. B. 2013 [1903]. *The Souls of Black Folk: Heart and Soul.* Chapel Hill: University of North Carolina Press.

Gay, Peter. 1968. *Deism: An Anthology.* Princeton: D. Van Nostrand.

Hoffmann, Christian H. 1995. *Zwischen alle Stühlen: Ein Deutscher Wird Muslim.* Bonn: Bouvier.

Özyürek, Esra. 2015. *Being German, Becoming Muslim: Race, Religion, and Conversion in the New Europe.* Princeton: Princeton University Press.

Ramadan, Tariq. 1999. *To Be a European Muslim: A Study of Islamic Sources in the European Context.* Leicester, UK: Islamic Foundation.

———. 2004. *Western Muslims and the Future of Islam.* Oxford: Oxford University Press.

Roald, Anne Sofie. 2004. *New Muslims in the European Context: The Experience of Scandinavian Converts.* Leiden: Brill.

Rogozen-Soltar, Mikaela. 2012. "Managing Muslim Visibility: Conversion, Immigration, and Spanish Imaginaries of Islam." *American Anthropologist* 114, no. 4: 611–623.

Wohlrab-Sahr, Monika. 1999. "Conversion to Islam: Between Syncretism and Symbolic Battle." *Social Compass* 46, no. 3: 351–362.

Woodlock, Rachel. 2010. "Praying Where They Don't Belong: Female Muslim Converts and Mosques in Melbourne, Australia." *Journal of Muslim Minority Affairs* 30, no. 2: 268–278.

FIVE

MERGING CULTURE WITH RELIGION

Trajectories of Slovak and Czech Muslim Converts since 1989[1]

GABRIEL PIRICKÝ

This chapter will analyze the trajectories of Slovak and Czech converts to Islam after the fall of communism in 1989. The two Slavic countries—Slovakia and the Czech Republic—are interesting to compare and contrast because from 1918 through 1993 they formed one state: Czechoslovakia. They also share a common history and held similar attitudes toward religion during the totalitarian era. After the communist takeover in 1948 institutionalized dogmatic Marxism-Leninism was introduced and atheism was promoted as the official ideology. Since religious faith in Czechoslovakia was supposed to be dying out and the spirit of atheism taking its place, individual citizens' religious beliefs were considered irrelevant. Although a few Muslims arrived in communist Czechoslovakia as students or immigrants, mostly from "progressive" Arab countries, their faith was played down. It was only after 1989 that freedom of religion started to be effectively respected.

Since very little has been written about Muslim converts in both countries, this chapter is an exploratory study. I will especially focus on the interplay of religion and culture and/or ethnicity connected to the conversion process. As many of the practices of immigrant Muslims are related to their cultures and not all of them share the same culture, this often creates "distance" between local converts and born Muslims. These differences include cultural elements that are perceived as Islamic only by immigrant Muslims from the Middle East, while converts simultaneously bring in native cultural elements as well. The immigrant Muslims also sometimes introduce concepts of a national and/or cultural version of Islam. Tariq Ramadan explained that, in Europe, immigrant Muslims often brought cultural traditions rather than Islam, which in turn created obstacles to their becoming true European citizens (Ramadan 1999, 2004). For instance, Turkish Muslims, including many scholars of Turkish Islam, promote the idea of a "Turkish Islam" that is said to be pluralistic, tolerant, and open to secularism and democratic developments (Yavuz 2004).

I will particularly investigate how converts merge their native Czech and Slovak culture and history with Islam. I will accordingly analyze the relationship between Islam and culture in the Czech and Slovak contexts. Consequently, I will address the following questions: What is the scale of conversion to Islam in Slovakia and the Czech lands, or Czechia? What are the issues and problems faced by converts to Islam, this "minority within a minority"? How do converts merge their native cultures with Islam? How is local history and mythology reappropriated by them?

I will analyze narratives of converts, particularly those published online (e.g., YouTube clips, egodocuments) and in the print media or collected from unpublished master's theses. I also conducted four interviews with mature and well-educated Muslim converts who were not in the early stages of conversion.[2] Almost all the converts in my research are reflection-based new Muslims whose conversion was a conscious choice rather than a sudden and abrupt change. These are men and women between their thirties and fifties, all of whom can be described as "pioneers" who converted without the large impact of mass Muslim immigration to Slovakia and Czechia.

In the first section of this chapter, I will provide a detailed account of Islam and Muslims in both countries with special attention paid to local Muslim converts. The second section will explore scholarly discussions about the intersection of Islam and culture/ethnicity in the field of conversion studies. The third will then illustrate this intersection within the specific Slovak and Czech contexts, analyzing local converts' views and attitudes. In the final section, I will focus on converts' reappropriation of local history and mythical facts for their own Muslim identity.

ISLAM AND MUSLIM CONVERTS IN SLOVAKIA AND CZECHIA

Conversion to Islam has negative meanings inscribed in the history of Central Europe, including Slovakia and the Czech Republic. Traditionally, in several languages of Central Europe, the expression "turning Turk" has signified "converting to Islam." Terms such as Muslim or Islam were unknown during conflicts with the Ottomans (in the sixteenth and seventeenth centuries), and the most common way to speak about their "exotic and foreign" faith was to call it "Turkish creed." Even in the nineteenth century, such terms as "Muslim" and "Turk" were quite frequently used synonymously throughout the region. In archaic Slovak or Czech, a person who converts from Christianity to Islam was often called a "*poturčenec*" (Turkish convert, renegade). Those who converted were considered to be "worse than a Turk" (*Poturčenec horší Turka*), which is a proverb still common in the Slovak language today.

Given the centuries-long struggle with "the Turk," Muslims—in Czech *muslimové* (singular *muslim*)—are often seen in collective memory as an enemy par example. Consequently, even today a Muslim convert must struggle with historical stereotyping of this nature. Certain segments of the population also use various abusive neologisms, such as *muslimáci*, which sounds like *slimáci*, the plural form of *slimák* (slug/snail), a word sometimes attributed to born and converted Muslims alike.

Many social spheres remain deeply insular and conservative in Central Europe, at least in those regions that were historically behind the Iron Curtain. The great social battles in the West—the sexual revolution, antiracism, gay rights, feminism, the massive impact of "foreign" religions—happened when much of Central Europe was still divided. The majority of this region is therefore still based on a single set of customs and languages.[3] No city in Czechia or Slovakia is really cosmopolitan, not even Prague, where masses of "foreigners" are mostly foreign tourists, along with Slavic immigrants from Slovakia, Ukraine, and Russia who are culturally very similar.

Immigration in Western Europe is a sociological fact, but not in Slovakia or Czechia; although cultural plurality does exist, it is not in the sense of new immigrant communities from very different cultures (Pirický 2010). If we consider that, unlike Western Europe, neither Czechoslovakia nor its predecessor Austria-Hungary had a colonial empire, we may better understand the abovementioned characteristics.

As far as Muslims are concerned, it is possible to say that both countries represent one of the most "Islam-free" regions in the European Union (EU). Muslim converts there are still regarded as strange, and veiled Muslim women even as dangerous. Especially in Slovakia, Islam has developed since the fall of communism practically ex nihilo. Slovakia, even more than Czechia, is a country with a relatively closed confessional milieu, and detraditionalization in the field of religion has been limited. Given that Slovakia is one of the youngest nations in Europe, Slovak identity is also very sensitive to influences from outside and Islam is viewed as a threat and an undesirable religion.

In this chapter, I seek mainly to illustrate the religious situation in Slovakia and Czechia with regard to the Muslim community. According to unofficial reports, Slovakia, with its clear Catholic majority and Protestant minority, has only about 5,000 Muslims (mostly immigrants) out of 5.3 million inhabitants. Because during the most recent census in 2011 Muslims living in Slovakia could be counted only in the categories "other" or "unknown," we do not have reliable statistics. We thus must rely on the 2001 census, in which 1,212 citizens declared themselves to be Muslims (Čikeš 2005: 195). The Pew Research Center's 2012 studies on religious composition estimated that there are 10,600 Muslims living in Slovakia (or 0.2 percent of the total population).[4]

There are fewer indigenous Muslims in Slovakia and Czechia than in neighboring Poland, which has a small minority of Polish Tatars (see Górak-Sosnowska and Łyszczarz, this volume). It is even more difficult to estimate the number of local converts to Islam. Of the roughly 150–300 local Muslim converts in Slovakia in 2006, the majority were educated, young, and female (Letavajová 2006: 91). This is small in comparison to neighboring Austria or Germany. For example, the number of converts in Germany is estimated to be between 20,000 and 100,000 (Özyürek 2009: 92). Whereas Muslim immigrants to Slovakia are mostly male, among Slovak converts women outnumber men to a ratio of 6:4 (Knapová 2007: 42).

The Czech Republic is usually mentioned among the most atheist countries in the world. Christians represent a minority, apart from southern Moravia, which is predominantly Catholic.[5] It is broadly believed that institutionalized religion is viewed with suspicion in Czechia. Unlike most Slovaks, Czechs have generally departed from traditional beliefs and either remained religiously indifferent or, more recently, started to search for new alternative spirituality of various kinds. In the 2011 Czech census, 3,385 of the almost 10.5 million Czech people chose Islam as their religion (Macháček 2013: 195). In 2012, the Pew Research Center estimated the proportion of Muslims to be less than 0.1 percent.[6] There are approximately 400 Muslim converts in Czechia, and the number is rising with dozens of new conversions every year (Macháček 2013: 196). One of my interlocutors, Větrovec, stated that there is a ratio of 2:1 between female and male Muslim converts in both Czechia and Slovakia, which diverges from Knapová's estimate made in the Slovak context.[7]

Although the community of Muslim converts in Slovakia and Czechia is heterogeneous, its members share some common characteristics with converts in neighboring countries relating to education, gender, and personal experience. In Czechia, as well as in Hungary, converts play key roles as leaders within the broader Muslim communities (Bureš 2010: 7). Historically, converts to Islam in the Czech Republic have been the most visible spokespersons of the community and the ones who invite non-Muslims to Islam.[8] In neighboring Poland, converts play the role of skillful cultural navigators who help translate various aspects of Islamic heritage into the Polish conditions (Górak-Sosnowska 2011). This is also true for many Slovak and Czech converts. Unlike in Hungary, however, there is no influential Muslim association of converts in Czechia or Slovakia.[9]

Emily Jane O'Dell (2010) asserts that Czech conversions to Islam are primarily related to vacations to Middle Eastern countries. She suggests that women in the Czech and Slovak Republics are not merely converting to Islam for the sake of marriage, but many have been inspired to convert after traveling to Egypt on affordable group tourist trips to Hurghada and Sharm al-Sheikh. O'Dell states:

> While many Czechs are introduced to Islam through tourism to the Middle East, others are introduced to Islam indirectly through the large presence of Arab tourists and immigrants in the spa-towns of Teplice, Dubí and Lázně Darkov. Thus, there seems to be a notable connection between tourism and conversion in the Czech Republic.[10]

Historically, Czech converts have been among the leading figures of Islam in Czechoslovakia. Important roles were played by converts such as Abdalláh (Bohdan) Brikcius (1903–1959), who was accused of collaboration with the Nazis in 1949, and Mohamed Ali Šilhavý (1917–2009), the chairman of the Center of Muslim Communities in the Czech Republic after the fall of the Iron Curtain (Mendel 1999: 24). The famous scholar Ivan Hrbek (1923–1993), a prominent Arabist, Islamologist, and Africanist and author of the highly respected translation of the Qur'an into Czech, was also a convert, although his scholarly interests later prevailed over his faith (Mendel, Ostřanský, and Rataj 2007: 365–366).

The overwhelming majority of converts in both countries are mainstream Sunni Muslims of the Hanafi legal school. Minority currents are represented, for example, by the Czech representative of Sufi Islam, Sálim (Vladimír) Voldán. Voldán sees Sufism as an important agent for conversion to Islam, similar to the role Sufism plays in countries in Western Europe (Mendel, Ostřanský, and Rataj 2007: 390–392; see also Yarosh, this volume). Also among the Sunni majority we find converts with different leanings, such as mainstream Sunnis, Muʿtazilite, Salafi, and self-made Islamic interpretations.

To understand the position of local converts, I will briefly discuss the legal status of Muslims in general in both countries. In Slovakia, Muslims have had no official recognition as a religious community since the establishment of the Slovak Republic in 1993, and they do not enjoy public funding of any kind. The 2007 amendment to the Act on Religious Freedoms and the Status of Churches and Religious Organizations set additional conditions for registration. Not only does it require signatures from 20,000 adult members of the religious community, who must be Slovak citizens with permanent residence in the country, it also requires the names, permanent addresses, and identity card numbers of all those people (Pirický 2010: 717–729; Drobný 2013: 587). Bratislava is quite often described by the local press as the last capital in the EU without a mosque, and Slovakia is the last EU country without a single one in the whole country.[11]

In Czechia, Muslim communities are not granted public funding either, although, in line with the "softer" Czech approach to minority religions, Muslims did get "basic" registration in 2004 and their application for "special rights" has been reviewed after a ten-year period. However, the Czech Ministry of Culture has postponed an upgrade of the Muslim community's rights until at least 2024.[12] There are only two established mosques in Czechia: in Prague and Brno, both without minarets, although the community's premises in Teplice, Hradec Králové, and Karlovy Vary are often described as mosques too.

The general atmosphere vis-à-vis Muslims may be epitomized by two statements made by leading politicians. On January 24, 2015, the Slovak press widely quoted Prime Minister Robert Fico:

> Given that Slovakia is a country where the Catholic Church dominates, and the second largest is the Lutheran Church, then perhaps we could not easily tolerate that 300 or 400 arriving Muslims would start building mosques and change the nature, culture, and values of the state.[13]

In August 2011, the current Czech president, Miloš Zeman, who had not yet taken office, said in an interview for the magazine *Respekt* that the term "moderate Muslim is the same contradiction as a moderate Nazi."[14] Moreover, as president he has supported the xenophobic initiative called "We do not want Islam in the Czech Republic" (*Islám v České republice nechceme*) as well as the Bloc Against Islam (*Blok proti islámu*), whose most well-known representative, Martin Konvička, currently faces charges of inciting hatred (Dizdarevič 2016: 125–126).

In both republics, we are witnessing not only rising Islamophobia but also strong representations of Islam as incompatible with local culture and traditions. The Czech-Slovak environment thus confirms the general atmosphere in the broader postcommunist Central European space. As Moreno observes: "Seeing the clash between Western European society and its Muslim minority, Central Europe is set to avoid greater diversity in order to prevent the same ethnic tensions from developing within its region" (2010: 80).

THE INTERSECTION OF ISLAM AND CULTURE OR ETHNICITY IN CONVERSION STUDIES

Before detailing how converts in Slovakia and Czechia merge Islam with culture, I will present a short overview of the scholarly discussions about the intersection of Islam and culture/ethnicity in the field of conversion studies in Europe. We live in a shrinking world where global trends continuously adapt to local conditions and the local and the global coexist in various forms and places. This state of affairs has also been described as a mixture of globalization and localization, or "glocalization" (Robertson 1998). Similarly, when mapping converts' ideas about belonging and citizenship, global Islamic tradition is always confronted with local cultural and ethnic contexts.

Generally, ethnicity is played down in Islamic discourse. The very idea that all people, Muslims and non-Muslims alike, are born in a state of Islam relegates the issues of ethnicity and culture to a subordinate and even undesirable position. Islam is, in fact, understood to be a non-national universal religion, and "the issue of ethnicity and nationality is important, yet it is condemned as '*fitnah*' and sinful" (Van Nieuwkerk 2006: 107). Its non-national quality is sometimes mentioned as one of the attractive features of the Muslim creed.

Usually, scholarly works on converts to Islam contain an element of comparison between religion and culture from a variety of perspectives that are of interest here. However, most focus especially on the Western European context (Allievi 1998, 2013; Roald 2004; Van Nieuwkerk 2006; Zebiri 2007; Özyürek 2014). Zebiri (2007), for example, mentions that "the relationship between religion, ethnicity and culture does not throw up quite the same set of issues for converts as for born Muslims" (Zebiri 2007: 98). McGinty argues that conversion implies not only a change to but also a change from something (McGinty 2006: 147).

Often, converts interpret Islamic sources and virtues through cultural filters, so the preconversion cultural context is extremely important. To illustrate this situation, I quote one of the Swedish converts in Roald's study: "'Swedish Islam' incorporates 'Swedish' values such as honesty, punctuality, a work ethic and the keeping of promises. She says that these virtues are also 'Islamic virtues,' but they 'are not particularly prominent among Muslims'" (Roald 2006: 57–58). These new Muslim communities that are the product of Scandinavian socialization formulate new views and ideas as a result of the cultural encounter between Islamic ideas and the converts' "cultural luggage" (Roald 2004: 347).

Roald also describes the process of conversion in three stages: love, disappointment, and maturity. She argues that after the first stage, which is emotionally characterized by an uncritical obsession with the new religion, there is a second period when converts feel strong disappointment with born Muslims and their ideas. It is actually during the third, "mature" stage that converts usually start to formulate their understanding of Islam with reference to their specific cultural or "national" context (2004: 347).

According to Allievi, who writes about new Muslims' "do-it-yourself culture" (*bricolage culturel*), converts enter a new phase after their conversion, which he calls "re-culturation" (Allievi 2013: 220–221). This process can probably best be understood as a hybridization between various aspects of local and Islamic cultures. In the field of cultural production and engagement in the media, book-writing, or popularization, converts are often more prominent proponents of Islam than their limited number would suggest.

Recently, Özyürek (2014; see also this volume) approached the problem of the relationship between Islam and ethnicity or culture from yet another angle. In her book *Being German, Becoming Muslim*, she demonstrates that German converts to Islam often share the suspicious attitude of German society toward the immigrant Muslim minority of Turkish or Arab origin. Therefore, to distance themselves from associations with immigrant and born Muslims and from what they see as "wrong" cultural-Islamic practices, German converts promote either a universal Salafi version of "culture-free Islam" or a German Islam that has nothing to do with Middle Eastern customs and mentalities. However, by accentuating an Islam based on German and European values, many German converts re-create the Eurocentric perspective. They reproduce representations of the "irrational Oriental mentalities" of Muslim immigrants in Germany. Özyürek summarizes:

> The flip side of a stress on an Islam compatible with Germanness sometimes involves the disqualification of immigrants as good Muslims. In order to claim Islam as German, converted Muslims and some born Muslims emphasize that Muslims and Islam are two different things. Like non-Muslim German intellectuals, many converts believe that second-, third-, and fourth-generation Muslims of immigrant ancestry need to be educated, integrated, and transformed. Yet for them, this transformation should happen not through leaving Islamic practices behind or reforming Islam but on the contrary, by making immigrant Muslims abandon their Turkish and other cultures as well as traditions, and persuading them to apply fundamental Islamic teachings to their everyday lives. In other words, they suggest, it is the immigrant Muslims in Germany who need to change and not Islam (Özyürek 2014: 133).

The German case is important for the Czech and Slovak context, not least because East Germany, formerly known as the German Democratic Republic (1949–1990), was ruled by an authoritarian and closed communist regime similar to the one in Czechoslovakia. Both before and after the fall of the Berlin Wall in 1989, Czechia and East Germany represented one of the least faith-based regions in Europe. Many of the Muslim converts in Czechia and Slovakia grew up as atheists and materialists, like their East German counterparts.

Apart from having been marked by similar experiences in the very recent past, Czechs and Slovaks have been inspired by the German nationalism that is based on shared culture and language for at least 200 years. Culturally, then, they were influenced mainly by the German conception of *Kultur*, the view that a specific culture *defines a people* (Kuper 1999: 32 ff.). Language, culture, and ethnicity have been the main building blocks of the Czech and Slovak national awakening on the road to their own statehood, first in the form of a common state called Czechoslovakia (1918–1939, 1945–1992) and since 1993 as two independent countries, Slovakia and the Czech Republic.

According to Özyürek, next to "Germanizing" Islam, it is particularly Salafism that attracts many converts in Germany, because it places new Muslims on the same level as born Muslims while simultaneously pushing aside cultural and ethnic differences (2015: 109–131). According to Roy (2008), Salafism represents a "pure religion," perceived to be superior to any culture. It is best adapted to globalization because it emphasizes Islam's own deculturation and aspires to universal validity.

As I will argue, on the one side it is true that contemporary Islamic discourse, especially the Salafi one, tends to devalue nationalism and ethnicity "as a component of identity, seeing it as subordinate to religious identity" (Zebiri 2007: 96). On the other side, patriotism—or even nationalism—and allegiance to their countries of origin is also very viable (Zebiri 2007: 96). Besides Swedish and German examples, there are plenty of other "ethnic Islams" in Europe, at least in the heads of converts, including Slovakized and Bohemized variants of it.

CZECH AND SLOVAK CONVERTS' VIEWS ON MERGING RELIGION AND CULTURE

Returning to the Slovak and Czech case study, I will now describe the preconversion cultural context and cultural filters of Czechs and Slovaks in order to analyze questions of national culture and belonging and citizenship. The Czech and Slovak context is different from Western European and Northern European studies because of the very few converts to Islam. Even fewer are those people who are ready to answer interviewers' questions, which is understandable given their low numbers and unease when answering questions about belonging in societies where they are viewed with suspicion.

As elsewhere in the European Union, a number of cultural concepts and symbols play an important role in the everyday lives of Slovaks and Czechs (Roberts 2005). Czechness, for example, is closely associated with a "dove-like character" (in Czech, *holubičí povaha*), or the positive trait of pacifism. An appreciation of hard work, succinctly expressed in the saying "work ennobles" (*práce šlechtí*), is another characteristic of Czechness. The superior talents and handyman abilities of the Czech nation are the essence of the idea of "golden hands" (*zlaté ručičky*) in Czechia (Roberts 2005: 131–132, 191). Slovaks also have a series of comparable concepts, one being a belief in "innate Slovak goodness." Another one presents Slovakia as a "hospitable nation" (*pohostinný národ*) whose guests are welcomed with bread and salt.[15]

Local converts are more aware of the above-mentioned concepts than born Muslim immigrants, so they introduce some of these attributes into their vision of how a good Muslim should behave. In fact, a strong work ethic, punctuality, societal engagement, and honesty stand at the forefront. One female convert, Iman, demonstrated this by saying "exactly because I am different in certain things, I go to work, but most [immigrant] Muslimas are not employed.... I also have various sporting activities.... simply, I am different." For immigrant Muslim women, "family is their duty ... but for me this is not enough" (Sedláková 2014: transcripts 579–583, 590–594).

With regard to merging Islam with local culture, I basically observed two groups of converts. For one group, local culture or ethnicity must be separated from Islam; the other group develops a local Islam that pays attention to Slovak and Czech culture/ethnicity. Whereas most of the people in the first group feel like foreigners in their own country, the second group of converts feels more at ease with the local context. Naturally, there are variations within both groups. For example, within the second group, one could differentiate between those who distance themselves openly from immigrant Muslims and those who do not.

There also exists a third group of converts who preach culture-free Islam, but I was unable to gather information from them. This may be because they feel threatened by exposing themselves due to their small numbers or simply because they have no intention to speak out.

For the first group, feelings of national belonging are nonexistent or secondary to religious identity. This is the case among many born Muslims in Europe as well as some converts, including those in Slovakia and Czechia. Jana, for instance, said:

> First of all, my children are Muslims. Of course, they have Czech citizenship, but they will not have, we hope, that Czech mentality. Given that my husband is a Palestinian and as a Palestinian he has lost his homeland, we encourage them to be emotionally linked with that homeland which we as a family have lost.[16]

Jana has a "combative convert identity" and stands close to what Allievi called "total converts" (Allievi 2013). By this, Allievi means those converts who enthusiastically promote their views within the wider society. Jana created two separate identities: one Muslim for her Palestinian family and eventually for all converts, and the other, Czech, for non-Muslims.

Within the first group, the wide variety of assertions concerning national belonging can be further illustrated using Beáta's example. She is a Czech convert married to a non-Muslim Czech, who said: "I live with a Czech, not with a Muslim" (Panýrková 2009: 82). Although the idea of two separate identities, Czech and Muslim, exists among many local converts, when Panýrková asked her Czech convert interlocutors to rank on a scale from one to five whether they feel completely Czech or entirely foreign, most of them chose three (Panýrková 2009: 97–98). Especially female Muslim converts feel uncomfortable living in Czech society; they feel like foreigners or Czechs, but foremost as foreigners in the Muslim component of their identity.

Within the second group, some converts distance themselves from immigrant Muslims. For Petr, "Islam is culturally foreign" in Czechia and the "cultures are not compatible." He went on to say that "every Muslim is a time-bomb" in the sense that "in a critical situation, he returns to his faith."[17] In his own words:

> Islam here in our country as it is spread by foreign missionaries, is intertwined, unfortunately—and without malice—with their local habits. This then leads to the formation of isolated ghettos of Muslim-foreigners and contributes to the anti-Islamic attitudes of those Czechs who confuse religious system as such with ethnic and cultural peculiarities of some of its holders (Mendel, Ostřanský, and Rataj 2007: 389).

According to Petr, Islam could become established in Czechia only if converts could create their own culture that would respect Central European and

Czech cultural and historical identity. His suggestion that Islam will not take root in Czechia unless it develops from local culture ties in with similar arguments that can be attributed to the increase in anti-Muslim sentiment and xenophobia toward immigrant Muslims and converts in Europe as a whole and in Czechia or Slovakia in particular.

His attitudes are comparable to those of some Hungarian converts who consider it "wrong" when people convert to Islam and try to develop their Muslimness not based on their own roots but on foreign culture or try to "Arabize" it.[18] Or as one convert informant put it, as a result, "the convert may feel losing his home both here and abroad."[19] All in all, Petr sees religion and culture as static and as separate concepts, and he seems to reproduce cultural and biological racisms vis-à-vis immigrant Muslims, similar to the attitudes of many converts in Germany (Özyürek 2014: 2). Paraphrasing Özyürek's statement, it is probably right to highlight that, in order to claim Islam as Czech or Slovak, some Muslim converts and certain segments of born Muslims emphasize that Islam and Muslims can contain two totally different sets of people.

Although converts are often critical of some aspects of Czech or Slovak culture, from my observations it seems that the majority of them do identify with local culture. Iman gave a good description of this attitude:

> I am neither an Arab woman nor a female from Asia, that means I am Czech, in fact I am a Muslima, but perhaps I identify closer with those people who are not in the mosque [meaning who are not Muslims]. . . . I invented for myself a Czech Islam (in Sedláková 2014: 68).

In the same way, Petr said, "I am Czech by upbringing, Muslim by faith, and so I will always be more Czech than Muslim."[20] Similar statements demonstrate that there are converts who, after embracing Islam, deem their new religion perfectly compatible with local culture. This idea is sometimes also the consequence of difficult experiences converts have with born immigrant Muslims who occasionally consider converts to be insufficiently "Islamic."

Meanwhile, there also exists a small segment of Slovak and Czech converts who think they represent minority views within the broader Muslim community. For example, Jozef, an independent, freethinking Slovak Muslim, stresses the Europeaness of his attitudes and reaches out to liberal traditions and individual choices when speaking about Islam, culture, and citizenship. Jozef feels that his views are somewhere between those of the Muʿtazila, an eighth-century Islamic movement and rationalistic school, and *taqwacore*, the Islamic punk movement named after the book by Michael Muhammad Knight. He explains:

> I personally do not think that I am a representative sample of Muslims in Slovakia. When I recently wrote one of the articles for our online page, IslamOnline.sk, my editor responded that it is somehow too much Muʿtazilite.

Both "the punk movement and aspects of Muʿtazilite rationalism and pragmatism are close to my heart," he says.[21] He explains how the ideas of Jan Werich (1905–1980), the prominent twentieth-century Czech actor, writer, and playwright, inspired him in 2004–2005 to do what he thought was right, that is, to convert to Islam.

Placed side by side with the highly esteemed non-Muslim personality of the Czech intellectual tradition personified by Werich, converts like Jozef promote the idea that conversion to Islam is compatible with claiming the Czech/Slovak cultural background. Jozef's statement merits special attention as it tries to connect Islam to the open-minded "enlightened" and democratically committed Czechoslovak icon, similar to the German converts' attempts to relate Islam to the German *Aufklärung* (Özyürek 2014 and this volume).

Mapping out how Czech and Slovak culture is reread and rerepresented by the converts should not lead us, however, to overstate both countries' specific cultural contexts. In his study on Muslim immigrants in Britain, Jacobson formulated an important argument when insisting on the distinction between ethnic culture and ethnic belonging among immigrant Muslims (Jacobson 1998). The concept of "Britishness" can be understood on two different levels: values and lifestyles versus citizenship. Whereas *ethnic culture* refers to the perpetuation or re-creation of cultural practices (e.g., gender and sex relations, language, cuisine), *ethnic belonging* refers to a particular ethnic origin—although often very loose—that is not identified with particular customs or behavior. Therefore, the disappearance or change of certain practices does not mean the end of ethnic identity. If this idea is applied to Czech and Slovak converts, we could summarize that, while they usually modify their cultural practices concerning various issues (e.g., marriage patterns, cuisine, gender relations, or even language), most of them still retain their ethnic belonging and citizenship.

Language, for instance, plays an important role in the self-image of local converts. The ex-imam of the Prague mosque, Emir Omič, a Bosnian Slav originally from the Bosnian town of Zenica, was very popular with Czech converts because he spoke good Czech and had a good understanding of the local mentality.[22] Both Czech and Slovak publics have only recently been introduced, albeit to a limited degree, to the basic Islamic terminology (e.g., Muslim, *shariʿa*, *ramadan*, *ʿid*, *bismillah*, *sira*, *hadith*, or *hajj*). Czechs and

Slovaks usually disdainfully perceive Arabic terms and idioms used by Czech or Slovak Muslim converts in everyday speech because they are incomprehensible. The usage of garbled Arabic terminology is widespread among some converts, whereas others—usually those with higher education, for example—strive to use foreign words carefully. Some converts prefer to use the nearest equivalent from the Czech cultural context to express the essence of a phenomenon in cases where Czech language lacks unambiguous terminology (Pelikán 2008: 45). They use Arabic words in Czech or Slovak speech only in those instances when foreign terms have already become established, although the terminology used in an intra-Muslim setting may often differ.

REAPPROPRIATING LOCAL HISTORY OR MYTH FOR SLOVAK AND CZECH MUSLIM CONVERTS' IDENTITIES

In this final section, I will focus more closely on how converts embrace historical or mythical facts and figures to inscribe themselves in the history of Slovakia and Czechia. Every nation and, in a certain sense, numerous religious traditions have their own ways of dealing with the past. Often, they create representations of the past, of their living space, mission, ancestral image, urban and regional affiliation, or national and religious symbols. Converts are no exception to this rule: they also have specific ways of dealing with their nation's past, often through myths turned into reality. George Schöplin suggested that myth "provides the means for the members of a community to recognize that, broadly, they share a mindset, they are in much the same thought-world. Through myth, boundaries are established within the community and also with respect to other communities" (Schöplin 1997: 20). In fact, myth is the system of cultural orientation that creates meanings and the "typical" form of collective thinking stored in collective memory. Conversion is never a complete abandonment of the old self, local history, mythology, or traditions. New and old beliefs, myths, and habits intertwine, and invented memories and heroes can emerge.

Reinventing Czech and Slovak religious history is one of the available options for connecting or reappropriating the history of the Czech lands and Slovakia with the converts' Muslim status. Two of the most respected figures from Czech and Slovak Christian religious history are the brothers and saints Cyril and Methodius. These two brothers from Byzantine Thessalonica introduced Orthodox Christianity among the Slavic peoples during the ninth century, primarily in the territory of the Great Moravian Empire with southern Moravia and southwestern Slovakia as its core territories. Since then, they have been venerated as "Apostles to the Slavs." The brothers also introduced a new Glagolitic alphabet and Slavic liturgy, and nowadays they are revered in both Slovakia and Czechia as national saints—July 5 is a national holiday—although both countries later changed to the Western liturgy and Catholic faith.

Today, some Czech Muslim converts try to reappropriate the legacy of Saints Cyril and Methodius to show not only that Muslims lead a normal way of life but also that their mission is very similar to that of the brothers. One anonymous convert likened today's Muslims in Czechia to the first Christians who arrived centuries ago from the faraway Middle East and then from Byzantium, among them Cyril and Methodius.[23] At that time, convert said, the brothers represented something alien and abnormal for the Czech and Moravian people, as well as for the Slovak pagan society. However, over time, people began to accept their teachings brought from distant lands, because "they appeared closer to the truth than their paganism, and thus they represented something more suitable for their own practical material and spiritual life."[24]

Converts argue that, like the Byzantine brothers, Czech Muslims are on a mission that is taking place in front of us. Jozef, a Slovak convert, also highlighted that the oldest preserved report on Islam in the Old Slavonic language probably originates from the territory of Great Moravia and can be found in the legend on *The Life of St. Constantine-Cyril* (Štefančík and Lenč 2012: 104–105). According to this legend, before Cyril came to Central Europe, the Byzantine emperor asked him to embark on a mission to the Arabs and the Khazars. His missionary activities included scholarly disputations with the Hagarens (Muslims) and Jews on Islam and Judaism (Štefančík and Lenč 2012: 104–105).

Modern national history is often as important for the convert's identity as religious history. National heroes can be won over through careful review of their life and work as the following case suggests. Ľudovít Štúr (1815–1856), the leader of the Slovak national revival in the nineteenth century and the author of the Slovak language standard, journalist, politician, poet, and philosopher, has been repeatedly voted as the most prominent and influential personality in Slovak history. The most pressing issue in Slovakia at the time of his life was not the revival of a prior literary norm but the formation of a new one, more closely related to the current vernacular. In the 1840s, Štúr created a version based on the language spoken in the central part of Slovakia, which is still in use today. In a letter from November 1841, addressed to Samuel Bohdan Hroboň, Štúr described his impressions from the northwestern Slovak city of Trenčín and presented his views of Slovak history after the demise of Great Moravia in the ninth century.

According to Štúr, after the invasion of Hungarians in the Carpathian Basin, the Slovaks gradually retreated to the mountain areas in the north, embodied by the Tatra Mountains. Trenčín became the last bastion of independent Slovakia under the Hungarian oligarch Matúš Čák Trenčiansky (of Trenčín), who is often portrayed as a "Slovak king." Štúr likened Matúš (Matthew) to El Zagnis Zaquir—Muhammad XII. Al-Zaghal, who ruled in al-Andalus from 1484 to 1489, was the last emperor of the Nasirid Arab-Muslim Granada (Macho 2013: 105; Ženka 2011: 122–136). Štúr paralleled his resistance to the Spanish *reconquista* with the resistance of Slovaks against the Hungarian "conquista" in the northern parts of the former Kingdom of Hungary. The comparison of Matúš Čák, "the last great Slovak," to the Moorish emir of Granada is unique in the Slovak context and makes a rather exotic impression. The same is true when Štúr attempts to compare Trenčín to Andalusian Granada, his Granada in Slovakia.

In short, it can be said that with this theory Slovak national historicism probably reached its highest peak in Štúr's writings. Also, within both wider Slovak society and much narrower Slovak intellectual elites, this analogy received no real response. Nevertheless, for a Slovak convert who made me aware of the whole story, the comparison represents a "footing" from which any Muslim could depart to reappropriate the "greatest Slovak" of all times as someone who, although not Muslim himself, held the Muslim ruler of Granada in high regard (Macho 2013: 105).[25]

Alongside historical characters and events, myth turned into reality can include historical buildings or book collections of major importance. The case of the demolished "mosque" in Bratislava is instrumental in this sense. Slovak Muslim converts striving for recognition and mosques refer to the multicultural character of ancient Bratislava, a town with a mixed population of Slovaks, Hungarians, Germans, Jews, and Czechs who lived in relative symbiosis up until World War II. Muslims like to point out that, in the 1960s, when the whole district of Vydrica in the foothills of Bratislava castle was insensitively pulled down, it was not only the magnificent synagogue of the Neologists that was demolished but also a small mosque. Although the "mosque building" itself was probably only an example of a summer house built in an Oriental style that was called a "mosque" in colloquial speech, some local Muslims, including Muslim converts, now understand it to be proof of their presence in the city at least since the nineteenth century (Janota 2008: 63–65). This helps converts and native-born Muslims alike to revive the image of Bratislava's multicultural past with its different national, religious, cultural, and linguistic traditions. It is a way to gain certain symbolic and cultural capital against those who are inclined to dismiss Islam as an adversary and an incompatible religion that was never present in the country.

Within the Czech context, a good example of an ancestral Czech mythic hero turned into an Arab-Muslim character gives proof that dealing with the mythical past can lead to creating new heroes. The old Czech legend about Bruncvík is probably well known to all Czechs. The mythical Czech prince Bruncvík, whose statue was erected next to the famous Charles Bridge in Prague, decided after the death of his father to travel the world and win the lion for his crest like a true brave knight. He returned home with a magic sword that beheaded on command. This heroic story from the fourteenth century was made famous by the Czech writer Alois Jirásek in his book *Old Czech Legends*. Moreover, Bruncvík's lion is said to be the two-tailed lion on the Bohemian coat of arms, while his sword remains hidden somewhere.[26] This legend was recently revised and adapted by Petr, a Czech Muslim convert who gave the story a fully "Arab-Muslim outfit" in the following way:

> Perhaps it would be a heresy to compare it with the older story of Sinbad the sailor from the Thousand and One Nights storybook. He ends his life in peace in his birth town of Basra instead of Prague, but otherwise his adventures are almost identical with our national hero. Instead of the Basilisk dragon slain by Bruncvík, Sinbad had to tackle a large snake; instead of the bird Noh, he was carried by bird Roc from the deserted island; however, reading their stories is like reading the diaries of two tourists travelling with the same agency on the same trip.... But perhaps our descendants will one day proudly show tourists a statue of Sinbad the sailor on the Charles Bridge or will praise the courage of stone bearded Turks guarding imprisoned Crusading aggressors at the Bridge Tower.[27] After all, how many times in the last two generations have we managed to proclaim heroes villains and villains heroes? At least in this respect I do not fear for the enduring survival of Czech identity (Pelikán 2011: 58–59).

Aside from the similarities between Bruncvík and Sinbad, the non-Muslim mythical environment appears to be recognized, at least in the convert's imagery, albeit only after being transformed into its Islamically more acceptable version through a process of cultural osmosis. However, similar metaphorical reminders may eventually serve the whole convert community in their effort to find a common orientation in a local environment that otherwise lacks Islamo-Arabic images.

CONCLUSION

As I stressed earlier, since very little has been written about converts to Islam in these countries, this chapter represents an exploratory study, and much work remains to be done on the subject. By focusing mainly on the interplay between Islam and culture, I am not suggesting that this is the only important issue for converts and their identity.

I have argued that converts to Islam usually represent alternative versions of being Czech or Slovak than born or immigrant Muslims. Converts sometimes also disassociate themselves from immigrant Muslims, whom they accuse of practicing "foreign" traditions and cultures instead of Islam. Slovak and Czech "norms" often continue to operate after converts' conversion to Islam, which creates a certain degree of particularism in the form of a "Czech" and a "Slovak" Islam.

The formation of Islam in the Slovak and Czech contexts indicates a tendency to view Islam through cultural filters that help converts invent a new tradition. Therefore, without jumping to quick conclusions, it may well be possible that we are witnessing a continuous process to accommodate "Czechness" or "Slovakness" with Muslim faith in a new pattern that is Islamically acceptable. Indeed, in their view, Islam may also be viewed as a continuation of Slovak/Czech culture.

Our limited sample suggests that it would be, however, misleading to totally bifurcate the converts' attitudes to issues of Czech/Slovak culture, citizenship, and belonging according to pro or contra standpoints. Although converts did change their views on Czech/Slovak culture and society after their conversion, they generally do not feel themselves to be outsiders. New Muslims are products of their Slovak and Czech socialization, and their particular social context shapes how they act and react (compare Roald 2004: 342).

The representational practices of local Muslim converts offer a wide variety of options that are usually less known to immigrant Muslims. As a result, Muslim converts insert new meanings into characters, historical events, myths, or symbols, not unlike Christians, nonbelievers, extremists, and others have done before them. Putting an Islamic frame around local historical narratives helps converts move toward a cultural orientation that creates meanings as well, as with the public image of Islam vis-à-vis the non-Muslim majority. Given that local history has often been considered a struggle for national ideas, exclusive identification with "imported" Islam by the converts could be seen as conflicting with the national interests of the non-Muslim majority.

Despite the limited sample, this analysis has also shown that Czech and

Slovak converts' views on Islam and culture in general correspond to those described in the Western European context. It appears that the "cultural luggage" Roald describes plays a significant role when Slovak and Czech converts merge their native culture and ethnicity with Islam. Similar to Özyürek's account of Germany, heated public debates and social controversy over Islam in Czechia and Slovakia have contributed to localizing Islam in a way that is sometimes very suspicious of immigrant Muslim culture. Indeed, unlike in Özyürek's case, it is not the culture-free form of Salafi Islam but rather the "Slovakizing" or "Bohemizing" variants of Islam that have been identified. This may also be the outcome of local conditions and a combination of small numbers and a fear of expressing opinions that identify a person too closely with "foreign" variants of Islam. My analysis also pointed out that since Slovak and Czech nationalism has been inspired by the German conception of *Kulturnation*, the accent on specific local culture that defines the people remains strong. Accordingly, this chapter described attempts by Slovak and Czech converts to reappropriate local history or myth and showed how they exploit local history and mythical facts for their own identity.

NOTES

1. The work on this chapter was supported by the Slovak Research and Development Agency under the contract No. APVV-15-0030.

2. The unpublished master's theses include the work of two students: ethnologist Ivana Knapová from the University of Ss. Cyril and Methodius in the Slovak town of Trnava, and Markéta Sedláková from the Department of Social Pedagogy at Masaryk University in Brno, Czechia. I would also like to mention Petra Panýrková's bachelor's thesis at the Department of Religious Studies and Philosophy, University of Pardubice, in Czechia.

3. www.economist.com/news/europe/21665050-one-man-epitomises-hostile-views-migrants-widely-held-his-people-orban-archetype.

4. www.pewforum.org/files/2012/12/globalReligion-tables-pdf.

5. The Czech Republic (Czechia) is composed of three historical lands: Bohemia, Moravia, and Czech Silesia. Moravia occupies the eastern part of Czechia and Moravians form a subgroup of Czechs.

6. www.pewforum.org/files/2012/12/globalReligion-tables-pdf.

7. I was given these numbers by the Czech convert Lukáš (Alí) Větrovec. Most conversions occur after marriage between a Muslim man and a non-Muslim woman.

8. See www.irex.org/sites/default/files/ODell%20Scholar%20Research%20Brief%20 2010-2011.pdf (p. 4).

9. The Hungarian Islamic Community (Magyar Iszlám Közösség, or MIK), led by Zoltán Bolek, was established in 1988 and is strongly "national" and patriotic, consisting

mostly of native Hungarians. The MIK dates to 1931, when it was founded by Hungarian, Bosnian, and Albanian Muslims. It is the smallest of three Muslim associations in Hungary and has the same rights as other Christian and Jewish communities. More on Muslims in Hungary and the region can be found in Rózsa (2010: 405–446).

10. www.irex.org/sites/default/files/ODell%20Scholar%20Research%20Brief%202010-2011.pdf.

11. domov.sme.sk/c/5571582/mesity-maju-cestu-zarubanu.html. However, this observation is partially incorrect since Athens is another European metropolis without a mosque. Estimates put the number of Muslims in the Greek capital at about 300,000. Also, the Slovenian capital, Ljubljana, only recently approved a project to build a mosque for local Muslims.

12. See www.lidovky.cz/islam-v-cesku-zvlastni-prava-neziska-nezverejnuje-vyrocni-zpravy-109-/zpravy-domov.aspx?c=A150117_142317_ln_domov_mct. The official reason for refusing the upgrade is that the community does not release its annual reports.

13. I. Tharoor, "Slovakia's Leader Said Islam Has 'No Place' in His Country. Now He's Taking a Leadership Role in the E.U." *Washington Post*, June 21, 2016.

14. www.reflex.cz/clanek/politika/42738/umirneny-muslim-je-stejny-protimluv-jako-umirneny-nacista-tvrdi-expremier-zeman.html.

15. The identification with national things can be further complicated on a more symbolic level. The Slovak national flag and coat of arms with a double cross standing on the middle peak of a dark blue mountain presents a problem for all Muslim converts and born Muslims alike because it displays Christian symbols. Slovakia's coat of arms consists of a red (gules) shield in early Gothic style, charged with a silver (argent) double cross standing on the middle peak of a dark blue mountain consisting of three peaks. Extremities of the cross are amplified, and its ends are concaved. The double cross is a symbol of Slovakia's Christian faith, and the hills represent three symbolic mountain ranges: Tatra, Fatra, and Mátra (the last one in northern Hungary). A modern interpretation of the double cross is that it represents Slovakia as an heir and guardian of Christian tradition, brought to the region by St. Cyril and St. Methodius, two missionaries from the Byzantine Empire.

16. www.ceskatelevize.cz/ivysilani/10119576319-fenomen-dnes/207452801370004.

17. www.youtube.com/watch?v=fRjbri5d1cg.

18. iszlam.com/iszlam-az-elet-vallasa/magyar-muszlimok/item/239-magyarkent-muszlim. This article states that the lives of old Hungarians shared many common traits with those of present-day Muslims, and the best proof is to visit any Hungarian village. In fact, Hungarian, Moravian, and Slovak female folk costumes look very much like a Muslim *hijab*.

19. See iszlam.com/iszlam-az-elet-vallasa/magyar-muszlimok/item/239-magyarkent-muszlim.

20. literarky.cz/blogy/tereza-spencerova/21842-petr-pelikan-kuvajane-v-teplicich-jako-ei-v-hurgad.

21. See komentare.sme.sk/c/7966868/jozef-lenc-kazda-bytost-stvorena-bohom-sa-rodi-ako-moslim.html.

22. Interview with Czech Arabist and Islamologist Bronislav Ostřanský on August 3, 2016.

23. website.informer.com/visit?domain=sharia4czechia.com.

24. See website.informer.com/visit?domain=sharia4czechia.com.

25. Interview on June 10, 2015.

26. Bohemia's coat of arms shows a silver double-tailed lion on a red background.

27. For non-Muslim Czechs, the figures of Turks on the Charles Bridge symbolize cruelty and lust.

REFERENCES

Allievi, S. 2013. *Les convertis à l'islam: les nouveaux musulmans d'Europe*. Paris: L'Harmattan.

Bureš, J. 2010. *Muslims in Visegrad*. Prague: Institute of International Relations.

Cenker, M. 2010. *Traditions Confronted: Muslim Migrants in Slovakia*. Saarbrücken: Lambert Academic Publishing.

Čikeš, R. 2005. "Registration of Churches and Religious Societies vs. Religious Freedom." In *Islam in Europe: Religious Freedom and its Aspects*. M. Moravčíková and M. Lojda, eds. Bratislava: Ústav pre vzťahy štátu a cirkví—Centrum pre európsku politiku. 194–198.

Dizdarevič, S. M. 2016. "Islamophobia in the Czech Republic: National Report 2015." In *European Islamophobia Report 2015*. E. Bayrakli and F. Hafez, eds. Istanbul: SETA. 115–130.

Drobný, J. 2013. "Slovakia." In *Yearbook of Muslims in Europe*, vol. 5. J. S. Nielsen, ed. Leiden: Brill. 585–591.

Górak-Sosnowska, K., ed. 2011. *Muslims in Poland and Eastern Europe*. Warszawa: University of Warsaw—Faculty of Oriental Studies.

Jacobson, J. 1998. *Islam in Transition, Religion, and Identity among British Pakistani Youth*. London: Routledge.

Janota, I. 2008. *Rehole, kostoly a kláštory v Bratislave*. Bratislava: Albert Marenčin—vydavateľstvo PT.

Kilpadi, P. ed. 2007. *Islam and Tolerance in Wider Europe*. Budapest: Open Society Foundation.

Knapová, I. 2007. *Konverzia na islam na príklade slovenských žien*. MA diss. Trnava: UCM.

Kuper, A. 1999. *Culture: The Anthropologists' Account*. Cambridge, MA: Harvard University Press.

Letavajová, S. 2006. "Náboženská konverzia ako dôsledok globalizačných procesov—prípadová štúdia o islamských konvertitoch na Slovensku." In *Reflexia globalizácie v lokálnom spoločenstve*. S. Letavajová, ed. Trnava: FF UCM. 91–133.

Macháček, Š. 2013. "Czech Republic." In *Yearbook of Muslims in Europe*, vol. 5. J. S. Nielsen, ed. Leiden: Brill. 195–208.

Macho, P. 2013. "Matúš Čák Trenčiansky—slovenský kráľ?" In *Mýty naše slovenské*. E. Krekovič, E. Mannová and E. Krekovičová, eds. Bratislava: Premedia. 104–110.

Mansson McGinty, A. 2006. *Becoming Muslim: Western Women's Conversions to Islam*. New York: Palgrave Macmillan.

Mendel, M., B. Ostřanský, and T. Rataj. 2007. *Islám v srdci Evropy: Vlivy islámské civilizace na dějiny a současnost českých zemí*. Praha: Academia.

Mendel, M. 1999. "Beginnings of the Muslim Religious Community in Former Czechoslovakia." ISIM *Newsletter* 2: 24.

Moreno, L. 2010. "Fearing the Future: Islamophobia in Central Europe." *The New Presence* 4: 73–80.

Özdalga, E. 2006. "The Hidden Arab: A Critical Reading of the Notion of 'Turkish Islam.'" *Middle Eastern Studies* 42, no. 4: 551–570.

Özyürek, E. 2009. "Convert Alert: German Muslims and Turkish Christians as Threats to Security in the New Europe." *Comparative Studies in Society and History* 51, no. 1: 91–116.

Özyürek, E. 2015. *Being German, Becoming Muslim: Race, Religion, and Conversion in the New Europe*. Princeton and Oxford: Princeton University Press.

Panýrková, P. 2009. *Konvertité k islámu v České republice*. Pardubice: Katedra religionistiky a filosofie Univerzita Pardubice (unpublished bachelor treatise).

Pelikán, P. 2008. "Předmluva překladatele." In *Zahrady spravedlivých: sbírka výroků proroka Muhammada*. I. J. An-Nawawí. Praha: Nakladatelství AMS. 22–53.

Pelikán, P. 2008. "On Death and Dying: The Ebb and Flow of Cultural Identities." *The New Presence* 4: 54–59.

Pirický, G. 2010. "Restrictive Legislation towards Minor Religions in Slovakia: The Case of the Muslim Community." *European Yearbook for Minority Issues 2007/8*. Leiden and Boston: Martinus Nijhoff Publishers. 717–729.

Ramadan, T. 1999. *Muslims in France: The Way Towards Coexistence*. Markfield, Leicester: Islamic Foundation.

Ramadan, T. 2004. *Western Muslims and the Future of Islam*. Oxford: Oxford University Press.

Roald, A. S. 2004. *New Muslims in the European Context: The Experience of Scandinavian Converts*. Leiden and Boston: Brill.

Roberts, A. 2005. *From Good King Venceslas to the Good Soldier Švejk: A Dictionary of Czech Popular Culture*. Budapest: CEU.

Robertson, R. 1998. "Glokalisierung: Homogenität und Heterogenität in Raum und Zeit." In *Perspektiven der Weltgesellschaft*. U. Beck, ed. Frankfurt: Suhrkamp. 192–221.

Rózsa, E. N. 2010. "Muszlim kisebbségek Közép-Európában, avagy Közép-Európa különlegessége," In *Az iszlám Európában*. Z. Rostoványi, ed. Budapest: Aula. 405–446.

Sabatos, Ch. D. 2014. *Mit ve Tarih Arasında: Orta Avrupa Edebiyat Tarihinde Türk İmgesi*. İstanbul: Bilge Kültür Sanat.

Sedláková, M. 2014. *Konstruování identity ženy v kontextu konverze k islámu*. Brno: Katedra sociální pedagogiky MU (unpublished MA diss.).

Schöplin, G. 1997. "The Functions of Myth and a Taxonomy of Myths." In *Myths and Nationhood*. G. Hosking and G. Schöplin eds. New York: Routledge. 19–35.

Štefančík, R., and J. Lenč. 2012. *Mladí migranti v slovenskej spoločnosti*. Brno: Tribun EU.

Topinka, D., ed. 2016. *Muslimové v Česku*. Brno: Barrister & Principal.

Van Nieuwkerk, K., ed. 2006. "*Women Embracing Islam: Gender and Conversion in the West.*" Austin: University of Texas Press.

Yavuz, H. 2004. "Is There a Turkish Islam? The Emergence of Conversion and Consensus." *Journal of Muslim Minority Affairs* 24, no. 2: 213–232.

Zebiri, K. 2007. *British Muslim Converts: Choosing Alternative Lives*. Oxford: Oneworld.

Ženka, J. 2011. *Pád Granady a zánik al-Andalusu*. Praha: Argo.

SIX

MOVING INTO SHIʿA ISLAM

The "Process of Subjectification" among Shiʿa Women Converts in London[1]

YAFA SHANNEIK

The religious and political factions as well as the ethnic and national backgrounds of Shiʿa communities in London are very diverse. There are a number of Shiʿa religious centers (*husayniyyat*) in London, generally divided according to the source of emulation (*marjaʿ altaqlid—pl. marajiʿ*) they represent. Women following *marajiʿ* that are close in their ideological understandings would gather together in one *husayniyya*. Many of these *husayniyyat* are within walking distance apart from each other, all centered in what is known as the "Shiʿa mile of London" in the borough of Brent in the northwest part of the city. The power dynamics between Shiʿa community members in London relate back to intranational relations in belonging to particular religious and social spheres in their countries of origin. Historical rivalries between the two shrine cities of Najaf and Karbala in Iraq play an enormous role within Shiʿa communities in London, competing for authority and status in the diaspora. Historical transnational conflicts between countries such as Iran and Iraq also play a role in the wider positionality and acceptance of the various Shiʿa organizations in London particularly in regard to their political and religious agendas in the Middle East.

These power relations are expressed particularly within religious gatherings (*majalis*)[2] that are organized on a regular basis throughout the year. The peak of Shiʿa religious rituals are in the first ten days (also known as *ʿashura*) of the Islamic calendar Muharram as well as in the mourning period for the following forty days (*arbaʿin*). Shiʿa commemorate in this period the death of Imam Husayn, the grandson of the Prophet Muhammad, and his family (*ahl al-bayt*), who is believed to have been killed on the plains of Karbala, southern Iraq, in 680 CE. These *majalis* are characterized by being hierarchical in nature. Social structures, which are shaped in terms of tribal and family backgrounds, and biographies of individuals provide certain women with religious and social capital (Bourdieu 1990; Rey 2007) and therefore the authority to set the tone in the *majalis* in terms of topics to be discussed, issues to be raised, particular rituals to be performed, and the manner in which they are performed. These women act as representatives and spokespersons to the religious and political factions of the *majalis*, which normally reflect the factions of the Shiʿa center they operate in. These social structures among community members still play a major role in the diaspora, providing individuals with authority within their respective communities.

Individuals are certainly influenced by these social structures. But those structures are also reflected within the wider Iraqi Shiʿa communities in London, mainly expressed through Shiʿa ritual practices that are characterized by being strongly culturally influenced—marginalizing those who are outside of these specific cultural contexts. This can, for example, be observed in the speakers invited to hold lectures and lead *majalis* at various *husayniyyat* in London. One of the very popular *ʿashura majalis* in London is the "Ashura camp," which in 2013 was a huge tent set up for the *ʿashura* commemoration ceremonies. The major speaker at "Ashura 2013" was Sayyid Muhammad al-Safi, a Baghdad-born scholar who gained much popularity in the last ten years, particularly among Shiʿa expatriates in Europe and the US. Sayyid al-Safi's vagueness about his allegiance to a particular *marjaʿ* plays a role in his increased popularity among Shiʿa in the West as it provides a space for Shiʿa following a variety of *marajiʿ* to listen to him. What characterizes Sayyid al-Safi is his traditional approach to holding a *majlis*. The stories he tells, the poetry he reads, and the *latmiyya* (rhythmic self-beating) he performs all mirror a nostalgic image of "Iraq in the old days" as born Shiʿa women describe it.[3] As explained above, *ʿashura* commemorations are ritual practices for remembering the historical events around the killing of Imam Husayn. Although it mainly concentrates on remembering the Battle of Karbala, it also reflects Iraqis' lives before migrating to Europe. A lot of his listeners enjoy participating in his *majlis*, as they are taken back to these personal memories and experience a kind of flashback to their lives in Iraq. This increases his popularity among the first generation of Iraqi migrants living in London in particular. As one of the women nostalgically says: "He reminds me of the *majalis* we used to do in Iraq while I was sitting with my mother, aunts and friends. This is the right way of holding a *majlis*."

Converts to Shiʿa Islam are outside of these aforementioned religious and political factions. They do not share the same national and ethnic or even religious and cultural fields that the first generation of Shiʿa migrants operate in. However, as one of the converts explains, these various intra-Shiʿa communal relations in London have an effect on the converts' positionality within the Shiʿa communities. As one of the converts highlights: "You get caught between the cultural, religious and national differences.... Your whole conversion is coming down to ideological intra-communal conflicts." This chapter will discuss these power relations among first-generation born Shiʿa and converts to Shiʿa Islam within various Shiʿa communities in London. How are converts positioned within these social structures? What mechanisms are brought into play by converts in order to position themselves within these power relations. And to what extent does this new position challenge existing power relations?[4]

In order to engage with these questions, I will first turn briefly to Michel Foucault's discussion on power and the reciprocal relationship between the individual and existing power relations within certain discourses (Foucault 1982). I then consider Jean Lave and Etienne Wenger's discussion on the "legitimate peripheral participation of learners" within what they refer to as "communities of practice" (Lave and Wenger 2002: 11–126).[5] Converts can be regarded as learners who through observations of certain religious ritual practices gain religious knowledge. Through this newly obtained religious knowledge, converts try to move from the periphery to the center of their communities. Michael Stausberg applies Lave and Wenger's discussions of communities of practice on Jain *pūjā* rituals and argues that the transition from periphery to the center is not granted solely after acquiring a degree of knowledge of particular religious ritual practices but rather involves a wide range of sociocultural, ethnic, national, and religious dimensions (Stausberg 2001).

This chapter discusses the representation of religion in the public sphere by converts as a form of self-assertion within their communities of practice. I argue that converts move from the periphery to the center, become spokespersons of their communities, and contribute to the production of knowledge through talking *about* religion. It is the talking *about* religion that offers them temporal access to the center of their communities. The converts' ethnic and linguistic backgrounds provide them with the social capital needed to be eligible, from their communities' point of view, to represent their communities at certain public events. Their temporal access to the center challenges to a certain extent existing power relations within their communities. At the end of this chapter, I will discuss converts' access to certain power dynamics when talking *about* rather than talking *within* religions (see Lave and Wenger 2002: 121–122).

POWER DYNAMICS WITHIN SHIʿA COMMUNITIES IN LONDON

Michel Foucault understands power as being generated within a particular discourse that shapes individuals through the government of their conduct. Individuals therefore operate within power relations that are deeply rooted in a "social nexus" (Foucault 1982: 791) or systems of social networks (Foucault 1982: 793). Structuring and shaping other people's actions according to particular norms of a given society or community might set limits on individuals but at the same time could provide certain forms of agency and individuality (compare Nixon 2013: 311). As Foucault argues in his later works, individuals, although still governed by power relations within particular discourses, exercise agency through a process of constructing their own subject positions through what he calls "the technologies of the self," which "permit individuals to effect by their own means or with the help of others a certain number of operations on their own bodies and souls, thoughts, conduct and way of being, so as to transform themselves in order to attain a certain state of happiness, purity, wisdom, perfection or immortality" (Foucault 1993: 203). I use Foucault's notion of the circulation of power (Foucault 1982) to analyze the ways in which converts try to position themselves within their communities. Power relations within communities of practice are not static but rather change according to members' degree of involvement in activities. I will adopt Foucault's understanding of new forms of individuality articulated through knowledge and networks of power when discussing converts' ways of finding their position within their Shiʿa communities in London.

Converts try to integrate themselves into their new religious communities and gain sufficient religious knowledge to take part in the various religious ritual practices. This socialization is governed by the existing social structures of their communities that direct certain behaviors and actions, on the one hand. On the other hand, the individuals' attempts to integrate themselves into their communities influence existing social structures and power dynamics (see Stausberg 2001: 607). These reciprocal power relations between the community and the individual, in which the latter constantly seeks self-assertion, cause a threat to existing power dynamics within their communities.

In regard to the relationship between the learner and the master in an apprenticeship context, Lave and Wenger argue that "legitimate peripheral participation" involves the process in which learners gradually gain knowledge and therefore are increasingly provided access to their communities of practice until they become full members of the community. The participation of learners, or newcomers, is constantly negotiated within existing power relations. In religious communities, the transition from periphery to the center is not granted solely after acquiring a degree of knowledge or of competence and performance[6] of particular religious ritual practices (Stausberg 2001: 612). The learners' transition to the center is an "ambivalent process" (Stausberg 2001: 612). After being granted access to the community, Shiʿa converts soon find themselves on its periphery. As one of the converts explains: "You sit at the back of the room. No one notices that you are here. No one notices that you have gone either." Converts try gradually to get access to the center. The way from the periphery to the center involves a variety of power struggles articulated within the various communities. Converts hope to develop over time their status in their communities from beginners to more established members. The peripheral position of converts and their move from the periphery to the center is not only dependent upon the degree of their knowledge but involves other sociopolitical, economic, national, and ethnic factors.

The question that needs to be discussed at this stage is how converts identify with their new religious communities. If, as stated above, they do not share any national, ethnic, or cultural capital with the majority of members in their communities, then what is the common denominator, or what Wenger terms the "shared repertoire" (see Wenger 1998: 82–83)? Lave and Wenger define community as the "participation in an activity system about which participants share understandings concerning what they are doing and what that means in their lives and for their communities" (Lave and Wenger 2002: 115). When talking about community coherence, Wenger identifies three sources: "mutuality of engagement,"[7] "accountability to the enterprise,"[8] and "shared repertoire."[9] It is the "shared repertoire" that is particularly relevant in regard to converts' identification with a Shiʿa identity. For Wenger this shared repertoire "combines both reificative and participative aspects. It includes the discourse by which members create meaningful statements about the world, as well as the styles by which they express their forms of membership and their identities as members" (Wenger 1998: 83). Converts try to identify with their new religious identity and establish shared links to their new religious communities through the construction of a shared repertoire.

THE CONSTRUCTION OF A SHARED REPERTOIRE AMONG SHIʿA CONVERTS

Female converts to Shiʿa Islam I interviewed construct various narratives of a shared repertoire. I will introduce two of these narratives: first, the construction of a global unified Muslim *umma*, and second, the sociopolitical marginalization of Shiʿa in the Muslim world.

The first narrative focuses on converts' description of an increasing secularization of societies in Europe and the growing public general discourse of separating religion from the state. Some converts feel attracted to an alternative political system that supports a fusion between religion and the state. The Islamic Republic of Iran and Ayatollah Khomeini's innovative interpretation of the political leadership and authority of clerics expressed through *wilayat al-faqih* (guardianship of the jurist) serve very well in this regard. Khomeini's understanding of *wilayat al-faqih* secures the centrality of religion within an Islamic state by giving ultimate executive, legislative, and juridical power to senior clerics. This perception and the particular religious understanding of Shiʿa Islam were supported by some converts' move to Iran and their intensive engagement with Iranian Shiʿa who support this politico-religious system. These converts criticize the tendencies and attempts of various European governments to separate religion from the state and argue that only God has the right to legislate, articulated first through the imams and then through particular *fuqahaʾ* (Islamic jurists) who see themselves as surrogates of the Hidden Imam until the end of his occultation. The converts agree with Khomeini's views that the concept of nationalism is an imperialist product that has caused, as one of them argues, "a lot of harm in the world." Similar to Khomeini, these converts believe in a Muslim *umma* as it once existed at the time of Prophet Muhammad and understand their religious identity as being part of a global, united Muslim community.

Converts' allegiance to *wilayat al-faqih* can be regarded as part of Foucault's understandings of "the technologies of the self." Khomeini's global, pan-Islamic, and revolutionary appeal transcends the narrow ethnonational identity understandings of many first-generation Shiʿa in the diaspora. Converts try to carve their place and position themselves within Shiʿa communities in the diaspora through the adherence to a Muslim *umma* narrative. As one of the converts describing her identity says: "It is not about being Shiʿa, or being Iranian or Iraqi. It's about being a Muslim."

The second narrative of a shared repertoire centers around the continuous political and social marginality of Shiʿa in the Muslim world and their long history of persecution. These converts highlight the maltreatment, execution, and displacement of Shiʿa under Saddam Hussein's regime in Iraq or other governments in the Persian Gulf as well as by al-Qaeda and the Islamic State (IS). These converts compare the Shiʿa political and religious context in the Middle East with similar European religio-political power struggles in countries such as Northern Ireland or Cyprus. Some of these converts, particularly those with friends at university level, engage in a variety of local civic work such as fund-raising events for the homeless or food-bank collections for the needy, as well as international civic engagement related to the most recent Syrian refugee situations in Europe or raising funds for orphanages in different parts of Africa. All these civic engagement activities are interwoven with a particular narrative of Shiʿa history. Shiʿa develop a particular group's "master narrative" (Connerton 1989) around the killing of Imam Husayn, which is also referred to as "the Karbala paradigm" (Fischer 1980: 19–26). This narrative produces a general sense of a homogenous unified group providing communities with a sense of oneness and unity (cf. Lambert et al. 2009).

This narrative of the Karbala paradigm is understood by the converts in the sense that Imam Husayn was a revolutionary who fought against the autocratic rule of the Umayyads. Twelver Shiʿa believe that ʿAli, the Prophet's cousin, companion, and son-in-law, should have been the successor of the Prophet Muhammad after his death. However, he became only the fourth Caliph and was assassinated during this period. Muʿawiyah (d. 680 CE) became the ruler and appointed his son Yazid (d. 683 CE) as his successor, thereby converting the caliphate into a dynasty—an act that was rejected by many, including ʿAli's son Husayn. Husayn was the most significant threat to this dynastic rule, since he was the only living grandson of the Prophet Muhammad. Yazid demanded therefore an official oath of allegiance from him as he believed that such an oath would grant him religious legitimacy. However, Husayn refused. He received many letters from Kufa in southern Iraq—a stronghold of opposition against the ruling dynasty—assuring him support and asking him to come and guide them to lead a revolt against Yazid. While making his way to Kufa, Yazid increased his pressure and forced the people of Kufa to change loyalty from Husayn to him. Just before arriving at Kufa, in a place called Karbala, Husayn and his entourage, including children and women, were intercepted by Yazid's army. The army numbered in the thousands and surrounded and prevented them from any water access for days. After ten days in battle on the tenth day of the Islamic month Muharram in 680 CE, Husayn was killed and decapitated, and his head was taken to Yazid in Damascus (al-Haidari 1999, Shanneik 2015).

Shiʿa converts as well as born Shiʿa Muslims in Europe present the narrative of the Karbala paradigm as an example of a resistance movement against oppressive regimes of all kinds.[10] It is framed particularly by converts in a way to stand for social justice as well as religious and social pluralism. Shiʿa Islam has been used, by born as well as by Shiʿa converts, as a counternarrative to Sunni militant movements in the Middle East. Shiʿa Muslims present themselves generally as an alternative *umma* that, different from their Sunni counterparts, denounces terrorism. Essentializing Shiʿa Islam functions as a "signifier of stability" (Bhabha 1994: 102) in the converts' identity understanding. It acts as a wider social assurance of joining "the good Muslims, the victims and . . . the oppressed," as one of the converts explains. This is particularly important for the converts' social environment of family and friends who might have a particular attitude toward Islam informed by recent political events. As one of the converts explains: "My mum was very sceptical and thought somebody had brainwashed me but I assured her that Shiʿa are the good Muslims and that they are being targeted by ISIS in the same way as Christians are. . . . Even worse." Essentializing Shiʿa Islam as a religion that stands for "a good deed," as another convert describes, in contrast to an Islam or any other religion that represents "a bad deed," can be read in Mahmud Mamdani's notion of "good Muslims [versus] bad Muslims" (Mamdani 2004; see also Scharbrodt 2011). Converts to Shiʿa Islam, in particular, repeatedly referred in our conversations to such narratives in order to justify their conversion within, what converts see as today's increasing public hostility toward Islam.

The narrative of the Karbala paradigm is a major part of Shiʿa *majalis*, in which throughout the year, but especially during *ʿashura*, a constant construction and presentation of Shiʿa as the alternative *umma* is articulated. As one of the converts explains, "Even if I do not come from an ethnic background, for example Iraqi, where the horrible story of Karbala would have been part of my life since childhood, the *majalis* I attend in London are so powerful. They go underneath your skin to the extent that you not only hear and see Imam al-Husayn, you even feel and smell him." The narrative of the Karbala paradigm is articulated in various Shiʿa *majalis* through the power of the senses. It is heard through verbal transmission in the form of various lectures and recitations of lamentation poetry. It is seen through visualizing the narrative through a variety of images and slogans as well as theatrical performances. And it is also felt through the rhythmic ritual self-beating on the face and the upper body. In addition, it is sometimes smelled through the blood that is shed during the performance of *tatbir*—the act of self-flagellation by using swords and knives for cutting one's body. Although this practice is highly controversial among the various Shiʿa communities across the world, it is gaining in popularity particularly among young women in London, despite the fact that traditionally it has been regarded as an act of "masculinity" (Shanneik, 2016).

Sally Promey and Shira Brisman introduce in this context the phrase "sensory cultures" (Promey and Brisman 2010), which describes the interaction between objects and individuals through their association with different smells, sounds, touches, and sights: "Sensory culture, like material culture, concerns not simply perception and its histories and theories but also things perceived and things produced for sensory apprehension" (Promey and Brisman 2010: 198). Using all of these forms of transmission to present the Karbala narrative helps converts to attach themselves emotionally to the narrative to the extent that it generates emotions that lead to weeping and self-beating as an expression of sorrow for the mistreatment and ultimate killing of Imam Husayn. As one of the women explains: "The story of Imam al-Husayn is a story of injustice, unfair treatment and murder. When you hear or see it you will of course cry—if you have a heart." Weeping as an expression of mourning and sorrow for the *ahl al-bayt* is part of Shiʿa rituals and is seen as a source of salvation.

The narrative of the Karbala paradigm helps converts particularly to feel integrated into their communities by building a "shared repertoire." By developing a communal emotional attachment, converts are able to strengthen their sense of belonging to their Shiʿa communities. It, however, also helps them to feel attached to their European environment as they use the narrative of Husayn—the revolutionary who stood for justice and fought for human rights—as an example to support Western attempts of fighting against terrorist Sunni groups in the Middle East they themselves are the victims of. This construction of an essentialized understanding of Shiʿa and Sunni Islam has the function of creating a clear and stable identity. This essentialism provides converts with what Bhabha refers to, in a different context, as a "static system" (Bhabha 1994: 102) of signifiers that constructs a counter-discourse to the existing public stereotypical discourse toward Islam within European societies. But these signifiers need to refer to universal meanings and values, such as human rights, as they are only "understood as if referring to things in a definite and unchangeable way. . . . Therefore they offer just one possibility of expression, or better: they provoke one certain way of understanding" (Hildebrand-Nilshon et al. 2001: 5). Through the construction of universal static and clear signifiers of a Shiʿa identity, converts are able to justify their conversion to Islam at a time in which Islam is presented as a definable entity within the public sphere of various Western societies. This definition of Islam refers generally to Sunni Islam and is associated with militant groups that use violence as a means to reach their aims. By presenting Shiʿa Islam as the alternative Islam, it functions as a counter-discourse to the existing assumptions of Islam—Sunni Islam in this case. By doing so, however, it also confirms and reproduces the status quo of the negative image of Sunni Islam in public media discourses in Europe.

The recent example of such static signifiers is the execution on January 2,

2016, of the Shiʿa cleric Shaykh Nimr Baqir al-Nimr, who lived in the Shiʿa-populated Eastern Province of Saudi Arabia. His arrest and subsequent execution generated international reactions from governments as well as individuals, including some converts living in London. Converts condemned the violent actions by the Sunni Wahhabi-oriented Saudi government and placed it in contrast to Shaykh Nimr's "democratic, non-militant and progressive" worldviews. In our various conversations, converts referred to the inhumane treatment of the Saudi government toward Shiʿa prisoners in general and toward Shaykh Nimr in particular, pointing out that the Saudi government is committing a thousand human rights violations in its treatment of Shiʿa prisoners. The sociopolitical situation of Shiʿa in Saudi Arabia is presented as an example of the contentious mistreatment of Shiʿa since the Battle of Karbala. Converts compare the political and religious influence of the Saudi government in the Middle East with the early Islamic dynasty of the Umayyads,[11] whose "goal [was] to eliminate the Shiʿa," as one of the converts explains. The imprisonment and execution of Shaykh Nimr, which received wide international media attention, functions as a stable signifier for converts who use this as an example to illustrate the ideological distinction between Sunnis and Shiʿa, the latter being suppressed, targeted, and executed. As another convert explains: "Shiʿa just want to live their lives without fear of persecution."

Essentializing Shiʿa Islam by presenting it as a counter-discourse to Sunni Islam, which represents violence and human rights violations, reflects what Bhabha refers to, in a different context, as the "mode of representation of otherness" (Bhabha 1994: 97). Sunni Islam as the "other" is presented continuously in various Shiʿa religious ritual practices and gatherings across Shiʿa *husayniyyat* in London as well as in private homes. Shiʿa Islam as the alternative *umma* to Sunni Islam, however, is also presented in public spaces such as during the yearly commemoration processions in London and other European cities (Shanneik et al. 2017). On the day of *ʿashura*, Shiʿa across the world organize processions commemorating the death of Imam Husayn and his family—the *ahl al-bayt*. Through visual representations (Hall 2013) such as the photo below, Shiʿa publicly use various modes of representing the "other" and oneself—thus deconstructing undifferentiated existing public stereotypical attitudes toward Islam in general. Through large banners, leaflets, on-street lectures, and one-on-one talks, Shiʿa publicly represent an alternative peaceful, although victimized and persecuted, Islam on the streets of London.

FIGURE 6.1.
Edgware Road London, ʿashura *procession, 2013 (Author photo).*

CONVERTS TALKING *ABOUT* RELIGION IN THE PUBLIC SPHERE

Speaking at the international Revert Muslim Association conference at the Islamic Centre of England in March 2015, one of the converts describes a dream she had one night of Imam Husayn warning her of getting isolated and asking her to get more involved in the Shiʿa community in London. A number of converts I interviewed vacillate in their relationship with the various Shiʿa communities between a strong feeling of integration and a sense of separation and stigmatization. How far are converts able to integrate themselves into Shiʿa communities that, as illustrated above, are characterized by intracommunal power dynamics? What mechanisms are brought into play by converts in order to position themselves within these power relations? What roles do they play therein? To what extent are these roles influenced by the geopolitical developments in the Middle East and to what extent does this new position challenge existing power relations?

Michel Foucault understands the process of subjectification as containing mechanisms used to transform oneself into a subject (Foucault 1982; Bhabha 1994: 95). Hildebrand-Nilshon et al. argue that it is the power of self-governing and self-articulation that is effective

> as a communicative, intersubjective practice based on existing societal constraints and conditions, and thus functioning according to present or future actions that aim to promote or to nullify possible relationships to others. Governing action is divided into both acting upon others and acting upon the self, and in this sense it could be understood as the various social rationalities and practices in which individuals employ strategies for their subjectification (2001: 2).

Shiʿa converts go through a process of subjectification by creating a self and positioning it within existing power relations apparent in their Shiʿa communities. By defining their position, converts challenge these power dynamics within their communities, to a certain extent, by securing a place and maximizing their own powers within existing discourses. They try, through particular actions, to move from the periphery to the center. When it comes to the public representations of Shiʿa communities in the UK, white European female converts to Shiʿa Islam occupy this role in the public space. During events such as the commemoration processions in London twice a year, on the tenth day of Muharram and forty days after, some converts become the female spokespersons of particular Shiʿa communities in London. In their

FIGURE 6.2.
Dr. Rebecca Masterton speaking at the commemoration procession in London, 2014 (Photo taken by Oliver Scharbrodt).

public speeches at these events, they recall the narrative of the Karbala paradigm interwoven with current political issues such as the violent terrorist activities of the Sunni militant movement of the Islamic State. One of the functions of these processions is to raise public awareness of Shiʿa Islam. This public space is used by Shiʿa community members and in most cases offered to white female converts to Shiʿa Islam to deliver a counternarrative to such Sunni militant movements in the Middle East. As illustrated above, political and public discourses are strategically informing the modes of representations of otherness. White European female converts to Islam present Shiʿa Islam at public events as the alternative Islam. Banners such as the one illustrated in the photo above with the acronym "ISIS" (the Islamic State in Iraq and Syria) crossed out and "No to Terrorism" show clearly the public message this event is presenting.

Representation is the production of meaning through language (Hall 2013: 2). Through converts' cultural and linguistic capital they gain power within their communities and gradually become community subjects.[12] They "learn the system and conventions of representation" (Hall 2013: 8) and contribute to the production of knowledge, out of which they gain power within their communities. However, converts' increase in power and their shift from the periphery to the center are only temporal and contextual.

Based on Jan Assmann's discussion on ritual continuity, Stausberg argues that communities need to have a functioning structure that enables the continuity of ritual practices. He continues by saying that ritual practices are produced and reproduced through the concept of mimesis, which is based on the observation of the performative dimension of rituals (Stausberg 2001: 608). Lave and Wenger refer to "informal" learning—through "observation and imitation" (Lave and Wenger 2002: 113). The learning process through performance in rituals is associated with material objects and symbols, emotions as well as spatial characteristics that have a "deeper" influence and effect on the learner (Stausberg 2001: 617). Stausberg distinguishes between two forms of ritual performances: some rituals require yearlong experiences, qualifications that involve understanding of religious and historical texts perhaps in various languages, and a deeper engagement with theological concepts and ideas. Other rituals, however, can be learned through mimesis and require neither a sophisticated engagement with various aspects of religion nor a particular ethnic, religious, social, or linguistic background (2001: 615).

The concept of communities of practice, understood as a set of relations among people who learn and share experiences from each other (Jean and Wenger 2002: 115), serves here very well in relation to religious communities, such as the Shiʿa community, for which ritual practices are central. The social structure of communities of practice defines the possibilities (cf. Jean and Wenger 2002: 115) for converts to learn the skills needed to participate in communal ritual performances. Converts imitating ritual practices willingly or unwillingly engage in ritual interpretations, thereby influencing their ritual performance. Ritual coherence provides believers with a sense of a coherent and stable identity and is based on the unchanging repetition and reproduction of rituals (Assmann 1992). The ways in which Shiʿa converts participate in Shiʿa ritual practices impact the communal power dynamics within Shiʿa communities, particularly among born Shiʿa Muslims. Very rarely, converts are allowed to hold *majalis* in London, but when they do they tend to move away from linking the Karbala narrative to the migration narrative and instead represent it as an example for current local issues such as political participation and/or civic engagement. Specific political and cultural topographies relevant to groups sharing a particular ethnic-national background are replaced by wider and more diverse topics to which particularly converts but also the second and third generations of Shiʿa born and raised in Europe feel more attracted. Shaykh Nimr's case, mentioned earlier and discussed in more detail later in this chapter, and the blood and water donation campaigns[13] are only two examples that illustrate how converts, but also second- and third-generation Shiʿa in Europe, try to make Shiʿa Islam more relevant to their everyday lives and to their moral values. These developments in the deviation processes in Shiʿa ritual practices cause the first generation of Shiʿa to feel threatened in their Shiʿa identity in the diaspora. Their experiences of persecution and displacement, which used to be the focus of Shiʿa *majalis*, are replaced by issues more relevant to the locality as well as to human rights values more generally outside any particular ethnic-national background and supported more explicitly by the younger generation as well as by converts to Shiʿa Islam.

As mentioned above, the *majalis* are hierarchal in nature. Family backgrounds of individuals are important signifiers that give women access to certain roles in the communities in general and in the *majlis* in particular. The religious capital of an individual is regarded as valid only when the social capital is existent. Reserving particular leadership positions within Shiʿa *majalis* to born Shiʿa is, on the one hand, an expression of power but, on the other hand, a way of securing an "authentic" Shiʿa identity in the diaspora. As one of the converts describes, "They [born Shiʿa] want to do it their way." Language could also be regarded as an important factor in getting access to knowledge and therefore power in the community (Lave and Wenger 2002: 119). One could assume that, the more qualification in the form of religious, theological, and linguistic know-how one acquires, the stronger one's position becomes within the religious community, leading to access to leadership positions within Shiʿa communities. This might be the case among born Shiʿa women, but not necessarily in relation to Shiʿa converts.

A number of female converts to Shiʿa Islam in London have a long experience in participating in Shiʿa ritual practices. They attended various religious classes in renowned *hawzas* (religious seminaries) in Iran and Iraq, acquired a high level of religious literacy, and are fluent in Arabic as well as in Persian. Despite their religious, linguistic, and cultural competency, they are hardly granted access to leadership positions in religious ritual practices among Shiʿa communities in London. As one of the converts explains: "*Majalis* are sometimes held by women less knowledgeable in religious matters than me just because I am not an Iraqi." Female converts struggle to be provided a space during religious gatherings inside the *husayniyya*. When it comes to the public image of the *husayniyya*, the "visibility" of the exercise of power changes. Whereas in communal spaces convert women are visibly underrepresented in leadership positions within their communities, in public spaces this visibility is turned around. Convert women occupy a significant public space and become spokespersons and representatives of their communities.[14]

TALKING WITHIN AND TALKING ABOUT SHIʿA ISLAM

Lave and Wenger distinguish between talking *about* and talking *within* a practice (Lave and Wenger 2002: 119–121). The distinction between the two types of talking is, however, porous, as talking within simultaneously involves talking about and vice versa. But as the authors highlight, both forms of talk fulfill certain functions: "engaging, focusing, and shifting attention, bringing about co-ordination, etc., on the one hand; and supporting communal forms of memory and reflections, as well as signalling membership, on the other" (Lave and Wenger 2002: 120). Within Shiʿa women communities in London, the circulation of power is particularly crucial in the context of representations inside as well as outside the wider Shiʿa context (cf. Hall 2013: 251).

In order to visibly express the existing power dynamics within Shiʿa women communities in London, highlighting who is in the periphery and who is in the center, certain leadership positions are guaranteed for certain people regardless of their religious knowledge. The social and political field these women occupy in their communities is the determining factor, the function of which is to provide a coherent secured Shiʿa identity in the diaspora. This identity is articulated particularly when talking *within* religion. This takes the form of constructing a narrative that highlights a shared Shiʿa heritage and a shared memory of the past but also of current shared experiences of persecution and displacement. As the photo below illustrates, at a demonstration in front of the Saudi Arabian embassy in London in October 2015, a young Iraqi Shiʿa woman, raised in Britain, is the spokesperson for the Shiʿa community and not a convert. Talking *within* and mainly for her Shiʿa community, Zena Hajjiya demonstrates against the maltreatment of Shiʿa in Saudi Arabia in general and of the torture of Shiʿa prisoners in particular. The weekly demonstrations in front of the Saudi embassy were organized particularly in order to prevent the execution of Shaykh Nimr, as well as to raise public awareness of the human rights violations against Shiʿa in the country. Having a young Shiʿa woman occupying such a public space illustrates the empowerment of Shiʿa communities in the diaspora expressed through their outspokenness and eloquence in expressing their thoughts publicly without fear. Whereas the first generation of Arab Shiʿa would tend to perform *taqiyya* (i.e., conceal their faith), the younger generation feels even more the need to express their faith publicly and to fight for injustice. As one of the younger Shiʿa Iraqis I interviewed says: "Maybe my parents were afraid of fighting back and might have in certain situations performed *taqiyya* back home. But we live in Europe now. We are not afraid. We want the whole world to know who we are. Who

FIGURE 6.3.
Zena Hajjiya in front of the Saudi Arabia Embassy in London, October 2015 (Photo taken by Chris Heinhold).

Imam Husayn was and what he stood for. We will fight against injustice until the end." This resonates with the active civic engagement of the younger generation of Shiʿa in London. Who therefore occupies which space in which context depends on the function it is supposed to fulfill.

The access to power has the function of fulfilling particular political, public, and communal discourses. Shiʿa women converts are able to articulate their subjectivity within these power dynamics and are granted access to the center only for a temporary period of time and only in particular contexts. Shiʿa converts are granted a public space to talk *about* Shiʿa Islam, the function of which is to raise awareness of Shiʿa Islam within a British public sphere. The access of converts to public and communal spaces is spatially and temporally limited and dependent on the function it is supposed to fulfill. Whereas for the *ʿashura* commemoration a white Shiʿa convert is better placed in talking *about* Shiʿa Islam, a younger Shiʿa woman raised in Britain fulfills, according to the organizers of the demonstration but also according to the converts I talked to, a better role in illustrating the empowered situation of Shiʿa in the diaspora fighting against injustice committed by certain governments in the Middle East.

CONCLUSION

The first generation of Shiʿa migrants in London operate in certain religious, national, political, and cultural fields within their wider social network. Since European convert women to Shiʿa Islam do not share these fields, they try to find other ways to position themselves within their communities through the construction of a shared repertoire. Some converts expressed their allegiance to Khomeini's *wilayat al-faqih* and to his global and pan-Islamic understanding of Shiʿa Islam, which transcended the narrow ethnonational identity understandings of many first-generation Shiʿa in the diaspora. Their adherence to a unified global Muslim *umma* helps them to position themselves within their communities. The second narrative of a shared repertoire centers around Shiʿas' long history of persecution. The current sectarian tensions in the Middle East through the rise of the "Islamic State," in particular, urge converts to engage in various local and international civic activities. The portrayal of members of Shiʿa Islam as victims of sectarian conflicts in the Middle East, by born as well as convert women, during public events helps the construction of a visible counternarrative to Sunni militant groups in Islam. Many convert women sympathize with the sociopolitical oppression and marginalization of Shiʿa in the Muslim world and the consequent displacement of many. They compare it with various political events in Europe's own history and thereby express their emotional affiliation and shared understanding of the political situation of Shiʿa.

Through the construction of these shared repertoires, converts try to move from the periphery to the center within their communities. This transition, however, is not granted easily by community leaders or individual members, as they fear the destabilization of their community structures. Converts go through a process of constructing their own subject positions by acquiring religious knowledge and advancing their language skills. They try to transform themselves into recognized subjects within their communities and occupy an important position therein through the representation of Shiʿa Islam publicly. I have argued in this chapter that converts move from the periphery to the center, become spokespersons of their communities, and contribute to the production of knowledge through talking *about* religion in the public sphere. When talking *within* religion—that is, within communal spaces to and for Shiʿa—convert women in leadership positions are visibly underrepresented. These positions are instead reserved for born Shiʿa women with certain religious and social capital. In public spaces, however, distributing leadership roles becomes more complex. The circulation of power relates to the kind and function of representation. During public processions, for example, talking *about* Shiʿa Islam involves also addressing non-Shiʿa. A convert woman is therefore better placed not only because she is a woman but also because of the shared repertoire with British society of being mainly white and European. During the demonstration in front of the Saudi Arabian embassy in London, however, a young British-born Iraqi Shiʿa is better placed as she shares, by being the daughter of Iraqi Shiʿa parents, a particular memory of persecution and displacement that the demonstration itself is articulating. The political function of the public representation of Shiʿa Islam in a procession is different than during a demonstration and therefore addresses a different audience. Who occupies which space depends on the context and function it is supposed to fulfill—thereby keeping the circulation of power within Shiʿa communities between the first, second, third generations and converts in constant flux.

NOTES

1. This chapter is part of the research project "Karbala in London": Transnational Shii Networks between Britain and the Middle East, funded by the Gerda Henkel Foundation and based at the Chester Centre for Islamic Studies (CCIS) at the University of Chester.

2. There are various ways of holding a *majlis*, but in short it consists of readings from the Qur'an and saying prayers for the particular member of the Prophet's family to be mourned within the *majlis* by a reader, in my case a female reader known as *mullaya* (pl. *malaly*). The prayers are standardized prayer texts found in Shiʿa prayer books. This is followed by a lesson on any topic. Blessings to the Prophet Muhammad and his family are said throughout the *majlis* in the form of a dirge in order to set the atmosphere in the room. Lamentation poetry sometimes in Classical Arabic but more often in colloquial dialects is chanted, which has a particular effect on the listener as it evokes emotions to the extent of weeping and self-beating to express sorrow for the maltreatment and ultimate murder of Imam Husayn. The poetry has various rhythmic beats from slow to middle to fast. Which type of poetry to chant depends on the woman and her ability to perform the poetry she had memorized. More on Shiʿa *majalis*, see Nakash (2007: 115–136).

3. As part of my ethnographic fieldwork on Shiʿa Muslims in London, I interviewed 107 Iraqi Shiʿa women of diverse political, socioeconomic, and educational backgrounds between 2013 and 2016.

4. This chapter is based on three years of ethnographic fieldwork among Shiʿa women converts as well as born Shiʿa women in London. I interviewed twenty-one women converts of various national, religious, socioeconomic, and educational backgrounds. As the Shiʿa convert community in London is so small, in order not to break the confidentiality agreement of my interviewees I am not able to reveal their countries of origin. However,

they come from a variety of European countries and have been living in the UK for at least ten years.

5. Robert Langer and Benjamin Weineck (2017) used this concept in analyzing the continuous reproduction of ritual practices of second-generation Shiʿa Muslims in Germany.

6. On aspects of the theory of syntax, see also Chomsky (1965).

7. This is understood as the ability to build a relationship with other members in the community and to establish an identity of participation and engagement. See Wenger (1998: 137).

8. This refers to the ability to understand the enterprise and to contribute to its actions. See Wenger (1998: 137).

9. For Wenger, a repertoire is the communities' set of shared resources that entails a history of mutual engagement. See Wenger (1998: 82–85).

10. Khomeini and the sociologist Ali Shariati both played a significant role in politicking and revolutionizing Shiʿa Islam in Iran. Khomeini used the narrative of the Battle of Karbala in 1963 to start protests and movements against the Shah. See Khomeini (1970); Algar (1981); and Shariati (1980).

11. A few years ago this narrative was related to Saddam Hussain, the American invasion, and the spread of militant Salafi-oriented groups in Iraq. See Shanneik (2015).

12. Hall talks in this context about "culture person." See Hall et al. (2013: 8).

13. On water and blood donation campaigns, see Spellman-Poots (2013: 7).

14. During *Muharram* 2015, Rebecca Masterton accompanied the major Shiʿa TV and radio station in the UK (*Ahlul-Bayt TV*) for media coverage during *ʿashura*.

REFERENCES

Algar, H. 1981. *Islam and Revolution: Writings and Declarations of Imam Khomeini*. Berkeley: Mizan Press.

Al-Haidari, I. 1999. *Trājīdīyā Karbalā: Sūsiyūlūjīyā al-khiṭāb al-Shīʿī* [The Tragedy of Karbala: The Sociology of the Shii Speech]. London: Dar Al Saqi.

Assmann, Jan. 1992. *Das Kulturelle Gedächtnis. Schrift, Erinnerung und politische Identität in frühen Hochkulturen*. München: C. H. Beck.

Bhabha, H. K. 1994. *The Location of Culture*. London and New York: Routledge.

Bourdieu, P. 1990. *The Logic of Practice*. Trans. Richard Nice. Cambridge: Polity Press.

Chomsky, N. 1965. *Aspects of the Theory of Syntax*. Cambridge, MA: M.I.T. Press.

Connerton, P. 1989. *How Societies Remember*. Cambridge: Cambridge University Press.

Fischer, M. 1980. *Iran: From Religious Dispute to Revolution*. Cambridge, MA: Harvard University Press.

Foucault, M. 1982. "The Subject and Power." *Critical Inquiry* 8, no. 4: 777–795.

———. 1993. "About the Beginning of the Hermeneutics of the Self: Two Lectures at Dartmouth." *Political Theory* 21, no. 2: 198–227.

Hall, S., ed. 2013. *Representation: Cultural Representations and Signifying Practices.* Los Angeles: SAGE.

Hildebrand-Nilshon, M., J. Motzkau, and D. Papadopoulos. 2001. "Reintegrating Sense into Subjectification." In *Theoretical Issues in Psychology.* J. R. Morss, N. Stephenson, and H. van Rappard, eds. Boston: Kluwer Academic Publishers. 289–300.

Khomeini, I. 1970. *Islamic Government: Governance of the Jurist.* London: Alhoda.

Lambert, Alan J., et al. 2009. "How Does Collective Memory Create a Sense of the Collective?" In *Memory in Mind and Culture.* P. Boyer and J. V. Wertsch, eds. Cambridge: Cambridge University Press. 194–217.

Langer, Robert, and Benjamin Weineck. 2017. "Shiite 'Communities of Practice' in Germany: Researching Multi-Local, Heterogeneous Actors in Transnational Space." In Shanneik et al., "Mapping Shia Muslim Communities in Europe: Local and Transnational Dimensions." *Journal of Muslims in Europe* 6: 216–240(special issue).

Lave, J., and E. Wenger. 2002. "Legitimate Peripheral Participation in Communities of Practice." In *Supporting Lifelong Learning: Perspectives on Learning.* R. Harrison, F. Reeve, A. Hanson, and J. Clarke, eds. London and New York: Routledge. Vol. 1, 11–126.

Mamdani, M. 2004. *Good Muslim, Bad Muslim: America, the Cold War, and the Roots of Terror.* New York: Pantheon.

Nakash, Y. 2007. "The Muharram Rituals and the Cult of the Saints among Iraqi Shiites." In *The Other Shiites: From the Mediterranean to Central Asia.* A. Monsutti, S. Naef, and F. Sabahi, eds. Bern: Lang. 115–136.

Nixon, S. 2001. "Exhibiting Masculinity." In *Representation: Cultural Representations and Signifying Practices.* S. Hall, ed. Los Angeles: SAGE. 291–336.

Promey, S., and S. Brisman. 2010. "Sensory Cultures: Material and Visual Religion Reconsidered." In *The Blackwell Companion to Religion in America.* P. Goff, ed. West Sussex: Blackwell. 177–205.

Rey, T. 2007. *Bourdieu on Religion: Imposing Faith and Legitimacy.* London: Equinox.

Scharbrodt, O. 2011. "Shaping the Public Image of Islam: The Shiis of Ireland as 'moderate' Muslims." *Journal of Muslim Minority Affairs* 31: 523–538.

Shariati, A. 1980. *Fatima Is Fatima.* Trans. Laleh Bakhtiar. Tehran: Shariati Foundation and Hamdami Publishers.

Shanneik, Y., et al. 2017. "Mapping Shia Muslim Communities in Europe: Local and Transnational Dimensions." *Journal of Muslims in Europe* 6 (special issue).

Shanneik, Y. 2015. "Remembering Karbala in the Diaspora: Religious Rituals among Iraqi Shii Women in Ireland." *Religion* 45, no. 1: 89–102.

———. 2016. "Re-thinking Women's Empowerment? The Practice of Self-Flagellation among Shia Women between Europe and the Middle East." Conference paper presentation at Glasgow University (April 18–19, 2016) on "The Unthought in Islam: Gender Perspectives."

Spellman-Poots, K. 2013. "Who Is Hussain?" *The Middle East in London* 9, no. 4: 7.

Stausberg, M. 2001. "Kohärenz und Kontinuität. Überlegungen zur Repräsentation und

Reproduktion von Religionen." In *Kontinuitäten und Brüche in der Religionsgeschichte: Festschrift für Anders Hultgard zu seinem 65. Geburtstag am 23.12.2001*. M. Stausberg, O. Sundquist, and A. van Nahl, eds. Berlin and New York: DeGruyter. 596–619.

Wenger, E. 1998. *Communities of Practice: Learning, Meaning, and Identity*. New York: Cambridge University Press.

SEVEN

CAN A TATAR MOVE OUT OF ISLAM?

KATARZYNA GÓRAK-SOSNOWSKA
AND MICHAŁ ŁYSZCZARZ

> My father claimed that he doesn't believe in God, but that was a windup. Man always believes, even if he says he doesn't. He might not practice, but he will always believe (Małgorzata).[1]

This study started as a personal and cognitive challenge for both of us. We have been studying the community of Tatars in Poland for around a decade, including its history, social structure, culture, and religion.[2] Moreover, Michał Łyszczarz is one of the few researchers who personally knows this community, having conducted a number of studies on their religiosity and the young Tatar generation (Łyszczarz 2013).

One aspect that has so far been neglected in studies of Polish Tatars is their movement out of Islam. And here the challenge began. Despite our wide network of personal contacts, neither of us could find even one Tatar who declared him or herself not to be a Muslim. It is true that the Tatar community in Poland consists of only around 3,000 people, but theoretically we should still have been able to find at least one non-Muslim Tatar, due to our good network and the close ties among the Tatar community.

We asked Tatars if they had heard of any Tatar who left Islam. The results were not promising: in the collective memory of our interlocutors, there were just three deceased Tatars who claimed to be atheists and one who converted and became a Jehovah's Witness in the 1980s, but "apparently ... he had some personality problems" (Małgorzata, the Tatar woman quoted at the opening of this chapter).

We were able to find only a few people who were not Muslim but had Tatar roots. However, Islam had been lost to them a long time before they, or even their grandparents, were born. What we did learn from this was that, in the perception of our interlocutors, as a general rule a Tatar is a Tatar as long as (s)he is Muslim. Losing Islam—either by conversion or by leaving religion entirely—means that a Tatar stops being a Tatar and turns into "a person of Tatar origin."

The relationship between religion and ethnicity, with the latter predefined by the first, seems to be unique to the Tatars and in contrast to other ethnic groups[3] in Poland.[4] It might thus indicate the important role religion plays in shaping the Tatar ethnos. Is it possible, then, to detach oneself from Islam and still be a Tatar? Or is ethnicity so strongly interconnected with religion that they cannot be separated? In other words: Is a non-Muslim Tatar still a Tatar? These are the questions that we will try to answer in this chapter.

It must be stressed that the Tatar's type of religion and religiosity is rather unique. It is neither the Islam of immigrants (as in the case of Western European Muslims) nor a traditional kind of Islam practiced in Muslim-majority populations. It is, rather, a unique and original form of religiosity that evolved in the specific sociocultural environment of Slavic and Christian Poland and is an example of a successful cultural adaptation. Thus, Tatar ethnicity should be understood as an interconnected ethnicity that is related to the context in which Tatars have been living for several centuries (Barth 1969). The Tatars define their ethnicity through interactions with the environment, and so it overlaps with Polishness (which used to be Slavicness), Christianity, and Western civilization. The contextual character of Tatar ethnicity is also shaped by Tatars' heritage, as well as by Turkish and Islamic traditions.

Intrigued by the lack of ex-Muslim interlocutors, we decided to interview several opinion leaders and stakeholders within the Tatar community and ask them whether a Tatar can leave Islam, what the conditions would be to do so, and why this process is so limited. We interviewed ten Tatar opinion leaders of different sexes, ages, and cities between December 2015 and February 2016. The interviews were semistructured and consisted of two sets of questions: the first addressed possible reasons and incentives Tatars might have to move away from Islam, and the second focused on the type of Tatar religiosity.

This chapter is structured in three sections. First, we will provide a general background about Tatars' history and their community in Poland. Then we will discuss the potential developments that could have propelled Tatars to move out. Finally, we will analyze why they generally stayed in their community.

TATARS OF POLAND

In 1997, the Tatars celebrated their 600th year of living in Poland. Indeed, their history is not only a long one; it is one that is also dominated by military achievements. The first Tatar settlements in the Grand Duchy of Lithuania date to the second half of the fourteenth century, when they mostly served as guards of Lithuanian dukes. In 1410, they bravely supported Grand Duke Vytautas and the Polish king Władysław Jagiełło in the Battle of Grunwald, one of the greatest battles in medieval Europe.

Only once (in 1672) did some Tatars (the Lipkas) rebel against the Polish state and join Turkey, which was in a state of war with Poland at that time. However, after only five years they decided to come back and declared their loyalty to Poland. They were then granted a status equal to that of Polish nobility. Together with the new status, most of the important Tatar military men also received a dozen villages in eastern Poland, and thus the settlement of Tatars in Poland began.

Since then, the Tatars have enjoyed a high social status. Before Poland's partition, they served as soldiers or craftsmen. They enjoyed civil liberties (including the right to practice their religion) and all the rights (except political ones) of the nobility (Łyszczarz 2013).

World War II brought significant changes to Tatar demography, as Poland's borders changed. More than half of the Tatars remained in eastern Poland (which became part of the Soviet Union), and many of the others were resettled and became scattered across Polish towns and villages. The villages of Bohoniki and Kruszyniany in eastern Poland became the new symbolic centers of Polish Tatars (Miśkiewicz 1990).

Until the 1980s, Tatars constituted the majority of Muslims in Poland, which can be seen in the ethnonym *Muślimowie*. Accordingly, Tatars were "the Muslims" in Poland. This situation started to change with the immigration of students from Islamic countries to Poland. In 2001, immigrant Muslims and converts to Islam founded their official religious community, named Liga Muzułmańska, and thus challenged Muzułmański Związek Religijny (MZR), the Tatar-based union established in 1925 (Tyszkiewicz 1989, 2002).

Currently, the Tatars constitute one of the smallest ethnic and national groups in Poland. While their estimated population has been set at around 3,000 people, only 1,000 belong to any of the Tatar religious communities registered at the MZR. The legal status of Polish Tatars is regulated by the Regional Language, National and Ethnic Minorities Act of January 6, 2005, on national and ethnic minorities and on the regional language (Dz.U. 2005 no.

17, 141) and by the Law of April 21, 1936, on the relationship of the State to the Muslim Religious Union in the Republic of Poland (Dz.U. 1939, no. 30, 241). This makes their legal status different from that of other migrant communities. Not only are they Polish citizens; they can also benefit from financial support for their cultural and educational activities.

The Tatars have been benefiting from this kind of support since it became available, but the proper social and cultural revival started around the mid-1990s. A tense relationship with the migrant Muslims has contributed to this process. Tatars have felt threatened by the growing number of migrant Muslims, and returning to their roots was a way to show that they are a different kind of Muslim (Łyszczarz 2013; Pędziwiatr 2011). This form of "ethnic mobilization" (Wróblewski 2007) seemed to be the best tool to avoid merging with the Muslim immigrant majority. It also explains to some extent why the revival was ethnic and not religious, as the latter would have the opposite effect—that is, of merging in.

It is worth stressing that, in the case of the Tatars, the religious element of their ethnicity is strongly linked to the ethnic one. In other words, religion is manifested through a Tatar ethnic framework. At the same time, Tatar ethnicity is much wider than merely rites related to religion. Ethnicity has been the driving force that propels religion, together with other significant elements of Tatar ethnos such as cuisine, folk dances, and folktales.

(POTENTIAL) REASONS FOR MOVING OUT

According to our respondents, almost no Tatar has ever declared that s/he has moved out of Islam. However, it is still worthwhile to identify and track possible incentives for losing religiosity (if not religion) among Polish Tatars. Based on our interviews, we identified four possible reasons for moving out of Islam, which we explain below.

The socialist legacy and the consequences of World War II

Unlike in Poland, it is not difficult to find a non-Muslim Tatar in the countries of the former Soviet Union (Benningsen and Wimbush 1979). The marginal number of Tatars in Poland is not the only reason; the history of religious politics in Russia seems to be much more important. Already in the sixteenth century, the Tatars of Kazan were forcibly converted to Orthodox Christianity and Russified. This practice continued until the mid-eighteenth century, when the Tatars became useful in the southern expansion of the Russian empire (Olson and Pappas 1994: 724).

The early twentieth century proved no better for the Tatars because, irrespective of their religion, none fit in to the new socialistic order due to its ideology of "materialism." Thus, institutional Islam had almost vanished, many mosques were closed, Muslim intellectuals and scholars were persecuted, and Islamic education was banned (Kemper 2009: 6). An interesting example of this atheization policy was the establishment of the Tatar Union of the Godless in the 1930s, even though it soon started to be persecuted due to its appetite for national autonomy (Benningsen and Wimbush 1979).

The Russian and then Soviet legacies largely eradicated institutional Islam but left unofficial religious life intact. One could publicly be a declared atheist but still privately observe Islamic rites of passage. At the same time, the religious and ethnic characters of these rites often blurred together, so the underlying Islamic character was harder to discover (Louw 2007: 3).

After World War II, Poland was incorporated under the Soviet umbrella, even though the country managed to maintain its official independence. Accordingly, Soviet influence was less severe, even though the activity and visibility of the Catholic Church in the public arena were limited and some of its assets were nationalized. Yet the church became one of the strongest pillars of Polish national identity. Our respondents often mentioned the socialist legacy and the consequences of World War II as one of the reasons for a "weaker religiosity" among Tatars:

> Islam was abandoned for political reasons. It happened because of the laicization of the society and the results of 50 years of socialism in Poland. In the PRL [Polish Peoples' Republic][5] we all used to be afraid, and we still are (Hanna from Gdańsk).

> The PRL period also meant that the state authority limited religious activity. If one wanted to make a career, he had to join the party. The PZPR [Polish United Workers' Party][6] was ideologically atheistic, so it was hard to combine it with our tradition (Bartłomiej from Białystok).

One should bear in mind that non-Muslims were also encouraged to join the Polish United Workers' Party, which at its peak had a membership of over 3 million people. Even though several decades have passed since the end of socialism, this era is still hard to evaluate, as there are fierce opponents and some shy proponents of the ancien régime. In the case of the Tatars, there are some other voices speaking about the PRL legacy:

> People criticize PRL a lot, saying that it deliberately banned Tatars from practicing their religion. But this was not the case. Sure, there was control over our activities, but no one ever closed our mosques. Today, PRL is compared to occupation because it is an easy thing to do. But I remember that we were useful for the authorities because we supported the state's policy toward Islamic countries. Now and again, we were taken to Bohoniki to welcome a delegation from some Islamic country, especially a socialist one. They wanted to show the tolerance and cultural diversity in Poland. So we had a secret agreement with the authorities: we would keep quiet and help them, so they wouldn't hurt us and would leave us alone (Felicja from Białystok).

> After the war, we had no opportunity to act on the ethnic level, as it was not allowed. Polishness was enforced. Only on the religious level could we stick out. It was not easy, but mosques were open, and people could travel through half of Poland only to reach Bohoniki for holidays (Małgorzata from Białystok).

Leaving the political debates aside, there seems to be a much more important issue when it comes to Tatar religiosity: the resettlements after World War II. While a minority of the Tatars could settle in the Podlachia region and maintain their ethnic identity and religion, others—the repatriates—were resettled and scattered all over the so-called Western Lands (Łyszczarz 2011: 54). This problem was mentioned by several respondents, including Bartłomiej:

> I believe that this [laicization] mostly has to do with the resettlements. After the war, our social bonds were destroyed, we got scattered. In the new environment, among new neighbors, the Tatars were afraid to show their otherness.

Another significant factor that induced laicization was the lack of a religious infrastructure and religious instruction. Even though there were still a few traditionally trained Tatar imams, they mostly lived in the Podlachia region and—even more important—had hardly any followers, as several respondents stressed:

> The biggest problem is the lack of practice and leaving the community. This tendency refers to the generation of people from 40–60 years of age, that is, people brought up in PRL. The reason is the lack of religious literature … and the scattering of the community, which resulted in breaking the bonds

> with mosques and imams. What only started to be established with such a great effort was stopped for 50 years (Piotr from Białystok).

> The problem of PRL was that there was no one to teach us religion, there was a lack of imams. There were such people in the main centers, but we were scattered all over. . . . There was awareness, but religious lacks were huge, especially in the generation born right after the war. This crisis weakened our religiosity and the results have been visible until now. This generation had neither any traditional knowledge transmitted by their parents, nor any new knowledge based on religious instruction (Felicja).

One example is the Arabic language. Although Tatars showed a great admiration for it as the sacred language of Islam, they had few chances to learn it during the socialist era. Pieces of paper written in Arabic, even if only on a candy wrapper, were sometimes kept because of the Arabic script. The limited access to religious knowledge made the sacred language magical (Górak-Sosnowska and Łyszczarz 2009). The gap in religious instruction was partially filled in the 1980s by Arabs who started teaching Tatar children. Still, the transmission of religious knowledge and practice had been severely distorted. Currently, Tatar children have greater religious knowledge than their parents, but it is the "globalized" version of Islam, which does not contain many traditional elements of Tatar heritage (see further Górak-Sosnowska 2012).

Secularization in Poland

Compared to other countries in the European Union (EU), Poland is quite religious. The 2008 European Values Study ranked Poland among the top three nations with the highest proportion of believers (96 percent); 88 percent of Poles claimed to be religious, while only 2 percent stated that they are atheists. On an institutional level, Poland is unusual in the EU in that 54 percent of Poles declared that they attend religious services at least once a week (this is the highest percentage in the EU aside from Malta; Ireland was in third place with 41 percent).[7] This data at best raises doubts about the notion of secularization in Poland.

"Secularization in Poland" means predominantly moving from the traditional religiosity to religiosity by choice, which can be illustrated by comparative data. In 1990, 50 percent of Poles were *dominicantes*, or those people who attended Catholic Mass; by 2014, it had shrunk to 39 percent. *Communiantes*,[8] or Mass attenders who also take communion, rose from 11 percent to 16 percent in the same period (ISKK 2018).

The same change might have occurred among the Tatars. However, due to Tatars' limited numbers, the consequences of these changes could be much more significant. Thus, some of our respondents attributed the secularization of Tatars to a general process of secularization:

> This process refers to everyone, not only to the Tatars. This is a global trend. We won't fight it; we must accept it (Hanna).

> The contemporary world has too much to offer, whereas in the past we didn't have so much to choose from. One went to the mosque not to pray, but to meet others. . . . If our imams had focused only on "imaming" it could have been better. I don't know. . . . The church acts on a macro scale; it has very broad structures, but it still cannot do anything about it (Mirosław from Wrocław).

As a matter of fact, the almost universal belief in God has been one of the pillars of Polish society. A Polish opinion poll found that more than 90 percent of Poles have declared that they believe in God since at least the 1990s, while no more than 8 percent have declared that they somewhat or completely do not believe. However, the number of people in the latter category has doubled since 2005. The same applies to the institutional dimension: there has been a significant decrease in the number of people who regularly attend religious services (from 58 percent to 50 percent) and an increase in those who do not go to church at all (from 9 percent to 13 percent) (CBOS 2015: 2–3).

Despite these changes, the claim of a "Polish laicization" seems to be at least exaggerated, even though it pops up occasionally in the public discourse. Two such occasions were when Poland joined the EU in 2004 and when Pope John Paul II died in 2005. Some Poles expressed their belief that greater exposure to Western European culture might negatively influence Polish national and religious identity, while the lack of a Polish Pope could decrease religion's attractiveness. However, despite some changes in religiosity after 2005, these claims seem to be unwarranted. Nevertheless, it is interesting to notice that some of our respondents link "Tatar laicization" to a similar process of secularization that they perceive to have occurred in mainstream Catholic society.

The bad image of Islam and the Arab stigma

The legacy of 9/11 and its aftermath, and that of the subsequent conflicts in the Middle East, including the activities of the Islamic State, have cast a shadow over the image of Islam in Poland as well. For quite a long time, Polish

Islamophobia was predominantly "Platonic," not only in terms of the marginal number of Muslims but also due to its declarative character: although Poles declared their dislike of Muslims, the lack of Muslims gave them few chances to really prove it. It also appears that of all the ethnic groups, Arabs—together with Roma—rank at the very bottom of Polish "likes."[9] Of all religious groups, Muslims are the most disliked.[10]

Poland's negative feelings toward Islam and Muslims are clearly visible when compared to the attitudes of other European nations, often with numerous Muslim populations, and sometimes with records of ethnic- and religious-based violence. Throughout the different cohorts of the European Values Study,[11] Poland—like other countries in Central or Eastern Europe—scored significantly higher in the declared level of intolerance of a Muslim neighbor.

A comparative study by Friedrich Ebert Stiftung that looked at eight European countries found not only a very high level of group-focused enmity in Poland (i.e., a declared dislike of different groups of "Others") but also relatively high levels of Islamophobia. This Islamophobia is in some ways comparable to that in Hungary, Germany, and Italy. However, it has nothing to do with the local Muslim population, because there are few Muslims in Poland and no history of problems related to their integration. However, almost half of the Poles surveyed claimed that there are too many Muslims in Poland, and two out of three believed that Muslims are too demanding (Zick et al. 2011: 61).

For a long time, the Tatars were excluded from this bad image of Islam, even though they are also Muslims. This is due to two reasons. First, they have been living in Poland for more than 600 years and are an established Islamic community, unlike Muslims of migrant origin who are still perceived as newcomers. Second, the Tatars have a special place in Polish history, as they bravely fought next to other Poles for their country.

Moreover, their religion is often limited to the private sphere and seems to deviate from mainstream Islam or from Islam as portrayed by the media. Thus, the public discourse has labeled the Tatars as the good, old Polish Muslims, in contrast to the new, alien, migrant ones. One popular anti-Islamic meme[12] has a picture of Tatars and says that these are Polish Muslims. Tatars are also opposed to Muslim immigrants, and while the latter are said to detest their assimilation into mainstream society, Tatars are well integrated.

However, the distinctive label of Tatars as the good Polish Muslims has slowly started to blur with the global Muslim one. In March 2015, Dominik Zdort, a journalist with *Rzeczpospolita*, a leading Polish weekly, publicly pondered the idea of deporting the Polish Tatars. He asserted that, even though they are part of Polish culture, they have not renounced their religion and so may become potentially attractive to Islamists who want to lure them into radical Islam.[13] Half a year earlier, a Tatar mosque in Kruszyniany was desecrated with offensive graffiti. There had never been such incidents before.

Our respondents pointed out that the bad image of Islam in Poland contributes to weaker religiosity among the Tatars, even though they mostly referred to the institutional level:

> This is a very complicated and delicate matter. Few Tatars go to the mosque, because I believe they don't want to meet Arabs in there (Józef).

> This is actually not moving out of Islam, but it is, for instance, ignoring our mosque. There are Tatars in Gdańsk who don't go there because they don't want to meet the Arabs (Hanna).

To draw a wider picture, we should add that both of those respondents come from the city of Gdańsk, where a conflict has arisen between the Tatar minority and the immigrant Muslim majority about the local (and only) mosque. Still, anti-Arab sentiment is quite widespread among some Tatars. One respondent attributed the Tatars' lack of religiosity directly to the Arabs:

> We are rooted in Poland and Arabs are not. That is why the Tatars don't want to be more religious, because they could be perceived as alien. We are the Tatars, not Arabs.... Islamization, which was led by the Arabs, aimed in fact at depriving us of our tradition (Adam from Białystok).

It might come as a surprise that Adam pointed to the Islamization of Tatars, as if Tatars were not Muslims themselves. However, he was referring to the ongoing struggle between the Tatar-style Islam and the Middle Eastern style of Islam, in which the Tatars are sometimes deemed to be not Islamic enough because they integrated a lot of customs of mainstream society into their religion (Pędziwiatr 2011). In addition, Tatar-style Islam is soaked with Turkish elements, which can easily be condemned as unorthodox. In fact, this notion popped up in a statement made by another respondent:

> It is said in Islam that we have the right to choose. They [the Arabs] sin by forcing us to behave in a specific way, but we sin twofold, because not only do we behave improperly, but we are also aware that we behave improperly and we don't follow their advice. That is why we have a problem with the Arabs, and this relationship frustrates us (Felicja).

In other words, Felicja knows that, in many ways, Tatar Islam does not fit Islamic orthodoxy. But the Arabs who tell her that only make things worse, because she does not intend to change her lifestyle or religiosity. By making her aware that her behavior is improper, she sins twice: once for not living in the proper way, and again for not taking their advice.

However, the bad image of Islam mostly causes fear of being ostracized, rather than representing an incentive to step out of Islam:

> This media hysteria won't cause the Tatars to move out of Islam. It will only cause fear about whether some lunatic fringe won't mistake us for these idiots on TV (Mirosław).

After several decades, the relationships between the Tatars and immigrant Muslims in Poland are still quite tense. There are fewer Tatars than immigrants, but the Tatars are perceived to be full Polish citizens of Muslim faith. The immigrants outnumber the Tatars at least fivefold, but they must struggle against the bad image of Islam that is attributed to them. Accordingly, both communities have some advantages and some worries and treat each other as aliens (Pędziwiatr 2011, Łyszczarz 2013).

The rising Islamophobia will probably not unite them but rather drive them farther apart, especially because some Tatar leaders have taken a clear stance against accepting Muslim refugees into Europe (see e.g., Chazbijewicz 2015). This stance seems to be motivated by the desire to maintain the distinctive Tatar customs and faith. Moreover, the presence of migrant Muslims in Poland has seemed to provoke a revival of Tatar culture and traditions—a desire to maintain their uniqueness not only in their own eyes but also in the eyes of Polish mainstream society.

Mixed marriages

While endogamy used to be one way that Tatars maintained ethnic and religious identity (Sowul 2009: 71–80), its enforcement became less strict after World War II for several reasons. First, there are relatively few Tatars: in a community of less than 3,000 people scattered all over Poland, it is hard to find a Tatar spouse. The second reason is related to the generation gap and, among young Tatars, a lack of interest in Tatar culture (Łyszczarz 2011). Third, there are practical reasons: not only is Catholicism the mainstream religion but, as mentioned above, it has become harder to be a Muslim. For all these reasons, some Tatars prefer exogamous marriages. Even if they keep their personal faith, they barely transmit it to their children.

We should add that exogamous marriages have not been uncommon in the past. Tatars never opted for a separatist strategy of acculturation, and marriages with Christian Polish women helped them integrate into mainstream society in the early times of their settlement in Eastern Europe (Dziekan 2000: 41), even if the children often followed their fathers into Islam.[14]

After World War II, exogamous marriages were perceived differently depending on the region of Poland. They were not uncommon in the Western Lands, where the Tatar population was scattered and forced to assimilate. Accordingly, they not only married Catholics; sometimes they also converted to Catholicism. In the Podlachia region, social control was much tighter. Our respondents shared some (rare) examples of marrying a non-Muslim and leaving Islam:

> There was only one such case here in Dąbrowa Białostocka. Felicja married an Orthodox and fully converted to Christianity. She got baptized and publicly wore a cross on her neck. It was a shock and a great shame; the elderly still point fingers at her. Her parents disowned her from their family. It could have been easier in a bigger city, but Dąbrowa is very traditional (Emilia from Białystok).

> Religious conversions, moving to a different faith, were not accepted. People who did it faced ostracism. Tatars from small villages like Suchowola settled in bigger cities, where it was easier to live without anyone pointing fingers at them. In my family, there was a man who married a Catholic and was buried in a Catholic cemetery. But there is no cross on his grave. No one knows if he converted fully, if he renounced Islam. It's embarrassing to talk about it (Piotr).

This strict approach to exogamous marriages recently changed for practical reasons. As another respondent put it:

> We have always tried to marry within our group, but it is very often impossible. There is no cure for love and we are so few, so it is hard to find a partner. Thus, there are mixed marriages (Felicja).

Emilia, a female respondent in her thirties, recalled that almost all her female friends married Christians. Although both religious traditions were cultivated at home, most Tatar wives decided to have their children baptized—either due to pressure from their husband's family or for practical reasons. In fact, religion in exogamous marriages is managed in different ways, and without quantitative study it would be hard to define the dominant pattern. Sometimes both religious traditions are cultivated at home, so there are both crosses and *muhirs* (paintings)[15] on the walls, and the spouses observe Christian and Islamic holidays—provided, of course, that the spouses are religious.

An apparently much bigger challenge is the religious upbringing of the children. Sometimes the parents let nature decide—a boy child will be Muslim and a girl will be Christian—but this often leads to conflicts. Another strategy adopted by parents is to skip any religious traditions and let their children decide when they grow up or—more frequently—to practice elements of both religious traditions and let their children choose one after becoming adults (interview: Józef, Schabieńska 2015).

Despite the four potential reasons to move out of Islam, as indicated above, we did not come across any Tatar who had actually done so. Therefore, the next section will identify the reasons for remaining Muslim and investigate the core elements of Tatar identity.

REASONS FOR STAYING MUSLIM

Tatar identity is built on three core components: ethnic, national, and religious traditions. Their role has been widely described in the literature (Warmińska 1999: 12; Łyszczarz 2013; Dziekan 2000). The ethnic component resides in the very heart of Tatar identity, defined by Tatar roots, tradition, and the collective memory of Tatar culture and history. Tatar ethnicity is bound to a certain territory and the sense of locality. After World War II, this local space—one where the Tatar ethnicity could be cultivated—was the Podlachia region, especially in two villages—Bohoniki and Kruszyniany—where old mosques and *mizars* (cemeteries) are located.

The national component refers to the Tatars' sense of Polishness. Having inhabited Poland for centuries, Tatars identify themselves as Poles and feel solidarity with the Polish nation (Warmińska 1999; Łyszczarz 2013; Miśkiewicz 1999; Tyszkiewicz 1989). Their own ethnic past has never been juxtaposed to Polish history but is instead perceived as an enrichment. Moreover, as described above, the Tatars have always been loyal to Polish rulers and have a long tradition of fighting alongside other Poles for the causes of their home country.

The third and last component is religious and refers to Islam itself. Even as the Tatars largely assimilated into local Polish culture they maintained their own religion: Islam. Even though it was not isolated from local influences and, except for holidays, became something practiced only in private at home, it was definitely the factor that helped the Tatars maintain their social identity as an ethnic group (Dziekan 2000, Łyszczarz 2013).

For many years, Islam was the dominant feature that identified the Tatars and made them different from mainstream society. Hence the Tatars were called *muślim* (archaic Polish plural for "Muslims"). As one of our respondents described: "There is a special bond between Islam and Tatarness.... Outsiders often say that we are of Tatar religion—so strong is this bond" (Hanna).

Based on this observation, two issues seem to be particularly interesting in terms of looking for the answer to why Tatars do not move out of Islam: On one hand, Tatar religion melded with their ethnicity; on the other, adaptation to the Polish majority resulted in a peculiar type of Tatar Islamic religiosity. These two processes are explained below.

Mixing religion and ethnicity

Tatar ethnicity and religion are interlinked, so the long-lasting debate about whether the Tatars are primarily an ethnic, religious, or regional minority remains unresolved (e.g., Janicki 2000). They could be an ethnic minority because of the Tatar ethnos and the Turkish roots. Islam—especially before immigration from Muslim countries took place—was a factor that distinguished the Tatars from any other Pole. At the same time, the Tatars mostly inhabited the eastern part of Poland (and neighboring Lithuania and Belarus), which could indicate that they are a regional group.

However, it was the religious element that proved to be the most important in creating their identity (Dziekan 2011: 29). Although one can easily find some elements of Tatar culture that are not directly related to Islam, the majority of them are. This refers not only to the pillars of Islam but also to all the rites of passage, such as birth, circumcision (called *siunniet*, that is, *Sunna*), and death. While there are some aspects of Tatar folk culture in their religiosity, these are also rooted in Islamic or Turkish culture, such as traditional healing methods or magic. The same holds true for the cuisine. Traditional Tatar food, especially the dish called *pierekaczewnik*, is most commonly served during religious holidays.

This interconnection of ethnicity and religion is clearly visible in the opinions of our respondents:

> A Tatar is definitely a Muslim, except in some unfortunate cases.... In history there were definitely such cases, but these people did not declare themselves to be Tatars, nor did we consider them as such (Hanna).

> Historically, one can easily trace the bond of ethnicity and religion. At the very moment when a Tatar left Islam—voluntarily or by force—he stopped being a Tatar. In Wrocław after the war, we had such a case when a Tatar married a Catholic woman under the condition of changing his religion. From that moment, this man was excluded from the community. It happened somehow spontaneously . . . nobody damned him, it's just that people stopped meeting him (Mirosław).

Both respondents above linked the core of being a Tatar to the Islamic religion. Conversion to another religion automatically means detachment from Tatar ethnicity.

At the same time, the sense of Tatarness seems to be related to how such a convert is perceived by the community. It is the Tatar community that decides whether one is a Tatar or not. However, this can also be regulated by mutual agreement—a Tatar perceives him/herself to no longer be a Tatar and is treated accordingly by the Tatar community.

There was another interesting case of a young man—a son of a Tatar mother and a non-Tatar Catholic father—who was very interested in Tatar culture. According to our interlocutor he is not a Tatar but, rather, a person of Tatar origin. The reason he is not a Tatar was not, however, his lack of interest in the religion; it was his lack of contacts with the Tatar community (Mirosław). Thus, membership in the Tatar community seemed to be a much more important factor than religion for perceiving someone as a Tatar.

Some other respondents were less strict about Tatarness and perceived it in a wider context. Usually they came up with their own categorization of Tatars, who were ranked according to their religiosity. Thus, Emilia divided the Tatars into "real Tatars"—Tatars who believe in Islam—and "cultural Tatars"—those who limit their religiosity to cultivating religious holidays. She believed that the latter category is becoming more and more numerous, especially through mixed marriages. Felicja gave another categorization: "aware Tatars" who are Muslim, pray in mosques, and cultivate Tatar traditions; "occasional Tatars" who go to the mosque only for the two main Islamic holidays; and "non-practicing Tatars" who have Tatar awareness but completely neglect religious duties (or even declare their atheism).

Unsurprisingly, these categories can be linked to similar ones that are used to describe Islamic religiosity in Europe by dividing people into religious, cultural, and ethnic Muslims (Pędziwiatr 2005: 43–44). Religious Muslims can be compared to "aware Tatars," as they both practice their religion (even though the Tatars also cultivate their ethnic traditions, many of which are linked to religion). "Occasional Tatars" resemble cultural Muslims, as they link their identity to Tatarness/Islam, but religion does not play any primary role in their life. Ethnic Muslims, similarly to "non-practicing Tatars," share Islamic/Tatar background and upbringing, but their contacts to religion are rather loose, if existent at all.

It is worth noting that these categorizations have an evaluative character. They judge which Tatar is better, either by labeling the religious one in positive terms as "the real Tatar" or by diminishing the nonreligious one as an "occasional Tatar." The link between religion and ethnicity is strongly present in these categorizations.

Lastly, some of our respondents provided an even wider and nonjudgmental definition of Tatarness that relates to one's self-perception and self-awareness as a Tatar. According to Józef, "Tatarness is wider than Islam . . . and Islam is not the rule." Another respondent, Hanna, a Tatar elder, went even further by describing her efforts to attract non-Muslim Tatars to the community:

> We actually take them in. We are so few in Gdańsk that we cannot behave differently. Moreover, one can't punish the kids for the mistakes of their parents. It is not their fault that their mother or father neglected their upbringing. We are happy for every person who comes to the mosque, even if this is just once a year. . . . And so they come and recall the tradition, and sometimes even pay the overdue fees to the community (Hanna).

It is hard to predict whether demographic and cultural changes will lead to a more inclusive definition of a Tatar. At the same time, it is evident that the community struggles to keep its sense of uniqueness and to cultivate its history and traditions. Accepting a non-Muslim Tatar is, on the one hand, a breach in the traditional definition of Tatarness, but on the other hand it might be a way to redefine and broaden the sense of collective identity. Although there are different ways of defining Tatarness, being a Muslim is generally seen as the essence of Tatar identity.

Tatar religiosity

The Tatars are Sunnis of the Hanafi *madhhab* (school of Islamic jurisprudence), the group that prevailed in the Ottoman Empire and among Turkish peoples. Due to its rich history and diverse ethnic origins, Tatar Islam has been influenced by pre-Islamic Turkish traditions as well as Christian religion. The Islamic core is in many aspects unique and built around Turkish and Arab influences. Since Polish-Lithuanian Tatars have always resided at the periphery of the Islamic world, with only limited contacts to mainstream Islamic civilizations, all these elements and influences have evolved in a particular way, making many aspects of the Polish-Lithuanian Tatars' Islam unique (Tyszkiewicz 1989, Łyszczarz 2013).

Tatars' links to religion can therefore be perceived in many ways: they can be based on Islamic doctrine, Islamic practice, or social aspects, such as being with relatives who cultivate Tatar beliefs and practices. From this perspective, Tatar religiosity can be very selective, as some respondents described to us:

> I call it a non-believing deism, which is a form of spirituality that is far from classical types of religiosity. It is a model in which occasional religious practice is not backed up with a real belief. . . . Such a Tatar goes now and again to the mosque, but he doesn't believe in what Islam says. Of course, this is an extreme example. Most often there are cases of selective religiosity—let's say I believe in God, but I don't feel like fasting or abstaining from alcohol (Rafał from Olsztyn).

> Even if they don't go to the mosque and don't believe, they are formally Muslims. I have never heard of a Tatar who would declare himself to be an atheist. . . . Maybe this is because religion is so important in our tradition (Mirosław).

Our respondents defined two different cases. The first is selective religiosity, which can lead to individualization of Islam—similar to that described by Frank Peter in the case of Western Muslims (Peter 2006: 107). The difference may be that, in the case of the Tatars, selectivity occurs regardless of religious authorities because they are generally lacking in the Tatar community. The second case refers to Tatars who—according to our respondents—do not believe in God but maintain some elements of Tatar rituals.

According to some of our respondents, the rituals, which are collectively practiced, form the very core of Tatar Islam. This is the fundament of the social bond and group identity:

> Today, Islam for Tatars is predominantly limited to the ritual aspect. This is due to the collective character of Islam for the Tatars. The Tatars go to the mosque to meet other Tatars. This is the most important thing (Rafał).

Family traditions take the central place in this collective practice, and the Tatars pay a lot of attention to them. Since the community is small, family ties are very important. Our respondents often referred to people by their first and last names to quote as an example, be they family members, neighbors, or distant persons. This might be because our interlocutors were community leaders and opinion makers, who we chose to interview because they have good personal networks of contacts. But it also indicates the sense of closeness that the community feels.

Although the family model has recently started to change due to the increasing number of mixed marriages, the traditional endogamous model still has great significance. It has helped the Tatars maintain the coherence of their ethnic group and close relations with their extended families and wider community (Sowul 2009). The importance of family and family traditions was mentioned by some of our respondents. They even claimed that this is the key incentive to stay Muslim:

> Much more important for the Tatars is that by changing religion they could lose their family traditions. This is much more probably the reason why they don't change their religion (Rafał).

> Tatars stick to Islam because they feel a bond with the tradition of their forefathers (Józef).

Academic literature has approached the specific type of Tatar religiosity in two different ways. First, Tatar Islam has been compared to mainstream Islam, with the differences pointed out and enumerated, showing Christian and Turkish influences. In this way, Tatar Islam becomes folklorized because it deviates from mainstream Islam and includes, for instance, some magical rituals (Dziekan 2000). This also builds a strong narrative of Tatars as the autochthonous and assimilated Polish Muslims, who are "our own Muslims" (in contrast to immigrants or converts). Second, Tatar Islam is presented as a privatized religion of people who are deeply rooted in Polish culture and tradition. They, for instance, drink alcohol, and hardly any Tatar women wear the *hijab*. Even in a mosque, Tatar women treat their headgear in a very symbolic manner: as a piece of cloth put on the head, but not necessarily covering all hair (e.g., Łyszczarz 2013; Górak-Sosnowska and Łyszczarz 2013). Privatization of religion is a manifestation of secularization and comes from the pressure to assimilate (Luckmann 1967). From this perspective, the Tatar strategy of leaving traditional religiosity for the sake of a more individualized one seems to be a vital part of an acculturation strategy.

Most of our respondents believed that Tatars feel at ease with their rather "loose attitude" toward mainstream Islamic rules. Only one elderly Tatar woman had a different opinion:

> They are aware, but they renounce it to decrease the discomfort caused by the fact that they don't behave as they should. One cannot be ignorant in the 21st century, when so many materials are available, not as it used to be. So Tatars can't claim that they don't know what religiosity should look like. They definitely have a guilty conscience (Felicja).

At the same time, she admitted that personally she feels at ease with mainstream Islamic rules and, for instance, wears short sleeves in public. This is her conscious decision, and she does not believe it makes her any less Muslim.

While Tatar religiosity has usually been compared to mainstream Islam, it has rarely been related to the religiosity level of mainstream Polish society. Interestingly, this was quite often a reference for our interviewees while discussing Tatar detachment from Islam:

> The whole society becomes laicized, and so do we. Religion becomes privatized, everyone chooses by his own conscience what he likes. The attitude toward faith is more declarative than real. I mean that it is not so deep as it used to be. These trends happen both in Catholic and Tatar communities. This means being a nominal Muslim—I keep some things, *adhan* [call to prayer], marriage, burial must be according to the tradition, but I forget the rest. However, these people still believe that they are Muslims (Mirosław).

> Tatars don't practice their religion, but they perceive themselves to be Muslims. I guess that it is to a great extent similar to the way Catholics treat their religion. I don't know the data, but definitely not 100 percent go to church (Adam).

While quite a few of our respondents related Tatar religiosity to the process of laicization in Poland, no one referred to the changing nature of Islam in Europe. If Muslims in Europe were mentioned, it was only in terms of the troublesome relations between the Tatars and immigrants. This again might indicate that Polish mainstream religiosity provides a better framework for understanding why the Tatars do not leave Islam. It is because Tatars feel Polish and they think Polish. Their approach to religion is different from that of migrants. Moreover, the Tatars feel comfortable with how they are Muslim, and they seem to treat their selective religiosity as a condition to being fully assimilated into Polish society. Yet further research is necessary to sustain this claim.

CONCLUSION

Tatar Islam belongs to the great variety of contemporary Muslim cultures and can be characterized by three distinctive features. First, it is a local type of Islam, one that is adapted to the Slavic and Christian environment and thus syncretic and quite selective when it comes to religious doctrine (Dziekan 2000, 2011). Second, ethnicity overlaps with religious practice. Third, the influence of mainstream Islam (i.e., Middle Eastern culture and traditions, except Turkish impact) is still limited.

Over recent decades, Tatar religiosity has diminished and changed its significance, and so the bond with Islam has grown weaker. Historically, the reason for that was the deep integration within the mainstream society, followed by assimilation. Further changes occurred after World War II and the socialist era: the Tatars were scattered across Poland and thus their traditional bonds became looser.

Another reason for diminished religiosity is mixed marriages, which have increasingly become the only choice for young Tatars. The generation gap has also made it harder to transmit religious knowledge and Tatar traditions to the next generations. The Tatar community has become increasingly secularized, while their religion has become privatized.

Despite these challenges, we found only a few cases of Tatars who completely moved out of Islam. For instance, some adopted an atheist stance—especially during the socialist era—while others converted to Christianity (mostly due to marrying Christians). It seems that conversion to Christianity was the dominant reason for moving out of Islam. Nowadays, the main reason lies in the mixed marriages and in insufficient willingness to bring up the children in one's religious tradition. However, it seems that in most cases the offspring do not actually move out of Islam but simply are brought up in the Christian faith from the very beginning. Thus, the Tatar spouse gives up the opportunity to introduce Islam to his or her children, rather than choosing to convert them.

Since the early 1990s, being Tatar has become fashionable, and Tatars have started promoting their ethnic heritage. However, this has not led to a religious revival.

As we have seen, Tatar Islam has greater cultural significance than strictly religious significance for the Tatars. One indicator might be the shared conviction among Tatars that belief is more important than religious doctrine or knowledge. In other words, one can say that Tatars simply do not need to move out of Islam unless they feel strongly attracted to a different belief system. They can maintain their religiosity at a low level, limited to the private sphere or less, and remain—as Felicja expressed—occasional or nonpracticing Tatars. Because leaving Islam would equate to leaving the whole community, the incentive to remain is quite strong. It is Islam in its particular Tatar form that constitutes the core of Tatar identity. Losing faith by individuals or the entire community would possibly mean losing the whole uniqueness and melting completely into mainstream society.

THE LIST OF RESPONDENTS:

- Emilia—female, born in the 1980s, lives in Białystok, interviewed on December 19, 2015.
- Mirosław—male, born in the 1950s, lives in Wrocław, interviewed on December 19, 2015.
- Piotr—male, born in the 1970s, lives in Białystok, interviewed on December 20, 2015.
- Bartłomiej—male, born in the 1960s, lives in Białystok, interviewed on December 20, 2015.
- Felicja—female, born in the 1930s, lives in Białystok, interviewed on December 20, 2015.
- Adam—male, born in the 1960s, lives in Białystok, interviewed on December 20, 2015.
- Małgorzata—female, born in the 1960s, lives in Białystok, interviewed on December 20, 2015.
- Rafał—male, born in the 1950s, lives in Olsztyn, interviewed on January 29, 2016.
- Hanna—female, born in the 1930s, lives in Gdańsk, interviewed on February 12, 2016.
- Józef—male, born in the 1970s, lives in Gdańsk, interviewed on February 12, 2016.

NOTES

1. To protect the anonymity of our respondents, we are using fake names. The task of choosing them was not an easy one. The community is very small, so the number of names is limited. Moreover, some Tatars use their Tatar names, others have Polish names, and some prefer universal Arabic names. Instead of modeling this variety, we decided to use regular Polish names.

2. Those in English include Górak-Sosnowska and Łyszczarz (2009; 2013) and Łyszczarz (2011).

3. According to the *Regional Language, National and Ethnic Minorities Act of 6th January 2005*, Tatars are one of four ethnic minorities; the others are Karaites, Lemkos, and Roma.

The law also stipulates what an ethnic minority is: Polish citizens who "are less numerous than the rest of Polish population, significantly differ from other Polish citizens by language, culture or tradition, they strive to maintain their language, culture or tradition, they are aware of their historical ethnic community, their ancestors have been living in Poland for at least 100 years, and they do not feel a part of any nation organised in their own country (provided there is one)" (Article 2.3).

4. A similar case occurs with a much smaller ethnic group, the Karaites, who only keep their religion and linguistic traditions.

5. PRL—Polska Rzeczpospolita Ludowa [Polish Peoples' Republic] was the official name of Poland from 1952 to 1989.

6. PZPR—Polska Zjednoczona Partia Robotnicza [Polish United Workers' Party] was the party that practically ruled Poland from 1948 to 1989.

7. *Atlas of European Values* (2011), www.atlasofeuropeanvalues.eu.

8. *Dominicantes* and *communiantes* are two indicators that have been used since the 1980s to estimate the institutionalized religiosity in Poland. The first indicator presents the proportion of Catholics who attend Holy Mass (selected Mass in October or November), while the second one describes the proportion of Mass attenders who take communion.

9. In 2010, 23 percent of the respondents liked Arabs and 46 percent disliked them. These results have been rather constant since 2002, when—probably prompted by the September 11 attacks—CBOS decided to include Arabs as a category in its yearly opinion poll about the national and ethnic preferences of Poles. Unfortunately, the survey stopped including Arabs as a separate category in 2012; instead a few Arab nationalities (e.g., Palestinians, Egyptians) were included from 2015. See CBOS (2012: 2).

10. In 2015, 44 percent of the respondents disliked Muslims and 23 percent liked them. See CBOS (2015: 3).

11. See www.europeanvaluesstudy.eu.

12. See images6.bibsy.pl/Adn3OVVr/polscy-tatarzy-zyjacy-w-zgodzie-z-polakami-na-terenach-polskich-od-300-lat-sa-muzulmanami-a-przy-tym-w-wiekszosci-sa-przeciwni-islamizacji-europy-dlaczego-poniewaz-naplywowi-muzulmanie-z-turcji-pakistanu-czy-czeczenii-ich.jpeg.

13. One of the most debated texts on this issue was Zdort's (2015).

14. There were far fewer exogamous marriages of Tatar females and non-Tatar males at that time. This was due to two reasons. First, there were generally fewer females from the beginning of Tatar migration to the Great Duchy of Lithuania and Poland; men could easily find a job in the army, but there were no proper jobs for females (and thus fewer incentives to migrate). Second, women were subject to ethnic pressure not to marry non-Tatars. It was not motivated by religion (a Muslim woman shall not marry a non-Muslim man) but rather by community ties and the need to transmit Tatar tradition.

15. *Muhir*, from the Turkish *mühür* ("seal") is a type of art—a painting, but also a relief, or type of installation, as long as it can fit into a frame and contains Islamic calligraphy.

REFERENCES

Barth, F. 1969. *Ethnic Groups and Boundaries: The Social Organization of Culture Difference.* Oslo: Universitetsforlaget.

Benningsen, A., and Wimbush, S. 1979. *Muslim National Communism in the Soviet Union.* Chicago: University of Chicago Press.

CBOS. 2012. "Stosunek Polaków do innych narodów." BS/22/2012. Warszawa.

CBOS. 2015. "Zmiany w zakresie podstawowych wskaźników religijności Polaków po śmierci Jana Pawła II." NR/26/2015. Warszawa.

Chazbijewicz, S. November 18, 2015. "Nie powinniśmy przyjmować uchodźców z Bliskiego Wschodu." Olsztyn: PiS. www.jednota.pl/index.php/ekumenia-i-religioznawstwo/spotkanie-z-islamem/369-tatarzy-polscy-muzumanie.

Dziekan, M. 2000. "Tatarzy—polscy muzułmanie." *Jednota* 8–9: 41–44.

———. 2011. "History and Culture of Polish Tatars." In *Muslims in Poland and Eastern Europe.* K. Górak-Sosnowska, ed. Warsaw: University of Warsaw.

Górak-Sosnowska, K. 2012. "The Place of Religion in Education in Poland." In *Islam (Instruction) in State-Funded Schools: Country Reports.* G. Lauwers, J. de Groof, and P. de Hert eds. Antwerpen: Universiteit Antwerpen. 194–205.

Górak-Sosnowska, K., and M. Łyszczarz. 2009. "(Un)Islamic Consumers? The Case of Polish Tatars." In *Muslim Societies in the Age of Mass Consumption: Politics, Culture, and Identity between the Local and the Global.* J. Pink, ed. Cambridge: Cambridge Scholars Publishing, 2009. 145–164.

———. 2013. "Perspectives on Muslim Dress in Poland: A Tatar view." In *Islamic Fashion and Anti-Fashion. New Perspectives from Eurpe and North America.* A. Moors, ed. London: Bloomsbury Academic. 93–104.

ISKK. 2018. Annuarium Statisticum Ecclesiae In Polonia Ad 2018. 39. iskk.pl/images/stories/Instytut/dokumenty/Annuarium_Statisticum_2018.pdf.

Janicki, W. 2000. "Tatarzy w Polsce—naród, grupa etniczna czy 'ludzie pogranicza'?" *Czasopismo Geograficzne* 71, no. 2: 171–185.

Kemper, M. 2009. *Studying Islam in the Soviet Union.* Amsterdam: University of Amsterdam.

Louw, M. 2007. *Everyday Islam in Post-Soviet Central Asia.* New York: Routledge.

Luckmann, T. 1967. *The Invisible Religion: The Problem of Religion in Modern Society.* New York: Macmillan.

Łyszczarz, M. 2011. "Generational Changes among Young Polish Tatars." In *Muslims in Poland and Eastern Europe.* K. Górak-Sosnowska, ed. Warsaw: University of Warsaw. 53–68.

———. 2013. *Młode pokolenie polskich Tatarów. Studium przemian generacyjnych młodzieży w kontekście religijności muzułmańskiej oraz tożsamości etnicznej.* Olsztyn: Uniwersytet Warmińsko-Mazurski and Muzułmański Związek Religijny.

Miśkiewicz, A. 1990. *Tatarzy polscy 1918–1939. Życie społeczno-kulturalne i religia.* Warszawa: Państwowe Wydawnictwo Naukowe.

Olson, J., L. Pappas, and N. Pappas. 1994. *An Ethnohistorical Dictionary of the Russian and Soviet Empires*. Westport, CT: Greenwood.

Pędziwiatr, K. 2005. *Od islamu imigrantów do islamu obywateli: muzułmanie w krajach Europy Zachodniej*. Kraków: Nomos.

Peter, F. 2006. "Individualization and Religious Authority in Western European Islam." *Islam and Christian-Muslim Relations*, 17, no. 1: 105–118.

Pędziwiatr, K. 2011. "'The Established and Newcomers' in Islam in Poland or the Intergroup Relations within the Polish Muslim Community." In *Muslims in Poland and Eastern Europe*. K. Górak-Sosnowska, ed. Warsaw: University of Warsaw. 169–182.

Postawy wobec islamu i muzułmanów. 2015. *CBOS*. NR/37/2015. Warszawa. cbos.pl/SPISKOM.POL/2015/K_037_15.PDF.

Sowul, M. 2009. "Odrębność Tatarów polskich badana narzędziami genetyki populacyjnej. Nazwisko jako wskaźnik izolacji genetycznej grupy." In *Tatarzy—historia i kultura*. S. Chazbijewicz, ed. Szreniawa: Muzeum Narodowe Rolnictwa i Przemysłu Rolno-Spożywczego w Szreniawie. 71–80.

Schabieńska, I. 2015. *Wychowanie i kształcenie w muzułmańsko-chrześcijańskich rodzinach Tatarów polskich*. Wrocław: Muzułmański Związek Religijny.

Tyszkiewicz, J. 1989. *Tatarzy na Litwie i w Polsce. Studia z dziejów XIII-XVIII w*. Warszawa: Państwowe Wydawnictwo Naukowe.

———. 2002. *Z historii Tatarów polskich 1794–1944*. Pułtusk: Wyższa Szkoła Humanistyczna.

Warmińska, K. 1999. *Tatarzy polscy—tożsamość religijna i etniczna*. Kraków: Universitas.

Wróblewski, P. 2007. *Mobilizacja i konflikt etniczny. Kraków: Semper*.

Zdort, D. February 6, 2015. "Dokąd deportować Tatarów." *Rzeczpospolita*. www.rp.pl/artykul/1177173-Dominik-Zdort—Dokad-deportowac-Tatarow.html&cid=44&template=restricted.

Zick, A., B. Küpper, and A. Hövermann. 2011. *Intolerance, Prejudice, and Discrimination: A European Report*, Berlin: Friedrich Ebert Stiftung.

SECTION III

TRANSNATIONAL MOVEMENT AND MOVING BETWEEN TRADITIONS

EIGHT

RELIGIOUS AUTHORITY AND CONVERSIONS IN BERLIN'S SUFI COMMUNITIES

OLEG YAROSH

This chapter addresses the issue of religious authority in Berlin Sufi communities in the context of native European converts to Islam and second-generation Muslims who are born to Sufi followers (*murids*). In the twentieth century, Sufism expanded beyond the geographical and cultural boundaries of the "Islamic World" and became a substantial element of Muslim religious life in the West. Furthermore, Sufism plays an important role in conversion to Islam in Western Europe and North America.

Larry Poston describes Sufism's role in spreading Islam in the West as "internal-personal missiology" aimed at the "conversion of individual persons within society followed by training in Islamic precepts, which will in turn enable each convert to induce further conversions" (Poston 1992: 62). Karin van Nieuwkerk also regards Sufism as a main agent for conversion to Islam in the West, which "has 'religious goods' to offer that contrast with those of modernist or Islamist versions of Islam" (Van Nieuwkerk 2006: 5). She also notices that converts are more likely to first associate themselves with Sufism and only afterward possibly embrace Islam (Van Nieuwkerk 2006: 5).

Scholarly publications have addressed conversion to Sufism and the converts' motives and strategies (e.g., Ali Köse 1996; Marcia Hermansen 2000; Haifaa Jawad 2006; and Julianne Hazen 2011, 2014). These works have focused mostly on the individual context of conversions while barely addressing the role of religious authority and institutional dimensions.

"Religious authority" means the power to define the proper way to interpret and practice Islam and to uphold the coherence and continuity of the Islamic tradition. Traditional forms of Muslim religious authority cannot simply be copied in Western countries. Muslims in the "minority situation" create forms of authority suitable to their new environment (Raudvere and Stenberg 2009: 9).

This chapter will discuss the following research questions. How is religious authority in Western Sufi groups constructed, and how does it affect interreligious and intrareligious conversions? How does the presence of many native European converts affect local Sufi communities? How do these European converts view Islamic normative tradition and express their religious identity? And how do they influence the defining discourses of local Sufi communities?

I will particularly address intrareligious conversion, regarded here as a process of religious learning and gradual adoption of religious norms and practices in Sufi communities. This chapter will also address the institutionalization and collective expressions of religious authority in some Sufi communities in Berlin, namely in the Sufi Center Rabbaniyya and the Tariqah Burhaniyya. It will especially focus on what Donald Taylor calls "awkward converts," or those who converted not by ritual but by behavior (Taylor 1999: 44). I will also examine their attitudes to Islamic normativity and positioning within Sufi communities[1] and explain why their presence is more visible in some communities than others. I presume that intraconversion in Sufi communities not only depends on the initial individual inclinations of its members and the authority of Sheikhs but also is determined by institutional patterns (i.e., hierarchy, communication) that constitute religious authority in these groups.

My research is based on twelve semistructured interviews with Rabbaniyya[2] and Burhaniyya community leaders, followers who converted to Islam, and those who have not formally declared themselves to be Muslims, the so-called awkward converts. I also conducted participant observations during Sufi gatherings[3] and held casual conversations with the participants.[4]

I will begin with an outline of the institutionalization of Sufi communities in Germany and their diversity. Next, I will discuss trajectories of conversions within Sufi communities in Berlin. Finally, I will address the construction and transformations of religious authority within these communities.

WESTERN SUFI COMMUNITIES: TRADITIONS AND CONTEXTUALIZATION

In her work on American Sufi movements, Marcia Hermansen uses a garden metaphor to classify Sufi communities as "perennials" or "hybrids" (Hermansen 1997: 155–158). She later developed this classification into the three-tier ideal-typical scheme (adding "transplants" as a separate category) (Hermansen 2013: 190–191). This chapter will mostly focus on the Sufi communities she characterized as hybrid.

Hybrid Sufi communities display different attitudes toward normative Islam: some are more varied in this regard, while others strongly rely on *Shariʿah* and aim to familiarize their members with Islam and change their lifestyles. This last type overlaps with "transplants" but differs from them in the greater number of converts among their members and their positioning within these communities.

Western Sufism has been developing in a social-cultural milieu that is marked by the "specialization of institutional domains, the pluralism of mass-culture, [and] the development of a market of world views" (Luckmann 1999: 256). The pioneers of Sufism in Germany were Abdul Halis Dornbrach, Muhammad Salah Id, and his disciple Hussein Abdul Fatah (Stefan Makowski), who founded the Institute for Sufi Research in Berlin in 1979 (Klinkhammer 2009: 136–137). In 1981, they moved to the Lüneburger Heide near Hamburg and opened a "Sufi healing school" known as House Schnede (Klinkhammer 2009: 136–137; Schleßmann 2003: 142). Their idea was to create an open Sufi Center as a meeting place for Sufi groups in Europe. Many famous Sufi teachers (e.g., Reshad Field, Muzzaffer Ozak, Sheikh Nazim) visited that place to deliver lectures and perform *dhikr* (remembering Allah's names). In the 1980s, House Schnede gradually transformed into the Burhaniyya Center. In 1992, Tariqah Burhaniyya Stiftung bought the house, and it has served as their meeting place ever since (Lassen 2009: 203).

Tariqah Burhaniyya is one of the most widespread Sufi communities in Germany today. It originates from Sudan as an offshoot of the Disuqiyya-Shadhiliyya. The forerunner of the order in Germany was Muhammad Salah Id from Egypt. After his death in 1981, forty German disciples went to Khartoum, where they were received by the leader of the Burhaniyya at the time, Sheikh Muhammad Uthman (Sidi Fahruddin) (Lassen 2009: 192–193).[5] His son and successor, Sidi Ibrahim, used to spend a lot of time in Germany, and his own son and current leader of the Burhaniyya *tariqah* (Sufi order), Sidi Muhammad, married a German convert and settled near Hamburg. Søren Christian Lassen describes the first generation of German Burhaniyya followers as a "small number of young middle-class Germans with little interest in Islam, but in search of experiential religious practices" (Lassen 2009: 190).

The second important Sufi group in Germany is the Naqshbandiyya-Haqqaniyya. Among the most prominent early figures within the German community were Sheikh Hassan Dysk, Sheikh Jamal al-Din Dirshl, and Sheikh Abd al-Jalil Stelzer. Gritt Klinkhammer calls the early followers of Sheikh Nazim "dropouts" from mainstream society and describes their path to the *tariqah* as follows:

> Some of them had traveled in the Near and Far East and later lived together as Sufis in Berlin while others moved to Mecca and Medina for religious studies in 1978, and from there went to Damascus for a while where Sheikh Nazim lived then. When they returned to Germany in the mid-1980s, they started to offer dhikr-groups in the name of the Naqshbandiyya-Haqqaniyya Sufi Order, named after Sheikh Nazim al-Haqqani who was by that time already known in Europe (Klinkhammer 2009: 139).

This is also typical for other Western countries, where many forerunners of Sufism emerged either from the heterogeneous milieu of alternative spirituality connected to the New Age movement or from "traditionalist" circles like Tariqah Mariamiyya of Frithjof Schuon. We can label them as "enlightenment seekers" who were shopping around for different religious alternatives. They were initially attracted by the mystical doctrines and practices, and they were not devoted to formal religiosity and doctrine.

Tomas Luckmann emphasizes that the New Age movement gathers diverse psychological, therapeutic, magical, and marginally scientific materials with older "esoteric" materials, repackages them, and offers them for individual consumption based on selective syncretism (Luckmann 1999: 255). These New Age movements are marked by a lack of institutionalization and an absence of canonized dogma.

The converts' early turn to Islam and Sufism is marked by a shift from religious individualism (not necessarily totally revoked in this process) to some collectively shared normativity that itself is a subject of continual reconsideration within the Sufi communities. The effects of these negotiations depend on different agents such as individual religiosity of the members, religious authority, and institutional structure. Some swing to an "exclusionary canon" based on adherence to Islamic norms and lifestyles, while others remain more or less diverse and "loose" in their religious attitudes (Luckmann 1999: 257).[6]

Today, Berlin hosts many Sufi communities or orders (*turuq*). A researcher from the Freie Universität Berlin, Nasima Selim, estimates that there are twenty-seven Sufi communities in Berlin (Selim 2015: 241). Some of them could be labeled as universalist, while others fall under the category of hybrid or even transplant. The universalist trend is represented by the communities related to the tradition of Hazrat Inayat Khan (1882–1927), who belonged to the Indian Chishti-Nizami *tariqah*. There are three independent branches of the transnational Inayati Universal Sufi networks active in Berlin; the most important is Sufi-Movement Germany (Sufi-Bewegung), established in 1925 by the local *murids* of Inayat Khan (Selim 2014).

Some Sufi communities in Berlin could be considered transplants. These include communities of Turkish origin, such as the Naqshbandiyya group of Mehmed Zahid Kotku Tekkesi, a local branch of the conservative İsmailağa Cemaati from Istanbul; the Kurdish Naqshbandiyya community in Semerkand Mosque that is connected with the mother lodge in the town of Menzil in Adiyaman Province; and the local community of the Qadiriyya Halisiyya *tariqah* of Hafiz Mustafa Efendi.[7] I should also mention hybrid communities such as the Sufi Center Rabbaniyya, which belongs to the international Sufi network Naqshbandiyya-Haqqaniyya, named after Sheikh Nazim al-Qubrusi al-Haqqani (1922–2014), and the Tariqah Burhaniyya.

The latter two, the Sufi Center Rabbaniyya and the Tariqah Burhaniyya, are the main subjects of this chapter. These two communities can be distinguished from the transplant groups by their multiethnic nature (including a significant number of native Muslim converts), their attitudes toward born Muslims, and their different approaches to normative Islam and religious authority.

TRAJECTORIES OF SUFI CONVERSIONS

In modern Western pluralistic societies, conversion trajectories depend on different social and cultural patterns. The most important is the absence of the one all-encompassing religious canon—or canon and distinct counter-canon—as highlighted by Luckmann. He argues that this condition complicates our understanding of conversions (Luckmann 1999: 257). Luckmann particularly applies the notion of conversion to the radical shift in religious beliefs and related social practices, thereby narrowing its meaning, while other scholars uphold more pluralistic approaches. Lewis Rambo gives a general definition of conversion: "turning from and to new religious groups, ways of life, systems of belief, and modes of relating to a deity or the nature of reality" (Rambo 1993: 3). He holds that a particular definition of "conversion" is related to concrete traditions and communities and involves special rituals and discourses.

Rambo identifies five ideal types of conversion: (1) apostasy, or defection; (2) intensification, or the revitalized commitment to a faith with which the convert has had previous formal or informal affiliation; (3) affiliation, or movement of an individual or group from no or minimal religious commitment to full involvement with an institution or faith community; (4) institutional transition of an individual or group from one community to another within a major tradition; and (5) tradition transition, referring to the movement of an individual or group from one major religious tradition to another (Rambo 1993: 13–14).

Some researchers distinguish between intrareligious or intrafaith conversions and interreligious conversions. Gilliat-Ray regards intrafaith conversion in Islam as a renewed and committed attachment to religious tradition, moving from a "position of indifference about the doctrines of their faith, towards a much deeper attachment and comprehension" (Gilliat-Ray 1999: 317). Thus, intrareligious conversion aligns with intensification and affiliation in Rambo's typology.

Donald Taylor, by contrast, classifies religious conversion as either inward, outward, or awkward. The last category is the most relevant for my research because awkward converts are present in great numbers in Western Sufi communities. Taylor understands the awkward conversion as an "in-between traffic": "It consists mainly in the participation of members of one religion in the festivals, pilgrimages and even worship of another religion" (Taylor 1999: 48). Taylor argues that liberal interreligious behavior has led to the emergence of new "multi-faith" individuals who "spun the idea of conversion" (Taylor 1999: 49). That notion is especially relevant to the Western pluralist societies underlined by Luckmann, where privatized social forms of religion have become a common type.

We can, to some extent, regard the Islamic canon adopted by Western converts as within the "transplant" class because it was initially established in a social form in Muslim-majority societies and then found its way into migrant religious communities that brought this canon to the West. However, this canon is permanently subject to negotiation and reconsideration in the Western context.[8]

Jane I. Smith maintains that despite growing interest in Sufism, both as a spiritual discipline and in the American Sufi orders, "those who actually 'convert' to Islam via Sufism are relatively few" (Smith 2009: 69). Marcia Hermansen seemingly shares this view. She stresses that the "appeal of Sufism to Americans usually occurs before formal acceptance of Islam, and many persons involved in Sufi movements never come to formally practice Islam" (Hermansen 2000: 161).

My own fieldwork experiences support these conclusions to some extent. A few people with whom I interacted during the Sufi gatherings could be referred to as "awkward converts." This is especially the case for the Rabbaniyya community. The other group of converts in this community embraced Islam through their affiliation with the Sufi community.

At the same time, some *murids* converted to Islam before formally joining the Sufi *tariqah* or giving *bay'ah* (an oath of allegiance) to the Sheikh (Hazen 2011: 25–27). During my visit to the Berlin Qadiriyya Center in 2008, I spoke to a German convert who revealed that he was a follower of a neofundamentalist Salafi group before becoming affiliated with the Sufi community. The last group of Sufi followers consists of second-generation *murids*. There are many of them in the Burhaniyya order, but few in the Rabbaniyya order.

Lewis Rambo and Charles Farhadian regard conversion as a step-by-step process that encompasses different stages: crisis, search, encounter or contact, interaction, commitment, and consequences (Rambo and Farhadian 2014: 23–24). They admit that this stage model should not be taken as universal or unilinear with an unchangeable order of stages. Sometimes it is characterized by a "spiraling effect" that goes back and forth between the stages (Rambo and Farhadian 2014: 23–24).

An example that perfectly fits the stage model is Marcus, who could be identified as an awkward convert.[9] He has not officially embraced Islam and does not identify himself as a Muslim, although he mentioned that a sheikh from the Netherlands gave him his Muslim name, Abdul Salam.[10] He said: "I'm not a Muslim. I'm not connected to any religion." However, he performs the ritual collective prayer (*salah*) with the Muslims at the Sufi Center Rabbaniyya.[11] Other awkward members of the group do not take part in the collective prayers with Muslims and sit on the side of the room during the ritual.[12]

The aide to Sheikh Eşref, Metin Arikan, who is authorized to lead *dhikr* and to deliver speeches on the sheikh's behalf, explained that some German converts hide their Muslim identity from other community members, especially strangers. They do this out of fear of disapproval from their relatives and colleagues, because Islam and Muslims are regarded with suspicion in Germany.[13]

Robert Rigney, an American journalist, wrote about a female convert in the Rabbaniyya community who wears a *hijab* in public but identified herself as a Sufi rather than as a Muslim because of social stereotypes about Muslims (Rigney 2014).[14] Rigney also reported that another German convert who bears a Muslim name, Abdul Cemal, asked him not to mention his given name because his colleagues and boss would be unhappy with his religious affiliation (Rigney 2014).

My interlocutor Marcus took a long path to Sufism. In his mid-50s as of November 2014,[15] he was raised by West German foster families since early childhood. He described these families as "Sunday Christians." Marcus formally left the church in 2003 and describes himself as a "rebel against the system." He has experienced personal problems throughout his life. In the mid-1990s, he became interested in Eastern religions and has since traveled across India, visiting Hindu *ashrams* (monasteries) and Sufi mausoleums:

> Religion woke up in my soul; religion is slowly coming to my soul. I have been talking to Hindi people, visiting Sufis in Ajmer. I've had no problem with singing to Shiva, Krishna, or praying to Allah. For me, these are merely names of God.

Marcus revealed that he experienced a severe depression in 2007, which resulted in his losing a sense of his life. He began searching for relief in different places. He visited a homeopath who sent him to a Reiki master. She then advised him to visit a therapeutic Sufi community, the Institute for Sufi Research, led by the Sufi teacher Hamdi Alkonavi, which meets in his private apartment in Schöneberg, a locality of Berlin.

This group mainly consists of non-Muslim Germans, although its leader was born Muslim (half-Turkish) and practices that religion. The group's practices comprise Naqshbandiyya-Haqqaniyya *dhikr* and the healing Sufi dance, as well as non-Islamic practices such as reading and discussing the Hermetic and Alchemical texts and Enneagram Aura Reading.[16] Alkonavi's followers claim that he has an authorization from Sheikh Nazim. Marcus explained: "He is a disciple of Sheikh Nazim, who is a one hundred percent perfect, accomplished man, and who directs him from Heaven." In this description, Marcus referred to a common Sufi belief that deceased sheikhs are not really dead but rather persist in the higher spiritual realm from which they direct followers.

Marcus's story matches the stage model developed by Rambo and Farhadian. At the beginning, personal problems inspired his interests in Eastern religious traditions and his initial quests for "spiritual healing." He then experienced much more intense psychological problems that were probably exaggerated by a midlife crisis, eventually leading him to contact the Sufi community.

As of November 2014 Marcus has interacted with this group for more than five years. At the beginning, he was attending only the Sufi gathering at the Institute for Sufi Research. Participation in its rituals and practices brought him much-needed comfort and inner peace and helped him to resolve other problems. He also developed a strong emotional link to Hamdi Alkonavi:

> I've found God in me. I've never prayed before. I'm finding my own way to God in this group. I'm not one hundred percent Muslim, but I open

> myself and say: Allah, Allah. My ego decreases and I'm so grateful to these people. I'm striving to become one hundred percent Marcus. . . . I thank Heaven because I've been directed to Hamdi. Whatever personal problem I have, Hamdi helps me.

His initial link to the Sufi community became stronger, and in 2013 he started attending Sufi gatherings in the Rabbaniyya *dergah* (Sufi lodge). Marcus also changed his attitude toward Islam and became more engaged in Muslim practices.

> I come here [to the *dergah*] and gratefully pray to Allah. Just being here automatically gives me inner peace. . . . I'm happy; I'm finding my way to God. I keep the Qur'an and a picture of Sheikh Nazim at home. It's not a formal way.
>
> I have started to regard Islam much better, and I like the *dergah* more and more. . . . I didn't like Muslims before, now I love them.
>
> . . .
>
> Jesus was Sufi, Moses was Sufi. I feel myself present in the world where my heart is shining, and I'm becoming one hundred percent Marcus. Thank you, Hamdi!

Obviously, he believes that Hamdi helps him find his own "real Self," or identity, which allows him to live a more authentic and meaningful life. Marcus identifies much more strongly with Hamdi's group than with the Rabbaniyya community. He explained that he relies on personal spiritual freedom and does not tolerate formal limitations: "No one is forcing me to do something; I feel freedom. I can pray again. I like to pray to Allah. Religious groups are suppressive."

Marcus upholds his individualistic and selective stance toward Islamic normativity and is more interested in the Sufi "technologies of selfhood" than in its religious side. His approach to Sufism is practical: he prefers the psychological therapeutic effects of its rituals and other "spiritual commodities" while avoiding the restrictions and obligations that belong to the "Islamic way of life" and avoiding submission to certain religious authorities.[17]

Nicolas Rose and Peter Miller introduce the idea of a "therapeutic authority," which I think is relevant to this example of an "awkward conversion" (Rose and Miller 2008: 142). They define therapeutic authority as "a complex of loosely connected expertise, technologies and representations addressed to managing problems of living, or the problematization of life from the perspective of its potential amenability to therapy" (Rose and Miller 2008: 142).

Another example of Sufi conversion in the Rabbaniyya community is that of a German convert named Abdul Cemal. His case clearly displays intrareligious conversion. Abdul Cemal joined Naqshbandiyya-Haqqaniyya ten years ago as a "techno-punk" with red hair and many piercings. He experienced a severe crisis, felt exhausted, and was looking for relief (Rigney 2014). At first he was suspicious of Islam and Muslims, but he soon changed his mind and became a devoted follower of Sheikh Eşref. He currently holds the position of caretaker in the *dergah*.

Inside the *dergah*, Abdul Cemal usually wears Muslim-style loose short pants, a long shirt with a standing collar, a waistcoat, and a maroon fez. He expresses his Muslim identity through his body language, as well as his manner of moving, sitting, and greeting others. Abdul Cemal reports:

> Because we try to imitate our Sheikh, we also copy his fashion.... And this, interestingly, has given rise to a feeling of belonging to a group, and that lends security, and in the time being it has become a trademark in Kreuzberg and Neukölln (Rigney 2014).

Abdul Cemal says that association with the community has brought positive changes to his life:

> Generally speaking, I can say that every person who goes there comes out a nicer person. I've made a number of very close friendships with brothers and sisters that developed over the years. Or there are those who come like comets every two years and then disappear again. But as a rule, everyone who passes through is changed positively. It's because everyone who has a question laying heavily on his breast finds an answer to his question (Rigney 2014).

Rigney claims that Sheikh Eşref once said: "I never wanted the normal ones. I prayed to God to send me the crazy ones, the abnormal, and that is what he has done" (Rigney 2014). Obviously, both examples refer to people from the same social background, the "dropouts" from mainstream society whose search was inspired by dissatisfaction and crisis. However, whereas Marcus remained religiously nonintegrated, Abdul Cemal successfully integrated religiosity into his life. As I will argue below, this difference could depend not only on their personalities but also on the agency of religious authority—that is to say, on how it is constructed and institutionalized inside the given community.

With regard to motives for conversion, John Lofland and Norman Skonovd identify the following six most typical "motif experiences": (1) intellectual, based on individual private investigation of possible "new grounds of being"; (2) mystical, based on sudden rapture or insight; (3) experimental, as a relatively prolonged period of trying different options; (4) affectional, as personal attachments or a strong liking for practicing believers; (5) revivalist, as inspired by collective emotional experiences; and (6) coercive, as in the case of forced conversion (Lofland and Skonovd 1981: 376–384).

Stefano Allievi distinguishes between relational and rational conversions. He further subdivides relational conversions into instrumental and non-instrumental ones based on personal interactions with Muslims. Rational conversions imply an individual search and include intellectual, mystical, and political motives (Allievi 1999: 283–300).

A notable example of a mystical motif experience conversion is that of Taufiq, a local *muqaddam* (representative) of Sheikh Bashir Ahmad Dultz of the Tariqah as-Safina.[18] This small community originates from the Libyan offshoot of the Shadhiliyya-Alawiyya of Sidi al-Fayturi Hamuda, one of Sheikh al-Alawi's successors. Tariqah as-Safina completely consists of Germans and is engaged in various public interreligious activities.[19]

Some of the *murids*, who formally joined the *tariqah* by giving *bayʿah* to the sheikh, do not profess Islam. Taufiq reports that some of them are Christian or Jewish and that they merely take part in the collective loud *dhikr* (recitation of divine names). *Salah* (prayer) is not compulsory for them, and they perform their own traditional prayers. They have regular *dhikr* sessions in Bonn, where Sheikh Bashir Ahmad Dultz currently lives.

Taufiq originally comes from East Germany and has a secular background, although his grandparents were religious. He studied Arabic and English at Leipzig University. I noticed no sign of personal crisis in his conversion narrative, although he experienced some dissatisfaction with the outer world after the "mystical experience" occurred (described below). As a student of Arabic, he also had some prior knowledge of Islam and Sufism and, as I can assume from his narratives, was interested in Sufi theosophy (*ʿirfan*). Therefore, we must also consider an intellectual motif for his conversion. He converted before his formal association with Sufism:

> I visited Israel as a student for the first time in 1992. I visited various Christian holy places, Bethlehem, the birthplace of Jesus. From Jerusalem, where it was snowing, we went to Eliat, where it was warm and sunny. I wanted to swim with dolphins, but even though I am a good swimmer I could not get close to the dolphins. Suddenly, one of the dolphins left the pod and swam toward me. He looked in my eyes, he was looking longer and longer, and

> it seemed to me that he was looking with an intention. I felt like sinking into the eyes of a dolphin. I looked at the red mountains of Jordan around me, and I suddenly realized that this whole world is just a breath of Allah. The dolphin showed me that he and I come from the same Creator: the attribute of Al-Rahman (Allah as the Most Gracious) and our return to it called the attribute Al-Rahim (Allah as the Most Merciful).... My friends and their concerns seemed completely empty to me; I could not understand how they could pass through the holy places like being in the supermarket. I wondered, who am I? It was a clear reference to al-Ahad (Allah as the One). I went back to Germany ... and three months later embraced Islam. I met my Sheikh in 1995.[20]

Allievi assumes that books on Sufism attract a wide Western readership, with many becoming acquainted with Islam through these works (Allievi 2006: 123). One of my interlocutors, a female Naqshbandiyya-Haqqaniyya follower named Miriam, held that Germans are mainly interested in the intellectual side of Sufism:

> Germans are attracted by Sufi music and poetry. Turks who are born in the Islamic tradition are different from them; for them, many things are natural. However, when they get together differences vanish, especially in the presence of the Sheikh, whom they equally respect.[21]

The Sufi Center Rabbaniyya, the Tariqah Burhaniyya, and Tariqah as-Safina generally accept people without demanding formal conversion to Islam. Annabel Böttcher reports that Sheikh Nazim al-Qubrusi approves "gradual familiarization with Islam and the rules of the Sufi network after the adherence" (Böttcher 2006: 258). However, formal conversion is a precondition for most Sufi networks, especially for *Shari'ah*-oriented ones.[22]

Medina, a female convert in the Rabbaniyya community, reports:

> He [Sheikh Eşref] has dedicated himself to a life of dignity to serve Allah, to help people. Not to turn them into Muslims. But rather to help them in spiritual problems, in normal everyday problems, whether that is in married life or with psychological issues. But, of course, in the name of Allah and with Sufi methods, Islamic methods (Rigney 2014).

The Tariqah Burhaniyya community in Germany, particularly in Berlin, consists mostly of converts and second-generation *murids*. Currently, the Burhaniyya community does not have many newcomers. Nevertheless, non-

Muslims are accepted here as a rule. A second-generation *murid*, Stefan, confirmed my assumption that many people go there for mystical experiences and do not want to go deeper into Islam. He reported that, in one of the Burhaniyya communities, three *murids* embraced Islam after being associated with the *tariqah* for three years:[23] "We come here and pray with the others. We are actually Muslims and there is no getting around it."

The other *murids* continued discussing this topic during my informal conversations with them later. They stressed the importance of personal connection with the sheikh in the process of conversion.

> Mathias:
> In our *tariqah*, *bayʿah* can be given to any member; it means that you give *bayʿah* to the Sheikh. Everyone can give *bayʿah*, whether Muslim or not. There were cases when someone said to the Sheikh, "I really respect you and want to take the oath, but I like to drink alcohol in the evening." The Sheikh accepts such a man and gives him a special *wird* (prayer or supplication) and, after a while, the person stops drinking.
>
> Alexander:
> Usually, for many people, conversion to Islam took several years.
>
> Stefan:
> It's a trap, man [laughs], in which you find yourself, and you have nowhere to go. It's as if someone said, "I do not want to live in Germany, and want to live in Berlin." They answered him, "Well, live in Berlin." And a few years later, he suddenly realizes, "Damn, I live in Germany."
>
> Alexander:
> Those who converted did it out of their love for the Sheikh.

Taufiq also confirmed that Tariqah as-Safina is not interested in proselytizing to its members:

> Some people accept Islam, but not a lot, since we are not engaged in the call to Islam. First, we regard it as an interreligious dialogue that enriches the tradition. . . . We do not need sermons about *jinni* [supernatural creatures made of "scorching fire"]. In one of the first visits to the Sheikh, I asked him about the correlation between the Essence of God (*Dhat*) and His Names (*Asma al-Husna*). He told me that one of the brothers needed a cup, the other needed a spoon, and I have to take care of it. I like his

> earthiness. . . . For me, Islam is a living tradition, not the history of the caliphs and sultans.[24]

At the same time, conversions to Islam due to marriage to a Muslim partner are not so important in the Sufi groups. In the Rabbaniyya community, some couples that marry by a *nikah* (Islamic matrimonial ritual) delivered by Sheikh Eşref have previously lived together.[25] In some cases, a widow of one community member marries another. Sheikh Eşref gives advice about matrimonial issues and checks the intentions of the spouses. Sometimes, interethnic marriages take place in the community. Sheikh Eşref has no objection to interethnic marriage in principle but discourages them when he notices great cultural differences between those intending to get *nikah*.

Mathias, a second-generation *murid* from the Burhaniyya community, reported that his brother had been dating his former girlfriend for two years before she became a Burhaniyya *murid*. Afterward, they married. Stefan reported that he married a Turkish spouse who follows one of the Turkish *tariqas* in Berlin.

The results of my research on Sufi conversions are in accordance with the conclusions drawn by Julianne Hazen, who studied the ʿAlami *Tariqah* in Waterport, New York. She points out that commitment to the sheikh plays an important role in the conversion process, especially for those people converted through the *tariqah* (Hazen 2011: 24).

In their narratives, members of Sufi communities expressed deep affection and respect for the sheikhs. As Taufiq reported:

> We need his view about daily affairs, education. He looks at things from a point that is two levels higher than we can imagine. People seek his advice in their daily activities when they need to make a vital decision. He has a connection to al-Haqq [Allah as the Truth]. His words always combine theological discourse with daily problems, social problems.

As the examples above show, the charismatic authority of the sheikh is essential to both interreligious and intrareligious Sufi conversions.

AUTHORITY CONTEXTUALIZED

Bruce Lincoln defines the main functions of religious authority as "preservation, interpretation, and dissemination of the group's defining discourse; supervision of its rituals; adjudication and enforcement of its ethics; [and]

nurturance, defense, and advancement of the community" (Lincoln 2010: 7). Alberto Melucci regards authority or leadership as a form of interaction: "The foundation of leadership should be sought not in the qualities of the leader or in the dependency of his followers, but in the relationship, the type of relations, that link the actors together" (Melucci 1996: 333). Therefore, the authority is based on transactions between the leader and his or her constituency: "As long as the leader pursues the goals of the group and satisfies the expectations of its members, s/he can rely on them for support and loyalty" (Melucci 1996: 333). Accordingly, authority is continuously negotiated by the leader and his followers and must be reinforced by the support of the group.

Charismatic authority in the Weberian sense is typical in Sufi communities.[26] The combination of charismatic and traditional authority is particularly relevant for the Sufi communities in Berlin, where hereditary leadership and gradual routinization of charisma occur.

In 2003, Shaikh Eşref Goekcimen opened the Sufi Center Rabbaniyya (previously called Sufi Center Berlin–European Center for Inter-spiritual Encounters) in Kreuzberg, a borough of Berlin. It later moved to Neukölln, Berlin's biggest multiethnic borough, which is home to a significant Muslim diaspora (predominantly Turkish).[27] Sufi Center Rabbaniyya has branches in Germany (Cologne, Radolfzell/Bodensee, Eigeltingen-Reute, Ludwigshafen) and abroad (Switzerland and Slovenia).

The Mevlana Sufi Center in Cologne opened in October 2012 and was reinstated two years later. It became the major Rabbaniyya branch in western Germany and a hub for further expansion to the neighboring countries.

The Sufi Center Rabbaniyya represents an example of a "hybrid" Sufi community. Its inner circle is composed of Sheikh Eşref, his brother Ayberk, and some senior members who are ethnic Turks.[28] The followers sometimes address them as "sheikhs," but they do not officially possess this spiritual rank. These senior members lead the *dhikrs* in the absence of Sheikh Eşref and give talks to the *murids* followed by questions and answers on Saturdays after the *dhikr* ceremony. In these talks, they usually discuss the topics raised in his *sohbet* (public conversation) on Friday.

We can depict the core membership in the Rabbaniyya as follows: A group of fifty followers (around half are women) regularly attend Sufi gatherings and take part in the ceremonies on Friday and Saturday evenings. This group is ethnically mixed and includes Turks, Kurds, and Arabs; German, Polish, Russian, and American converts; Kazakhs; and African nationals. Germans are the major ethnic group within the community. Apart from this core group, there are others who Abdul Cemal described as "those who come like comets every two years and then disappear again" (Rigney 2014).

Böttcher points out that, due to a minimal institutionalized infrastructure, the Naqhsbandiyya-Haqqaniyya is created and held together by the charismatic appeal and religious authority of its network leader. This is based on the Sufi doctrine of "a spiritual master having to guide a disciple's spiritual training and the disciple having to trust and obey his spiritual master" (Böttcher 2006: 243).

The *murids* attracted by the charisma of the sheikh are connected to him through a spiritual link (*rabita*). The sheikh appoints regional representatives (*hulafa*) and creates social links among followers by initiating and organizing marriages and subnetworks for ritual and social purposes (Böttcher 2006: 243). Böttcher states that stability and development of the network depends on how the Sheikh's charismatic authority is exercised within the network. After the death of Sheikh Nazim on May 7, 2014, his elder son, Mehmet Adil, who lives in Istanbul, became his successor.

In the Sufi Center Rabbaniyya, direct communication with Sheikh Eşref and his deputies, whom he has authorized to speak publicly, plays a key role in maintaining and reproducing the center's defining discourse. In addition, all the sheikh's public speeches are filmed and posted on the community website.[29]

The space inside the assembly room in Sufi Center Rabbaniyya is organized in such a way that the sheikh or his representative is central, sitting in a decorated chair in front of which lies a sheepskin, while the rest of the community sits in a semicircle around him on carpets or pillows. Men occupy the front seats and women sit at the back. This organization of space is the material expression of the sheikh's authority within the community.

A key communication medium in the Rabbaniyya and the Naqshbandiyya *tariqah* in general is the *sohbet*, which is recognized as one of the basic religious practices. One of the founders and eponym of the *tariqah*, Shah Bahauddin Nakshband (1318–1389), proclaimed that "*tariqah* is based on *sohbet*. Goodness is always with *jama'at* (assembly)." *Sohbet* can be described as an enlightening speech given publicly by the sheikh to his followers on religious topics considered the most beneficial to the whole community. During these speeches he also gives general instructions on spiritual matters. As Metin Arikan stated:

> The Sheikh speaks out of his spiritual state, provides the knowledge from the living book, of lived experience.... *Sohbet* is addressed to the spiritual side of a person who learns how to be a good person. *Sohbet* goes from the heart of the Sheikh to the hearts of his students.[30]

In Sufism, especially in the Naqshbandiyya *tariqah*, the sheikh is regarded as a "living Qur'an," and he embodies Qur'anic norms and inner meanings. Tayfun Atay underscores that for his own students the sheikh is the "primary source of Islamic knowledge." Even the simple presence of a sheikh is regarded as a symbol of "superior knowledge." Atay quotes one of his informants from the London Naqshbandiyya—Haqqaniyya, who said of Sheikh Nazim that "he is our Qur'an." The informant never read the Qur'an but knows half of it by heart from the discourses of Sheikh Nazim (Atay 2012: 246).

The *sohbet* is usually delivered late on Friday evenings, after the *dhikr*. On Saturday evenings, one of the sheikh's deputies also delivers a speech to the assembly. He further discusses topics from the previous *sohbet*, but this is not regarded as a proper *sohbet*. As noted by Metin Arikan:

> I'm not actually a Sheikh such as Tahir and others. I just have the right to deliver what I've learned from the Sheikh, not to speak on my own behalf. It will not be a *sohbet*, just talk. The transfer of knowledge from others is always safer. I know you do not treat me as a Sheikh, we are rather friends.[31]

He reported that Sheikh Eşref usually addresses questions with great importance to the whole community during his *sohbet*. Sometimes, the *sohbet* covers topics discussed earlier in private conversations with students. Informants also noted that, because of the presence of both Muslims and non-Muslims within the community, Sheikh Eşref avoids direct reference to purely Islamic topics and presents these issues more generally in terms of religion and spiritual development. According to Metin, Islamic knowledge is present here as a "source of truth."

Sheikh Eşref also holds individual meetings with students. Most of them are looking for advice on matters about everyday life. The religious classes, Qur'an recitation training, and training in prayers and other rituals are organized according to the community's needs. Most converts learn prayers and rituals by imitating other Muslims.

Many of the people I met during the Sufi gathering in the Rabbaniyya *dergah* on Fridays and Saturdays could be described as "awkward converts." They had not formally professed the declaration of faith (*shahada*) and did not consider themselves to be Muslims. Some of them stood with Muslims during collective ritual prayers, while others ignored this ritual. The latter group also displayed their "otherness" through their special body language—sitting in a yogic lotus posture with the tips of their index fingers and thumbs touching

(*Vardhak Mudra*)—during the performance of the collective *dhikr*. They received an embodied knowledge by incorporating practices such as performing Sufi rituals, which develops their belonging within the community. Yet their "awkward Muslimness" was not necessarily tolerated by born Muslims, who consider themselves to be "heirs" and "repositories" of Islamic tradition.

Sheikh Eşref Effendi usually accepts such eclectic attitudes and behavior from the so-called awkward converts. He developed a healing system called "Hayy-Kraft Yoga" that combines elements of Sufi *dhikr* and *muraqaba* (meditation) with yogic practices. This was primarily designed for the non-Muslim "seekers" who are usually familiar with yoga and meditative exercises and is intended to introduce them to the basics of Sufi practices. Notably, Sheikh Eşref explained the need to separate women and men during the meditation because their energies have different qualities. Women are assembled behind men in the same room and are not isolated by a curtain or other barriers.

Some of the awkward female participants take a seat close to the men's circle (*halqah*). This caused dissatisfaction on the part of the born Muslims of Turkish origin, who complained about this to Sheikh Eşref. After he rejected their demand to introduce strict separation between women and men during the Sufi gatherings, they complained to Grand Sheikh Mehmet Adil Efendi.

As a result, Shaikh Mehmet Efendi authorized a split in the Rabbaniyya community. He disbanded the Sufi Center Rabbaniyya in Berlin and ordered it to move to another location. He also insisted that German members of the Sufi community meet separately from the Turkish followers and banned the Turks from attending the "German" meetings. Sheikh Mehmet dissolved the Sufi ensemble and suspended all the community's public activities. The German group is allowed to work only with Germans and other European converts.

In the case of the Rabbaniyya community, we see a hierarchical communication model based on the collective direct interaction between the sheikh and his students organized as a ritual. The effectiveness of this model largely depends on affective identification with the sheikh's extraordinary qualities and consolidation of his religious authority within the community.

As we can see from this example, religious authority in the Rabbaniyya Center is not properly consolidated, and thus the community is fragmented along ethnic lines. The presence of many awkward converts in this community allows them to uphold a distinct collective identity within the Sufi group. This, however, hinders the intrareligious conversion inside the community.

Let us now turn to the Tariqah Burhaniyya. The current sheikh, Muhammad Ibrahim, lives permanently in Germany, so his German followers have easier access to him and can directly ask for his opinion in solving their problems. He usually does not respond to messages sent by email, especially from German students. However, students can visit him personally. The sheikh spends hours in individual communication with his students.[32]

Matias reported that, after the death of Sheikh Muhammad Uthman in 1983, disputes over the succession caused internal splits. That is why only Muhammad Ibrahim is considered to now be the sheikh, and this title is applied to other senior members of the *tariqah* only in a figurative sense. Therefore, the structure of the Burhaniyya network is more formalized than that of the Naqshbandiyya-Haqqaniyya.

Tariqah Burhaniyya in Germany consists almost completely of converts and second-generation Muslims of German origin. There are also a few Sudanese *murids* who are widely respected by other members. Kinship ties play a very important role in the communities. For example, in the Berlin center, many *murids* are relatives of the local *murshid* (mentor) Abdullah. Recently, the community has mainly developed through marriage and new generations, not by acquiring new members.

Religious authority in Tariqah Burhaniyya is mediated by the regional network of representatives. The sheikh appoints local representative-mentors (*murshids*). In the regional communities, guiding (*irshad*) committees are set up hierarchically: the local *murshid* is a mentor for senior students, who in turn are responsible for the newcomers. Each community member should entrust her/his needs and problems to her/his own mentor, who will try to resolve them. If necessary, the mentor may consult with the local *murshid*, who in turn may apply directly to the sheikh. On Saturday evenings, the Berlin *zawiyah* (assembly) hosts "family meetings" of community members. They come together to prepare and share a meal, discuss issues of community life, and read and discuss discourses and speeches by sheikhs such as Sheikh Hussein and Sheikh Muhammad Ibrahim.

The attitude toward Islamic normative tradition in Tariqah Burhaniyya is more rigorous than in Rabbaniyya. In 2003, Sheikh Ibrahim banned women's "bodily participation" in the *dhikr/hadra* ceremony. Since then, women in this community can perform *dhikr* only "spiritually," like a meditation, while separated by a curtain from the men who are actively engaged in the *dhikr* ceremony. Matias complained to me that, once Sheikh Ibrahim introduced these restrictions, it became difficult to attract new female followers because they regard this separation as a form of discrimination.[33]

Thus the Burhaniyya community looks more homogeneous; its structure is more formal, and religious authority is consolidated to a greater extent than in the Rabbaniyya. These conditions have a positive impact on intrareligious conversions in this community, where almost all members have formally embraced Islam and are practicing it religiously. Meanwhile, the current shift toward Islamic normativity makes the Burhaniyya less attractive for newcomers who are socialized in a liberal interreligious milieu.

CONCLUSION

Religious authority in the Western Sufi communities represents a form of interaction between the charismatic leader, or sheikh, and his followers. In other words, it is a kind of exchange in which the leader satisfies religious and everyday life expectations of community members and receives their loyalty in return. At the same time, the presence of a significant number of converts in Western Sufi communities makes a noticeable difference in terms of discourses, practices, and religious authority.

Western converts often express their religious identity in modern forms characterized by selective and individualist attitudes toward the Islamic tradition. "Being Sufi" and "Being Muslim" are not similar, at least for some of them. They are the so-called awkward converts who attend Sufi meetings and take part in Sufi rituals without formally professing the declaration of faith. They are not involved in the process of "intrareligious" conversion based on religious learning and the adoption of Islamic normativity.

The defining discourse within the Rabbaniyya community and its relation to the Islamic tradition has been negotiated by different actors, including local agents (sheikh, converts, born Muslims) as well as translocal actors (other Haqqaniyya groups in Berlin and Germany, as well as the central authority of the Naqhsbandiyya-Haqqaniyya network). We can regard it as pluralistic in that it appropriates Western social and cultural patterns as well as contextualized Islamic norms. The awkward converts feel more comfortable within a group like the Rabbaniyya, which tolerates their ambiguous attitudes toward Islamic tradition.

Therefore, the expectations of many Sufi converts are different than those of born Muslims. What converts consider to be an advantage—such as the absence of gender segregation within the community—some born Muslims refuse to accept. This can lead to a situation in which a group within the community, or the central authority in the network, withdraws its support for the local leader. That is what happened at Sufi Center Rabbaniyya in December 2014.

Because of the availability of other Haqqaniyya groups in Germany, converts can shop around for different alternatives: the more *Shariʿah*-oriented versus the more eclectic. This allows them to form a new transcommunal framework of loyalty, which in turn weakens the consolidation of religious authority within the Rabbaniyya community.

Meanwhile, religious authority in Tariqah Burhaniyya appears to be more consolidated because of its developed infrastructure, formalized communication, and ethnic homogeneity. This enables the sheikh to control the defining discourse of the Sufi network and to promote the intrareligious conversion of its members based on the gradual adoption of Islamic norms and lifestyles. At the same time, it makes the Burhaniyya community less attractive to novices with a secular or an eclectic religious background.

NOTES

1. The problem of Sufi followers who do not formally embrace Islam has been partially addressed in the works of Marcia Hermansen and Jane I. Smith (Hermansen 2000: 161, passim; Smith 1999: 68–69).

2. During the period of my fieldwork in Berlin, a major event dominated the situation in the community: a formal split of the Rabbaniyya on the command of Sheikh Mehmet Adil Efendi and the relocation of Sheikh Eşref Efendi to Bodensee. This situation will be discussed below.

3. I actively participated in the Sufi rituals while maintaining my "outsider" status within these groups.

4. The fieldwork took place from October through December 2014 in the Rabbaniyya *dergah* and the Burhaniyya *zawiyah* in the Neukölln borough of Berlin. I appreciate the support of the Berlin Graduate School Muslim Cultures and Societies (BGSMCS), which provided me with a fellowship that enabled my research. The names of my interlocutors (except Metin Arikan and Taufik Mempel) are pseudonyms.

5. The Burhaniyya *murids* repeatedly told this story (whether true or partly fictional) to newcomers. Over time it has been transformed into a ritualized "origin narrative." (Lassen 2009: 193). Meanwhile, Khalid Duran, who himself functioned for a while as imam at Haus Schnede (Hoffman 1995: 322), presents an alternative account of this event, namely, that several years before his death Salah Id had taken forty German followers to Khartoum to pledge allegiance to Sidi Fahruddin (Duran 1991: 467).

6. According to Luckmann: "Canons originate in social processes, or more precisely, in institutionalized communicative interactions. The aim of these interactions is to regulate communicative interactions and their results. The processes consist of selection and elimination (censoring), as well as systematization of those collective representations which are central to the world view of a society. The result, an exclusionary canon (defining orthodoxy and orthopraxis), is given institutional support by routines of transmission and enforcement" (Luckmann 1999: 257).

7. I visited all these communities between October and December 2008. Their mem-

bership, with a few exceptions, consists of born Muslims of Turkish and Kurdish origin. As Margaret J. Rausch notes: "The 'transplanted' Sufi orders provided familiar communal structures and a sense of home in exile" (Rausch 2009: 159).

8. Here we refer to Lewis Rambo and Charles Farhadian's notion of context: "The context is the ecology in which converting takes place. It could be argued that the context is not strictly speaking a stage but rather the total environment of religious change" (Rambo and Farhadian 1999: 24).

9. Collecting the conversion narratives was not a major concern in my fieldwork, so the design of the interview and questions did not follow Rambo and Farhadian's stage model. That is why his example is notable.

10. On the significance of the choice for an Islamic name, see Allievi (2006: 124–125). At a meeting in the Rabbaniyya Center, I asked Sheikh Eşref "What is the significance of giving Muslim names to your followers"? He asked me first if I wanted to receive a name from him myself and then replied: "Those who experience a 'rebirth' in the community get two names for the convenience of their socialization in the Western world. They can use Christian names at work or at university, while here they can be referred to by Muslim names."

11. Interview with Marcus at the Rabbaniyya *dergah* in the Neukölln borough of Berlin, November 2014.

12. My assessment is based on their interreligious behavior. According to Metin Arikan, the aid to Sheikh Eşref, German converts usually perform ritual prayers in the *dergah* on Friday and do not regularly pray at home.

13. Interview with Metin Arikan at the Sufi Center Rabbaniyya, Berlin, October 2014.

14. Robert Rigney is a freelance journalist from California who was visiting Sufi communities in Berlin at the same time I was.

15. Interview with Marcus at the Rabbaniyya *dergah*, Berlin, November 2014.

16. Nasima Selim writes: "The Berlin Sufis invest a lot of energy in either designing or promoting newly constructed rituals, a diverse set of 'innovative body practices' to mobilize their distinct therapeutic politics" (Selim 2015: 242).

17. Jeremy Carrette and Richard King claim: "At a cultural level, the shift in interest from 'traditional religion' to 'private spirituality' has overwhelmingly been presented to us as consumer-oriented, that is as reflecting the concerns of the modern, 'liberated' individual to free themselves from the traditional constraints of religion, dogma and ecclesiastical forms of thought-control" (Carrette and King 2004: 27).

18. Interview with Taufiq in Berlin, November 2014.

19. See www.sufi-tariqahh.de.

20. Interview with Taufiq in Berlin, November 2014.

21. Interview with Miriam in Berlin, December 2014. She is a 25-year-old, second-generation Naqhsbandiyya-Haqqaniyya *murida*, born to an ethnically mixed couple.

22. For example, in the Kyiv Centre of the al-Ahbash movement, connected to the Rifai'yya-Qadiriyya *tariqah*, novices are required to attend individual lessons with the teacher to acquire an Islamic basis before they are allowed to take part in the Sufi rituals.

23. Interview with Stephan in Burhaniyya *zawiyah* in Berlin, November 2014.

24. Interview with Taufiq in Berlin, November 2014.

25. Interview with Metin Arikan at the Sufi Center Rabbaniyya, Berlin, October 2014.

26. Weber describes charisma as "a certain quality of an individual personality by virtue of which he is set apart from ordinary men and treated as endowed with supernatural, superhuman, or at least specifically exceptional powers or qualities. These are such as are not accessible to the ordinary person, but are regarded as of divine origin or as exemplary, and on the basis of them the individual concerned is treated as a leader" (Weber 1947: 358–359).

27. The other Naqshbandiyya-Haqqaniyya *dergah* in Berlin is located at Bundesplatz. This multiethnic community, where German converts predominate, is led by Shaykh Ahmed Kreusch. Shaykh Ahmed reported that, during his voyages across Europe, Shaykh Nazim used to stay there. They traditionally hold *dhikr* sessions on Thursday evenings. I also noticed some of the Rabbaniyya followers there.

28. Annabel Böttcher distinguishes between the three categories of the Naqshbandiyya-Haqqaniya followers: *mubtadi/mubtadi'a* (novice), *murid/murida* (advanced follower), and *muhibb/muhibba* (nonconnected "sympathizer"). The last category is most numerous in the Haqqaniyya (Böttcher 2006: 258).

29. See sufi-zentrum-rabbaniyya.de.

30. Interview with Metin Arikan at the Sufi Center Rabbaniyya in Berlin, October 2014.

31. Participant observation at the Sufi Center Rabbaniyya in Berlin, November 2014.

32. Interview with Matias in the Burhaniyya *zawiyah* in Berlin, December 2014.

33. Interview with Matias in the Burhaniyya *zawiyah* in Berlin, November 2014.

REFERENCES

Allievi, S. 1999. "Pour une sociologie des conversions: lorsque des Européens deviennent musulmans." In *Social Compass* 46, no. 3: 283–300.

———. 2006. "The Shifting Significance of the Halal/Haram Frontier: Narratives on the Hijab and Other Issues." In *Sufis in Western society: Global Networking and Locality*. R. Geaves et al., eds. Oxon: Routledge. 120–153.

Atay, T. 2012. *A Muslim Mystic Community in Britain: Meaning in the West and for the West*. Bremen: Europäischer Hochschulverlag GmbH & Co. KG.

Böttcher, A. 2006. "Religious Authority in Transnational Sufi Networks: Shaikh Nazim al-Qubrusi al-Haqqani al-Naqshbandi." In *Speaking for Islam: Religious Authorities in Muslim Societies*. G. Krämer and S. Schmidtke, eds. Leiden: Brill. 241–269.

Carrette, J., King R. 2005. *Selling Spirituality: The Silent Takeover of Religion*. London and New York: Routledge.

Duran, Kh. 1991. "Muslim Diaspora: The Sufis in Western Europe." *Islamic Studies* 30, no. 4: 463–483.

Gilliat-Ray, S. 1999. "Rediscovering Islam: A Muslim Journey of Faith." In *Religious Conversion: Contemporary Practices and Controversies*. C. Lamb and M. D. Bryant, eds. London, New York: Cassel. 315–333.

Hazen, J. 2011. "Beyond Whirling and Weeping." *Polyvocia: The SOAS Journal of Graduate Research* 3: 17–32.

———. 2014. "Conversion Narratives among the Alami and Rifaʿi Tariqa in Britain." In *Sufism in Britain*. R. Geaves and Theodore Gabriel, eds. London: Bloomsbury Academic. 137–157.

Hermansen, M. 1997. "In the Garden of American Sufi Movements: Hybrids and Perennials." In *New Trend and Developments in the World of Islam*. P. B. Clarke, ed. London: Luzac Oriental. 155–158.

———. 2000. "Hybrid Identity Formations in Muslim America: The Case of American Sufi Movements." *Muslim World* 90, no. 1/2: 158–197.

———. 2013. "American Sufis and American Islam: From Private Spirituality to the Public Sphere." In *Islam v multikulturnom mire: Musulmanskie dvizenia i mehanizmy vosproizvodstva ideologii islama v sovremennom informacionnom prostranstve*. D. Brilyov, ed. Kazan: Izdatelstvo KFU. 189–208.

Hoffman, V. J. 1995. *Sufism, Mystics, and Saints in Modern Egypt*. Studies in Comparative Religion. Columbia: University of South Carolina Press.

Jawad, H. 2006. "Female Conversion to Islam: The Sufi Paradigm." In *Women Embracing Islam: Gender and Conversion in the West*. K. van Nieuwkerk, ed. Austin: University of Texas Press. 153–172.

Klinkhammer, G. 2009. "The Emergence of Transethnic Sufism in Germany: From Mysticism to Authenticity." In *Sufis in Western Society: Global Networking and Locality*. R. Geaves et al., eds. Oxon: Routledge. 136–137.

Köse, A. 1996. *Conversion to Islam: A Study of Native British Converts*. London: Kegan Paul International.

Lassen, S. C. 2009. "Strategies for Concord: The Transformation of Tariqah Burhaniya in the European Environment." In *Sufism Today: Heritage and Tradition in the Global Community*. C. Raudvere and L. Stenberg, eds. London and New York: I. B. Tauris. 189–209.

Lincoln, B. 2003. *Holy Terrors: Thinking about Religion after September 11*. Chicago: University of Chicago Press.

Lofland, J., and N. Skonovd. 1981. "Conversion Motifs." *Journal for the Scientific Study of Religion* 20, no. 4 (December): 376–384.

Luckmann, T. 1999. "The Religious Situation in Europe: The Background to Contemporary Conversions" *Social Compass* 46, no. 3: 251–258.

Melucci, A. 1996. *Challenging Codes: Collective Action in the Information Age*. Cambridge: Cambridge University Press.

Poston L. 1992. *Islamic Daʿwah in the West: Muslim Missionary Activity and the Dynamics of Conversion to Islam*. New York and Oxford: Oxford University Press.

Rambo, L. R. 1993. *Understanding Religious Conversion*. New Haven: Yale University Press.

Rambo, L. R., and C. E. Farhadian. 1999. "Converting: Stages of Religious Change." In

Religious Conversion: Contemporary Practices and Controversies. C. Lamb and M. D. Bryant, eds. London, New York: Cassel. 23–35.

Raudvere, C., and L. Stenberg. 2009. "Translocal Mobility and Traditional Authority." In *Sufism Today: Heritage and Tradition in the Global Community.* C. Raudvere and L. Stenberg, eds. London and New York: I. B. Tauris. 1–13.

Rausch, M. J. 2009. "Encountering Sufism on the Web: Two Halveti-Jerrahi Paths and Their Missions in the USA." In *Sufism Today: Heritage and Tradition in the Global Community.* C. Raudvere and L. Stenberg, eds. London and New York: I. B. Tauris. 159–177.

Rigney, R. 2014. "*Hippy Muslims.*" www.exberliner.com/features/zeitgeist/hippy-muslims.

Rose, N., Miller P. 2008. *Governing the Present: Administering Economic, Social, and Personal Life.* Cambridge: Polity Press.

Schleßmann, L. 2003. *Sufismus in Deutschland. Deutsche auf dem Weg des mystischen Islam.* Köln: Böhlau-Verlag GmbH.

Selim, N. 2015. "*Healing the City: Sufi Prayers in Berlin's Towers.*" www.medizinethnologie.net/sufi-prayers-in-berlins-towers.

———. 2015. "Sufi Body Practices and Therapeutic Politics in Berlin." In *Somatisierung des Religiösen.* G. Klinkhammer and E. Tolksdorf, eds. Bremen: Univ. Bremen: Veröffentlichungen des Instituts für Religionswissenschaft und –pädagogik. 237–282.

Smith, J. I. 1999. *Islam in America.* New York: Columbia University Press.

Taylor, D. 1999. "Conversion: Inward, Outward, and Awkward." In *Religious Conversion: Contemporary Practices and Controversies.* C. Lamb and M. D. Bryant, eds. London, New York: Cassel. 35–51.

Van Nieuwkerk, K. 2006. "Gender and Conversion to Islam in the West." In *Women Embracing Islam: Gender and Conversion in the West.* K. van Nieuwkerk, ed. Austin: University of Texas Press. 1–19.

Weber, M. 1947. *Theory of Social and Economic Organization.* New York: Oxford University Press.

NINE

DERADICALIZATION THROUGH CONVERSION TO TRADITIONAL ISLAM

Hamza Yusuf's Attempt to Revive Sacred Knowledge within a North Atlantic Context

HAIFAA JAWAD

In a recent interview, professor John Voll spoke on the future of Islamic studies in academic institutions. He called the American convert scholar Hamza Yusuf a "committed public intellectual," rather than an academic scholar, whose primary aim is to present traditional Islamic scholarship to the public in an enlightening manner (see Nalla 2011). Since the mid-1990s Hamza Yusuf has acted out this role as a committed public intellectual. Initially, this role comprised lectures and courses that attracted English-speaking Muslims from a variety of ethnic backgrounds in Canada, England, and the United States. He also taught with other scholars at an intensive course known as the Rihla, which first started in England in 1995. His scholarship, charisma, and oratory ability led to an increasing popularity culminating in interviews in international media outlets and a brief advisory role to the George W. Bush administration after 9/11. In 2009 he cofounded Zaytuna College, a Muslim liberal arts college based in Berkeley, California, that was the first accredited Muslim undergraduate institution in the United States.

Despite the international importance, influence, and appeal of Hamza Yusuf, and despite a vast output of publicly available lectures, teaching material, books, and media work, he has not been the subject of detailed scholarly inquiry. Hamza Yusuf is mentioned only briefly in academic surveys of Muslims in the Western diaspora (Schmidt 2005) and in his role as a translator (Nguyen 2008). One of the few studies to focus exclusively on Hamza Yusuf, using discourse analysis to examine some of his public speeches that are distributed via the internet, was done by El Naggar (2012). However, in labeling Hamza Yusuf as a "Muslim Televangelist"—an often pejorative term associated with evangelical Christian speakers—El Naggar fails to examine his role as "committed public intellectual" or his scholarly output. The Rihla course and the foundation of Zaytuna College has not previously been the subject of scholarly inquiry.

This chapter will address this lacuna by focusing on the contributions of Hamza Yusuf to public intellectual debate, community activism, and scholarly endeavor in English-speaking Muslim communities in the United Kingdom, Canada, and the United States. The specific focus is on his role in encouraging people to move into a traditional form of Islam via the revival of sacred knowledge within this English-speaking context. I argue that two distinct groups identify with the teachings and personality of Hamza Yusuf: (1) non-Muslims who converted and became Muslims; and (2) born Muslims from different ethnic identities who moved into the narrative of Islam advocated by Hamza Yusuf. The latter group is of special importance because, as I will show, the teachings and public engagement of Hamza Yusuf have helped born Muslims negotiate a complex path between their religious and cultural identity within a Western context. In this sense, born Muslims' move back into Islam, or confidently reengaging with their Islamic identity, is akin to a conversion experience (Rambo and Farhadian 1999; Rambo 1993; Dutton 1999; Winter 2000). In this chapter, I will therefore examine and assess how far and by what means Hamza Yusuf's message, teachings, and activity have encouraged people to move into a traditional form of Islam.

METHODOLOGY AND ANALYTICAL FRAME

In this study, qualitative data was used to examine how Hamza Yusuf influences Muslim and non-Muslims to move into Islam. In order to fulfill the research objectives, I conducted semistructured interviews via email. The online interview method was particularly useful for this research because it gave me access to individuals regardless of their geographic location (Meho 2006). By using this technique, I contacted people who are not easily accessible or who are geographically distant. After they completed and sent me the questionnaire, I asked them follow-up questions based on their responses.

Participants were recruited through a combination of snowball and purposive sampling. I have personal contact with some people who are connected with Hamza Yusuf; using the snowball technique, I was able to identify participants and receive the names and emails of some converts and born Muslims. In the recruiting sample, Imam Zaid Shakir[1] also played a particularly important role in providing potential subjects for my study. I used Imam Zaid and a friend[2] who has a close relationship with Hamza Yusuf[3] as gatekeepers to help me make contact with possible respondents. I then interviewed Imam

Zaid for thoughts on his teaching and intellectual development as well as on the prospect of the mission of Zaytuna College.

Using the online interview method, I contacted forty-six people; thirty-six of them (eleven females and twenty-five males) agreed to take part in the study. Of the thirty-six interviewees, six are converts and thirty are born Muslim. The average age of the participants is thirty-seven years old. Their nationalities vary: twenty-seven are British, three are Australians, three are Americans, two are Turkish, and one is Canadian.

In addition, the level of rapport differed from one person to another. This is an anticipated disadvantage of conducting online interviews. While some respondents seemed more comfortable than others in writing their experiences about Hamza Yusuf and his role in their conversions and transformation, others were not as effective writers as they are speakers.

The information obtained in the study is confidential. In order to protect the anonymity of the participants and maintain the confidentiality of the data, I didn't identify individuals by their names in the study and used pseudonyms in the data analysis. These interviews form the basis of this chapter but were supplemented by textual and content analysis of Hamza Yusuf's lectures, writings, media work, and other publications related to this research.

One unexpected dominant theme that emerged from these interviews was the attraction of Salafi groups, extreme, radical Islamist groups such as the Islamic State (ISIS), and political groups such as Hizb ut-Tahrir (see Taji-Farouki 2000) for converts and born Muslims alike prior to becoming aware of the teachings of Hamza Yusuf. The majority of interviewees were attracted to such groups in a pre-9/11 world in the radical 1990s, when Salafi, political Islamist groups, and even jihadist groups operated with impunity and openly on university campuses and within the Muslim community (Song 2012). At that time there was no political will to counter these groups despite the public nature of their teachings.

This theme on the attraction of radical and militant Islamist groups, particularly in the 1990s, is an important and necessary part of this chapter. I will analyze the reasons given for joining or following such groups. I then show the hitherto unstudied role of Hamza Yusuf in deradicalizing people. This was done by disseminating the sacred knowledge he has studied overseas via the Rihla course, which continues to run, via lectures and talks, and via institutions such as Zaytuna College. Hamza Yusuf was and continues to be supported by a range of scholars of similar views such as Zaid Shakir, Nuh Keller, and Timothy Winter who further spread his teachings.

After 9/11 there was a focus on institutional efforts by Yusuf (and Shakir) with the foundation of Zaytuna College in California and the further development of Rihla courses worldwide. The importance of Zaytuna College and the Rihla program in providing an institutional base to help draw people into Islam has not been previously considered. This chapter considers the importance of Zaytuna and further emphasizes how this influenced other institutions and organizations in Canada (Toronto), Australia, the UK (Liverpool and Cambridge), and Spain. These institutions are, for the most part, not explicitly linked to Zaytuna, yet their founders came out of the same scholarly milieu of the 1990s and 2000s as Hamza Yusuf and retain close personal and intellectual ties. Understanding these institutions is crucial to understanding the international influence of Hamza Yusuf in attracting people. Finally, I discuss the role and importance of Hamza Yusuf in the Muslim world, in particular his engagement with scholars and political leaders in Morocco, Jordan, and the Gulf States. This engagement, I argue, situates him as part of an ongoing revival of traditional, Sunni scholarship, which in turn has attempted to influence Muslims within the Muslim world.

However, it is impossible to analyze the importance of Hamza Yusuf without exploring and understanding the scholarly, intellectual, and academic context that produced him. This necessitates a brief mention of his early studies, including his studies overseas. We know that Yusuf after his conversion to Islam at the age of eighteen left America for England and studied Islam for a few years. He then traveled to the Middle East (United Arab Emitates, Saudi Arabia, Algeria, Morocco, and Mauritania), where he studied Arabic and Islamic sciences in a traditional way from some of the great traditional scholars, chief among them being Murabit al-Hajj from Mauritania. It was these studies, in addition to his scholarly works,[4] that gave him authority and legitimacy when he returned to the West, helping his rise to prominence among converts and young Muslims in the 1990s. I argue that this authority and his scholarly credentials, coupled with a cultural affinity and awareness of the West, helped him to transcend the plethora of politicized Muslim groups that emerged in the United Kingdom, Canada, and the United States at that time.

MOVING INTO ISLAM IN THE 1990S

In his article "The Radical Nineties Revisited: Jihadi Discourses in Britain," Jonathan Birt (2009) recalls and analyzes jihadist Salafi groups in Britain. This was an important historical moment before 9/11 and the Terrorism Act 2000. Crucially it was a time before political Islam had entered the consciousness of the general public. There was no Global War on Terror, no Axis of Evil, and no constant reporting in the global media of terrorist events carried out by minority Muslims. Coverage of political Islam was restricted to nationalist terrorist groups in the Middle East or airplane hijackings. These events were often in seemingly remote lands (i.e., the Middle East) and occurred or were reported on occasionally. They were not events that impinged upon the collective American or European consciousness, and they were not used as political capital, as political rhetoric, or to form policy. The pre-9/11 political climate regarding Muslims differed considerably from the 2016 US presidential debates and from recent debates over immigration and integration in European Union countries (see further de Koning, this volume).

There was also another important difference between pre- and post-9/11 reporting on Muslims. The internet, live reporting, online streaming, and twenty-four-hour news networks were still in their infancy, especially in Europe. Smart phones, such as the iPhone, with an always-on cellular internet connection, were yet to be invented. There were no YouTube channels, no WhatsApp groups, no Twitter or Facebook, and no Telegram messaging service. This lack of online technology had three important consequences. First, it impacted on how much time and space news networks could devote to political Islam. This, in turn, meant that there was little political will or a need to respond to stories concerning Islamist extremism. Second, groups such as Hizb ut-Tahrir, al-Muhajiroun, and militant Salafi groups were not able to recruit or spread their messages as easily as they can now. This is in direct contrast to the methodology of ISIS and its supporters who use Twitter, Telegram, and online forums to recruit followers and spread propaganda. Third, the lack of online resources meant that radical Islamist groups in the 1990s had to recruit in person or by holding events. Jonathan Birt also notes that radical groups were largely left alone by the state, provided their activities did not impinge on the safety of the United Kingdom. In this he confirms my premise that political Islam was perceived as something foreign, not important, not frequent, and not part of the political discourse.

Birt's contribution focuses on Salafi groups in Birmingham prior to 9/11. While he briefly mentions dissident voices coming from other Muslim groups such as the Deobandis and Hizb ut-Tahrir, the emphasis is very much on the jihadist Salafi ideology and its adherents during that time. It is, nevertheless, an important contribution given the insider access he had at that time. One point noted by Birt is that those Islamist dissident groups, whether Salafi or political groups, were instrumental in persuading young Muslims to reject the quietest Barelvis-influenced Islam of their parents. In the 1990s, young Muslims, especially those who were university-educated, increasingly saw the Islam of their parents as folkloric, cultural, or somehow not representative of the pure Islamic teachings of the early generations of Muslims. The Islam of their parents was not politically engaged, although many first-generation immigrants from the Indian subcontinent engaged with politics through secular political parties such as the Labour Party. It is important to note that the Salafi groups of the 1990s, alongside political groups such as Hizb ut-Tahrir, were fundamental in moving people into Islam (Abou El-Fadl 2009; Taji-Faruki 1996). This happened in one of two ways: (1) Some converts became Muslim through these groups or joined them shortly after their conversion; or (2) born Muslims rediscovered their faith through the teachings of these groups. In both cases the attraction was political engagement, a perceived return to the purity of early Islamic teachings unencumbered by culture, and the use of the English language in promotional materials, literature, and talks. These were groups who engaged their young English-speaking audience.

In my interviews with Muslims who started listening to Hamza Yusuf during this time I find a similar trajectory. A number (twenty-eight) of converts and born Muslims I interviewed converted or became politicized due to the influence of hard-core Salafi *daʿwah*, joining Salafi groups immediately after their conversion or transformation. A number became, in their words, "Wahhabis."[5] This was the case in the three settings: the United States, Canada, and the United Kingdom. Their reasons for joining such groups are varied but contain some common themes. In some instances, Salafi Islam was the only form of Islam they were familiar with, and understandably so given the role these Salafi groups played in their conversion or transformation.

Bookstores devoted to Salafi ideology were opened in major UK cities such as Birmingham and in areas of the United States such as New Jersey and New York. There were also bookstores devoted solely to the teachings of political Islam, such as the now defunct Kalifah Bookshop on City Road in Cardiff. This particular bookshop was mentioned several times by the interviewees. It was a front for Hizb ut-Tahrir, and while it stocked books written by scholars outside of Hizb ut-Tahrir, the emphasis was on works that agreed with the group's ideology. Aside from a few Arabic titles, such as collections of *hadith*, all the books were in English, on relevant subjects, and smartly presented. The staffs were friendly and engaging. The emphasis at that time on English-language books, English-language speakers, English-language talks on cassette, and books on relevant political or theological topics added to the appeal of these groups in moving people into Islam. Interviewees noted how they felt welcomed or "at home." They could identify with the writings and the speakers. These writings and talks seemed like an expression of true Islam, rather than an ethnic, cultural, or folkloric form.

This use of well-produced English-language books and talks mirrors the current use of technology by Salafi and Islamist groups. As previously noted, current Salafi and Islamist groups use social media, messaging apps, and internet forums to spread their message. In the 1990s, books could be printed cheaply due to the emergence of desktop publishing software on home computers and printing presses in the local community. Tape cassettes facilitated the spread of talks. Salafi and Islamist groups used the current technology of the time. However, in the absence of the internet, human contact was still essential. Our interviewees attended gatherings (*halaqas*) in the back of bookshops or in people's houses. This gave them a sense of brotherhood and, in some cases, a sense that they were part of an inner circle. Food was shared at these gatherings, heightening the sense of brotherhood.[6] What emerged from my data is the idea of a Salafi or Islamist social support system engaging speakers and personalities, speaking in English, and coupled with the technology of that time, alongside friendship and brotherhood to attract both converts and born Muslims, moving them into a certain form of Islamist identity.

Identifying the location of these groups is also crucial in understanding how they operated. A cursory glance through the comments sections on the websites of the right-wing press, following the reporting of the indictment of Muslims on terrorism charges, reveals that some people believe the promotion of terrorism occurs inside mosques in the United Kingdom and United States.[7] My data does not support this view. While Salafi mosques existed during the 1990s, the larger ones in the United Kingdom were part of the nonpoliticized Pakistani Ahle Hadith movement. It is difficult to find examples of militant or jihadist Salafi mosques from that time. There were, however, according to the interviewees, either study circles or one-off talks led by members of political Islamist groups such as Hizb ut-Tahrir held in some mosques. One interviewee mentioned a talk in a large mosque after the Friday prayer given by a prominent Chechen jihadist raising funds for jihad against the Russians. He recalled how the Chechen jihadist explicitly requested that people should not go to Chechnya to fight, that "they had enough fighters" but needed financial donations.[8] In a post-9/11 world, such a person would not be allowed to speak by either the mosques or the government. The fact that he could speak openly at various mosques around the country validates Birt's contention that such speakers were largely left alone by the government and security forces as long as they posed no direct threat to the UK.

If the mosques were not sites of radicalization, then the question of locating the activities of radical groups remains. As pointed out, bookshops and private houses played an important role, but another seemingly unlikely site was identified over the course of my research. The 1990s witnessed the emergence of private gyms aimed at practicing Muslim men. While local authorities provided women-only classes and gyms for non-Muslim and Muslim women, practicing Muslim men wanted to exercise in an environment free from music and the opposite gender. This led to the opening of private gyms catering to this need. One such gym owner outlined his understanding of why some Muslims in these gyms were attracted to Salafi ideology. Such gyms are usually located in areas of high economic deprivation and low educational achievement. These areas are also known locally for drug- and gang-related activity. The gym owner I interviewed pointed out that a number of his clients are violent young men regardless of their Muslim identity. He elaborated further on this point: if these young men are already invested in gang-related violence, or live in violent areas, then they are found in testosterone-fueled locations such as gyms, and the violence of militant Salafism is attractive.[9] In effect, he said, it gives a religious legitimacy to violent behavior and enables them to channel their aggression into a religious cause. Furthermore, these locations are out of reach for many Muslim scholars and elders—they are not able to exert a calming influence.

Thus far the emphasis has been on men or brotherhood. I conducted an interview with Asma, a young Bangladeshi Muslim female from London. She recorded her feelings prior to meeting with Hamza Yusuf and engaging with his teachings. Her interview is important, as she is from the same area, community, and ethnicity as the three "Jihadi brides" who left their homes in February 2015 for ISIS-held territory in Syria. She records her extreme "anger" and her "confusion." She felt she had "no purpose" and "no role," that she "felt rejected by society," and that she and others like her had been "written off by society."[10] Pointedly, she was aware of the young people who had left her community to fight in Syria, and she could relate to their anger and sense of dislocation. Her view was that, in committing acts of religiously motivated violence, they could show people that they "don't care" about how society views them and that "they are not scared by anyone."[11] She went on to say that in carrying out such terrorist acts there is a false sense of "pride, independence, and strength."[12] Finally, her internal motivation for thinking about terrorism was to "make people listen or see that I needed help."[13] She wanted to attract the attention of the society that she felt rejected by.

Her feelings of anger need unpacking. It is important to point out that she was not radicalized by either ISIS or any other militant Salafi group. She was not recruited, nor did she listen to their talks or read their writings. She was not influenced by any Islamist scholar or by her own personal understanding of Islam. In fact, the opposite is true: she also felt angry at religious scholars, her own community, and even at God. The motivation for her anger came instead from mainstream media images of events in Syria and elsewhere in the Middle East. To be clear, she was not blaming the media, nor did she mention anti-Muslim bias in the media. Rather, the fact that she could simply observe injustice or killing, coupled with her sense of powerlessness and rejection by society, made her want to do something. Again, we can see the role of technology in attracting people to radical Islam, though in this case, perversely, it was more likely to be images from the BBC than from ISIS-inspired internet forums.

The anger she talks about can be linked to the anger mentioned by the gym owner. In both cases there is a feeling of senseless rage. This feeling of anger and the will to commit violence is present before any radicalization by Muslim groups. Rather, the individuals concerned are angry at society, their parents, their community and circumstance, and even their teachers. At this point Asma was almost nihilist in her beliefs. She talks about "turning her humanity off,"[14] and at this early stage there is no sense of her being committed to the cause of radical Islam. However, when these young people come into contact with radical groups that encourage violent acts, they give a cause into which their anger can be channeled. At this point their anger has, in their minds, a legitimate cause, and a process of radicalization can begin.

HAMZA YUSUF'S PROJECT ON TRADITIONAL SACRED KNOWLEDGE

Thus far this chapter highlighted how converts and born Muslims were drawn further into Islamist practice by the groups that they associated with. Some of these people were exposed to the radical political groups of the 1990s; others were exposed to more recent extremism in the form of ISIS-inspired terrorism. This section considers how people moved out of these radical groups into more traditional sacred Islamic teachings. I identified two key reasons among my interviewees explaining why they moved away from these groups. First was a realization about the "hypocrisy," "inadequacy," or "inauthenticity" of the teachings of the groups they were involved in. Second, they were eventually exposed to traditional, normative Islamic knowledge via scholars able to deliver these teachings. A third, less reported reason was the exposure to a more spiritual practice and the growth of their spiritual life that enabled them "to calm down," "overcome the feelings of despair," and help with some of "the pent-up anxieties" and anger people were feeling. Sajda, a female born Muslim from the UK, stressed the importance of spirituality in the following way: "There was something missing. I was always quite angry and rebellious. I feel this was all due to emptiness.... I was looking for spirituality."[15]

A number of people I interviewed were involved with the group Hizb ut-Tahrir and had firsthand experience of their deported former leader, Omar Bakri Mohammed, who was highly influential on UK university campuses during the 1990s. Often there was an ideological battle between Hizb ut-Tahrir and Salafi groups on campus. According to some of my interviewees, the principle problem was that Omar Bakri Mohammed was "the Shaykh with no clothes." By this, they meant that he passed himself off as a traditional Islamic scholar, calling people to normative Islam, with readings from "the books of *usul-al Fiqh*, *tafsir*, *hadith* etc."[16] For some converts and young born Muslims, this seemingly authentic Islamic knowledge was reassuring and attractive. Those talks were delivered in English and Arabic, unencumbered with Indian subcontinent cultural practices, which only added to the attraction. However, interviewees soon experienced rank hypocrisy. They noted that the practices of the group and its leaders were rather different from the theory. They recall obligatory prayers being deliberately missed, as the leaders viewed their talks as being more obligatory (*wajib*) than the prayer. They were horrified by the appalling lack of manners or knowledge of basic Islamic *adab*[17] among senior members and leaders. They saw that the leaders and senior members perceived themselves as part of an intellectual elite intent on controversy and argumentation wherever they went. Crucially, they came to understand that the supposed traditional Islamic qualifications of senior members were a sham. These senior members knew more about *Mein Kampf*—which was in their recommended reading list—than the books of *sira*[18] or *fiqh*.[19] There was no grounded sacred Islamic knowledge. The ex-members of Hizb ut-Tahrir I interviewed now say they were "really woken up by Hamza Yusuf"; his lectures "were a breath of fresh air."[20] It was the teachings of Hamza Yusuf that helped these people and others move out of radical/politicized Islam and into the traditional sacred knowledge of Sunni Islam.

The question, then, is how and why people were initially attracted to Hamza Yusuf's teachings? Hamza Yusuf (and other scholars like him, such as his colleague Imam Zaid Shakir) emerged at a time when there was a need for a more moderate and pragmatic teaching of Islam, as Khan, a born Muslim from the UK, states:

> There was a huge thirst for classical Islamic scholarship in those days. There were few books and most of the activism you would come across was in the

> form of Salafist ideas or Islamist groups, so the chance to [be] with people like Hamza Yusuf, Nuh Keller, and other luminaries of traditional Islam was incredible.... There was quite a close knit community of young people interested in Sufism and classical Islam in those days.[21]

It can be argued, therefore, that Hamza Yusuf might be aware of the need to counter the influence of the Salafists and politicized Islamist groups prevalent at the time. In addition, he seemed to have identified a crisis among Western Muslims in which many seemed to lack solid knowledge in the basic tenets of their creed and the essentials of practice, such as the rituals of purification, prayer, and, most important, the path and struggle of character refinement. These politicized Islamist groups tended not to care about the inner individual character and focused more on their own party politics. Jessica, a female convert from the US, stressed that Hamza Yusuf seemed to have realized that there were urgent needs to bring "the heart of Islam" back to life and to demonstrate how "the intellect and the heart can work in balance with one another." For her, Yusuf succeeded in showing her and her generation "the intellectual rigor, nuance, and the beauty of the faith."[22]

The assumed lack of sacred knowledge[23] among some Western Muslims may have sparked an early awareness on the part of Hamza Yusuf of the need of Muslims in the West to have potential scholars well versed in both traditions to deal with future problems they might encounter. Khan, who attended the early Rihlas, alluded to this issue:

> Other than teaching the students the fundamentals of their religion I think one of their aims was to talent spot young men and women who had the potential to become the next generation of scholars and guides for Western Muslims. I think they realised that Muslims in the West would face distinct problems which would need to be addressed by people from that culture who were conversant with Islamic theology, law, culture etc.[24]

The exposure of those people to the teachings of traditional Islamic sciences via Shaykh Hamza Yusuf (and other like-minded scholars, chief among them Tim Winter, Imam Zaid Shakir, and Nuh Keller) played a major role in their moving from radical/politicized Islam into a more Sunni Sufi-oriented Islam. This happened through many avenues such as the Rihla, his tapes, and finally Zaytuna College, which he cofounded with his colleague Imam Zaid Shakir. These modes of knowledge will be addressed below.

The Rihla

The Rihla program was designed by Shaykh Hamza Yusuf in the 1990s to teach dedicated students (both males and females, though there seem to be more female attendees than males) the traditional Islamic sciences and their obligatory knowledge of the religion. With this core objective in mind, classes were organized via a traditional model in which the teacher sits at an elevated position in the classroom and students sit at his or her feet, signifying the humility that is deemed essential in the learning process. That being said, the classes and style of teaching have been modified over time. From lectures and lessons that were initially modeled after a *madrassa* model—where the student quietly absorbed the knowledge shared by the teacher—they now have classrooms that use modern presentation methods including Keynote and PowerPoint presentations, interactive discussions and Q&A, and study sessions where students gather to review and revise lessons given earlier in the day. Course materials include not only Arabic/English texts but also note-taking guides and lesson-related workbooks to help facilitate retention of the salient points.[25] However, Khan commented that early Rihlas

> were cheap and cheerful. Conditions were quite basic and food was utilitarian, but it was more accessible because of the lower price and I think more instructive to live simply. I believe subsequent Rihlas (have) become more expensive and professional.[26]

Apart from the didactic components that are at the core of the program, the Rihla also aims to provide a spiritual recharge for its participants. The venue is chosen with great care to cultivate an atmosphere of introspection and devotional practices. Because many of the venues have been in historical locations (i.e., Fez, southern Spain, Istanbul, Konya), organized visits and tours to prominent sites are intertwined with the program. The culmination of these aspects is what makes the Rihla program unique and why many who attended have found it to be life-changing.[27]

Since its inception, the program has graduated over 4,000 students, most of whom have said that the program was a life-changing experience. For many, it provided an understanding of the religion that they would not have received in their local communities.[28] They reported that it guided them to a more serious practice of their faith with an emphasis on regular self-improvement. Salwa, a female born Muslim from Turkey, said that "it deepened my knowledge of Islam," it has "changed my attitudes to others," it has "made me more humble," and it has corrected "my understanding of the

Deen" (Islam).[29] Imran, a male born Muslim from Turkey, stressed that the "teachers practice what they teach" and the "people are caring."[30] With regard to the content of the Rihla, Khan, a male born Muslim from the UK, mentioned that students "gained a deeper appreciation of classical Islam, beyond the individual facts of knowledge.... Students got to live with their teachers ... and could pick up their attitudes and approach to life and religion."[31]

The Rihla appears to be a catalyst for a sizeable number to pursue a traditional Islamic education with Arabic studies and certificates (*ijazas*)[32] in the core subjects. These students, now teachers, have started their own learning institutions that have impacted many communities. There are now institutions that teach traditional Islam in many Western countries such as Australia, Canada, Spain, and Britain. Knowledge of the Islamic tradition is now convenient and accessible, with a sharp rise in translations and critical editions of landmark traditional texts. Although it is hard to quantify the long-term impact of the Rihlas, they have led to an emergence of traditional Islamic education in the West and a commitment to preserving the normative teachings of Islam.

Tapes

Hamza Yusuf's taped lectures deal with various Islamic subjects, as well as with Muslims in Britain and America, Islamic radicalism, interfaith relations, and Islam and the West. The Islamic subjects he lectures on include the core texts of Islam such as the Qur'an, *hadith*, Islamic law, especially Maliki law, and other guiding precepts of the faith, but he also speaks on current social, political, economic, and moral/ethical issues. It is important to stress that Yusuf's approach or message, whether in his lectures or sermons, is orthodox and

> rooted so deeply in the "original" of the Islamic tradition. The best of what he speaks (and writes) about in his many talks and lectures is traditional Islam—the teachings of the Qur'an and of the Prophet, orthodox *fiqh*, and the spiritual principles of normative Sufism. It is this Islam—faithfully transmitted from generation to generation, an Islam that is broad and deep, legally circumspect and spiritually rich, ethically demanding and aesthetically sensitive—that he learned from his traditional shuyukh, and it is this that he in turn (expresses) and teaches to the best of his ability.[33]

These lectures, which are transmitted through tapes, were and continue to be vital in attracting converts and young born Muslims to move into the form of Islam advocated by Hamza Yusuf.

Two interviewees, Khalid and Shah, based in the United Kingdom, further explained the importance and influence of the tapes in attracting them to the message of Hamza Yusuf. They noted that, while some tapes were available in their home town, the majority were available only from a shop on Park Road in central London. They and their peer group would often travel down to London specifically to buy the tapes or make a special trip to the shop selling the tapes when in London for other reasons. They contrasted this effort with the relative ease of downloading talks on the internet or with watching talks on YouTube, noting:

> There seemed to be immense *Baraka* in those days. We had to travel two hours down to London, then spend £2.50 on each cassette, sometimes a lecture would spread over two cassettes. We would treasure these, then bring them home, and listen to them not distracted by other things going on around us. We absorbed the teachings of Hamza Yusuf on these cassettes.[34]

The titles of these taped lectures were then spread by word of mouth. Interviewees report how in the 1990s people would compare which Hamza Yusuf tapes they had with peers in order to determine what other talks were available.[35] The situation was broadly similar in the United States. Muslims were buying bootlegged video recordings of Hamza Yusuf's talks from bookshops in cities where there were major Muslim populations.[36]

The institutionalization of Zaytuna College

Since the September 11 attacks on the United States, Yusuf has assumed an even more prominent role not only in the US but also worldwide. His views are sought regularly not only by the media but also by leaders and heads of state (including the former president George W. Bush, who sought his advice after the attacks). In Britain he is a familiar face in the British media and a sought-after interviewee by BBC radio and television, as well as by newspapers, chief among them being the *Times* and the *Independent*. Faced with an increase in alienation and disenchantment among Western Muslim youths and converts, he seems to have decided to institutionalize Zaytuna College (the first accredited Islamic institute in the United States) in 2009 to revive and consolidate the teaching of Islamic traditional sacred knowledge in order to counteract violence and radicalization. The aim of the college is

> to educate and prepare morally committed professional, spiritual, and intellectual leaders who are grounded in the Islamic scholarly tradition

> and conversant with the cultural currents and critical ideas shaping modern society.[37]

The College acquired a good reputation, and its module has been replicated in the UK, Canada, Spain, and other Western countries. However, Jessica, a female convert from the US, thinks that, despite its importance, Zaytuna is available only to those Muslims in the West who can afford it; for those Muslims who are struggling to make ends meet, Zaytuna is beyond their reach.[38]

In the next section, the influences of Hamza Yusuf's teaching—through his Rihlas, tapes, and Zaytuna College—on born and converted Muslims will be analyzed.

HAMZA YUSUF'S IMPACT

Hamza Yusuf's influence on converts and born Muslims appears to be considerable. Nearly all of the interviewees who went to the Rihlas said they attended because of him. Others mentioned that his traditional teachings encouraged them to go to the Rihlas. Louay, a born Muslim from the UK, said: "It changed the course of my life. I have been dedicated since then to understand the traditional Islamic sciences."[39]

They spoke of him with passion and admiration, almost like a cult leader; once they had met him and spent time with him, their lives were changed for the better. When asked which aspects of Shaykh Hamza Yusuf ultimately led them to commit to his path, they mentioned different aspects. First was the influence and change upon Hamza Yusuf himself by his own teachers. My interviewees expressed their appreciation at the positive influence of his teachers that made him the way he is now: "al-Hajj" and Bayyah's "teaching seemed to exemplify the teachings of the early Muslims,"[40] and they loved "his utmost respect to his teachers."[41] Second, many interviewees stressed that they like the way that he practices what he teaches in the same way as the early generation of Muslims: "I feel his great influence and inspiring nature is true because he lives what he preaches,"[42] said Suha, a female born Muslim from the UK. Further, Michael, a male convert from the UK, stated: "I have always been struck by his . . . deep conviction and integrity. When meeting him in person he radiated calm and was extremely down to earth in his demeanour."[43]

Third, they mention his character. Jessica commented:

> He's had a tremendous influence on my religious life. He has kept me grounded in Islam despite the many, many difficulties of choosing that

> path. With him I had a visceral realization: whatever path this man is on, I want to be on it, because if it can produce a human being like that, it's a true path. That realization has carried me through many, many trials as an American Muslim. I find it very affirming that when I have consulted with him on difficult matters, he has consistently responded with mercy. This to me is another sign of a true path: that the more learned the scholar, the more merciful they become.[44]

His grounding in Western civilization was also mentioned as one of his attractions together with his ability to guide Muslims on how they can live in the West and negotiate the complex interplay between their Western identity and Muslim identity (Franceschelli and O'Brien 2015; Robinson 2009). Benn, a male convert from the US, said the following:

> Hamza Yusuf helped to reintegrate me into American society and helped me to see that one can be both a Muslim and an American at the same time. ... As a convert himself we can identify with a lot of his experiences. He certainly increased my confidence and ability to navigate in both worlds.[45]

Interviewees also mentioned his ability to articulate Islam in a "culturally relevant" way and with no dilution in the main principles of the faith. Benn, a male convert from the US, explains this: "He represents someone who can be an orthodox Muslim but [also] maintains his Western cultural identity."[46] On the latter issue, many of my interviewees think that he has popularized Islam "amazingly," especially among native-born Americans and Canadians. Ahmed, a male convert from Canada, explained this as follows:

> Yusuf is able to articulate an Islam that was culturally relevant to me but still appealed to my then intense desire to oppose Western sensibilities regarding race, religion and political activism on a global level.[47]

Jessica said: "He made Islam relevant to me.... Islam felt foreign and inaccessible—until I began to listen to Hamza Yusuf ... and I feel proud to be Muslim when I see Hamza Yusuf at his best, behaving with such dignity and integrity as a leader."[48] John, a male convert from Australia, said Hamza Yusuf (and Imam Shakir) "presents Islam as living faith not as a dry rule book and this kind of faith is compatible with my culture, so I can now embrace both my Australianess and my faith."[49]

Further aspects mentioned in the interviews include his ability to communicate effectively with his audience, not only in the English language but also—and most important—in the classical Arabic that he is so well versed in, fascinating ordinary Arab people who speak only colloquial Arabic.

The *Guardian* described his speech as follows:

> [Hamza Yusuf] has a rare cultural fluency, shifting easily between the Bible and the Koran, taking in, within a few breaths, Shakespeare, Thoreau, John Locke, Rousseau, Jesse James, Dirty Harry and even, at one point, the memoirs of General George Patton (Roald 2004: 224).

A number of the female interviewees mentioned his physical attraction as a factor in drawing them into Islam, at least in the initial stage when they had met him. Jessica has this to say about Hamza Yusuf:

> He seemed both very familiar to me—as an American with some similar sensibilities . . . and very daunting and imposing. . . . In his presence I was overwhelmed. More than his words affected me, his state of being did. As his words settled in my mind, my heart responded to who he was. It was truly a disconcerting experience. After I said goodbye to him I felt like I was in love.[50]

Hamza Yusuf is also highly popular among some prominent people and world leaders and as such has worldwide connections—for example, he was once the guest of the king of Morocco. Also, he has a relationship with Prince Ghazi of Jordan, who worked with him on several research projects. Prince Ghazi says of Yusuf:

> Unlike many leading Muslim scholars [Hamza Yusuf] seems to know every aspect of Islamic culture, art, civilization, history and politics. . . . He also seems to know and understand the modern world, world history, world religions, science and philosophy. Moreover, as regards Western culture, he is a kind of "Renaissance man" that knows, discerns and appreciates what is worth appreciating in that great tradition. He has definitely affected and enriched the lives of millions of Muslims, not just in the West but all over the Islamic world, and I dare say mine is one.[51]

All these connections have added to his overall aura and increased his popularity among ordinary people.

One of the most important aspects of his popularity is by far his solid grounding in traditional sacred knowledge. His knowledge of the Qur'an, *hadith*, and other classical Islamic sciences combines with a broad and deep knowledge of Western thought and culture. One of our interviewees described him as "a walking encyclopedia."[52]

DERADICALIZATION

In an age when radicalization of young Muslims has increased, programs like the Rihla and Hamza Yusuf's sacred knowledge project provide tools to counter the agenda of Salafi and political groups. Asma, a female born Muslim from the UK who attended the Rihla during summer 2016, described the positive effect of the program on her after she was distressed and on the verge of contemplating an act of violence. She says:

> Going to Rihla was my way of reaching out for help. I felt I had no purpose, no role, I felt rejected by society, I managed to leave the UK and thought, now I am out why should I go back? Whisperings flooded my head about all the things I could do.[53]

The teachers were particularly important in her transformation:

> They were so kind that I was angry at not being able to respond in anger/hate.... They changed my life. They gave their time to me. I left feeling cared and a bit clearer about my purpose.... I went back home [and] since become a lot stronger in myself.... I do not feel despair and overwhelming sadness anymore because I met teachers [in the Rihla] who care about me and gave their time to me selflessly. I learned to be selfless.[54]

A good number of our male and female interviewees said explicitly that the teaching of sacred knowledge and the traditional approach[55] of Hamza Yusuf played an important role in moving them from Salafi/politicized Islam into more Sunni/Sufi–oriented form of Islam. This process, for them, constituted a major shift in ideological orientation and was therefore akin to a deradicalization process. Here is what Benn, a male convert from the US who underwent such process, said:

> As a Muslim convert in the [1990s], I adopted the Salafi approach to Islam. Hamza Yusuf was greatly responsible for changing my perspective on Islam and bringing me to a more Sunni/Sufi oriented approach to Islam and also making me more easygoing in my dealing with other Muslims who I may have disagreed with.[56]

Mariam, a female born Muslim from Australia, explains her transformation:

> Growing up in Sydney, the "default" Islam was a more hard-line approach/Wahhabism. . . . It was just all I knew . . . all the talks at uni by chaplains and shuyookh were following a more hard-line approach. . . . I felt a vacuum because there was always an emphasis on the outer that led to a lot of judgment. And that never sat right with me. . . . When I started listing to scholars like Shaykh Hamza . . . I found their teachings were more aligned to spirituality. . . . Shaykh Hamza opened up the gateway to honing in on the potential to reach a higher level of spirituality.[57]

Fatimah, a female born Muslim from Australia, alluded to the same situation:

> I grew up in Sydney and the only way we were taught Islam was through a hard-line approach. We really didn't know any other way. . . . I was a lot younger . . . and I believed it at face value. . . . At that time, listening to any scholar was . . . the worst thing I could think of. I was sick of the shouting and the telegraphing and would much prefer to listen to Radiohead or an alt rock band [but when I started listening to Shaykh Hamza] I started to enjoy it—it was different. There was depth, there was an intellectual air [and after that] I scoured every Islamic store to find as many VHS tapes and cassette tapes of Shaykh Hamza that I could get my hands on. I would listen to them daily and never tired of hearing him speak. . . . [He] changed my life . . . changed my thinking. . . . The most profound impact [he] had had on me was his *aqeedah*[58] class in 2009. . . . He taught me to love Allah. That Allah [is] love. This was a spiritual game changer and that shift was palpable.[59]

Ahmed, a male convert from Canada, refers to his change in this way:

> I accepted Islam with staunch Wahhabism who discouraged me from listening to Hamza. . . . Being a student of sociology and student of color and having been exposed to racism and prejudice from a young age, I gravitated to anything that was anti-Western . . . [but] I began to feel more isolated [and] separated from the rest of my society. What I was looking for was a way out of a meek, minority status as a person of color who had to fit in with the dominant society around me. Sidi Hamza gave me a way out of that by teaching me that Islam [is] noble, universal, uniting of all people and races. . . . . [Hamza's] impact on my religious and spiritual life is immense, even to this day.[60]

Jessica, a female convert from the US, describes the transformation that has taken place to her husband as a result of Hamza Yusuf's approach to scared knowledge: Yusuf "has revitalized Islam in the hearts of native-born Muslims (and converts) who feel almost as if they have had their own conversion experience through listening to his teaching."[61]

CRITIQUE AND CONCLUDING REMARKS

It is hard to find critiques from people around Hamza Yusuf or those whom he works with. The criticism tends to come from people who are theologically and ideologically opposed to him. That being said, I have managed to identify some criticisms or complaints from some of the interviewees, but also beyond the group that I engaged with. One of my interviewees, Farhan, a British-born Muslim, seems to be very critical of Hamza Yusuf. He thinks that although Yusuf is a man of great impression, and played an important role in giving him a sense of pride to be a Muslim for a while, Farhan felt that Yusuf was unfriendly and rather standoffish.[62] For him, Yusuf's influence in his religious-spiritual life is now negligible, as Farhan decided to move away from Yusuf's traditional interpretation of Islam and from Islam altogether. The catalyst event for this change was Farhan's personal encounter with Yusuf, during which he felt that Yusuf had let him down[63]: "I had a severe mental breakdown while I was at the Rihla of 2001, and instead of giving me medical treatment, or even waiting for my father—who pleaded with him to wait, saying that he would come and get me, Yusuf got his acolytes to put me on the next flight. That was a traumatic event for me.... It literally took me years to get over it, and I'm not sure if I'm entirely over it yet."[64] After this episode, Farhan discovered that he was idolizing Yusuf's personality, "and any personality cult is likely to fail, as we are always dealing with fallible human beings."[65] He also thinks that Yusuf has been not true to his words in his recent remarks on the Black Lives Matter movement[66] when he initially refused to admit his remarks (more on this below). For Farhan, "These 'slippages' ... are unconscionable, especially for a public persona of Yusuf's renown."[67] When asked about the impact of Yusuf's writings and public sermons, Farhan's response was critical: "I have come to wonder—while examining his more recent lectures—to what extent he is actually teaching anything of substance, at least insofar as academic scholarly standards are concerned."[68] Farhan thinks that Yusuf's uncompromising belief in the role of traditional Islam forms a major obstacle in his and his followers' ability to understand how Islam works in the modern world. His view is that, for Muslims to have their voices being heard seriously in the West, they need to think outside of the box of traditional Islam.[69] Further, Farhan questions the relevance of *taqlid* in contemporary situations and believes that the idea that no one can question or criticize teachers or scholars has done more harm than good for Muslims. He stressed that he himself had suffered a lot at the hands of other scholars. He used to have total faith in their views and asserts that "Muslims need to . . . be more critically and intelligently engaged with the Islamic tradition—which is far easier said than done, of course. Far too often people leave their intelligences at the door of the Masjid."[70]

I also asked my group a few questions related to the long-term effectiveness of Zaytuna, the Rihla, and other activities such as his public appearances and lectures. With regard to Zaytuna, some expressed appreciation regarding the work of the college. They said that the combination of liberal arts, social sciences, and Islamic traditional sciences is the best way to counteract Salafism/politicized Islamist groups and therefore radicalism.[71] But others said it is elitist and that not everyone can afford it. Here is what Jessica has to say:

> Better education in Islam naturally counters radicalization or an Islamist mind-set, but the impact of Zaytuna seems analogous to the impact of the organic food movement on addressing hunger. What I mean by that, only the affluent can afford organic food, and for those who struggle to afford the most basic sustenance the organic food movement is irrelevant.[72]

For her this is the case with Zaytuna:

> It is available to Muslims, who are socio-economically successful in the West, and perhaps these folks are the least likely to become radicalised. For those who are most vulnerable to radicalisation—who have seen the collapse of their society on so many levels, and who see no job opportunity except for with IS—Zaytuna is irrelevant.[73]

This opinion resonates with the views other interviewees who questioned whether Hamza Yusuf is reaching out to the ghettos and gangsters or whether he is accessible to ordinary people or just the media. Ahmed, for example, said that for young Muslims who are affected by the extremist's ideologies Hamza Yusuf "comes off as elitist."[74] Farhan agreed, believing that it is playing a relevant though limited role "given that it is one institution in a vast country, and it is still largely dependent on the charisma of one or two individuals."[75]

For the Rihla, they all referred to its importance but stressed that it has become very expensive, which would deter students with limited financial resources. His tapes were and are by far the most popular mode of knowledge transfer for those who want to follow the path of traditional Islam. A few of the interviewees emphasized that his popularity, especially since the September 11 attacks, has taken a downturn. This is probably due to his brief role as an adviser to President Bush after 9/11. But it is also related to some of his charging statements immediately after the attacks, as well as his position regarding the Arab Spring of 2011. This disappointed some of those who looked at him as a role model. His recent remarks at the RIS (Revival of Islamic Spirit) convention in Toronto—where he criticized Black Lives Matter members for being unable to help themselves, the Arab Gulf states (in which he stressed the existence of Arab privilege over non-Arabs), and the politicized Islamic groups (in which he put ISIS, al-Qaeda, and the Muslim Brotherhood on the same platform)—did not earn him much favor.[76]

His comments on Black Lives Matter specifically brought him a scathing criticism in social media and led his colleague and friend Imam Zaid Shakir to defend him on Facebook and on the New Islamic Directions website.[77] Criticism also came from some respectable members of the black community in America. For example, Mr. Evan from the American Learning Institute for Muslims commented on Yusuf's statement regarding Black Lives Matter: "Shaykh Hamza's commenting on black violence and the breakdown of the black family in connection with the value of black life and police brutality is unacceptable. [He has to be informed] that the fact of white privilege precludes the possibility of his being able to make such comments with any integrity."[78] Those who are close to Yusuf believe that the attacks on him as a privileged white man who lacks sensitivity to black suffering amounts to character assassination.

The theme that Yusuf is a white and privileged person and thereby attracts followers has also surfaced recently in academia, especially with the emergence of a wave of activism based on critical theory. One of those related works is an article published in 2013 by Mahdi Tourage. His approach is rooted mainly in theories on color, racism, patriarchy, and power. I will focus on his critique of Yusuf's role as a white and privileged leader in the RIS (Revival of Islamic Spirit) conventions. The article essentially argues that Hamza Yusuf attracts followers not because of his knowledge but because of his charisma and whiteness. For Tourage, nonwhite people are subconsciously drawn to Yusuf because he is white and because there is a deep subconscious obsession with white people among colored people who form the majority of those who attend the Revival conventions. In this context, immigrant Muslims value white convert speakers (like Yusuf) more than they do black American converts. The normative model performed by Yusuf in these conventions lead to the empowerment of a disempowered community in America. Hamza Yusuf is, according to Tourage, in the business of "belief production." He writes: "In these conventions the effects of performance go beyond the construct of identity, they include the performance of belief" (Tourage 2013: 212). Also, "the fetishist function of prominent white converts becomes apparent: through discursive repetition of gestures of power they are authorised to empower the Community [and they] bring about outward manifestations and proofs of Islamic belief. . . . In effect they believe for the rest of the Muslims" (Tourage 2013: 219).

Based on my research, I do not agree with these assumptions. First, all members of the group that I interviewed said that before they saw the color of his skin they heard the power of his ideas. This rebuts the assumption that all brown people listen to Yusuf only because of an unconscious fetish for whiteness. Even if there are few who view him in this way, the majority considers him a well-versed Muslim scholar. And they turn to Yusuf for guidance, not "to perform and believe for them" (Tourage 2013: 222). In my view, Tourage essentially denies agency for the individuals (who happen to be educated and well informed) who listen to Yusuf and suggests that, instead of using their intellect, they are just automatons, unconscious of their desire for whiteness. Tourage's assertion that immigrant Muslims value white over black speakers also has no ground due to the popularity of many black scholars such as Jackson and Imam Shakir. His claim that Yusuf is in the industry of belief production is unfounded; Yusuf is a transmitter of knowledge rather than a belief-maker.

In this chapter I have examined and assessed how far and by what means Hamza Yusuf's message, teachings, and activity have encouraged people to move into a traditional form of Islam. This is done through three modes of knowledge: lectures, Rihlas, and Zaytuna College. The importance of his works in this context resides in the fact that he managed to reach a confused generation during the 1990s and early 2000s, a generation that had been exposed to politicized/Salafi narratives of Islam that were attractive because they were the loudest voices and were the best organized. Those who encountered such narratives accepted them readily because they were the only ones they were confronted with. The Muslim communities, especially the mosques, did not offer solid knowledge of Islam or anything more than basic *fiqh* and how to read the Qur'an without even understanding Arabic. Many of them, therefore, including converts, followed narrow versions of politicized/Salafi Islam.[79]

Hamza Yusuf (and scholars like him)[80] provided people with a very expansive interpretation of what Islamic civilization and theological heritage represented, and he opened up an understanding of culture, poetry, literature, arts, and theology of other civilizations and how Muslims could incorporate these into their worldview. When he did so this narrative was like a revelation for his followers. They compared his narrative with an us-versus-them approach to the politicized group,[81] and they realized the huge difference. Therefore they decided to leave the politicized narrative of the faith and to embrace traditional Islam as advocated by Hamza Yusuf.

Hamza Yusuf has and continues to play a pivotal role in encouraging disfranchised and radicalized people to move into his moderate form of Islam. Those who follow his path—traditional Islam—play an increasingly important role in the slow but sure emergence of a traditional version of Islam that addresses vital issues relevant to Muslims in the West, such as radicalization and the lack of integration in the UK, the US, Canada, and beyond.

NOTES

1. One of the founding faculty members of the Zaytuna College. He is also one of the most respected scholars and well versed in traditional Islamic science. Online interview, July 14, 2016.

2. I am particularly grateful to Aftab Malik, Ahmed Weir, and Imam Zaid Shakir, who responded to all my questions.

3. Despite the efforts of a contact to have an online interview with Hamza Yusuf, I was unable to achieve that.

4. He wrote on the subtleties of the Islamic faith that show a solid knowledge of traditional Islam. He also translates classical Islamic works and poetry. Among his major works, which have had a major impact on British Muslims, especially Muslim youths, are the *Purification of the Heart* and the translation of the Creed of Imam Al-Tahawi, one of the respected classical texts that deals with the articulations of Islamic faith and Muslim belief.

5. Online interview, June 25, 2016.

6. Online interview, October 14, 2016.

7. See www.dailymail.co.uk/news/article-2404078/NYPD-secretly-branded-entire-mosques-terrorist-organisations-allow-surveillance-sermons-worshippers.html#comments.

8. Online interview, October 16, 2016.

9. Online interview, October 15, 2016.

10. Online interview, September 1, 2016.

11. Online interview, September 23, 2016.

12. Online interview, September 15, 2016.

13. Online interview, September 16, 2016.

14. Online interview, September 23, 2016.

15. Online interview, October 4, 2016.

16. *Usul al-fiqh* means "methods of reasoning and rules of interpretation and deduction." See Mohammad Kamali, *Principles of Islamic Jurisprudence* (Cambridge: St. Edmundsbury Press, 1989). *Tafsir* is the Arabic equivalent for "exegesis," especially the Qur'an, the main source of Islamic law. "Hadith" means "collections of the reliable sayings of the Prophet Muhammad" and are regarded as the second source of guidance for Muslims after the Qur'an.

17. This is a key Islamic concept that denotes a high level of courtesy and good manners. To possess *adab* means to have courtesy and good manners, and this includes the mind, body and soul. See Nasr (1987: 101–102).

18. Biography or the life of Muhammad.

19. Online interview, September 15, 2016.

20. Online interview, October 1, 2016.

21. Online interview, June 28, 2016.

22. Online interview, September 15, 2016.

23. On the philosophy of sacred knowledge in Islam and other religions, see Nasr (1989).

24. Online interview, June 23, 2016.

25. Online interview, September 15, 2016.

26. Online interview, September 20, 2016.

27. Online interview, September 15, 2016.

28. Online interview, September 15, 2016.

29. Online interview, September 17, 2016.

30. Online interview, September 27, 2016.

31. Online interview, September 28, 2016.

32. It is an Arabic word equivalent to a certificate in English, which entails that the person who holds it is given the authority and permission from a higher authority to transmit and teach traditional Islamic sciences.

33. Reza Shah-Kazemi, "Shaykh Hamza Yusuf: A Response to Nadeem Azam," Q-News (London), August 1998, 18.

34. Online interview, October 6, 2016.

35. Online interview, October 6, 2016.

36. Online interview, September 12, 2016.

37. Online interview with Imam Zaid Shakir, September 2016.

38. Online interview, September 19, 2016.

39. Online interview, October 28, 2016.

40. Online interview, October 9, 2016.

41. Online interview, June 3, 2016.

42. Online interview, October 10, 2016.

43. Online interview, August 6, 2016.

44. Online interview, September 19, 2016.

45. Online interviews, August 25, 2016.

46. Online interview, August 29, 2016.

47. Online interview, September 30, 2016.

48. Online interview, August 27, 2016.

49. Online interview, June 28, 2016.

50. Online interview, June 12, 2016.

51. HRH Prince Ghazi bin Muhammad, chief adviser to HM King Abdullah II, for *Religious and Cultural Affairs*. Online communication, October 4, 2016.

52. Online interview, October 5, 2016.

53. Online interview, October 15, 2016.

54. Online interview, October 20, 2016.

55. One male interviewee stressed that he read the works of both Philips and Deedate and was troubled by their confrontational approach, contrary to the approach of Hamza Yusuf. Online interview, October 2016.

56. Online interview, June 25, 2016.

57. Online interview, November 8, 2016.

58. Meaning the fundamental belief principles of Islam.

59. Online interview, November 7, 2016.

60. Online interview, November 5, 2016.

61. Online interview, September 3, 2016.

62. Online interview, November 10, 2017.

63. For more on this issue, see www.taseelcommons.com/politics/wolves-in-shepherds-clothing-nouman-ali-khan-hamza-yusuf-and-pastoral-power.

64. Online interview, November 3, 2017.

65. Online interview, November 10, 2017.

66. See m.youtube.com/watch?v=40qlvuQqET8.

67. Online interview, November 10, 2017.

68. Online interview, November 10, 2017.

69. Online interview, November 10, 2017.

70. Online interview, November 3, 2017.

71. Online interview, June 28, 2016.

72. Online interview, August 20, 2016.

73. Online interview, August 19, 2016.

74. Online interview, June 23, 2016.

75. Online interview, November 10, 2017.

76. See 5pillarsuk.com/2016/12/25/hamza-yusuf-stokes-controversy-with-comments-about-black-lives-matter-and-political-islam.

77. See newislamicdirections.com/nid/articles/shaykh_hamza_yusuf_is_not_a_racist.

78. See islamicate.co.uk/restraining-the-tongue.

79. Sohail Nakooda, executive director of Abu Dhabi, UAE, Skype interview, November 30, 2016.

80. Tim Winter was one of the most important people at that time because he put

an academic footing on the study of Islam. Sohail Nakooda, Skype interview, November 30, 2016.

81. Sohail Nakooda, Skype interview, November 30, 2016.

REFERENCES

Abou El-Fadl, K. 2009. *The Great Theft: Wrestling Islam from the Extremists*. San Francisco: HarperCollins.

Birt, Jonathan. 2009. "The Radical Nineties Revisited: Jihadi Discourses in Britain." In *Dying for Faith: Religiously Motivated Violence in the Contemporary World*. Madawi Al Rasheed and Marat Shterin, eds. London: I. B. Tauris. 105–111.

Dutton, Yasin. 1999. "Conversion to Islam: Quranic Paradigm," In *Religious Conversion*. C. Lamb and M. Bryant, eds. London and New York: Cassell. 151–166.

El Naggar, Shaimaa. 2012. "Intertextuality and Interdiscursivity in the Discourse of Muslim Televangelists: The Case Study of Hamza Yusuf." *Critical Approaches to Discourse Analysis across Disciplines* 6, no. 1: 76–95.

Franceschelli, M., and M. O'Brien. 2015. "Being Modern and Modest, South Asian Young British Muslims Negotiating Multiple Influences on their Identity," *Ethnicities* 15, no. 5: 696–714.

Jawad, Haifaa. 2011. *Toward Establishing a British Islam*. London, New York: Continuum.

Meho, L. I. 2006. "E-mail Interviewing in Qualitative Research: A Methodological Discussion." *Journal of the American Society for Information Science and Technology* 57, no. 10: 1284–1295.

Nalla, Zarina. 2011. "Interview with Professor John O. Voll on the Future of Islamic Studies." *Islam and Civilisational Renewal (ICR)* 3, no. 1: 235–240.

Nasr, S. H. 1987. *Islamic Spirituality: Foundations*. New York: The CrossRoad.

———. 1989. *Knowledge and the Sacred*. New York: State University of New York Press.

Nguyen, Martin. 2008. "Hermeneutics as Translation: An Assessment of Islamic Translation Trends in America," *The Muslim World* 98, no. 4: 485–501.

Rambo, Lewis. 1993. *Understanding Religious Conversion*. New Haven: Yale University Press.

Rambo, Lewis, and C. Farhadian. 1999. "Converting: Stages of Religious Change." In *Religious Conversion, Contemporary Practices and Controversies*. C. Lamb and M. Bryant, eds. London and New York: Cassell.

Roald, Ann Sofie. 2009. *New Muslims in the European Context: The Experience of Scandinavian Converts*. Leiden: Brill.

Robinson, L. "Cultural Identity and Acculturation Preferences among South Asian Adolescents in Britain: An Exploratory Study." *Children and Society* 23, no. 6: 442–454.

Schmidt, Garbi. 2005. "The Transnational Umma—Myth or Reality? Examples from the Western Diasporas." *The Muslim World* 95, no. 4: 575–586.

Song, Miri. 2012. "Part of the British Mainstream? British Muslim Students and Islamic Student Associations." *Journal of Youth Studies* 15, no. 2: 143–160.

Taji-Faruki, Suha. 1996. *Fundamental Quest: Hizb Al-Tahrir and the Search for the Islamic Caliphate*. London: Grey Seal Books.

———. 2000. "Islamists and the Threat of Jihad: Hizb al-Tahrir and al-Muhajiroun on Israel and the Jews." *Middle Eastern Studies* 36, no. 4: 21–46.

Tourage, M. 2013. "Performing Belief and Reviving Islam: Prominent (White Male) Converts in Muslim Revival Conventions." *Performing Islam* 1, no. 2: 207–226.

Winter, Tim. 2000. "Conversion as Nostalgia: Some Experiences of Islam." In *Previous Convictions, Conversion in the Present Day*. M. Percy, ed. London: SPCK.

TEN

ESCAPING THE LIMELIGHT

The Politics of Opacity and the Life of a Dutch Preacher in the UK

MARTIJN DE KONING

Here you can be Muslim.

ABU BASHIR[1]

The above quote is from an interview I held with Abu Bashir, a Dutch Muslim preacher, now living in the UK, who identifies himself as a follower of the Salafi method of Islam and who was very active in Dutch Salafi circles between 2000 and 2008. In that same period—after 9/11 and the murder of film director and writer Theo van Gogh in 2004—the "Salafism" phenomenon became the main target of the Dutch counter-radicalization policies, as it was regarded as a threat to social cohesion and national security. In this chapter I address how Abu Bashir, as a Muslim preacher who explicitly associates himself with the Salafi *daʿwah* (mission, proselytizing), responds to the increased public visibility of Salafism as a radical phenomenon, as well as the extent to which visibility plays a role in his life and work.

Abu Bashir was raised in a small country village in the south of the Netherlands and converted (or in his words "reverted") to Islam in his teens. In young adulthood, he became one of the founders of three major Dutch websites and, although he remained invisible to the general public, over a short period of time he quickly became a well-known figure within Dutch Salafi circles.

In this chapter I argue that Abu Bashir engaged in what could be called a "politics of opacity" that regulated the distinction between his visibility and invisibility to a wider audience. This means that I am not so much interested in the question as to whether Abu Bashir's work is an example of a particular Islamic position or not, as this would imply that his engagement with the public is determined by his "belonging" to a particular trend and its doctrines (Schielke 2010). Rather I am presenting and analyzing Abu Bashir's life story and work, as this provides insight into the particular conditions that make

Muslims who are active on behalf of Islam engage in more and less visible contestations about the public presence and representation of Islam.

First I discuss the concept of visibility and demonstrate how different, but related, dimensions of this visibility create a regime of surveillance, a regime that obliges people to ask how they are to live and behave in a society in which they are problematized as belonging to a group that poses a threat to social cohesion and national security. After a brief discussion of Abu Bashir's life story and conversion I explore the methods he uses in his attempt to evade the regime of surveillance, an attempt that is only partly successful and that is driven by a desire not only to escape the surveillance but also to avoid the intra-Salafi debates about what "good" Islam is and what makes good preachers. I conclude with a few notes on what Abu Bashir's life story means for wider debates on public visibility, activism, and claiming a "Muslim voice."

VISIBILITY AND A REGIME OF SURVEILLANCE

In this chapter I thematize the issue of visibility by exploring the life story of Abu Bashir, a Dutch preacher who claims to follow the Salafi *manhaj* (method); according to many Salafi preachers and scholars, this is the methodology for interpreting and gathering Islamic knowledge through which people acquire a sense of "what Islam really says." When Abu Bashir talks about his life and how to live within the particular context he is in, he often reflects on the consequences of ascribing himself to a particular community and of being more or less visible as such. But there is one constant: Abu Bashir always remains hidden from the wider public. By very carefully regulating his visible presence and keeping out of the spotlight, he is able to engage in all kinds of activities on behalf of Islam without being targeted by government agencies or the press. He was not, however, invisible enough to be shielded from intra-Salafi scrutiny and politics, nor was he left untouched by the Dutch debates on Islam.

If we look closer at this brief introduction to Abu Bashir, we can identify three different modes of visibility: first, there is the general context of religion in the public sphere (i.e., the "problem" of Islam as a visible religion in the public domain). This is closely related to the discussion about a "secular notion of religion" that is being forced upon religion in Western Europe. The second mode concerns the hypervisibility of the Salafism phenomenon and the regime of surveillance that is a product of it. The third mode of visibility is one of authority and recognition. In this chapter I focus on the latter two modes but would like to make some brief remarks on the first, as this provides the background in which people operate and are interpellated.

Islam in public

The term "public" pertains to matters and groups characterized by openness and accessibility (Amiraux and Jonker 2006). At the same time, "public" is related to attempts by European governments to regulate religion into a fixed place within the public sphere. It is often argued, sometimes by scholars of religion but more often by politicians and opinion makers, that Islam came to Europe at a time when the public relevance and presence of religion was declining. The visible public presence of Islam, for example, evidenced by the women with headscarves or face veils or the men going to mosque, and the audible presence, evidenced through the public call to prayer, are then seen as the opposite of this development. Salvatore (2004: 1018) calls this, referring to Luckmann's (1967) thesis, a "mechanistic reversal of paradigms of 'invisible religion.'" Salvatore (2004) correctly points out that the issue is more complicated than simply the "coming out" of Islam and Muslim religiosity and identity. Salvatore (2004: 1018) argues that the "entry of Muslim tradition into European public spheres" should be "understood in relation to the history of the European formulas for the separation of religion and politics, and private and public spheres." The relationship between both separations has been crucial in the state's attempts to assign autonomy to the religious field within the wider secular field and to be able to monitor and regulate it.

The more familiar Dutch argument in this regard describes Muslims as having entered the Dutch religious field at a time when pillarization in the Netherlands was collapsing or already had collapsed. They were "too late to the party," so to speak. Both Thijl Sunier (2000) and Sarah Bracke (2013) have effectively challenged this notion, Sunier by pointing to the idea of nation-state building as an ongoing process and Bracke by not treating the demise of the pillarization and the institutionalization of Islam as two separate processes but by analyzing them as two related dynamics instead. According to Bracke, the depillarization, at least in the structural sense of the term, has less to do with the decline of religious institutional affiliations after the 1960s and more with the logic of "Islamization" (or civilizational logic, as Bracke calls it) in which, and through which, Islam and Dutch culture and identity are construed as their mirror opposites. It is here where the racialization of Muslims and secularism in the Netherlands overlap. Referring to, among others, the late populist Pim Fortuyn (murdered in 2002), Tebble (2006) identifies the emergence of the discourse of "identity liberalism" and describes it as being characterized by its opposition to multiculturalism, its strong focus on advocating a national culture based upon shared values, and its appeals to the state to protect this national culture against allegedly intolerant forces so as to safeguard liberal democracy. The emphasis in the pleas made by Fortuyn (and before him by Frits Bolkestein, leader of the conservative liberal VVD party at the time) was not only on having a people with a shared culture (which for them was liberal and secular) but also on building a strong defense of liberal principles in the face of an illiberal force that was increasingly exemplified by Islam (de Koning 2016).

This identity liberalism is strongly connected to a vision held by politicians and opinion leaders about the importance of the Netherlands being a secular society. Many opinion leaders and politicians (such as, in the past, Fortuyn) see the depillarization and reduction of the societal and political influence wielded by Dutch churches as liberation from the "constraints of religion" (Van der Veer 2006). The dominant ideal vision of the identity of Dutch society is that it is a modern society of secular (including sexual) freedoms that has to be defended against a religion that is either not yet modern (so-called moderate Islam) or is even antimodern (fundamentalist or radical Islam) (de Koning 2016). In particular, the visible presence of Islam, such as women wearing head scarves or face veils, the various mosques, plus the audible presence of the public call to prayer, is then seen as actively opposing the so-called secular and/or Judeo-Christian tradition of the Netherlands. This particular vision of the visible presence of Islam is often expressed and summarized in the slogans about the Islamization of "our" culture or the Islamization of society.

As the late Pim Fortuyn (2002 ed.: 42) stated in his book *Against the Islamization of Our Culture*:

> For anyone who wants to see, it is clearly visible that many Islamic women are being hindered in developing themselves in the public domain. Wearing long dresses and little headscarves is less innocent than it may seem. Furthermore, we do not know enough about what is happening in all of these mosques. As far as it does undermine our core values or acting in public, outsiders have nothing to do with it. As far as that is the case, a public answer is necessary.

Fortuyn's and others' now common argument against the Islamization of our culture transforms the incorporation of Islam into the secular arrangements of the religious field into a cultural conflict. It is an argument that has evidenced itself, in particular, through opposition to mosques, the public call to prayer, and occasionally the headscarf. Therefore, the ideas about what an ideal secular society should be are constructed in opposition to a racialized vision of Islam and Muslims. After 9/11, the focus in the media and in policies on integration shifted almost entirely to Islam and Muslims and their alleged threat to Dutch society (Vliegenthart 2007; De Graaf 2012). This is certainly not an exclusively Dutch development; recently several researchers throughout Europe have delved into the issue of the process of securitization (Fekete 2004; Edmunds 2012; Cesari 2009; Croft 2012; Mavelli 2013). Transforming a particular group from being treated not as an ordinary political issue but as a security threat legitimates the adoption of exceptional measures that may go beyond (or even undo) existing legal benchmarks and rights (Edmunds 2012) but, crucially, allows it at the same time to become part of the daily political, bureaucratic security logic (Mavelli 2013).

The hypervisibility of Salafism

It is within this context that the phenomenon of "Salafism" emerged as a matter of security, and it is this securitization of Islam that raises the second aspect of visibility that I want to highlight: the hypervisibility of what is called "Salafism." The term "hypervisibility" is borrowed here from critical race studies (Reddy 1998; Yancy 2008) and refers to the processes that make racialized people become intensely visible as objects of the state's gaze (e.g., as a threat to security). In this logic the body plays an important role; Muslim men wearing beards and who are (sometimes because of the beards) thought to be "Salafi" are often referred to as "hate beards." The wearing of the face veil by women is seen by the Dutch government as a symbol of a form of Islam that does not fit Dutch society (Moors 2009: 401). These traits are often regarded as features of Salafism, and people who wear the face veil or refuse to shake hands are thought to be Salafi.

Much of the literature on Salafism in Europe focuses on the processes of radicalization among Muslims (Amghar 2007), on its attraction to Muslim youths because of its compatibility with the search for religious identity among second-generation Muslims seeking "pure" religion (Hamid 2009), or on the contradictions between daily life and Salafi ideologies and the tensions and uncertainties that ensue from this (Adraoui 2009; Dumbe and Tayob 2011). A recent special issue of *Comparative Islamic Studies* contained several articles that focused on the social dimensions of Salafism; the articles attempted to show the empowering and transformative dimensions of Salafism and how they produce and inform solidarities and conflict. Sedgwick (2012) correctly noted that much of the literature on Salafism is focused on doctrines (but see Gauvain 2012) and tends to neglect the social life of Salafis. In this chapter I address Abu Bashir's social life in general and examine how he deals with the visibility of Salafism in particular.

To be clear, mosques, networks, and individual preachers claiming to follow the Salafi *manhaj* (method) have been present in the Netherlands since the 1980s. During the 1990s the main Salafi networks in the south and the west of the country fragmented as a result of local and transnational debates among Salafis, which focused in particular on the different views held about the presence of US soldiers in Saudi Arabia during and after the Gulf War and on (violent) opposition against Middle Eastern regimes.[2]

All of the major Salafi networks in the Netherlands try to provide Muslim youths with incentives to acquire the right kind of knowledge and behavior (de Koning 2013b). They strive to teach insiders what it means to belong to a particular kind of community, how to recognize that community, and how to identify themselves as members of it. Through these activities, the different Salafi networks try to establish and present themselves as moral guardians of a Muslim community that, according to Salafi authorities, is characterized by moral crisis. According to Salafi preachers this moral crisis has risen because Muslims adopt Dutch customs and values and leave the path of Islam. The preachers try to persuade their constituency to reorganize their daily routines and to focus on "returning" to Islam according to Salafi interpretation (de Koning 2013b). In doing so they challenge the discourse of integration propagated by the Dutch state, which is increasingly focused on compliance with Dutch (secular) standards and democracy (instead of God's law) and undivided loyalty (instead of the transnational loyalties of the Salafi movement) under the label of "active citizenship" (instead of "true" Muslims worshipping only God) (cf. Geelhoed 2011; H. Moors and Jacobs 2009).

Although Salafis shied away from any public visibility during the 1980s and 1990s, let alone from participating in public debates, from 2002 onward Salafi visibility increased in the public's image of Islam and Muslims because of a number of incidents (de Koning 2012a and 2012b). In 2003 the term "Salafism" became apparent to a wider audience. That year a trial took place of twelve people accused of recruiting young men for the military jihad, in particular for the violent struggles in Kashmir, after two young men from the city of Eindhoven were killed there in 2002. According to the newspapers, the public prosecutor stated that the twelve men belonged to "Salafism," a "radical Islamic branch with extreme ideas about Quran interpretation and Islamic law. Salafism pertains to establishing the Islamic state (not, of course, referring to IS at the time), the caliphate, the Islamic rule of law [and sharia]."[3]

What is important here is that Salafism is being referred to as a clearly distinguishable Islamic ideology, one that people can belong to—two features that are highly contested by Muslims, and certainly when it is stated that Osama bin Laden "belongs to it." The intra-Muslim contestations about the Salafi *manhaj* or "Salafism" as a clearly defined ideology are usually not taken into account. "Salafi" or "Salafist" as a label is highly contested among Muslims; some refuse to use it, some use it to denounce other Muslims (Abu Bashir is an example of this trend), and some (even those who refuse to use the label in religious circles) use it in public debate to describe themselves. Furthermore, it should also be noted that there are many groups of Muslims, other than Salafis, who regard the Prophet Muhammad and the first three generations of Muslims as exemplary Muslims and their teachings as an inspiration for current reform. These range from other Islamic movements to socialists and feminists in the Middle East. For many individual Muslims, whether or not they are affiliated with a particular branch or movement, the lives and teachings of the first generations and the Prophet Muhammad are attractive "ideals," although there is no clear concept of what form they actually take.

It is not a coincidence that the first time the notion emerged in the consciousness of the general public was in the context of a terrorism trial. This has put Salafism in the context of a matter of security, and the term "Salafism" itself has become part of the hypervisibility of Muslims as bearers of an intolerant and violent religion. After the murder of the Dutch writer and TV director Theo van Gogh by someone who frequented the Salafi centers, Salafism became the focus of the Dutch counter-radicalization movement and was regarded as a threat to social cohesion, integration, the democratic order, and national security. The question of how dangerous Salafism is, or who Salafis are, has underpinned much of the media coverage and policy attention. In public debates, Salafism is often equated with radicalism and vice versa; so-called radical Muslims are often called Salafi or Salafists. In this way so-called Salafi Muslims have become radically visible and visibly radical.

The regime of surveillance

In assessing what this political context means for Salafi Muslims, in particular for those who are preachers or imams who affiliate themselves with the so-called Salafi *manhaj* (method), I focus on its relationship to the answers they give to the question "How should one live?" The result of the ongoing racialization of Muslims and the securitization of Islam (regarded here as the reduction of Islam to a topic of security and the reduction of security to Islam) is that Muslims, especially after the murder of Theo van Gogh, feel increasingly under scrutiny. In a recent research project on militant activists, we referred to such an idea as the experience of a "regime of surveillance" (de Koning, Roex, Becker, and Aarns 2014). In the context of the securitization of Islam, Edmunds (2012) makes a distinction between "hard" and "soft" regimes of regulation and surveillance. Regulation of this sort could include 24/7 monitoring, wiretapping, disturbing all kinds of activities, etc. but also includes the tendency of the intelligence services and the Dutch national coordinator of counterterrorism to focus on Salafism, defining it as the main security threat in general and the main Islamic security threat in particular. The hard regimes of regulation target and affect a small number of people (e.g., those who support foreign fighters or plan to go to Syria themselves) and also have implications for a wider group: those who are suspected of being supportive to foreign fighters and/or plan to go abroad to fight. The hard regime of surveillance can also come into play, as many meetings in Salafi mosques appear to be monitored by the security services (or at least this is what the audiences present believe).

The soft regime involves what Edmunds has called "the 'hyper-legalization' of perceived cultural threats," which refers to banning particular Islamic clothing such as the headscarf (Korteweg and Yurdakul 2014) or face veil (Moors 2009) or outlawing minarets (Lentin and Titley 2012) because they are deemed to be a security risk. Note that the examples given here pertain to visible markers of Islam; this is significant given that the debate on secularism focuses on the separation of the private versus the public and of religion and politics. In the debates referring to those markers, it is their visual nature that is often regarded as an obtrusive presence of Islam in the public sphere and a symbolic reference to political Islam that is deemed to be rejecting "our" cultural values.

In our notion of the regime of surveillance we use the concept of the soft regime of surveillance but build upon it and develop it to take into account the experiences of people themselves. I regard a "regime of surveillance" as the sum of discourses and practices that are experienced by people who experience being singled out and labeled as a problem because of their religious and/or ethnic identity. Their experiences of the debates on Islam and integration—which have included topics ranging from how Muslims take a shower after sports, how they treat women, right through to national security issues—all trickle down to the work floor or school playground. Muslims feel that they are questioned and interrogated for what others do in the name of Islam. Suspected and proven practices of ethnic profiling also contribute to this idea of being singled out and scrutinized.

At a general level I assess a wider array of policies and discourses, all of which problematize Islam, and Muslims in particular, in relation to integration and security. I then look specifically at the answers Muslims give to the question "How should I live?" (cf. de Koning 2013a). Following Lakoff and Collier (2004), I treat such ideas as particular ethical formations that emerge in uncertain circumstances. Lakoff and Collier developed the idea of "regimes of living"

> as congeries of moral reasoning and practice that emerge in situations that present ethical problems—that is, situations in which the question of how to live is at stake. Methodologically, the regime of living is abstract: a given regime of living can identify common ethical configurations in diverse situations, and, thus, takes diverse actual forms (Lakoff and Collier 2004: 420).

Elsewhere I have used the idea of regimes of living to analyze how Salafi Muslims constitute their identity as Muslim (de Koning 2013a).

In this chapter I want to focus on the hypervisibility of Salafism, which to a certain extent reduces Salafism to a matter of security. Speaking out as a Salafi preacher and focusing on piety and individual reform (as many preachers do) can then be a way of achieving recognition as a Muslim. However, this rather positive idea of visibility should be problematized (Amiraux 2016). Establishing visibility in the public sphere also means being visible to others and being subjected to, in the case of religious authorities, debates about the place of religion in public and, in the case of securitized subjects such as Salafi preachers, increased scrutiny in terms of security, belonging, and Islam. We can regard this as a classic dilemma for organizations and activists who aspire to bring about social change, ranging from people like Martin Luther King (Roberts et al. 2008) to more mainstream Muslim organizations, as Monnot (2016) illustrates regarding Muslim associations in Switzerland.

And so we arrive at the third aspect of visibility I want to highlight. One of the moral, but also strategic, questions that many people with a public presence raise relates to visibility and invisibility. How should they be present in public? Indeed, should they be present at all? And, if so, what kind of image do they want the public to have of them, and how is this related to their status as converts or, as in the case of Abu Bashir, a white convert? First, conversion to Islam by white Dutch men and women produces a visibility that is specific for this category. As shown by Moosavi (2015a) for white converts in the UK, their white privilege is disrupted in several ways. In the Netherlands, for some people white converts are traitors, while for others their Dutchness is questioned (Vroon 2014; Van Nieuwkerk 2004). Second, many studies about conversion show how white converts often acquire a privileged position within Muslim communities as an example of people who consciously choose Islam, who can speak for Muslim communities, and who act as mediators between Muslims and non-Muslims (Tourage 2012). This is a privilege that can become a burden as well because of the high expectations that come with it. Third, and related to the former, this ascribed position between us and them also causes white converts to be regarded with suspicion. White Muslims are sometimes suspected of being informants for the security services by other Muslims (Moosavi 2015b), while the state sometimes fears the radicalization of white converts (Özyürek 2015). Fourth, the conversion to Islam by white people is sometimes regarded by friends and family or in the media as being at odds with or questioning the idea of white people as secular and modern (Özyürek 2015).

Of course, white converts can live life unmarked as a Muslim when they do not wear a headscarf (or other accoutrements) and do not use other visible markers that are regarded as typically Muslim. Their white privilege never disappears entirely but gets disrupted as their existence clashes with the ideas of Europe as a modern secular continent and white people as unmarked, non-Muslim, or even areligious and Islam as racially marked, foreign, and different (Rogozen-Soltar 2012). Here it is important to note that initially I planned to present a second case beside Abu Bashir. However, this second person requested to remain out of the spotlight because he feared the attention would be damaging. As I had strong doubts whether or not I could protect this person's anonymity, I decided not to include this person in my analysis here. As I will demonstrate, Abu Bashir does not make a choice between being visible or invisible; he engages in what Brent Crosson (2014) has called a politics of opacity—the constant play between degrees of visibility and invisibility. By focusing on the politics of opacity we are able to transcend the opposition between visibility and invisibility. As Crosson explains in studies on activism, visibility is often seen as empowering and as a form of recognition, as well as a condition in which one becomes a target of a particular racializing or sexualizing gaze. Invisibility is often treated as the erasure of particular bodies in public. The story of Abu Bashir and how he became an Islamic preacher after converting in his teens complicates this dichotomy because, as I will show, one of the ways he constructs his authority is via a constant and well-thought-out play between degrees of visibility and invisibility, not only in relation to the gaze of the media and state but also in relation to intra-Salafi debates.

ABU BASHIR—INVISIBILITY, FISSION, AND AUTHORITY

Abu Bashir was born and raised in the south of the Netherlands. He converted to Islam at fifteen; with a group of friends from the same village he went to a Salafi center, Al-Islam Mosque, in the south. There he befriended a new young preacher in the Eindhoven mosque: Abu Khalid, also a convert, who was following the Salafi teachings of Rabiʾ al-Madkhali. Al-Madkhali is a Saudi Salafi scholar who preaches unconditional loyalty to the religious and political authorities in Saudi Arabia and condemns Sahwa (Awakening) scholars like Salman al-ʿAwda. The Saudi authorities supported the al-Madkhali current, hoping that it would counteract the growing support shown for the Sahwa movement, which had become increasingly vocal in its criticism during the 1990s (Meijer 2009).

In the Netherlands, the first major conflict took place in the Al-Islam Mosque when the imam left at the end of the 1990s after being accused by his congregation of being "too political" and "too controlling." The imam founded a new mosque in the south, but in 2001 a few of his students rejected his political teachings and became followers of the Saudi al-Madkhali. These students established their own circle in Tilburg and called themselves "Selefies" (the Dutch pronunciation of Salafis). In 2002 and 2003, these Selefies disseminated a blacklist containing the names of preachers who were accused of being "people of innovation" (*bidʿa*) and "excommunication" (*takfir*) and of dividing the Muslim community.

Abu Bashir was heavily influenced by the teachings of al-Madkhali via Abu Khalid. When Abu Khalid was studying in Saudi Arabia (at the University of Medina) in 2000 he sent cassette tapes to the Netherlands denouncing all major Dutch Salafi imams (including the ones at the Al-Islam Mosque) and advised the young Muslims in Al-Islam to attend the lectures of a different preacher, Abu Redouan.

Abu Khalid established the Dutch version of a major international Salafi website, at that time a major outlet of the al-Madkhali teachings. The first initiative was established in 2001 but ceased to exist within a year after several arguments among the preachers took place and a number of financial problems occurred. At the time, Abu Bashir was already studying in Saudi Arabia as well and, together with Abu Khalid and another Dutch convert, decided to build a new website that included Arabic and English texts translated into Dutch by the three men. They published so-called refutations against Dutch preachers and in 2002 and 2003 sent a blacklist of preachers to their friends. This proved to be the start of a major expansion of the Selefie network in the

Netherlands, which continued to thrive until 2006 when Abu Khalid and Abu Bashir parted because of ideological differences and financial problems.

In terms of visibility, Abu Bashir and his friends did many things at the same time with the blacklist. The blacklist was devised partly as a response to the hypervisibility of Salafism: according to Abu Bashir it was preachers who falsely claimed to be on the Salafi *manhaj* who were giving Salafism a bad name. As the regime of surveillance makes a distinction between people who are potentially acceptable (safe) and potentially unacceptable (dangerous), Abu Bashir felt they needed to do something against what they regarded as an unjust classification. Using their network, they tried to expose and make visible the other Salafi networks as "false" while making their own network more visible (as the "true" Salafis) among the Dutch Salafi networks. Although, according to Abu Bashir and several others, the release of the blacklist was an accident, it did give this Salafi circle its fame and made a lot of people very curious. Yet, as this was an internal Salafi affair, they remained invisible as individuals for a large audience. The blacklist was particularly effective in making the Selefie network visible as a whole, but not the individuals within it, as most preachers were still not widely known.

Interestingly, Abu Bashir very rarely refers to his conversion to Islam. If he talks about it, he explains it (as many converts in the Salafi circles do) as "reverting" to Islam. In doing so he regards his turn to Islam as a return to a natural spiritual state and to an authentic Islam. He often emphasizes that he was already on the correct path of Islam before he started visiting Al-Islam Mosque. He did so, according to himself, "without having much knowledge and without knowing what Salafi *daʿwa* actually was."

In his talks with me Abu Bashir presented himself in three different ways but as a Muslim first and foremost. Wearing a long and full beard and long dress are part and parcel of following the "correct path of a Muslim," and in his conversations with me he shows that he is aware that this look makes him appear "more Muslim" in the eyes of outsiders. Then, second, he is very careful to point out that, "although there is only one Islam," not everyone is practicing Islam in the correct way of the *salaf al-salih*—the pious ancestors, or the first three generations of Muslims—as it is commonly understood. According to Abu Bashir he was "always on the line of the Salafi, but without having much knowledge and without knowing what Salafi *daʿwa* was" until he went to the Salafi center and met a teacher who later became his friend: Abu Khalid.

Third, he emphasizes that he obtained his knowledge of Islam from a *talib al-ʿilm* (a student of knowledge). And fourth, he presents himself as being a member of a particular circle of Dutch networks of Muslims who associate themselves with the Salafi *manhaj*, yet at the same time he stayed in the background and shunned public attention, although his name can still be found on some of the translations and publications. He was known within the Al-Islam Mosque he visited, by (former) Medina students, the inner circle of the Selefies, and by some of his adversaries, but outside these circles people had only occasionally heard of his name and had never met him face to face. This was not uncommon within these Selefie circles: of the people Abu Bashir worked with, only Abu Khalid and Abu Redouan could be described as being widely known, and this was only within larger Salafi circles. They never took part personally in public debates about Islam, only rarely gave interviews to journalists (I know of only three occasions), and refrained as much as possible from having contact with local and national Dutch authorities.

His carefully crafted public image and his isolationist attitude toward wider society, combined with the more confrontational approach displayed to other Muslims (in particular Salafi circles), show how Abu Bashir played with shades of visibility in order to establish and maintain his authority. This reached an entire new level when he moved to the UK.

OUT OF THE SPOTLIGHTS: (PARTIAL) *HIJRA* TO ENGLAND

In 2006 Abu Bashir returned from Saudi Arabia to live in the Netherlands, but according to his own statements he couldn't adjust anymore and grew tired of the intra-Salafi politics and the Dutch Islam debate. Abu Bashir, in sharp contrast to the majority of Salafi preachers, did not take part in the public debates and preferred a life in the background. He and his wife wanted to migrate to what they saw as an Islamic country (and making *hijra*), but Saudi Arabia proved to be impossible. After hearing about the UK from acquaintances, they decided that it would be a suitable place for them to live. After arriving in a city in the north with his family, Abu Bashir started working in a migrant area of that city with many people of Somali and Pakistani descent. After two years he left again, to a city in the south of the UK.

Abu Bashir was certainly not the only Muslim who moved from the Netherlands to the UK. Some of the Dutch Salafis (it is impossible to provide accurate numbers here, but, based upon the stories I heard and the people I met in the Netherlands and the UK, I would estimate a few dozen) left the Netherlands to go to the UK. Before we continue it is important to establish the fact that these Salafi Muslims were not the only Dutch Muslims leaving the Netherlands for the UK. Somali Muslims have migrated to the UK in particularly large numbers, not only from the Netherlands but also from other European countries as well. The motives for this migration were similar to those expressed by other Dutch Muslims I have spoken to in the UK, including Abu Bashir. I will, therefore, briefly highlight these based on research by van Liempt (2011a; 2011b) and van Heelsum (2011).

Van Liempt (2011a) and van Heelsum (2011) both note that around 2000 it became clear that large numbers of Somali Europeans were relocating within the European Union (EU), many of them from the continent to the UK, ending up in cities such as Bristol, Liverpool, Sheffield, Birmingham, and Leicester. This internal relocation within the EU consisted of about 10,000–20,000 people, as is estimated by several researchers, although no reliable statistics exist. According to research by van Liempt (2011b), the reasons Dutch Somalis moved to the UK included job and career opportunities, the changing political climate after 9/11, the fact that many had already made plans to move to the UK, and the idea that the Netherlands had never been the final destination in the first place. In many of these narratives, arguments are put forward about never being accepted as more than allochthonous (a categorization that in practice denotes black non-Western immigrants and their descendants, including Muslims), having fewer opportunities on the labor market, and the rapidly changing political environment in the Netherlands, with growing anti-Muslim sentiments contradicting their initial idea of the Netherlands as a tolerant country (Van Liempt 2011ab). As van Liempt notes, a combination of the expectation of more economic opportunities in the UK and an environment expected to be more tolerant to people expressing their religious and ethnic affiliations is at the heart of many relocation narratives (Van Liempt 2011a). Van Heelsum (2011) suggests that the desire to live in a relatively closed community of family and clan members might also have contributed to why so many Dutch Somalis located to the UK, although this point is made somewhat complicated by the fact that many of them went to Birmingham and Leicester—cities with very small Somali communities initially.

In my talks with Abu Bashir and other Dutch Salafi Muslims in the UK, as well as Dutch Somalis in the UK, I encountered similar narratives. There was a very strong view that the UK would provide more economic opportunities, more religious freedom, and greater chances of being accepted and being able to lead a life "the Muslim way" (see also Van Liempt 2011b: 575). In a few other cases the men I interviewed had married a woman who was already living in the UK or a Middle Eastern woman who was not allowed into the

Netherlands but who could get married and live in the UK. The latter was important for Abu Bashir as well: he married a woman whose family already lived in the UK.

Abu Bashir regards his move from the Netherlands to the UK as part of *hijra*; for him a complete *hijra* would entail a migration to an Islamic country, preferably Saudi Arabia. This is still an option in the future, but for now he chooses to live in the UK. As such this partial *hijra* can be seen, I suggest, as part of what Abu Bashir regards as both being and becoming a "true" Muslim. Conversion, or "reversion" in Abu Bashir's terms, refers then both to a status (to which he seldom refers to) as well as a dual process of becoming by returning to an authentic spiritual essence and moving forward to a more Islamic life in a more Islamic environment.

When he first moved to the UK he had several jobs, but after a year he started working as a teacher in two *madrassas*, including one of the British Salafi circles, and a Salafi bookshop. He had to leave the latter job, as it did not pay well enough: the shop was hardly making a profit and could not afford him, he said.

Abu Bashir's memory of the Netherlands and his current experiences in the UK show he has mixed feelings about both countries. According to Abu Bashir, Islam is restricted in the Netherlands. "This could happen in the UK as well but until now it is much easier to be a Muslim in the UK." He also says that many things in the UK are much worse compared to the Netherlands: it is dirty. In fact, one of the first things he asked me when we walked up to his house during our first meeting, is: "So, what is your first impression of [this area] except that it is dirty?" Abu Bashir was and still is concerned that "things will go into the same direction as the Netherlands, maybe not in 10 years, but in 20 years maybe. In the Netherlands, Muslims have to do a lot of things that go beyond the law, and if they don't do the law is adjusted. This is what Islam says as well: if more people will practice Islam, there will be more persecution."

Although other interlocutors also noted that racism in the UK can be much tougher than in the Netherlands, they also feel more protected and less judged. As Abu Bashir states: "Here you can be Muslim." Furthermore, Abu Bashir notes that as someone "who looks Muslim" he is able to blend in more in the migrant area where he lives, as it is dominated by Pakistani and Somali Muslims, which I have noticed as well when observing the streets in that area after Friday prayer. The fact that Abu Bashir is white apparently does not negate his experience of blending in.

Yet in the UK he misses the Dutch food—slices of meat, cheese, and so on. According to him, the quality of bread, houses, and public services is much lower compared to the Netherlands. Abu Bashir still keeps in contact with the Netherlands, especially with his family and some fellow Salafi "brothers and sisters," saying that he still identifies himself as Dutch. He still follows the Dutch Islam debates but also watched the abdication of Queen Beatrix, which he in fact heard about before I did when I was visiting him:

AB: Hi Martijn, did you hear the news?
M: What happened?
AB: Beatrix is going to leave as queen.
M: When did that news break?
AB: An hour ago or something.

If the Netherlands had more space for religion, he would go back this instant. But some issues are now dealt with so hypocritically in the Netherlands, he said, for example, polygamy: "You can have several girlfriends, mistresses and so on, but an official marriage? No that is not an option."

Interviews and internet chats with Abu Bashir and several other Dutch Muslims from the Salafi circles and a few Somali Dutch Muslims who migrated to the UK indicate that they consider living in the UK to be "easier," which for them appears to mean that they feel they are less scrutinized compared to in the Netherlands. Living in cities such as Birmingham, Manchester, or Leicester, where many more migrants from similar backgrounds reside, they feel less targeted or under surveillance as "Muslims," "radicals," "foreigners," and "allochthonous" than they did in the Netherlands, where they experienced both a lack of recognition and the prospect of being treated forever as foreigners.

In his conversations with me, Abu Bashir equals being Muslim with being categorized as an outsider: "When people know you are a Muslim, you are regarded as outsider. Only sometimes my skin tone confuses people." For Abu Bashir, his conversion appears to disrupt his whiteness in the eyes of other people but does not completely erase it. Also, in the migrant area he lives in, his identification as a Muslim goes unquestioned most of the time, even when he is categorized as white by other Muslims, according to him. Yet, it is his skin color that makes people ask where he comes from. As soon as he then replies he is from the Netherlands, he is categorized as a convert, he told me. He tries to resist such categorization by saying: "I'm a Muslim for more than 25 years now. How long do I remain a convert"?

Furthermore, Abu Bashir makes a distinction between past and present. In the past, according to him, people asked all kinds of questions about Islam. They still do, but things have changed at the same time: "In the Netherlands people are very suspicious. In the past people asked you all kinds of questions about Islam, but that was because they were curious. Nowadays you have to answer for everything and people distrust you." The regime of surveillance is not something that pertains only to public debates, policies, and security measures; it trickles down into people's daily lives as they experience being interrogated and treated with suspicion. In response, Abu Bashir appears to be trying to create a space where he is less affected by the processes of categorization that he experiences as being based on hostile definitions of Islam. In almost all accounts given by Dutch Salafis in the UK, the pressure of being categorized and held accountable (by non-Muslims and Muslims) was mentioned as either one of the reasons for migrating or (more often) as the main difference between the Netherlands and the UK. Nevertheless, Salafi Muslims who are associated with sympathizing (or engaging in) armed struggle are very aware of the fact that they are under counterterrorism surveillance, an experience that they find much more intrusive than anything they experienced in the Netherlands. For most of them, however, their lives are spent in relatively isolated neighborhoods in London, Manchester, and Birmingham, which appears to shield them from the situations they experienced in the Netherlands.

Because Abu Bashir was known in the Netherlands among a small public as being associated with one of the Salafi circles in the south, he became involved in the intra-Salafi debates. Ideological differences and personal issues that arose because of, and during, these debates often resulted in fragmenting the existing circles Abu Bashir was working in. In 2002, 2006, 2010, 2012, and 2014 the networks (already the smallest faction among the Dutch Salafis, consisting of just a few hundred people) split into about six much smaller networks that today contain less than a few dozen people.

For Abu Bashir these intra-Salafi politics were a burden, as even a minor dispute or the minor misbehavior (or what was regarded as such) of one preacher led to fragmentation, accusations (which often surfaced outside the networks as other Salafi networks made them public), and broken friendships: "People got hurt." Nevertheless, he also contributed to these debates himself by his release of the blacklist.

It was difficult in the UK too because his reputation in the Netherlands followed him: other Dutch Salafi Muslims noticed him, he said, which resulted in rumors and gossip about him not living in the correct way of the Salaf. Other "brothers" warned against him. After a while he moved to another city in the UK because he expected it would be easier to find a job and also because it would allow him to hide particular aspects of his past that he feared would create all kinds of expectations among people he worked with:

"Here no one knows who I am, that I studied in Medina. If they do know, they immediately expect things from you such as teaching. I prefer people not to know." After some time he found a job as a youth worker while also teaching young children to learn Arabic and the Qur'an: "They pay well and they are not affiliated with other organizations." He also noticed that the same fragmentation of the Salafis also occurs in the UK, but he said that he does not meddle, as he does not want to be involved: "It is one of the reasons I left the Netherlands. Tell me, what good does it do? I'm all done with it, that whole mess."

CONCLUSION: SOME NOTES ON THE POLITICS OF OPACITY

The intersection of Islamophobia, secularism, securitization, and counter-radicalization produces the hypervisibility of so-called Salafi Muslims (the label itself is actually part of the surveillance regime) who are regarded as a threat to national security, social cohesion, and the integration of Muslims. But the hypervisibility that Abu Bashir tries to evade is not only the "gaze" of the state and the media but also the intra-Salafi debates about what constitutes the correct Islam and a good preacher. We often tend to forget that the Muslim publics they aim at are as much a part of the wider public sphere as the media is, for example. And yet intra-Salafi disputes get their dynamics from the wider debate on Salafism as we saw with the blacklist, which was partly developed as a response to the "bad preachers" who gave Salafism a bad name. Here the different dimensions of visibility overlap: Islam in public (with its focus on Islam as a security topic), the hypervisibility of Salafism (as the main threat and object of counter-radicalization policies), the regime of surveillance (pertaining to the question for Salafi preachers of how they engage with the public debates on Islam, if at all), and the disruption of whiteness (regarding himself as an outsider in the Netherlands but relatively unmarked in the migrant areas in the UK). These are fueled and informed by the actions and statements of preachers and other individuals who (heavily contested by others) claim to follow the Salafi *manhaj*.

This hypervisibility leads to some Salafi preachers, such as Abu Bashir, engaging in what Brent Crosson (2014) has called a politics of opacity, where the individual is constantly playing between degrees of visibility and invisibility in front of different publics. With Abu Bashir living in two geographical contexts and with different modes of opacity enabled and, in themselves, made necessary by the hypervisibility of Islam, we may revisit (as Brent Crosson argues) the assumption that visibility is necessarily equated with power and recognition and that invisibility is the opposite of that. Abu Bashir's story provides us with some insight into how individuals deliberate on how they are interpellated, how they can position themselves, and the consequences of the politics of opacity for people's everyday lives.

Of course, with regard to Islam the whole debate on the public visibility of religion in general and Islam in particular plays a role. In the Netherlands these debates are often discussed against the background of a diminishing pillarization of Christian denominations (and therefore a waning of the public role of religion) that coincided, or was followed by, the emergence of a visible Islam in a largely secularized country. It is this context through which Abu Bashir has tried, in different ways, to navigate his (in)visibilities. His reasoning is informed by both moral and practical reasoning and taking into account the secular sensitivities about Islam in public, as well as different voices and opinions about what makes a good Muslim and an authoritative preacher among the various Muslim publics. His move to the UK, mainly for reasons of marriage, has not shielded him from intra-Salafi politics.

He had to make a conscious decision not to disclose his past as a student in Medina and to stay away from Salafi organizations so that he would not be subjected to intra-Salafi debates in the UK and the Netherlands. Abu Bashir's case teaches us how an individual is able to make use of degrees of visibility and invisibility to enhance his authority as a Muslim on the correct path—without making himself too vulnerable to public attack. An appreciation of Abu Bashir's use of the politics of opacity, therefore, is important if we are to understand the agentic possibilities that individuals have when situations in which they are subjected to racialized and securitized public scrutiny, as well as the intra-Salafi gaze pertaining to the "correct" Islam, seem almost inescapable and all-encompassing.

NOTES

1. This research is part of the project "Forces That Bind and/or Divide," a project of the Department of Cultural Anthropology at the University of Amsterdam (funded by the NWO program Religion in Modern Societies) and part of the project Identity, Lifestyles, and Memories of the Department of Islam Studies at the Radboud University Nijmegen. My conversations with Abu Bashir have taken place in the Netherlands and the UK between 2010 and 2018: three formal interviews, thirteen informal conversations, and ongoing conversations on Telegram and WhatsApp.

2. The next three paragraphs are taken from de Koning (2012b).

3. De Volkskrant, "Preek of Propaganda," May 14, 2003. www.volkskrant.nl/buitenland/preek-of-propaganda~a727271.

REFERENCES

Adraoui, M-A. 2009. "Salafism in France: Ideology, Practices, and Contradictions." In *Global Salafism. Islam's New Religious Movement.* R. Meijer, ed. London: Hurst. 364–384.

Amghar, S. 2007. "Salafism and Radicalisation of Young European Muslims." In *European Islam: The Challenges for Society and Public Policy.* S. Amghar, A. Boubekeur, and M. Emerson, eds. Brussels: Centre for European Policy Studies. 38–51.

Amiraux, V. "Visibility, Transparency, and Gossip: How Did the Religion of Some (Muslims) Become the Public Concern of Others?" *Critical Research on Religion* 4, no. 1: 37–56.

Bracke, S. 2013. "Transformations of the Secular and the 'Muslim Question': Revisiting the Historical Coincidence of Depillarization and the Institutionalization of Islam in the Netherlands." *Journal of Muslims in Europe* 2, no. 2: 208–226.

Cesari, J. 2009. *The Securitisation of Islam in Europe.* Paris: CEPS.

Croft, S. 2012. *Securitizing Islam: Identity and the Search for Security.* Cambridge: Cambridge University Press.

Dumbe, Y., and A. Tayob. 2011. "Salafis in Cape Town in Search of Purity, Certainty, and Social Impact." *Die Welt Des Islams* 51, no. 2: 188–209.

Edmunds, J. 2012. "The 'New' Barbarians: Governmentality, Securitization, and Islam in Western Europe." *Contemporary Islam* 6, no. 1: 67–84.

Fekete, L. 2004. "Anti-Muslim Racism and the European Security State." *Race & Class* 46, no. 1: 3–29.

Gauvain, R. 2012. *Salafi Ritual Purity: In the Presence of God.* London: Routledge.

Geelhoed, F. 2011. *Purification and Resistance: Global Meanings of Islamic Fundamentalism in the Netherlands.* Rotterdam: Erasmus Universiteit.

De Graaf, B. 2012. "Religion Bites: Religieuze Orthodoxie Op De Nationale Veiligheidsagenda." *Tijdschrift Voor Religie En Samenleving* 2, no. 2: 62–81.

Hamid, S. 2009. "The Attraction of 'Authentic Islam': Salafism and British Muslim Youth." In *Global Salafism: Islam's New Religious Movement.* R. Meijer, ed. London: Hurst. 384–404.

Heelsum, A. van. 2011. *Why Somalis Move? An Investigation into Migratory Processes among Somalis.* Paper for the ECAS Conference 2011 in Uppsala, Sweden, June 15–18.

de Koning, M. 2012a. "Between the Prophet and Paradise: The Salafi Struggle in the Netherlands." *Canadian Journal of Netherlandic Studies/Revue Canadienne D'études Néerlandaises (CJNS/RCÉN)* 33/34, no. 2: 17–34.

———. 2012b. "The 'Other' Political Islam: Understanding Salafi Politics." In *Whatever Happened to the Islamists? Salafis, Heavy Metal Muslims, and the Lure of Consumerist*

Islam. A. Boubekeur and O. Roy, eds. New York and London: Columbia University Press/Hurst Publishers. 153–176.

———. 2013a. "How Should I Live as a 'True' Muslim? Regimes of Living among Dutch Muslims in the Salafi Movement." *Etnofoor* 25, no. 2: 53–72.

———. 2013b. "The Moral Maze: Dutch Salafis and the Construction of a Moral Community of the Faithful." *Contemporary Islam* 7, no. 1: 71–83.

———. 2016. *De ideologische strijd tegen de islam. Fortuyns gedachtegoed en de racialisering van moslims*. Uithoorn: Karakter Uitgevers, 2016.

de Koning, M., et al. 2014. *Eilanden in een zee van ongeloof—Het verzet van de activistische da'wa in België, Nederland en Duitsland*. IMES Report Series. Nijmegen/Amsterdam: Radboud Universiteit.

Korteweg, A. C., and G. Yurdakul. 2014. *The Headscarf Debates: Conflicts of National Belonging*. Stanford: Stanford University Press.

Moosavi, L. 2015a. "The Racialization of Muslim Converts in Britain and their Experiences of Islamophobia." *Critical Sociology* 41, no. 1: 41–56.

———. 2015b. "White Privilege in the Lives of Muslim Converts in Britain." *Ethnic and Racial Studies* 38, no. 11: 1918–1933.

Lakoff, A., and J. Collier. 2004. "Ethics and the Anthropology of Modern Reason." *Anthropological Theory* 4, no. 4: 419–434.

Lentin, A., and G. Titley. 2012. "The Crisis of 'Multiculturalism' in Europe: Mediated Minarets, Intolerable Subjects." *European Journal of Cultural Studies* 15, no. 2: 123–138.

Van Liempt, I. 2011a. "'And then one day they *all* moved to Leicester': The Relocation of Somalis from the Netherlands to the UK Explained." *Population, Space and Place* 17, no. 3: 254–266.

———. 2011b. "From Dutch Dispersal to Ethnic Enclaves in the UK: The Relationship between Segregation and Integration Examined through the Eyes of Somalis." *Urban Studies* 48, no. 16: 3385–3398.

Luckmann, T. 1967. *The Invisible Religion: The Problem of Religion in Modern Society*. New York and London: Macmillan.

Mavelli, L. 2013. "Between Normalisation and Exception: The Securitisation of Islam and the Construction of the Secular Subject." *Millennium—Journal of International Studies* 41, no. 2: 159–181.

Monnot, C. 2016. "Visibility or Invisibility: The Dilemma of the Muslim Associations of Switzerland." *Journal of Religion in Europe* 9, no. 1: 44–65.

Moors, A. 2009. "The Dutch and the Face-Veil: The Politics of Discomfort." *Social Anthropology* 17, no. 4: 393–408.

Moors, H., and M. Jacobs. 2009. *Aan de hand van de imam. Integratie en participatie van orthodoxe moslims in Tilburg- Noord*. Tilburg: IVA.

Özyürek, E. 2015. *Being German, Becoming Muslim: Race, Religion, and Conversion in the New Europe*. Princeton: Princeton University Press.

Reddy, M. T. 1998. "Invisibility/Hypervisibility: The Paradox of Normative Whiteness." *Transformations: The Journal of Inclusive Scholarship and Pedagogy* 9, no. 2: 55–64.

Roberts, D. D., et al. 2008. "The Invisible Work of Managing Visibility for Social Change:

Insights from the Leadership of Reverend Dr. Martin Luther King Jr." *Business & Society* 47, no. 4: 425–456.

Rogozen-Soltar, M. 2012. "Managing Muslim Visibility: Conversion, Immigration, and Spanish Imaginaries of Islam." *American Anthropologist* 114, no. 4: 611–623.

Salvatore, A. 2004. "Making Public Space: Opportunities and Limits of Collective Action among Muslims in Europe." *Journal of Ethnic and Migration Studies* 30, no. 5: 1013–1031.

Schielke, S. 2010. "Second Thoughts about the Anthropology of Islam, or How to Make Sense of Grand Schemes in Everyday Life." *ZMO Working Papers*, vol. 2.

Sedgwick, M. 2012. "Introduction: Salafism, the Social, and the Global Resurgence of Religion." *Comparative Islamic Studies* 8, no. 1: 57–70.

Tebble, A. J. 2006. "Exclusion for Democracy." *Political Theory* 34, no. 4: 463–487.

Tourage, M. 2013. "Performing Belief and Reviving Islam: Prominent (White Male) Converts in Muslim Revival Conventions." *Performing Islam* 1, no. 2: 207–226.

Van der Veer, P. 2006. "Pim Fortuyn, Theo Van Gogh, and the Politics of Tolerance in the Netherlands." *Public Culture* 18, no. 1: 111–124.

Van Nieuwkerk, K. 2004. "'Veils and Wooden Clogs Don't Go Together.'" *Ethnos* 69, no. 2: 229–246.

Vliegenthart, Rens. 2007. *Framing Immigration and Integration: Facts, Parliament, Media, and Anti-Immigrant Party Support in the Netherlands.* Amsterdam: Vrije Universiteit Amsterdam.

Vroon, V. 2014. "Sisters in Islam: Women's Conversion and the Politics of Belonging: A Dutch Case Study." PhD thesis. University of Amsterdam.

Yancy, G. 2008. *Black Bodies, White Gazes: The Continuing Significance of Race.* Boulder: Rowman & Littlefield.

SECTION IV

NARRATIVES AND EXPERIENCES OF MOVING OUT OF ISLAM

ELEVEN

BRITISH MUSLIM CONVERTS

Comparing Conversion and Deconversion Processes to and from Islam

MONA ALYEDREESSY

In this chapter, I will explore the experiences of British converts to Islam who later on decided to leave the faith. Much research has been carried out on conversions to Islam (Köse 1994; Al-Qwidi 2002; Van Nieuwkerk 2006; Zebiri 2007; Brice 2010; Moosavi 2011; Neumueller 2012; Suleiman 2013), and some research has been conducted on Muslim apostates (Griffel 2008; March 2010; Cottee 2015; see also Cottee, this volume). But little attention has been paid to the social challenges British Muslim converts face when they decide to leave Islam.

Britons' conversion to Islam has been well known since the nineteenth century, when Abdullah Quilliam founded Britain's first mosque in Liverpool. Despite Islam's poor reputation in the media after 9/11 and 7/7 and the spread of Islamophobia, conversion to Islam has become statistically significant only in recent years (Brice 2010).[1]

Nevertheless, recent reports (such as Raiyaan 2012) and case studies found on the Solace website[2] show an increase in the numbers of Muslim converts who have decided to leave the faith. Usama Hasan, a part-time imam and senior researcher at the Quilliam Foundation, an antiextremist think tank, has said that "many converts leave the faith. We don't have exact statistics but some stats say fifty per cent will leave within a few years" (Shahid 2013). Numerous reports within the foundation claim that a high number of individuals who chose to deconvert had cited religious doubts, bad experiences with Muslims, and the lack of community support as their main reasons for doing so (Shahid 2013).

Having conducted a PhD study of British Muslim converts between 2012 and 2015, I became aware of the variety of challenges many interlocutors experience that may lead to deconversion from a former faith group, conversion to Islam, and then deconversion from Islam. I will compare both conversion and deconversion journeys in order to discover if there are any shared crises and experiences that occur in individuals' lives that compel them to search for a solution in Islam or to abandon Islam if their crises increased, worsened, or remained unsolved.

The aim of this chapter is to explore the narratives of five converts among the thirty-four participants I have interviewed. They had converted to Islam hoping that it would provide solutions to their problems, but they later deconverted as a result of failed expectations. Each conversion and deconversion journey is unique, so it is important to recognize the processes as variable phenomena. The time it takes someone to convert varies alongside crises, context, social matrix, motives, personal needs, and aspirations. In this chapter, conversion will be looked at as stages of identity transformation and will be studied from the participants' own personal perspectives to provide a better understanding of their experiences and points of view, including the emotional, psychological, and social implications of religious conversion and deconversion. I will compare the crises, elements, motives, turning points, differences, and similarities found in the conversion and deconversion stages and processes.

CONVERSION AND DECONVERSION PROCESSES

Contemporary studies have explored conversion in sociological terms, reflected in the theoretical contributions of Lewis Rambo and Charles Farhadian (1999; 2005), who claim that "conversion" is the term for all forms of religious change, whether physical, mental, psychological, emotional, or intellectual. Rambo (1993) examined a variety of theories and disciplines—including religious studies, psychology, and missiology—to establish why people convert. Conversion is perceived by him as a problem-solving solution, and he attempts to understand the types of crises and problems that contribute to the decision to convert. Rambo created a framework of seven interlinked conversion stages to explain his theory, although he acknowledged the vast differences between individual cases when it came to experiences, influences, and decision-making processes: (1) context; (2) crisis; (3) quest; (4) encounter; (5) interaction; (6) committing; and (7) consequences. Sociologists such as Henri Gooren (2010) perceived conversion to be a "career" and reckoned that the "disaffiliation" stage is important to analyze, as it illustrates that conversion is not always a positive experience. In this chapter I will use Rambo's stage model and will consider "disaffiliation" to be part of the "consequences" stage.

I will further use Helen Ebaugh's (1988) study of ex-nuns to analyze the causes and processes of deconversion from Islam. She explores the general process of "role-exit," defining it as "the process of disengagement from a role that is central to one's self-identity and the reestablishment of an identity in a new role that takes into account one's ex-role" (1988: 1). Ebaugh created four distinct stages to analyze the pattern of role-exit in which individuals begin to question their role commitment. The stages are: (1) first doubts; (2) seeking and weighing role alternatives; (3) a turning point; and (4) establishing an ex-role identity. The first stage involves the experiences of general dissatisfaction with individuals' present lifestyles that stems from previous crises, events, and turning points that lead them to have intellectual doubts. In the second stage they admit dissatisfaction with their role and search for alternatives. The third stage—the "turning point"—is where they realize they cannot continue to occupy their current role. The fourth stage involves creating a new role and/or adapting to an ex-role. Both Rambo's and Ebaugh's frameworks include crises and turning points as major influences behind the decision to convert and deconvert.

The interconnectedness and flexibility of the stages make both frameworks suitable to use. Each stage sets the appropriate foundation for the next, so that they link together as a collection of life experiences that individuals encounter during their childhood, adolescence, and adulthood development periods.

Conversion: Context

Lauren, a 29-year-old white English woman, was raised in a nonreligious, single-parent household. But being Christian was part of her identity, as she came from an area where religion is more of an ethnic/cultural identity than a belief. Even so, Lauren had held strong beliefs in God since she was a child, though she was not a practicing Christian. Janet, a 32-year-old white English woman, was raised in a nonpracticing Christian household and witnessed the period when her parents became atheists as a result of not being able to cope with their hardships and doubting the existence of God because of global crises. For Janet, being Christian merely meant being a part of a community, as she was not raised to have any religious beliefs or values. Luke, a 39-year-old black Caribbean man living in the UK, was raised by an atheist father and a religious Christian mother, which created confusions that encouraged him to question religious beliefs and God while growing up. Mark, a 34-year-old white Englishman who had been raised by a religious Italian mother, believed in God and Jesus, but he did not believe in the concept of heaven, hell, angels, and devils. Lina, a 37-year-old white English woman, was the only participant out of the five who had been raised in a religiously committed Christian household. As she grew older she became a Sunday school teacher and claimed that her parents had raised her to have excellent Christian morals and deep religious beliefs.

Crisis

Various scholars (Rambo 1993; Erikson 1968; Wohlrab-Sahr 2006) have suggested that individuals experience crises during the early stages of their conversion journeys, crises that trigger the search for problem-solving solutions within a religious context. These might come after they exhaust other potential solutions or represent their first and only solution. Crises usually range from religious doubts and questioning the purpose of life to being abused and experiencing the illness or death of a loved one.

Lauren said, "I believed in God very strongly as a young adolescent.... It helped me cope with the emotional and psychological problems that were caused by my upbringing." She had held suicidal thoughts because she had been emotionally and physically abused throughout her childhood by her father, who was an alcoholic. She was also troubled as a result of her parents' divorce and thus blamed them for her crises and also claimed to have had an existential crisis in high school that depressed her, so she began questioning the meaning and purpose of life. She went on to say, "I was extremely depressed and felt unloved and all alone in the world.... I decided that God had to guide me to what was 'right.' I began to read up on the monotheistic [Abrahamic] religions and the '*tawheed*' or monotheism in Islam was very attractive from my point of view.... I desperately needed God." Seeking a spiritual connection with God or His help has been a way in which many individuals have dealt with crises, as it may improve self-esteem.

Lina had an intellectual crisis after attending a public Islamic awareness event and reading a book about the science of the Qur'an, which made her doubt her Christian beliefs. Experiencing religious doubts may be very distressing because it causes individuals to question what they had been raised to believe in. She began to suffer from anxiety and worried about her fate in the afterlife. For Lina, a logical and intellectual belief system with a clear guide that encourages morality and a connection with one's inner spirituality and one God was attractive, as she felt that it extended and emphasized the moral values and beliefs she already possessed. Janet also doubted her Christian beliefs regarding Jesus as God when she was in high school after learning about Islam and making Muslim friends. This caused an intellectual and emotional crisis, as she was unable to obtain any logical answers to her questions from her parents and other Christians. Presenting religious practices as a part of

British culture confused many of the participants when they were growing up, especially if the parents did not believe in God or follow religious rules but nevertheless attended church services at Christmas and Easter.

Mark and Luke both experienced major emotional crises linked to family illnesses and deaths that they blamed on God. Experiencing depression from the loss of a loved one during adolescence raises questions about the purpose of life, especially when the deceased has a religious burial. The significance of religion in an individual's burial encouraged Mark, who attended his grandmother's Christian funeral, to think more deeply about the meaning of life, death, and what happens after death within a religious context.

Luke also had a troubled adolescence because his younger brother died in a car accident, which caused him to lose faith in God's mercy:

> When he didn't get better and died I was disappointed with God. I felt deep resentment towards God and stopped believing in Him. My mother didn't lose her faith. . . . In fact her visits to the church became more frequent but I decided to become an atheist like my dad, as I felt that God had rejected my prayers or just simply didn't exist.

These crises and their aftermath accord with findings by Lofland and Skonovd (1981), who state that emotional stress arising from the death of close kith and kin and other major personal problems often lead to a search for logical answers and encourages some people—especially those who were raised in religious households or held previous beliefs in God—to explore other religious beliefs.

Quest

The challenge of the quest stage is to reach a place that helps active seekers transform the anger, confusions, anxiety, depression, and other negative emotions into hope, comfort, and peace. For this to happen, they must be certain that what they are aiming toward is something positive that will benefit their lives.

Mark, Lauren, and Janet were active seekers who attempted to find answers in religion by researching the purpose of life within various theologies. Mark said:

> I made it my mission to learn about different religions during and after my years at university. I had an urge to speak to all my colleagues at work

> who were from different religions and [had] open discussions about them. I sat with Sikhs, Muslims and one Jewish guy and we debated about God and the afterlife.

Studying and observing different religious groups helped some individuals to make the decision to convert to Islam as they identified the theology that suited them best alongside important problem-solving elements found in the faith they believed to be missing in their lives, such as personal and social discipline, life goals, community, logical reasoning regarding the purpose of life, and/or spirituality. Islamic ethics and lifestyles also appealed to Lauren and Janet, who felt they needed moral and spiritual guidance as they wanted a way of life to commit to. Some do not feel comfortable living in a society where "everything is allowed." A lifestyle with clear guidance that encourages an ethical code and a connection with one's inner spirituality can be attractive to people who wish to follow clear moral guidelines.

Encounter and interaction

Unlike the others, Lina and Luke were non–active seekers and had come across Islam and Muslims at university and public events. Lina did not initially experience a significant crisis but, later, experienced an intellectual crisis when she began to develop religious doubts after learning about Islamic teachings during her time studying religious theologies at university and at work, where she interacted with Muslims for the first time. She said, "Being a religious person I was naturally curious about other religions and what they believed in." It wasn't until later in her life, after she had had her first baby, that she became an active seeker and developed a deeper interest in Islam, believing it was more logical and simpler than other religious beliefs. Luke learned about the fundamental teachings of Islam from kind missionaries who offered him books and other types of literature about the faith and invited him to attend an Islamic awareness open day, after which he became an active seeker and pursued his interest in Islamic teachings. "I was warmly greeted by Muslims at the event and they offered tea, drinks and cakes to the visitors. They were really well mannered in how they discussed religious subjects."

Since 9/11, British Muslim organizations have made an effort to educate and change the public's understanding of Islam by portraying it in a more positive way by hosting Islamic awareness events, such as Islam Expo and the Global Peace and Unity event, to tackle media stereotypes and negative portrayals of Muslims. Luke kept in contact with the man who told him about lectures and debates about God he was keen to attend.

Mark, Lina, and Luke become inspired to learn about religions and Islam from interacting with Muslims they met or knew and who recommended Islamic books, websites, YouTube lectures, and university talks. Janet and Lauren, however, who did not know any Muslims personally, felt comfortable meeting them via social media networks and online discussion forums to inquire about their faith. Janet said, "My husband was always expressing his concerns at how 'obsessed I was getting over it all' and we used to argue because I would always be online researching and reading [about Islam]." Lauren also took it upon herself to learn about Islam independently from a young age and said, "I was like a sponge, I just memorized and processed every single information of Islam I got my hands on. I knew more about the *hadiths* and chapters of the Quran than people who had been religious Muslims their whole life."

The five participants had all spent some time observing Islamic practices, such as the Friday prayers, to learn the customs and to obtain an idea of what kind of life they would lead and what would be expected of them. The experimental element of the conversion journey also often appears within the interaction stage, as individuals communicate with and befriend Muslims, many of whom encourage them to experience the spiritual phenomenon found in religious practices, such as fasting the month of Ramadan and wearing a *hijab*, before making a final decision to convert. Lauren mentioned that she had tried wearing the *hijab* for a week and enjoyed the confidence it gave her as a woman. "There was something special about it."

Committing: The Shahadah

The five individuals had all taken their *shahadah* (the Muslim testimony of faith) in a mosque or in front of other Muslims. Juliette Galonnier (this volume) states that the recitation of the *shahadah* is usually considered to be the rite of passage that marks one's entry into Islam. Under this conceptualization, the conversion moment is expected to be precisely situated in time, with a clear date of record, marking a discontinuity between a "before" and an "after." The *shahadah* ceremony is powerful for many individuals: not only does it provide a profound transformation for their experience of the conversion process; it also provides a means by which to consolidate their beliefs and involvement in a faith group. The decision to become a Muslim often signifies individuals' desire to take on the worship and moral obligations of membership, which they believe is necessary on the path to spiritual transformation. The ceremony is celebrated by local Muslims who shower the new Muslims with hugs, embraces, and small gifts, such as a prayer mat, head scarf, and Islamic books. All five participants had taken their *shahadah* in a local mosque or among Muslim friends and had perceived it to be a major turning point in their lives.

Lauren felt greatly welcomed by Salafi Muslims in the mosque, as they embraced her and showered her with attention. Luke also said, "He [Muslim friend] met up with me, took me to his local mosque where people greeted me warmly and offered their help and support.... I was overwhelmed by the number of people who came to hug me and congratulate me. I felt excited and happy to be a part of this community." Mark had expressed his interest in Islam to a Sufi Muslim imam who held a small interview with him first to make sure that he was willing to commit to Islam. "The process of converting was surprisingly easy, I just had to take my *shahadah* with two witnesses and that was it. Some other people were there and they congratulated me on my conversion. It was a nice day."

Janet said, "I went to a local mosque and asked them how I can convert. The secretary told me I would need to come and take my *shahadah* in front of people, get a conversion certificate, take a bath afterwards and then change my name!" At the time, Janet was not ready for such a change, but she was told later by a Muslim she met that as long as she believed in her heart that there is one God and that Muhammad is His messenger then she was already a Muslim. She declared her testimony of faith later on in a mosque among Muslims she met in order to make her conversion more official and "authentic." Lina's conversion ceremony was also low-key; she declared the *shahadah* in front of a few Muslim friends and the imam.

Committing: "Coming out" and being a Muslim

The element of surrender in the commitment stage requires an individual to give up various habits for the benefits of the new faith (Rambo 1993: 134). However, some may not feel ready to give up certain things straight away for the sake of complying with religious rules and the moral requirements of the new community, such as drinking alcohol or giving up a boyfriend or girlfriend. Therefore, some do not like to declare their conversion in public, to avoid being pressured by practicing Muslims into things they are not ready for. They may also feel the need to move away from the Muslim community and to keep a low profile and avoid being unfairly judged by others.

Lauren was very keen to start practicing straight away and was happy to wear the *hijab* and even the *burqa* as a way of expressing her commitment to the new faith, but in order to do this she had to cut ties with her family, who could not accept her new beliefs and Muslim dress. She also started praying and fasting on a regular basis. Lina, by contrast, was not able to wear the *hijab* around her family or in her non-Muslim community, as a result of being a victim of Islamophobic verbal abuse, but she would happily wear it when being in the safe company of Muslims in Muslim communities. "I had some English neighbors who would call me a Paki and I would get eggs thrown at my window, which was very distressing." The term "Paki" is as offensive as the word "nigger" and has been linked to racist abuse for many years (Bhatia 2007). Lina felt that those who attacked her perceived her to be a traitor and that she was being punished for wanting to belong to a "dangerous" foreign community linked to terrorism and the likes of ISIS and Al-Qaeda. She mentioned how her children have also been affected negatively by her conversion and were confused about their identities, as the white kids at school teased them for having a "Paki" mum because she wore a *hijab*. "My daughters hated it and refused to go out with me when I wore it, they found it very embarrassing. Raising my daughters to be good Muslims was just too hard a task and a burden for me." It took her a while to learn the prayers and start praying all five of them regularly.

Janet suffered the most during the commitment stage, as she was told by Muslims that she could no longer be married to a non-Muslim man if she wanted to be a "good Muslim." She had many arguments and problems with her husband at the time, as she was interested in Islam whereas he was not, and their differences in beliefs had created a distance between them in their marital relationship. As a result, Janet decided to separate from him in order to be able to live a proper Islamic lifestyle among other Muslims, which also caused her to have problems with her family. She said, "I must say getting a divorce was the biggest sacrifice I made for Islam." She was also pressured by heritage Muslims—that is, people born and raised as Muslims by ethnic Muslim parents—to find a Muslim husband, to start wearing the *hijab* straight away, and to change her name to a Muslim name. However, after she did so she was abandoned by them and was left alone to figure out Islam for herself and had to teach herself how to perform rituals such as *wudu'* (washing for prayers). This created a new crisis in her life, as she began to suffer from anxiety and loneliness. Mark did not make any significant changes in his life when he committed to Islam, such as changing his name and wearing Muslim clothing, and started practicing in a low-key manner gradually over time by praying in quiet areas and by abandoning fundamental things that were forbidden, such as eating pork. Luke had a similar experience, but he never told his family about his conversion and was able to attend Islamic classes and pray properly only when he visited the mosque in the nearest local Muslim community.

As Rambo (1993) has suggested, the main challenge of the commitment stage is "coming out" to others as a Muslim, establishing a new identity, and surrendering to the laws of the faith. The attitudes converts tend to experience from their families often seem to reflect the current attitudes of the society they live in. As a result, their conversion may have negative impacts on their most meaningful relationships and result in, for instance, disownment, as Lauren experienced, or divorce, as Janet experienced, as her husband could not accept her conversion to Islam.

Mark and Luke chose to not inform their friends and family of their conversion to avoid any negative consequences and confined their prayers and other practices to their bedrooms or secluded places. Lauren had also started this way but felt later that she was unable to hide her faith, as she wanted to be a "good practicing Muslim" and was compelled to "come out" to a mother who dislikes Muslims. She wrote a letter that she described as being "dramatic" to inform her mother of her conversion, as she considered this to be an easier task than having to tell her face to face. "She reacted very badly, it caused a crisis and [she] made me 'retract' my conversion." Lauren lived as a secret Muslim again for a while before coming out a second time, which is when she was forced to leave her home before turning nineteen. Lauren's mother had used Lauren's weakness of being unable to sever her ties with her siblings as an emotional tool to persuade her to abandon Islam. Her mother even blamed Lauren for the problems her siblings were having at school and did not allow her to accompany them on family trips. After many attempts to gain acceptance, however, Lauren chose to give up her family for Islam and also to avoid the emotional and psychological bullying. "That might sound crazy, but the indoctrination was so strong that Islam and God had to come first before anything else, or else you would end up in hellfire." Like others, Lauren perceived her hardships and crises that appeared in her life as a Muslim to be "tests from God."

Becoming a closeted Muslim can be challenging for many because of the religious obligations, such as the daily prayers, so some tend to move away from their previous locations to find comfortable and private environments in which they can practice freely away from negative influences and temptations. This choice usually comes with the difficulties of either sacrificing relationships with family members and friends or living a double life (see Cottee, this volume). However, some converts, such as Mark, made the effort to fit in and to keep relationship ties with loved ones by negotiating a new Muslim identity and compromising on some non-Islamic practices (e.g., socializing in pubs) even though it made them feel uncomfortable, as what was previously "normal" to him had now become "immoral." Following Islamic rules and beliefs was sometimes perceived to be a personal challenge and a disciplinary test of strength and willpower to see how well they would do in abstaining from what had become forbidden to them after becoming Muslims.

Alongside the problems, the participants faced with their families, they also experienced problems in their relationship with their new Muslim community and its members. Lauren's experience with heritage Muslims was described as being "highly frustrating":

> I early on saw the misogyny, oppression and subjugation of women amongst the Muslim community, which was even practised by the "nobler" Imams, *Shuyookh* [Sheikhs], and preachers. The culture was more oppressive than the religion seemed to be. . . . I also realized that a lot of Muslims did not "understand" or practice Islam, in the way I thought was correct and right, and some of the very devout and pious Salafi Muslims even committed crimes such as fraud and stole money through the social services etc.

On account of her literal understanding of Islam and being under the influence of more "radical" Muslim teachers, Lauren described herself as a "staunch Salafi jihadist" and a "fish out of water" during the start of her commitment stage because she felt she had taken radical steps very early on in her conversion, as a Salafi Muslim, to follow all the rules. She claimed that, despite feeling uncomfortable in a *hijab*, because it was hot in the summer and restricted her movement and freedom to eat properly, she wore it for the sake of pleasing God.

Some converts join Salafi groups because they find the lack of Muslim cultural practices in these circles appealing and believe they are following a purer form of Islam not affected by external influences (see Özyürek, this volume). However, many individuals leave these groups because the "pure forms" of seventh-century Islam in Salafism are very difficult to practice, are inflexible, or deemed to be unrealistic. Mark thought the lifestyle many Salafis want to lead does not suit Britain or the modern age. He remarked: "It's a part of human nature to adapt. I mean we can't live like eighteenth century Victorians in modern day Britain that would be absurd but that's unfortunately what a lot of Muslims are doing." All five participants found many Muslim cultural practices, attitudes, and behavior to be incompatible with Islamic and British values. Mark also claimed to have been interrogated by unwelcoming "ignorant" Salafi Muslims who suspected he was a spy (as he was new to the area). Mark learned a year after his conversion that he had converted to the

Sufi Muslim group rather than the mainstream Sunni Muslim group and had developed doubts in Islamic teachings as a result of his struggles with Sufi spiritual practices and rituals. He said, "I thought every Muslim was a Sunni Muslim." He claimed, for example, to feel uncomfortable with the "loud and exhausting" chanting of God's names, which made him feel that he belonged to a cult, as the practices were becoming "weirder" and more cult-like the more members advanced in their spirituality levels.

Luke mentioned how he found it very difficult to wake up for the *fajr* prayer (the first of the five daily prayers, performed at dawn) and complained about poor Islamic classes run for new Muslims in the local mosque and imams who did not take into consideration people from other ethnicities, as their talks and sermons were given in Urdu rather than English. He also had no luck finding a Muslim spouse and felt Muslims discriminated against him for having *kafir* (non-Muslim) parents and family members, alongside the fact of being a black convert, which was perceived to be a social disadvantage. He believed this attitude to be against Islamic teachings and thought the Muslims he met did not implement Islamic values or manners into their lives and did not practice what they preached. "Hypocrisy" and "contradictory behavior" adopted by heritage Muslims was one of the main causes that drove these five individuals away from Islam.

Consequences: Deconversion

The various forms of hardships, crises, and negative social consequences these converts faced after conversion triggered the deconversion process from Islam. The social context and circumstances linked to deconversion are very important in determining how and when individuals decide to take the difficult decision to deconvert from Islam, as this may be perceived as an act of treachery. Leaving a religion can be so socially challenging that it may make some hide the fact they no longer share the same beliefs. Concealing the lack or loss of belief is particularly prevalent in heritage Muslim communities, as reported by the Council of Ex-Muslims of Britain, yet it may be argued that the façades that people construct in such circumstances are actually part of their identity and not necessarily hidden—from their perspective, at least. Cottee (2015) suggests that apostasy from Islam in the West among heritage Muslims is perceived by the Muslim community to be a moral issue rather than a religious or political problem that may carry stigma and various negative consequences. Fear of stigmatization is likely to encourage the majority of disaffiliates to become community disaffiliates or to conceal their beliefs, which prevents them from becoming open disaffiliates. It is therefore vital to investigate how individuals live with hidden identities and how it affects their lives and well-being.

As Ebaugh (1988) suggested, it was found that all the participants who had decided to deconvert experienced intellectual doubts as a result of the hardships they faced, whether with Muslims, society, or family, the Qur'an and *hadiths*, or on a personal level. It was found that individuals often questioned Islamic teachings when encountering problems they found difficult to deal with, such as being a wife to a strict Muslim husband or being pressured to conform to Islamic practices they did not believe in or were not ready for.

Intellectual doubts

Lauren mentioned that, in the last few years as a Muslim, Islam began to have a relatively lesser impact on her life both spiritually and intellectually until she decided to deconvert after a slow and gradual process of disaffiliation: "It became more and more obvious that the Islamic teachings discriminated towards women and went against scientific facts and truths we have about our universe." She struggled to make sense of Islamic teachings that seemed to support her husband's antifeminist views. As a result of her continuous hardships and failed attempts to connect with God and the Qur'an, she began to question His existence. Lauren felt from her own understanding of Islam that it limited her choices, since the dichotomy between *haram* (forbidden in Islam) and *halal* (permissible in Islam), alongside Islamic obligations, controlled her life and every choice she made. She also felt resentment toward Islam, as she understood that as a Muslim she could not have any social ties with her non-Muslim family and that her strict practicing of the religion made her family turn away from her:

> [Islam] basically bereft me of a lot of joyous moments in my life because your whole life had to revolve around worshiping God and thus following His commands. I lost all contact with my old friends because of my new radical lifestyle, which still has detrimental effects on my social and professional life.

Lauren, who had converted into a strict Salafi Muslim, started to change two years after her daughter's birth when she became more concerned with women's rights and feminism. The stress and pressure to be good Muslims may cause converts, women in particular, to rebel and deconvert. Janet and Lina felt they were becoming more "backward" as Muslims, as they thought the West had moved on from the limitations of gender roles that feminists had fought for over many years until women were given more rights and freedom in modern-day Western society. They felt that these rights had been taken away when they converted to Islam and married Muslims. Janet, Lina, and Lauren all criticized the Qur'an regarding their intellectual understanding of its views on gender relationships in Islam and blamed God for their suffering, as a result of being married to so-called religious and patriarchal Muslim men. These women had all claimed that their husbands had justified and manipulated many Qur'an verses and *hadiths* to suit their controlling motives, which made them feel that Muslim wives were meant to be slaves to their husbands. In general, all five participants were unable to accept some Qur'an verses and *hadiths* because they were taken out of context and went against their own Western values, ethics, principles, and beliefs. Lauren attempted to find different meanings for them to make them more acceptable so she would not be perceived as a bad Muslim for not accepting what was considered by traditional and renowned scholars to be authentic: "I couldn't hide behind 'different interpretations' anymore and I couldn't reconcile the Islamic texts with what I knew was right."

Turning points

In addition to intellectual and religious doubts, my interlocutors mentioned specific experiences they faced that triggered their final decisions to leave Islam. Mark, for example, claimed that the more he questioned "cult-like" Sufi practices, rituals, and beliefs, the more he was told that he was having "satanic thoughts," which made him question and doubt Islamic teachings. He also became confused, as Sufi teachings were different from mainstream Sunni Muslim teachings. For Janet and Lauren, losing friends and family members was one of their biggest issues, as this resulted in their isolation from those they loved. Loneliness and feeling vulnerable were two major elements that contributed toward an unhappy Muslim lifestyle for all the participants, especially if they were unable to find help and support from Muslims. Janet said:

> Ramadan came and I was virtually ignored by the women in the mosque. I would take some food each day around the time of breakfast at sunset and would eat alone in the mosque. It was the longest, loneliest month of my life.

Luke struggled to deal with the racial discrimination he experienced among heritage Muslims. He began to feel that there was nothing special about being

Muslim and that his own, non-Muslim society was more tolerant of other races than were Muslims. Mark felt his new Islamic lifestyle was too restrictive and also felt the need to leave his Muslim community to live a "normal" life among those he felt most comfortable with. Feeling alienated and in need of family drove the participants back to their former lives in which they found love, security, freedom, and social acceptance.

Lauren, like Lina and Janet, whose issues were mainly gender-related and connected to her Muslim ex-husband's patriarchal understanding of Islam, spoke about his treatment of her as a main reason why she decided to deconvert, as she felt he gradually destroyed all her ambitions, hopes, hobbies, and dreams because of the Islamic doctrine and idea of morality alongside his "dictator attitude," which stopped her from accomplishing anything in her life that was "a threat to him and his ego." She felt he had feelings of jealousy, "backward" cultural interpretations, and personal insecurities. She said, "As if it wasn't bad enough Islam already limiting my life, he made it worse by enforcing his Asian culture on me and prohibiting me from going anywhere and having to ask his permission to do anything. I found it unbearable."

Lauren abandoned her university education because of his Islamic ideas regarding gender segregation and claimed they did not have a TV set or go out with friends because, apparently, it was *haram*: "I got the impression Islam didn't want you to enjoy your life at all." She blamed her husband for portraying an awful image of Islam to herself, her family, and the public: "I regret it badly, however, I was so keen on being a good Muslim I just accepted all the Islamic texts that he somehow managed to justify in order to get his way all the time." Lauren had trusted and relied on her husband's knowledge, as she expected him, as a heritage Muslim, to know better.

According to Kevin Brice's (2010) report and Karin van Nieuwkerk's (2006) study, many women convert to Islam after being attracted to the rights and protection that Islam gives Muslim mothers, wives, daughters, and sisters, and they expect to receive those rights and protection in a marriage from a supposedly practicing Muslim man. Lina, who had also suffered greatly in a patriarchal marriage—the result of having daughters from a previous husband—said:

> His attitude ruined my life. Everything I had read about the status of Muslim women in Islam did not apply in my case. I was extremely disappointed. He didn't treat me like a Muslim husband or father should. He was extremely suffocating, for example the girls couldn't sing and dance or whistle, as it was "devilish" and he hit my eldest badly. He would even hit me if I defended them.

Some converts who adopt a Muslim female identity long for the security of marriage, a traditional nuclear family, spirituality, discipline, confidence, and self-value in their lives. However, Lina, Janet, and Lauren were disappointed to find that their Muslim husbands lacked even the basic Islamic values and claimed their husbands were physically abusive, suffocating, and had a tendency to interpret Qur'an verses and *hadiths* about male authority in a harsh manner, which made them resent God and Islam. Janet said, "I [also] found that he didn't pray all five times a day and he would sometimes swear at me and break things in the house if I refused to "obey" him. I really hated that." They came to believe that God preferred and loved men more than women by giving them authority to control and oppress women as they pleased.

Those who experienced abuse in their relationships and remained within them were reluctant to admit to their families that their lives worsened after becoming Muslims and that the men they had often previously been warned about indeed turned out to be abusive. Suleiman (2013: 53–54) found domestic abuse and patriarchy to be a problem in a Cambridge University study on female Muslim converts in Britain and claimed that women cannot escape from these relationships for various reasons, such as the lack of family support and because they do not want to be shamed in front of their families and friends.

Obtaining a divorce was one of the hardest struggles Lina had to go through, as her husband did not make the procedure easy and dragged it out for a long period of time by not answering the legal letters sent by the Islamic Sharia Council dealing with the divorce case. Janet mentioned that her (non-Muslim) ex-husband had more Islamic qualities, manners, kindness, compassion, and love for her than did her Muslim husband. What made matters worse later on was discovering that her Muslim husband had abandoned her once he received his residency visa, which she helped him get. Unlike Lina, she was able to get an Islamic divorce easily, as he no longer had any need for her. Janet said:

> I was enraged that I had given up so much to be Muslim, that I had such high expectations of being a Muslim and of the community. I sacrificed my family and no one who hadn't gone through that would understand how that felt. I was majorly depressed.

As a result of her marital problems her emotional issues had become worse rather than better. This caused her to burn her headscarves, along with pages from the Qur'an and her conversion certificate. Janet struggled to deal with the regret, the disappointment, and the reality of the loss of her time for Islam and remarked: "I didn't believe in God anymore. . . . If this is what being a Muslim is like, then I don't want Islam." Lina as well mentioned "getting rid" of material things connected to her life as a Muslim:

> The first thing I did when I announced my deconversion was put all my *hijabs*, prayer mat, Qur'an and Islamic books in black bin bags and dumped them at the local mosque. I felt like I had relieved the burden from my shoulders.

Luke disaffiliated as a result of being a victim of racial discrimination on a number of occasions in the Muslim community and felt that the *daʿwah*—the practice or policy of preaching, proselytizing, and inviting people to Islam—that he received had been misleading, as missionaries had "sugarcoated" the assumed benefits he would get by being a Muslim in the community.

Seeking alternatives

In my study, I found that people are more likely to explore their options and seek alternatives after they experience turning points and significant negative experiences that trigger a deconversion process. It is important to explore these stages on account of the personal and social consequences that may occur as a result of a deconversion from Islam. This will also provide a broader insight into the identity transformation processes that leads individuals to the establishment of an "ex-role identity."

Lauren was the only closeted disaffiliate who endured hardship as a result of her fear of abuse from strict Salafi Muslim community members and her "radical" ex-husband, who took matters such as apostasy "very seriously":

> The risk of me getting physically hurt, and my daughter being taken away from me permanently [by her husband and his family] was a very real threat and reality for me and still is. There have been incidents where the radical husband has run off with the child and the apostate be physically, verbally and emotionally abused.

Lauren had become paranoid because she had heard stories of people having their house and car windows smashed on a daily basis. Her husband had reacted with great shock and anger and for a while was in denial about her deconversion, claiming that she had been possessed by evil spirits. "I am now in a bitter custody battle in order to protect my child from abduction and Islamic indoctrination, and I have suffered both financially and socially when

I left Islam and my former Muslim life." Lauren was later rejected and exiled from the Muslim community by her in-laws in much the same way as she had been rejected and made to leave her home when she converted. The repetition of the same experience and crisis has contributed to her depression and has made her feel bitter toward Islam.

Lauren is also the only participant who can be considered to be a "whistle-blower." She set up an active blog under the protection of the Council of Ex-Muslims, where she publicly warned people about joining Islam. Others, such as Janet and Mark, warned people quietly and in private about issues related to being a Muslim if they were asked about Islam and for advice on conversion. Because Janet did not leave a religious community or supportive Muslim friends, her deconversion, like Luke's, went unnoticed.

Lina, although an open disaffiliate, encountered a similar experience to that of Lauren when she informed her husband and his family of her choice to deconvert. She claimed that she is now completely ignored by them and her former Muslim friends who have distanced themselves from her out of fear for their own reputations. She also fought for custody of her youngest daughter, as she feared she would be radicalized if raised in a Muslim community. She chose to return to her non-Muslim society after the court supported her and granted her custody on potential grounds of radicalization, so that her children can grow up like "normal white Britons."

Mark cut ties with the Muslim community in order to move on peacefully with his life and to avoid any negative consequences. He felt he did not owe anyone an explanation for his deconversion: "I was just a bit worried because I didn't know how they [the Muslim community] would react with apostates and so I didn't tell anyone that I had left Islam." Although Mark did not live in the Muslim community as a closeted disaffiliate, he had to endure the inconvenience of moving to another apartment and also kept his distance from Muslims at work. Despite his deconversion, Mark did not lose his fundamental belief in God, but he did abandon his Islamic beliefs and returned to his former society.

A new ex-Muslim identity

During this stage, my interlocutors decided what they wanted from life and the type of identity with which they were most content and comfortable, whether by returning to a former religion or by becoming atheists. After many struggles and hardships, they tended to be more appreciative of things they had previously taken for granted in their former lives.

Lina realized from her experiences that her former life was more liberated and decided to go back to Christianity, which in her opinion offered a great deal more than Islam and its members who were more helpful and friendly. Her conversion journey helped her to realize that being a Christian was part of her true identity and was what made her happy.[3] Despite her negative experiences as a Muslim, however, she did claim that Islam had helped her to stop smoking and drinking, which improved her health. She also claims to appreciate the freedom she has after experiencing a lack of it when married to a Muslim and enjoys going out without being covered and asking for permission to do so; this helped her regain her confidence and self-respect.

Luke found it easy, after a period of gradual and silent disaffiliation from his local Muslim community, to go back to his previous secular lifestyle, as he had not informed his family and friends of his conversion to begin with. He became an atheist after reaching the conclusion there is no God: "God hasn't helped me with anything in my life; when I depend on God to help me or show me the right way my life gets worse." His response indicates that he had many expectations of life as a Muslim that were not fulfilled, one of them being that his new Islamic beliefs would solve his emotional crisis—which resulted from the death of his younger brother and losing faith in God—which did not happen. Converts such as Luke are able to give up their Muslim identities without feeling guilt, as they feel that God has failed them rather than feeling that they have failed God and are unable to be good Muslims.

Janet mentioned that many of the Muslims she knew did not attempt to help her come back to Islam when they found out about her disaffiliation. This disappointed her to begin with, but she later perceived this to be an advantage, as her deconversion, like Luke's, did not trigger any negative social consequences. She blamed her bad experiences of conversion on Muslims who had failed to support her during difficult times and, like others, realized that being in an environment where people loved her, cared about her, and supported her was more important than following a religion that isolated her. Janet had decided to return to her nonpracticing Christian community in which she found love, care, and family: "I was lucky enough to have my parents take me back in after everything that happened. They were just so happy I didn't have any children and that I had left Islam."

Lauren mentioned how she was much happier and content with her new life, as she was able to see a bright future for herself. She claimed to value her life much more now than she ever did before. Like Luke, Lauren now calls herself an atheist and is no longer interested in the idea of any religion governing her way of life. She had initially perceived her conversion to be a temporary problem-solving procedure for the emotional and existential crisis she faced as a teenager, and it had helped to get rid of her suicidal thoughts, but she now felt she no longer needed religious guidance:

> Islam made me more confident. . . . I grew as a person and had a lot more courage to stand up for my opinions even though everyone was against me. . . . The Islamic code of conduct and morality [how a "good" person should be] helped me become a more mature and better person.

Because she felt that God could not help her, however, she decided to pursue her search for the truth and the purpose of life within a nonreligious context.

Mark realized that he did not need to belong to a religion to know who he was or have a spiritual connection with God, and he rediscovered himself and his identity in his own and "normal" former society. He describes his former life as being "normal," referring to the typical secular British lifestyle and culture that he perceives as being contrary to the Islamic lifestyle. He also claimed that his conversion did not transform his character or his worldviews in any significant manner and that the conversion journey was an exploration of his identity and morality within a religious context. Mark did not make many sacrifices to be a Muslim, and unlike Janet and Lauren, he did not feel any regrets about converting. Also, it was a relatively easy process for him to leave, as he did not get married or have any children. He perceived his conversion to Islam to be a learning experience and was happy to know how it feels to be a Muslim and how the journey helped him to find himself:

> It helped me to discover who I really am and what I really believe in. I have no regrets doing what I did. I am at peace now. I would say that maybe I am a more understanding and compassionate person now, as I can see how people can be easily brainwashed and manipulated into following religious groups.

CONCLUSION

This chapter aimed to compare the narratives of conversion and deconversion of five of my interlocutors in order to discover if there are shared crises and experiences that compelled them to embrace Islam and abandon the faith when it appeared that their crisis worsened or when they were faced with new problems. It is important to note that the five interlocutors do not necessarily represent the experiences of other deconverts from Islam in Britain. Because of the sensitive nature of this subject, it was difficult to find more participants who were willing to share their personal experiences. Deconversion is therefore an area of research that requires further investigation. Nevertheless, this chapter aims to provide an insight into the episodes some may experience throughout their conversion and deconversion journeys.

I have shown that my interlocutors experienced various crises that led them on an Islamic conversion journey in the hope that finding God and spirituality, belonging to a community, and having religious beliefs would solve their problems. Instead of finding solutions, however, their conversion to Islam brought more problems. Lauren, Lina, and Janet suffered from new patriarchal relationships and a lack of personal freedom, whereas Luke suffered from racial discrimination, which did not help his self-esteem and emotional well-being, especially as he was trying to overcome the loss of his brother. Mark was the only participant who did not regret his conversion, as it made him feel that he had learned about himself throughout the journey. He was also the only one who felt that he had solved his crisis and settled on the opinion that there is a God, however following a religion was unnecessary.

Those such as Lauren and Janet, who felt isolated from their non-Muslim friends and family members, believed that their crises had increased due to a lack of emotional support and that religion made their lives more difficult, as it limited them from many things that were considered wrong, such as socializing with loved ones in places that did not implement Islamic values (e.g., pubs). Also, the Islamic education they had obtained from "extreme Muslims" had been greatly influenced by "foreign cultural practices." In addition to negative experiences such as abuse, being abandoned by Muslims, and pressure to conform to Islamic practices, the general lack of support had contributed toward their previous crises and added more complications and problems to their lives. These issues had compelled them to deconvert after experiencing turning points that confirmed or triggered the questioning of intellectual and religious doubts that had surfaced during various stages of the journey, especially when they felt that their crises were not being solved by what they believed to be potential solutions.

Each turning point was significant in its own right and highlighted the main disappointments and failed expectations of a better life, God, and being a Muslim. Some converts left Islam if they felt it did not "make sense," if they did not find anything positively unique about it or its followers, or if they felt their previous lives, beliefs, and societies were better. They were also likely to deconvert if they felt that the religious teachings went against their own personal and British values.

The encounter and interaction stages differ in both trajectories, as they are often positively influenced in the conversion journey by group members, whereas in a deconversion journey encountering and interacting with problematic and nonsupportive Muslims—such as strict husbands and unfriendly neighbors—was more likely to drive them toward a deconversion.

Finding God was important to converts who had previously experienced crises such as an illness or death of a loved one, whereas in a deconversion process individuals are less likely to seek God but more likely to seek a new practical solution to their problems, such as visiting a counselor, psychologist, or therapist or by returning to a previous environment in which they felt their problems were lessened. This shows that the deconversion journey does not necessarily involve a search for God but rather a more comfortable lifestyle alongside personal freedom and family and friendship ties and/or support, which were often found in their previous lives and might have been taken for granted. Lina, who reverted back to Christianity, showed a continuation of her spiritual journey and national-religious identity experimentation. The inability to successfully integrate both British and Muslim elements into one identity in the society they lived in encouraged the disaffiliates to return to their former groups, where they did not have to juggle between different identities, beliefs, cultures, values, and lives.

"Coming out" as a disaffiliate was not a major challenge for all five. Some chose to remain as "closeted disaffiliates" and kept their options open until they were sure that they did not wish to remain in the faith group or if they feared abuse. Disownment, stigmatization, isolation, and divorce encouraged individuals to search for solutions outside an Islamic frame.

Those who deconverted unanimously agreed that the positive elements they took away from their time as Muslims were an opportunity to experience life as a Muslim, alongside an improvement in their character, morality, and health. Each participant had been through a process of identity change and construction throughout the entire journey and realized and believed that the identity each became happy and comfortable with, alongside the beliefs each was more inclined to hold after deconversion, was his or her "true" identity.

NOTES

1. The white Muslim population count in the 2001 census was estimated at 61,000, which had almost doubled by 2011, as shown in the 2011 census report. Kevin Brice's (2010) study found that London accounts for almost 4 percent of the Muslim population in the UK and more than 50 percent of its white and black converts to Islam. British converts are estimated to make up 4–5 percent of the Muslim population in Britain.

2. See www.solace.org. Solace is a charity that provides help for female converts to Islam who are in difficulties.

3. Solace (www.solace.org) reported a growing number of Muslims who deconvert and become Christians because they found the support they needed from Christian missionaries, friends, and families rather than from Muslims.

REFERENCES

Ahmed, S. 2010. *The Promise of Happiness*. Durham and London: Duke University Press.

Al-Qwidi, M. 2002. *Understanding the Stages of Conversion to Islam: The Voices of British Converts*. PhD thesis. Leeds: University of Leeds.

Bhatia, R. June 11, 2007. *After the N-Word, The P-Word*. BBC online. news.bbc.co.uk/1/hi/magazine/6740445.stm.

Brice, K. 2010. "A Minority within a Minority: A Report on Converts to Islam in the United Kingdom." *Faith Matters* online. faith-matters.org/images/stories/fm-reports/a-minority-within-a-minority-a-report-on-converts-to-islam-in-the-uk.pdf.

Cottee, S. 2015. *The Apostates: When Muslims Leave Islam*. London: C. Hurst & Co. Publishers.

Ebaugh, H. 1988. "Leaving Catholic Convents: Toward a Theory of Disengagement." In *Falling from the Faith: Causes and Consequences of Religious Apostasy*. D. Bromley, ed. Newbury Park, CA: Sage. 100–121.

Erikson, E. 1968. *Identity: Youth and Crisis*. New York: Norton.

Gooren, H. 2010. *Religious Conversion and Disaffiliation: Tracing Patterns of Change in Faith Practices*. New York: Palgrave Macmillan.

Griffel, F. 2008. "Apostasy." *Encyclopaedia of Islam*, 3rd ed. Gudrun Krämer et al., eds. Leiden: Brill.

Köse, A. 1994. *Conversion to Islam: A Study of Native British Converts*. London and New York: Kegan Paul International.

Lofland, J., and N. Skonovd. 1981. "Conversion Motifs." *Journal for the Scientific Study of Religion*. 20, no. 4: 373–385.

March, A. 2010. *Apostasy: Oxford Bibliographies Online Research Guide*. No city: Oxford University Press.

Moosavi, L. 2011. *Race, Islamophobia, and Belonging in Muslim Converts' Experiences*. PhD thesis. Lancaster University.

Neumueller, C. 2012. *The 21st Century New Muslim Generation: Converts in Britain and Germany*. PhD thesis. University of Exeter.

Raiyaan, U. August 7, 2012. "Why Are New Muslims Leaving Islam?" Islam 21C online. www.islam21c.com/islamic-thought/5823-why-are-new-muslims-leaving-islam.

Rambo, L. 1993. *Understanding Religious Conversion*. New Haven: Yale University Press.

Rambo, L., and C. Farhadian. 1999. "Converting: States of Religious Change." In *Religious Conversion: Contemporary Practices and Controversies*. C. Lamb and D. Bryant, eds. London and New York: Cassell. 23–34.

Rambo, L., and C. Farhadian. 2005. "Conversion." In *Encyclopedia of Religion*, 2nd ed. L. Jones, ed. Detroit: Macmillan. 73–79.

Shahid, O. May 17, 2013. *Confessions of an Ex-Muslim*. www.newstatesman.com/religion/2013/05/confessions-ex-muslim.

Suleiman, Y. 2013. *Narratives of Conversion to Islam*. Cambridge: Prince Alwaleed Bin Talal Centre of Islamic Studies.

Van Nieuwkerk, K., ed. 2006. *Women Embracing Islam: Gender and Conversion in the West*. Austin: University of Texas Press.

Wohlrab Sahr, M. 2006. "Symbolizing Distance: Conversion to Islam in Germany and the United States." In *Women Embracing Islam: Gender and Conversion in the West*. K. van Nieuwkerk, ed. Austin: University of Texas Press. 71–92.

Zebiri, K. 2007. *British Muslim Converts: Choosing Alternative Lives*. London: Oneworld.

TWELVE

IN THE CLOSET

The Concealment of Apostasy among Ex-Muslims in Britain and Canada

SIMON COTTEE

This is Hanif, a 27-year-old ex-Muslim from Britain, describing, in an online forum post, the time he nearly blew his cover:

> On my way back from work, I was walking through the City Centre and I walked past a shop called "Urban Pie." I thought that I might try that, so I walked in and ordered a Lamb and Rosemary Pie (which was beautiful might I add). Anyway, I was eating my pie and my cousin who works in a shop nearby saw me through the window and walked in. He saw what I was eating and said "What you eating that for?!!!"
>
> I think I blagged it, luckily. I said that I had heard so much about this place and I really wanted to try it and I gave in. Then I went on to say that everyone sins. I told him that not eating *haram* [forbidden] and not drinking are not the only two points of being a Muslim and there are much worse sins. So, somehow, I managed to give him an Islamic lecture while eating a *haram* lamb and rosemary pie!

To most non-Muslims, this story probably won't make a lot of sense. But to ex-Muslims, who frequently recount and share similar episodes in secret online ex-Muslim forums, it will no doubt strike a familiar chord, because all ex-Muslims know what it means to lie about, or conceal, their status as ex-Muslims. Ex-Muslims also share, no less frequently, their "coming out" stories, in which they relay who they disclosed their apostasy to, how, and with what consequences. In fact, much discussion on ex-Muslim forums revolves around these twin poles of "in the closet" and "out of the closet."

When I first started researching ex-Muslims, in 2011, I was struck by just how ill-equipped theoretical approaches in the sociology of religion were for illuminating the fundamental moral experiences of those I had met who had left, or were in the process of leaving, Islam. In the sociology of religion, apostates are invariably characterized as "native informants" who use their special status as "exes" (Ebaugh 1988) to testify against their former coreligionists (see esp. Bromley 1998a, 1998b). According to this characterization, the apostate inhabits a role that is "socially constructed" by "anti-cult" activists, whose primary concern is to abolish or control the apostate's former group. Correspondingly, their "exit narrative" or testimony reflects not their "true" experiences inside the group but rather the control-imperatives of their anticult sponsors (see Beckford 1983). Indeed, apostates, from within this perspective, are career exes who capitalize on "opportunities of status enhancement" provided by the "countermovement coalition" that creates their role (Wright 1998: 97). They are also, moreover, prototypical "true believers" (Hoffer 1951) whose "intensity and zeal" and "salvific claims of redemption" represent "a type of quasi-religious conversion in its own right" (Wright 1998: 97).

Far from being "native informants," however, most of my interlocutors were, in their own terminology, "in the closet" and had not disclosed their apostasy. Indeed, their apostasy was a closely guarded secret, revealed only to the most trusted confidants—or to distant strangers under the protective cover of a pseudonym. And although some, clearly, were zealous and intense in their rejection of Islam, many were simply confused, unsure of how to understand and fully come to terms with, much less narrate, their departures from the faith.

This chapter is about the closeted experiences of these ex-Muslims and the strains and stresses of managing what Goffman (1963) calls a "spoiled identity." Its central themes are secrecy and moral stigma and how both define and color the leaving process for ex-Muslims. In a seminal 1991 article published in *Social Forces*, Stuart A. Wright (1991) suggested that the process of leaving a high-commitment religious group can be compared to leaving a marriage. Drawing on life-history interviews with thirty-five ex-Muslims in Britain and Canada, this chapter explores the usefulness of Wright's comparison in the context of apostasies from Islam. It also advances a further comparative reference point for capturing crucial aspects of these exits: namely, gay departures from the heterosexual world.

APOSTASY AND RELATED CONCEPTS

Apostasy is more than just an exit or departure; it is an act of *renunciation*, whereby the exiter disavows the very epistemological and moral tenets of the group. It goes without saying that the renounced group must have been a previous source of belonging or identity for the leaver: one cannot apostatize from a group to which one did not belong or with which one did not identify. Apostasy is also an act of *personal transformation*: the leavers' very self-identity undergoes a dramatic change and they become, as a matter of personal self-definition, an ex- or former member of the departed group.

To exit a group is to withdraw from it, but this need not imply actual physical separation. It is perfectly possible to publicly renounce the norms of a group and still live among, or in close proximity to, its members as an outcast. Diogenes of Sinope is a good example of this. Although he sharply distanced himself from the social conventions of the Athenian society in which he lived, he did not remove himself from its public setting and did little to conceal his scorn for its norms: indeed, he would fart loudly in crowded places, defecate wherever he chose, and masturbate in the marketplace, knowing full well that these activities would scandalize the Athenians who witnessed them and invite their public censure. Diogenes thus fits into that category of persons whom Robert K. Merton (1938: 677, emphasis in original) describes as "*in* the society but not *of* it." He is like "the stranger," whom Simmel (1971: 14) describes as "near and far at the same time."

It is also possible to withdraw from a group and yet remain an outwardly compliant participant in its practices and life-world. That is, it is possible to privately reject the fundamental beliefs and values of a group and still involve oneself in its affairs to the effect that one fully subscribes to them. Merton's (1968: 204) description of the "ritualist" is pertinent here. The ritualist relinquishes the conventional aspirations of the wider culture, and in this sense he is deviant. But he does not reject the "institutionalized means" for achieving conventional aspirations; on the contrary, he continues to adhere "almost compulsively" to these. Merton (1968: 205) characterizes this "clinging" to "safe routines" as a form of self-protective "*private* escape from the dangers and frustrations" inherent "in the competition for major cultural goals." Thus, outwardly the ritualist is conformist, but inwardly he is deviant. All this strongly suggests that exits can be emotional as well as physical and that one can simultaneously be both tied to and distant from a group.

In the sociological literature on religion, apostasy has been defined in a variety of ways. C. Kirk Hadaway and Wade Clark Roof (1988: 29) suggest that an apostate is someone "who held a religious identity at one time, but who now has rejected that identity" and chosen "not to identify with any religious group." That is, an apostate is someone who disaffiliates not only from their former faith but also from organized religion altogether. Apostates, Hadaway and Roof clarify, belong to the "the unchurched" population, as do "nones,"[1] but they are distinctly unlike "invisible affiliates" who, while rarely if ever attending religious services, may still retain a religious identity (Hadaway and Roof, 1988: 29). Nor are they synonymous with nones, since the "none" category "contains persons who have never had a religious identity."

David G. Bromley (1998a: 5) specifies a more restrictive definition of apostasy. The apostate, he suggests, not only renounces his former religion; he *opposes* it. Indeed, he is at war with it: "Apostate refers not to ordinary religious leavetakers but to that subset of leavetakers who are involved in contested exit and affiliate with an oppositional coalition."

Stuart A. Wright (1998: 96) similarly makes a distinction between "the typical *leavetaker* and the *apostate*." Whereas the former "decides to terminate his or her commitment and disaffiliate in a non-public act of personal reflection and deed," the latter is "a defector who is aligned with an oppositional coalition in an effort to broaden a dispute, and embraces a posture of confrontation through public claimsmaking activities."

Anson Shupe (1998: 209) echoes this. Apostasy, he argues, is not just "a loss or wilful abandonment of faith"; it is an act of political opposition, and the apostate is "an outspoken, visible critic" of their former group. This emphasis on rejection and rebelliousness is no doubt well placed. An apostate does not merely challenge or critique their faith; they reject it. Apostasy is an act of disavowal. This, indeed, is its core definitional feature. But it is unduly narrow to stipulate that apostasy is *necessarily* a political act of rebellion, since this excludes the many personal and private apostasies that are not politically shaded (Carter 1998: 227). Bromley prefers to categorize these apostasies as acts of "leavetaking," but "leavetaker" is vague and unhelpful. It is more useful and sensible to talk of public and private apostasies. A silent apostasy is no less an apostasy than a loud one—and is certainly no less interesting.

Nor is it quite right to suggest, as do Hadaway and Roof, that apostasy is necessarily synonymous with irreligion, since it is eminently possible to exchange one religious faith for another. The fact that a person has joined another religious group doesn't alter the fact that they have apostatized from their former group.

For the purposes of definition, it makes better sense not to prejudge the issue of the apostate's motivations and destination. In deciding whether someone has apostatized, the essential question to ask is "Did they reject the faith into which they were born or converted so that they no longer subscribe to its core beliefs nor personally identify with it?" If yes, the person counts as an apostate.

Apostasy must be distinguished from conversion, although the two can be deeply entangled. As already suggested, one can exit a group to join (or rejoin) another; in this case the act of joining (or rejoining) is simultaneously an act of apostatizing. That is, "someone could be an apostate and a convert at much the same time, and the motives for leaving one group might largely overlap with those for joining another" (Wilson, 2004: 2; see also Reinkowski 2007: 414).

But it is also possible to exit a group without joining another: one may leave and remain *un*affiliated or independent. For example, none of the ex-Muslims I interviewed converted to other groups; many, in fact, remained within—but at a vast emotional distance from—the Islamic fold as "closeted" apostates. Indeed, one of the greatest challenges that nonreligious ex-Muslims face is adapting to a life *apart*—not only from their former coreligionists but also from non-Muslims who show little interest in, or understanding of, their situation. Scot McKnight and Hauna Ondrey (2008: 7) are thus assuredly wrong: not all apostasies are, as they insist, conversions.[2]

Connectedly, apostasy is not defection, at least not necessarily. "Defection" refers to the act of exiting a group for another (Cragun and Hammer, 2011: 157). It implies a realignment of allegiance, a switching of sides in a competitive struggle. To defect is thus necessarily to apostatize, but, as we have just seen, to apostatize is not necessarily to defect (i.e., to transfer one's loyalties to another group). To put it more succinctly: all defections are apostasies, but not all apostasies are defections.

One must also sharply distinguish apostasy from heresy. The heretic does not renounce the group (Wilson 2004: 18–19). Quite the contrary: he professes to embody its highest and truest ideals. As Coser (1956: 70) puts it, "Unlike the apostate, the heretic claims to uphold the group's values and interests, only proposing different means to this end or variant interpretations of the official creed." Or, to use Albert O. Hirschman's (1970) terminology, the heretic chooses *voice* over exit, fighting to change the organization from within. Moreover, the heretic continues to compete for the loyalty of existing group members (Coser 1956: 71). This, Coser (1956: 101) argues, makes him a more ambivalent figure than the apostate: "In his conflict with the group he still maintains the group's basic values" and thus "is apt to create more confusion in the group" than the person who outright rejects them. Self-perception, in other words, is the crucial determinant: whereas the apostate ceases to view himself as a member of the group, the heretic grandiosely self-identifies as the group's true guardian of orthodoxy (Kurtz 1983: 1088). Indeed, the heretic, as G. K. Chesterton (1923: 11) observed, furiously denies the charge of heresy, redirecting the self-same accusation against his condemners.

The terms "disengagement" and "disaffiliation" frequently recur in the sociological literature on religious exiting. Whereas the former refers to minimal participation in the routinized activities of a religious group (Albrecht, Cornwall, and Cunningham 1988: 63–64),[3] the latter refers to termination of organizational identification with a religious group (Albrecht, Cornwall, and Cunningham 1988: 70–71).[4] Neither disengagement nor disaffiliation is proof positive of apostasy. For example, there are Mormons who, despite becoming inactive in the life of the church, "retain an organizational identification with Mormonism and would, if queried, define themselves as a member of that church" (Albrecht, Cornwall, and Cunningham, 1988: 63).[5] There are also ex-Mormons who terminated their organizational identification with the Mormon Church and yet continued to adhere to certain Mormon beliefs (Albrecht, Cornwall, and Cunningham, 1988: 77).

APOSTASY AND DIVORCE

Leaving a closely knit religious group, Wright (1991: 127) suggests, is like leaving an unhappy or unsuccessful marriage:

> Focusing on the social and psychological dynamics of disaffiliation, it may be shown that the processes, experiences and symptoms of leavers are strikingly similar to those evidenced by persons facing marital dissolution. The disentanglement of affective bonds, the disillusionment that accompanies renunciation of an intense loyalty or sacred commitment, the sense of personal failure, the feelings of confusion, anxiety, anger, frustration and the diminished ability to function following the break-up are characteristics of marital disengagement that may be aptly applied to departures from new religions.

Apostasy and divorce, Wright (1991: 128) elaborates, "are disengagement processes sharing important key traits because they both involve deeply felt emotions surrounding the abandonment of highly valued identities and intimate social relations." Furthermore, both marital love and cultic devotion "entail considerable levels of selflessness, duty, devotion and sacrifice." Thus, "disengagement from the religious group may be more akin to divorce than most observers recognize."

Describing the experiences of voluntary defectors from three new religious movements (the Unification Church, Hare Krishna, and Children of God), Wright (1991: 130) convincingly shows how these parallel those of marital divorcées in terms of "patterns of withdrawal," "post-involvement effects and reactions," and "aspects of adjustment and rebuilding."

Wright is clearly on to something here, and it is worth focusing in some detail on Robert S. Weiss's (1975) seminal research on marital separation to better bring out the force of his analogy. According to Weiss, the dissolution of a marital relationship is marked by multiple pains and losses. It is neither a single event nor one that moves inexorably in a single direction. Accomplishing it can take many months, even years. As one of Weiss's (1975: 17) interviewees put it:

> For years I really wanted to be out of the marriage and wasn't able to do it. Cutting loose was a tortuous thing. I knew that I wanted a divorce and couldn't look at it, because there was guilt and fear and, you know, shit going on inside me, so I just couldn't face it.

Reluctance to separate was widely reported among Weiss's interviewees, because "separation means starting over, alone. It means setting off without the partner on whom one has, perhaps for years, relied. It means new vulnerability and perhaps isolation and loneliness" (Weiss 1975: 25).

Weiss (1975: 17) found that many who "had tried for years to make the best of a bad marriage mourned not the marriage itself but rather the years they had given to it"; they regretted "tolerating the marriage for so long." He also found that the euphoria his interviewees reported feeling just after they had separated was often short-lived. One interviewee said:

> I found that I felt quite euphoric for about three months. I sort of did everything that I wanted to do. I hadn't gone out much, so I went to the theatre. I didn't do these things before I was married. I sat in a bar, drinking, just talking to anybody. I met just lots of different people. After three months and having met just one or two people who were really interesting, I found it was an empty life. I realized that my family meant a great deal to me and that there was no family anymore (Weiss 1975: 54).

Guilt is a prominent theme in Weiss's interview material, especially among those who had initiated the separation: they regretted the "damage their departure inflicted on those they were pledged to cherish" and felt that the condemnation of others was partially deserved. By contrast, those on whom separation was imposed often felt "misused" and questioned their self-worth. Among both parties, there was a strong sense of self-blame simply for having failed at marriage (Weiss 1975: 64).

Another prominent theme is isolation and how the end of a marriage can decimate a person's entire social network. Furthermore, Weiss (1975: 69) observes, "most among the separated suffer the loss of some of the social scaffolding on which their self-definition had rested" and as a consequence "may no longer feel themselves to be quite the same people they had been when they were married." The "constant, uninterrupted custom of years together," "the years of going places together, sitting down to dinner together, consulting each other on management of the children and the house, presenting ourselves to others as a couple, sharing a house, a car, a bedroom": this is what "makes our marriage a part of ourselves" (Weiss 1975: 71). And this, Weiss explains, is why leaving it "may be experienced by us as akin to loss of a limb" (Weiss 1975: 71). In losing their former self-definitions, he says, the separated must create new ones: "They are, as it were, between selves"(1975: 70). For some, the major task is to "battle through to an autonomous self, distinct from the self they had maintained during their marriage" (1975: 73). But "what self that is may now have become uncertain" (1975: 70). Eventually, however, "the individual will develop a new coherent self, but its formation is a slow process, and for a time the separated may feel confused and without direction"(1975: 76).

Wright illuminatingly details how his own research interviewees underwent similar experiences in leaving the cultic milieu. My own research on ex-Muslims, to which I shall now turn, also testifies to the fruitfulness of Wright's analogy. However, it also highlights its limitations and provides support for a potentially richer parallel, related to gay exits from the heterosexual world.

ISLAMIC APOSTASY AND DIVORCE

Between September 2011 and February 2013, I conducted life-history interviews with thirty-five ex-Muslims.[6] Interviews lasted between two and three hours. Some subjects were interviewed more than once. I also engaged in written correspondence with many respondents after they had been interviewed and traced some of their online footprints where possible. In addition to this, I attended numerous ex-Muslim "meetups" in both Britain and Canada over a two-year period.

All respondents, except one, were born and raised as Muslims. Eight had been Shiʿa Muslims, while the remainder had been Sunni. All self-identified as "ex-Muslims"—though not without reservations—and all were nonreligious, defining themselves as either agnostic or atheist. There were fifteen women and twenty men. The youngest was eighteen, the oldest forty-eight. At the time at which they were interviewed, nine were based in Canada and twenty-six in the UK.

I recruited respondents exclusively from the online forum of the Council of Ex-Muslims of Britain (CEMB), a refuge for mainly secular and nonreligious ex-Muslims. The forum was established in 2007 and attracts members from all over the globe, although the core of the membership is from Britain and Canada.[7] In several posts on the CEMB forum, between May 2010 and February 2012, I advertised my interest in speaking with ex-Muslims, explaining that I was a sociologist and that I wanted to know what it was like to leave Islam, how this occurs, and with what consequences.

Some forum members I interviewed had only the most fleeting engagement with the forum, whereas others were longtime, although not necessarily active, participants in its life. All respondents signed a participant consent form promising confidentiality, and they were all given pseudonyms to protect their identities. In most cases, respondents chose these themselves.

Recruitment through an online self-help group may invite the suspicion that the sample is unrepresentative, since, it might be supposed, ex-Muslims who seek out a self-help forum are more troubled than those who do not. My sense is that many respondents undoubtedly were troubled and that some were not—or rather not any more averagely troubled than anyone else. More generally, though, the overwhelming picture that emerges from my research is one of trauma and suffering: leaving Islam, for many of the unknown numbers who leave, is a prolonged and psychologically costly process, marked by feelings of uncertainty, guilt, self-doubt, loneliness, and depression (Cottee 2015a).

Many of the ex-Muslims I interviewed would probably scoff at the suggestion that their exits from Islam resemble exits from marriage. But the parallels are in fact striking, especially at the levels of "post-involvement effects and reactions" and "aspects of adjustment and rebuilding." This is Khadija, describing how she felt just after renouncing Islam:

> At the beginning it felt exciting. Very exciting. I felt so free. That didn't last forever. I became quite depressed. Very depressed. I didn't leave my house for a long time. I just debated online because the only time I was feeling okay was when I was online talking. As soon as I would switch off the computer I would just be depressed again. Everything just seemed pointless. It all seemed empty after the initial buzz of being free wore off.

Ahmed echoed this:

> The real struggle came a few years later [after he had apostatized] when I was in my early twenties. I became really, really depressed, where I would just think there's no point in life and I went through this huge stage of de-

> pression where I couldn't function, I couldn't work, I couldn't do anything, I couldn't get out of bed. I felt that my life had lost meaning and that there was nothing to live for.

Tasnim described feeling "lost" in the months after she had apostatized:

> Why do I do the things I do? Why do I even exist? Why do I exist—what does this mean? I used to think you live your life to please God and get into heaven, but I don't have that anymore. So where do I go from here? How do I live the rest of my life without a purpose?

For Aisha, the dominant feeling wasn't one of pointlessness but of uncertainty. Before she left Islam she had a script, and now she no longer did:

> I was just in the biggest state of confusion afterwards. My conception of the world is going to be completely different now. What am I supposed to do? Everything I said and everything I did was in accordance to Islam. What am I supposed to do now? That's my whole life shattered, I don't know what to do, even about the little things. What music do I like now? Because I avoided music for quite a while. It was all so confusing.

Feelings of confusion over self-identity were also common among interviewees, since in renouncing Islam they had not only abandoned the guidance and consolations of the faith but also put into question the very foundations of their self-definition. They were once Muslims, but they were Muslims no longer. So who were they? Many interviewees said that it took months, even years, to work this out—or at least to establish categorically who they were *not*. As Tasnim confided to me, for a long time, "I didn't know who the fuck I was anymore."

One of the greatest challenges ex-Muslims face is reconciling their post-apostasy self with the expectations, demands and intrusions associated with an Islamic-oriented family life. This involves a delicate round of negotiation that lasts as long as the relationships last. In this sense, there is no "beyond Islam"; there is no "moving on," and Islam continues to be a central reference point. As Manzoor ruefully put it, sounding not unlike Michael Corleone in the third—and least satisfying—installment of *The Godfather* film trilogy: "You may leave it but it never leaves you."

This, however, is where the analogy between leaving Islam and leaving a marriage falls down. Marriages end, and there is typically a point at which the former marital partners adjust to a life beyond the marriage, step out of its shadow, and move on. According to William J. Goode (1956: 19, emphasis in original):

> The post-divorce adjustmental process is one by which *a disruption of role sets and patterns, and of existing social relations, is incorporated into the individual's life pattern, such that the roles accepted and assigned do not take the prior divorce into account as the primary point of reference*: In more commonsense terms, the woman is no longer "ex-wife," or "divorcee" primarily, but first of all "co-worker," "date," or "bride."

Despite their best efforts, Islam was still a central reference point in the lives of the ex-Muslims I interviewed. The analogy is also inapt in the sense that leaving Islam is a *deviant exit*, whereas leaving a marriage no longer is. In this key respect, and as I suggest below, it is more directly analogous to contested gay exits from the straight world.

ISLAMIC APOSTASY AND SEXUAL STIGMA

In his classic study of stigma, Erving Goffman (1963) suggested that if a stigmatized person's stigma—that is to say, "an attribute that is deeply discrediting"—is not immediately apparent, the issue is "not that of managing tension generated during social contacts, but rather that of managing information about [their] failing." For the "discreditable" person, whose stigma is hidden but always at risk of being discovered, the issue is: "To display or not to display; to tell or not to tell; to let on or not to let on; to lie or not to lie; and in each case, to whom, how, when, and where."

This conundrum—"to go public or to pass"—is richly explored in the context of gay men's lives in Ken Plummer's *Sexual Stigma* (1975: 189, 135), as is the process of "becoming homosexual." Plummer contends that there are four key stages through which "some homosexuals pass in adopting homosexuality as a way of life": (1) "sensitization"; (2) "signification"; (3) "coming out"; and (4) "stabilization" (Plummer 1975: 134). "Sensitization" refers to "those first conscious and semi-conscious moments in which an individual comes to perceive of himself potentially as a homosexual: with the general process of constructing sexual meanings, modifying them, and in many instances, neutralizing them" (Plummer 1975: 135). "Signification," by contrast, is "a heightened homosexual identity," developed over time in a process marked by confusion and ambivalence (Plummer 1975: 141). This is because homosexuality is "bedeviled by ban" and regarded as "sinful" or as a "sickness" by the wider society. In this context, "the neophyte comes to perceive his initial experience with increasing anxiety and possible guilt" (Plummer 1975: 142). In addition to this, he is likely to feel lonely and isolated, unable to communicate his anxieties and concerns to others. "Neither spoken about openly, nor immediately visible," homosexuality is something that must "be kept to oneself, debated inwardly and defended from public gaze" (Plummer 1975: 144). According to Plummer, there are two aspects to the neophyte's sense of isolation. One comes from a lack of contact with other homosexuals ("for as long as he guards his secret well, the chance of ever meeting somebody else who experiences the world in the same way remains slight"); the other comes from a lack of support from heterosexual companions:

> The first source of isolation may mean that the neophyte comes to perceive himself as "the only one in the world." . . . If one is confronted naively with a societal reaction that says homosexuality is odd and that nobody should be engaged in it, it is difficult for the neophyte to actually believe that many people are so engaged. . . . The second source of isolation comes from a (justified) unwillingness to broach the subject with family, peers or "officials." . . . Not only are peers and families generally inaccessible on the subject, official agencies have not developed any well-defined and "well-known" paths to offer "help." Recently, of course, there has been an increase in organizations developed to help homosexuals and to provide forums for discussion, but in the past such bodies were non-existent (Plummer 1975: 145).

"Coming out" is the process by which individuals are "reborn into the organized aspects of the homosexual community" and "come to identify themselves as 'homosexuals'" (Plummer 1975: 147). It marks the transition from "a world characterized by secrecy, solitude, ambiguity and guilt to a subworld where homosexual-role models are available, where homosexuality may be temporarily rendered public, and where a belief system is on hand to legitimize the experience" (Plummer 1975: 148). Plummer adds that this is "neither an inevitable nor a necessary stage in becoming a homosexual." It is possible, he says, to "develop self-conceptions as homosexual without contact with this world," although it is a crucial step "in taking on homosexuality as a way of life" and reaffirming a positive self-image.

The last stage, "stabilizing homosexuality" (Plummer 1975: 148), involves the "adoption of a permanent homosexual role." This is made possible by a broader subculture that positively affirms and legitimizes this role.

Plummer (1975: 175) also writes insightfully about "the interaction problems confronted by the homosexual who attempts to conceal his identity," as well as the various methods, including "information control" (i.e., avoiding the use of stigma symbols), used to "pass" as heterosexual.

It is more than four decades since *Sexual Stigma* was published, and the stigma attached to homosexuality in contemporary societies has progressively faded, though by no means vanished, in the interim. In polite or progressive circles at least, homosexuality is no longer seen as a stigma or pathology. But the account it sketches of a deviant identity, and the pressures and shame associated with, respectively, both its concealment and exposure, resonates strongly with the accounts relayed by the ex-Muslims I interviewed and in online ex-Muslim testimony.

THE EX-MUSLIM CAREER: DOUBTS AND DISCLOSURE

Many ex-Muslims liken the onset of doubt to contracting a painful illness and describe the process as fundamentally unsettling. Omar, for example, recalled: "The doubts just kept coming into my head, and I would say to myself, 'stop that,' I don't want those thoughts to come, that's the devil whispering in my ear." Farhad, who "was always doubtful of Islam," similarly remarked of his doubts that he "would try to suppress them, because I knew they were wrong." Kareem told me, "I would feel arrogant and ashamed if I asked too many questions."

Omar said that his greatest fear in doubting Islam was that others would discover this and shame him for it:

> I was aware of another fellow, who was a few years older than me. He was having his own doubts. He actually became an atheist long before I became an atheist. And everybody would talk behind his back, "Oh, he's completely gone off his rocker" and so on. That basically shut my questions up. I didn't want to seem like an idiot, so I just forgot about those questions and they didn't resurface until later.

Tasnim similarly remembered concealing her doubts:

> Because I was scared that those doubts might be seen as negative, and that they'd think I'm possessed. I remember my brother used to say that people who are possessed are put in a circle and beaten to get the ghost

> out of them. And I was scared of that and I was scared that they would think something has possessed me and that's why I'm having these doubts.

Because many interviewees felt that they could not openly share their doubts for fear of social ridicule and rebuke, the process of doubting was a punishingly lonely business. This is Tasnim again:

> I was scared of questioning, because I was always taught, never question. But when I did, and I had all these questions, I knew that I couldn't talk to anyone. I couldn't ask my mum. I couldn't go to my Arabic teacher. I couldn't go to the mosque and ask somebody. I was scared of how they would react, so I just didn't really speak to anyone.

Farhad, too, "kept it all in because there was no one I could talk to. I lived in a predominately Muslim area and everyone around me was Muslim. I didn't want it to get out that I was having doubts. So I just kept it to myself. Not having anyone to talk to was horrible."

Only one respondent—Samir—contradicted the above picture: "I can't remember anyone telling me not to ask questions or that something was true 'just because.' This includes my parents who were pretty open-minded and discussed things with me in a mature way." However, it is instructive to note that this respondent fiercely concealed his apostasy from his extended family and that when he announced it to his uncle, whom he counted as the most "liberal-minded" member of his family, "he was the one who took it the worst."

Nearly all respondents said that their doubting and eventual apostasy made them feel strange and that before coming across other ex-Muslims, invariably online, they had felt, just like Plummer's "neophyte homosexual," that they were "the only one in the world." Nabilah, remembering the first time she came across the CEMB forum, said, "I was floored.... It's like, whoa, you guys actually exist, oh my god! There are ex-Muslims in the world. And I appreciate that, just knowing that ex-Muslims exist. That's fantastic. It validates us, yes we exist." Tasnim, on first discovering the CEMB forum, was similarly taken aback:

> I was just typing in Google searching stuff. Then I came across the forum and it was so strange because I don't know anyone who went through the same things as me. Anyone at all. It was strange reading the bios and to see everyone just gathered to talk about the struggles they had and the life experiences they had. They were so similar to mine. It was just like, you know what, I'm not alone.

Or as Amina more succinctly put it, referring to the CEMB forum: "It was good just feeling like there were other people out there who were just like me."

Respondents who disclosed their apostasy to family and Muslim friends invariably encountered negative reactions, ranging from condemnation, shock, hurt, rejection, banishment, and denial. In most cases, their apostasy was met with resistance and they were encouraged to return to Islam.

Wahid told me that when he came out to his mother she had initially "seemed cool with it," but within the space of just a few hours she began to behave hysterically. "She was crying, saying stuff that didn't make any sense." Wahid's concern wasn't what his mother would do to him but what she might do to herself: "I thought she'd do something stupid." For a day or two, nothing was said between them. And then shock turned to anger: "She attacked my character, she attacked my personality, and she attacked my living habits."

Masood said that, when he anonymously disclosed his apostasy in a Muslim online forum, the response was uniformly negative, and he was accused of never having been a "true" Muslim in the first place. "I still don't understand how you could leave Islam," said one commenter. "I just don't get it. To me it's like you never had Islam in your heart, because if someone understands the true meaning of Islam (and this life) and the beauty of Islam, they will not be able to leave it. You can give me an explanation and all that, but like I said—I will never understand."

Among the younger contingent of ex-Muslims I spoke with, many said their parents had dismissed their apostasy as youthful rebellious exuberance, something they would grow out of once they had regained their senses. Mustafa said his parents "thought I was going through a phase. They didn't think that it was going to be something permanent."

Other ex-Muslims said that, when they disclosed their apostasy to relatives, not only was their knowledge of Islam held up to scrutiny, but so was their very sanity. "My family thinks that I'm crazy," Khadija told me. "My step-mum told the imam everything that had happened. And the imam said it sounded like I'd gone crazy. So I was declared, like, insane."

And nearly everyone I interviewed who had disclosed their apostasy to others expressed their annoyance at having their motives assailed: "They think that you just want to live a life of sin, that you want to sleep around and get drunk and go hedonist," said Abdullah, referring to his family and friends.

No one I interviewed has been subject to physical violence *because* they renounced Islam, although since concluding my research study I interviewed an ex-Muslim who relayed to me how she was stripped naked by her father and a group of his friends and violently shaken and spat on as part of an exorcism carried out to purge her of her "waywardness" (Cottee 2015b). I have also met a young Pakistani British woman who said her parents threatened to kill her if she didn't recant her apostasy and return to the fold. Other ex-Muslims have publicly spoken about the countless online death threats they have received.

THE EX-MUSLIM CLOSET

During the time I interviewed respondents, just over half were actively concealing their apostasy from their parents, other family members, and other Muslims in or outside their local communities. They all used the term "closeted" to describe their lives as secret ex-Muslims. Less than five were fully "out"—another term all respondents used to refer to the disclosure of apostasy—in the sense of making a public declaration of apostasy using their real identities. Just under half had disclosed their apostasy to a parent or a sibling.

The most commonly cited motives among respondents for remaining closeted was that they did not want to hurt their parents by failing to meet their expectations and that they did not want to risk ostracism or censure from the family. So they resolved to keep their apostasy a secret. But this came at a cost.

Many closeted respondents told me how profoundly "trapped" they felt and tried to convey the nature and immensity of the frustration this caused. They spoke of their frustration of having to fulfill obligations that they had come to detest, like praying and fasting. For example, Abdullah said that, at home during university holidays, he is expected to pray: "I just hate doing it. I don't know, maybe because of the principle of it." He remembers that it was especially bad in the first Ramadan after he had apostatized. He was still living at home. He was fasting. That was okay. He could fast. But the praying he found "hellish," especially the Taraweeh prayers:

> In the 30 day period they recite the whole Quran, so they do about 50 pages a day, all by standing in prayer. So it takes about 2 hours a night just standing there in a room with 30 men. And that was while I was depressed and the last place I wanted to be was in my own head, so having 2 hours a night just to do nothing but think was pretty hard.

Farhad, referring to Friday prayers, which his family expect him to attend, similarly said: "I really don't like being in a mosque, it's a horrible experience for me. It's the ultimate feeling of being trapped. I sort of feel like a zombie."

Respondents also spoke of their frustration at being prevented from engaging in activities that are Islamically off-limits for fear of "blowing their cover." Masood, for example, enjoys a drink—a beer, a cocktail, a glass of wine. But he lives with his parents, for whom he is currently acting as a de facto caretaker outside his working hours, and so he has to rein it in:

> I might go for a pint or two after work, but I'm constantly aware that they [Masood's parents] might smell it on me and I'll then have to go and chew some gum or eat some peanuts or whatever. And it's annoying that I have to do that, that I can't just have a relaxing pint after work and then just go home.

Returning to this theme at another point in our interview, he said:

> I'd like to be able to walk into a restaurant, maybe order a glass of wine and some pork chops or whatever, and be able to indulge in that without people going, "Oh my god, aren't you a Muslim?" I want to live my own life in freedom but I've accepted that I can't in some ways.

Hanif also has to lie about his enthusiasm for alcohol and his love, in particular, of wine. He told me that he'd like to be able to share this with his wife, but he can't, because she is a practicing Muslim and because wine is *haram* in Islam. About this, Hanif said, resignedly: "So living my own life how I want to live it, it kind of causes a difficult situation in that sense."

Many respondents said that in the immediate aftermath of their apostasy they felt angry, especially at themselves: for not having renounced Islam sooner, for wasting time, for missing chances. Hanif's worry isn't about this, not anymore. It isn't about lost time; it is about a lost *future*. He is worried that in remaining closeted he is depriving himself of joys and opportunities that he will never be able to recapture later on, once it is too late. It's not the things that he *could* have done that concerns him but rather the things that he *can* conceivably do but is *not* doing:

> It is something that really does concern me and I think about it a lot. I do feel like I'm wasting my twenties a lot of the time. That is probably one of my biggest concerns in this whole not coming out thing. For example, all my mates went on holiday to Paris last year and I couldn't go and I was just thinking, what am I doing? It's little things like that which make me think I might be wasting the best years of my life. My twenties should be the best years of my life.

Farhad similarly worries that "this is the only life that I will get" and that the longer he remains closeted the less time he has to live it as he would like.

This is also Amir's chief concern: that he may never experience the future he longs for, that "I may never be able to be myself in public, never be able to defend atheism as I would like to, to be able to drink and eat pork openly." "I would love a life," he continues, "where I have a secular wife, secular children, and have alcohol in my house, etc."

In addition to these frustrations, respondents also alluded to the annoyance of having to suppress thoughts and feelings for fear of offending the sensitivities of others, provoking their censure, or giving away the game. This, Luqman recalled, was one of the most maddening aspects of his time in the closet:

> It was particularly annoying. I had to bite my tongue basically. Every time they tried to preach to me I was dying to tell them, to shout out I don't believe all this. I completely don't believe it. I had to bite my tongue for many months.

Farhad also conveyed something of the weight of frustration he feels at always having to self-censor in the face of his mother's preaching:

> I never ever speak out against Islam. I usually keep quiet and mum nags me and I just ignore her. Try and blur it out of my head because it is always the same stuff. You need Islam. You need Islam to go to university. You need Islam to succeed in life, because, obviously, if you don't believe God won't give you anything, so if anything goes wrong in my life, if something has gone bad, it's always because of Islam, it always comes back to Islam. Sometimes I do want to lash out verbally, but I always hold it back. It's really frustrating.

For some respondents, an even greater source of frustration lies in having to suppress not only thoughts and feelings but also key aspects of an entire identity. This is Nubia, referring to the *hijab*:

> I just hated it because people assumed things about me. For example, at university I wasn't really included in any of the fun things. People just treat you a lot differently. I think it's because they're trying to be respectful. Or they think you have certain lines that you don't cross or whatever. But I just found it really suffocating and annoying. Even in discussions I'd go to,

> like the Atheist and Muslim Society events, people just assume that I'm on the side of the Muslims. Obviously I can understand where they're coming from, but to me it was really annoying. I remember I was in this lecture and they asked all the Muslims in the room to raise their hands and I had to reluctantly put it up because of my headdress.[8]

Aisha, in the last few months of wearing the *hijab*, had also become exasperated by the very misperceptions she had helped create:

> Like when you're talking to people and they make some sexual reference. It's like I'm not allowed to hear it because of who I am. And obviously it wasn't who I was and I hated having to be this symbol of Islam. It just really annoyed me, because whenever somebody would talk about the Republic of Iran or how much they hate theocracies people would automatically assume that I support Iran or theocracy but I actually don't.

A further source of frustration for closeted respondents is the burden of having always to be "on" and in a permanent state of self-watchfulness. Abdullah, for example, tellingly remarked that one of the greatest changes in his life since moving away to university is that

> I'm not conscious of the things I do. Before I always had to act a certain way and be a certain way and say certain things and it was annoying. But here just having that sense of freedom to do what I want is sort of liberating and not having to worry about who will see me or what people will say.

Maryam, since moving away from her hometown, is similarly less self-conscious about how she acts and the impression she gives off:

> I'd say it's less stressful since I've moved to Durham. When I was in Birmingham I would be quite scared because my dad, his shop and his restaurant are in Birmingham. I'd often be scared if I was out with friends just wearing normal clothes, my perception of what is normal to me anyway. That my dad or any of his friends might see me or if I was out with my boyfriend that they might see us as well. And it was quite stressful. Now that I'm here it's not so bad.

For some respondents, the fear of blowing their own cover was so pronounced that they would often dream about it. Nubia, for example, said:

> This is funny, because I had a dream last night and, oh my God, basically I went to a CEMB meet-up and on the way back I went into a corner shop for something. And then my cousin called me and she said, "Where are you?" And I said, blah, blah street and then she said, "Can I come and see you?" And I thought, oh no, I'm not wearing my *hijab*, she's going to know. And then I thought, you know what, she's actually nice, this will be okay, she's open minded. So then I met her and she was with my mum and my two brothers. And they saw me and it was just a shit storm. It was horrible. And I woke up straight away.

Aisha's closet dreams follow an almost identical script:

> It used to be quite frequent, like every night. They'd find my Christopher Hitchens book or they'd find the website for CEMB, and this is something I still worry about. It feels horrible lying to my parents, but I haven't got an alternative.

Interviewees also spoke of the shame they felt in remaining closeted. Nasreen, for example, recalled how humiliating it felt to have to wear the *hijab* in her local community, "because I completely disagree with this scarf, this religion, this whole sexist way women are treated, and yet I have to pretend to be happy with it." Nasreen has since discarded it, but she is not yet "out" to her parents since "it would destroy them." Tasnim also said this, registering what she sees as the absurdity of having to constantly pretend: "If I'm supposed to be in prayer and I hear someone coming I'll quickly go to the prayer mat and pretend to pray. It does feel ridiculous but I know if I don't pray I'd hear the whole 'Oh, why aren't you praying?' It is really ridiculous." Some respondents also felt shame not only for betraying themselves but also for deceiving others, especially loved ones.

Finally, all closeted respondents testified to how lonely and isolated they felt in concealing their apostasy. Because they wanted to avoid the "righteous scrutiny" (Matza 1969: 151) of other Muslims, they would purposively curtail relationships or interactions with them. At the same time, they also avoided developing decent and emotionally satisfying relationships with non-Muslims for fear that these would raise suspicions about their faith commitment. Masood, for example, had met a woman and embarked on a relationship with her. After months of dating, she asked him if he would consider moving in with her. He did consider it. But it was impossible. She wasn't a Muslim. And, in the eyes of his parents at least, *he was*. If he were to move in with her it would have all come out—the whole story—and he wasn't prepared to face the fallout that this would involve. "I thought at the time that they [his parents] would probably disown me," Masood said, adding, "and I didn't want to hurt them like that." So the relationship ended, although "I'm still friends with her and occasionally she gets maudlin when she gets drunk and texts me saying I wish you'd fought for me." Tasnim, too, has had relationships, but these have gone nowhere because she very deliberately decided that they would go nowhere. "I can't be bothered with the heartache," she said. Of one doomed relationship, she commented: "There was a friend who wanted more than just friends. He was agnostic and I just said, 'It's not a good idea, my family won't accept you. You'd have to be a secret, you don't want that.'"

CONCLUSION: SECRET APOSTASY AND THE SOCIOLOGY OF RELIGION

The consensus in the sociology of religion is firm on the matter: it is possible to be religious without belonging to, or participating in, a religious organization. As Hadaway and Roof (1988: 29, emphasis in original) observe, among the "unchurched population" there are "*invisible affiliates*—those who identify with some religion, but who rarely if ever attend religious services." Similarly, Albrecht et al. (1988: 63) write of Mormons who, despite becoming inactive in the life of the church, "retain an organizational identification with Mormonism and would, if queried, define themselves as a member of that church."

By contrast, the countervailing possibility that one can be irreligious and yet belong to, or participate in, a religious organization has scarcely been registered, much less empirically investigated, by scholars in the sociology of religion. This in part reflects the dominant thematic concerns of the sociology of religion. These—understandably and legitimately enough—center on the varieties of religious experience and on what it means to acquire or possess religious belief and to belong to or identify with a religious community. But it also reflects the common definitional and thematic emphases of the existing sociological research on apostasy. As we saw earlier in this chapter, Bromley (1998a; 1998b)—one of the leading lights in the sociology of religious apostasy—defines an apostate as someone who not only leaves a religious group but also actively and very publicly speaks out against it. For Bromley, the "apostate role" is "socially constructed" by organized opponents of the apostate's former group in an asymmetrical conflict in which the departed religious group lacks all the power. The apostate's specific task is to delegitimize his former group by exposing and amplifying its "atrocities."

The explanatory power and richness of Bromley's work on the "social construction of subversive evil," as he phrases it, cannot be doubted. However, by focusing almost exclusively on militant and politicized apostates from subversive religious organizations, Bromley in effect ignores the experiences of ordinary, nonpoliticized apostates who apostatize not only in silence but also in *secret*, remaining in the group as available but emotionally distant members.

Other notable work in the scholarly study of religion similarly conspires to shift attention away from the possibility of secret apostasy. Heinz Streib and Barbara Keller (2004: 191), exclude a priori the possibility that one can simultaneously deconvert and yet remain involved in the ritualized life-world of the group from which one deconverts. My aim in this chapter has been to acknowledge this possibility and to convey some of the texture of this experience among ex-Muslims.

It is impossible to know just how many closeted ex-Muslims there are in any given time or place. But the fact that they exist cannot be disputed—nor can the reality of their apostasy. The respondents I interviewed reject the fundamental tenets of Islam. They do not identify as Muslims. Indeed, most self-consciously defined themselves as "ex-Muslims" or "apostates," despite—or perhaps because of—the negative baggage attached to these two terms. Yet they do not exist in the sociology of religion, because the field predominantly defines (and disparages) apostates as outspoken agitators against their former groups, whose public visibility is there for all to see.

Steven Seidman (2002: 123), reflecting on the alienating impact of the gay closet, perceptively observes that "to be isolated is to live with a keen sense of being both inside and outside of the social world." This is not unlike the situation of the closeted ex-Muslims I interviewed, who must contend with the challenge of living both inside and outside the faith communities from which they have become psychologically, if not physically, estranged. How ex-Muslims and secret apostates from other faiths negotiate this challenge—and the consequences for their emotional well-being—is an immensely rich area for future social research.

NOTES

1. A "none" refers to someone who, when asked in a survey what his or her religion is, stated "none" (Zuckerman 2009: 950). "Nones," Roof and Landres note, "are people who reject an institutional religious affiliation. . . . Their doing so may or may not correspond with a personal affirmation of faith" (Roof and Landres 1997: 82). The term "nones," in others words, encompasses both atheists and believers.

2. This conflation between apostasy and conversion is also implicit in Bromley's (1998b: 36) definition of apostasy, according to which the apostate undergoes "a total change of loyalties by allying with one or more elements of an oppositional coalition."

3. "Dropping out," a term also in wide currency in the sociology of religious exiting, is broadly synonymous with "disengagement." Hoge (1988: 82), for example, uses it to refer to "the cessation of Catholic Mass attendance." Yet another widely used synonym for "disengagement" is "disinvolvement." Bromley (1997: 48–49), for instance, uses it to refer to "distancing and pulling back from investment of self in the group."

4. Hoge (1988: 82) prefers the term "disidentification," since disaffiliation, he argues, "has to do with being on formal membership lists," which renders it inapplicable to the many religious groups—including the Catholic Church—which do not keep them.

5. This is also true of large numbers of Protestants (Perry et al. 1980: 388–404), Jews (Lazerwitz and Harrison 1979: 656–666), and Catholics (Hoge 1988: 81–99). In an illuminating study of gay Christians who had "completely withdrawn from participating in the Church," Yip (2000: 129, 130) found that "almost all still maintain their Christian identity."

6. This research (Cottee 2015a) was funded by the Economic and Social Research Council (RES-000-22-4308).

7. The other major forum for ex-Muslims—established and funded by Faith Freedom International—attracts greater numbers of ex-Muslim converts to Christianity and is more overtly political in its concerns.

8. For closeted ex-Muslim women, the *hijab* is what Goffman (1963: 60) would classify as a "disidentifier": a symbol that serves to distance the "discreditable" person from their discreditable identity. It is the polar opposite of what Plummer (1975: 191) calls a "stigma symbol."

REFERENCES

Albrecht, S. L., M. Cornwall, and P. H. Cunningham. 1988. "Religious Leave-Taking: Disengagement and Disaffiliation among Mormons." In *Falling from the Faith: Causes and Consequences of Religious Apostasy*. David G. Bromley, ed. Beverly Hills, CA: Sage. 62–80.

Beckford, J. 1983. "Talking of Apostasy or Telling Tales and 'Telling' Tales." In *Accounts and Action*. N. Gilbert and P. Abel, eds. Aldershot: Gower. 77–97.

Bromley, D. G. 1997. "Falling from the New Faiths: Toward an Integrated Model of Religious Affiliation/Disaffiliation." In *Leaving Religion and Religious Life*. Mordechai Bar-Lev and William Shaffir, eds. Greenwich, CT: JAI Press. 31–60.

———. 1998. "Sociological Perspectives on Apostasy: An Overview." In *The Politics of Religious Apostasy: The Role of Apostates in the Transformation of Religious Movements*. David G. Bromley, ed. Westport, CT: Praeger. 3–16.

———. 1998b. "The Social Construction of Contested Exit Roles: Defectors, Whistleblowers, and Apostates." In *The Politics of Religious Apostasy*. David G. Bromley, ed. Westport, CT: Praeger. 19–48.

Carter, L. F. 1998. "Carriers of Tales: On Assessing Credibility of Apostate and Other Outsider Accounts of Religious Practices." In *The Politics of Religious Apostasy*. David G. Bromley, ed. Westport, CT: Praeger. 221–237.

Chesterton, G. K. 1923. *Heretics*. New York: Dodd Mead.

Coser, L. 1956., *The Functions of Social Conflict* London: Routledge and Kegan Paul.

Cottee, S. 2015a. *The Apostates: When Muslims Leave Islam*. London: Hurst.

———. 2015b. "I Escaped an Arranged Marriage." Vice, February 26. www.vice.com/en_uk/read/i-escaped-an-arrange-marriage-494.

Cragun, R. T., and J. H. Hammer. 2011. "'One Person's Apostate Is Another Person's Convert': What Terminology Tells Us about Pro-religious Hegemony in the Sociology of Religion." *Humanity & Society* 35, no. 1–2: 149–175.

Ebaugh, H. 1988. *Becoming an Ex: The Process of Role Exit*. Chicago: University of Chicago Press.

Goffman, E. 1963. *Stigma: Notes on the Management of Spoiled Identity*. London: Penguin.

Goode W. J. 1956. *After Divorce*. Glencoe, IL: The Free Press.

Hadaway, C. K., and W. C. Roof. 1988, "Apostasy in American Churches: Evidence from National Survey Data." In *Falling from the Faith: Causes and Consequences of Religious Apostasy*. David G. Bromley, ed. Beverly Hills, CA: Sage.

Hirschman, A. O. 1970., *Exit, Voice, and Loyalty: Responses to Decline in Firms, Organizations and States*. Cambridge, MA: Harvard University Press.

Hoffer, E. 1951. *The True Believer: Thoughts on the Nature of Mass Movements*. New York, Harper & Row.

Hoge, D. R. 1988., "Why Catholics Drop Out." In *Falling from the Faith: Causes and Consequences of Religious Apostasy*. David G. Bromley, ed. Beverly Hills, CA: Sage. 81–99.

Kurtz, L. R. 1983., "The Politics of Heresy." *American Journal of Sociology* 88, no. 6: 1085–1115.

Lazerwitz, B., and M. Harrison. 1979. "American Jewish Denominations: A Social and Religious Profile." *American Sociological Review* 44, no. 4: 656–666.

Matza, D. 1969. *Becoming Deviant*. Englewood Cliffs, NJ: Prentice-Hall.

McKnight, S., and H. Ondrey, 2008. *Finding Faith, Losing Faith: Stories of Conversion and Apostasy*. Waco, TX: Baylor University Press.

Merton, R. K. 1938. "Social Structure and Anomie." *American Sociological Review* 3, no. 5: 672–682.

———. 1968. *Social Theory and Social Structure*. New York: The Free Press.

Perry, E. L., et al. 1980. "Toward a Typology of Unchurched Protestants." *Review of Religious Research* 21, no. 4: 388–404.

Plummer, K. 1975. *Sexual Stigma: An Interactionist Account*. London: Routledge & Kegan Paul.

Reinkowski, M. 2007. "Hidden Believers, Hidden Apostates: The Phenomenon of Crypto-Jews and Crypto-Christians in the Middle-East." In *Converting Cultures: Religion, Ideology, and Transformations of Modernity*. Dennis Washburn and A. Kevin Reinhart, eds. Leiden: Brill. 409–433.

Roof, W. C. and J. S. Landres. 1997. "Defection, Disengagement, and Dissent: The Dynamics of Religious Change in the United States." In *Leaving Religion and Religious Life*. Mordechai Bar-Lev and William Shaffir, eds. Greenwich, CT: JAI Press.

Seidman, S. 2002. *Beyond the Closet: The Transformation of Gay and Lesbian Life*. New York: Routledge.

Shupe, A. 1998. "The Role of Apostates in the North American Anticult Movement." In *The Politics of Religious Apostasy*. David G. Bromley, ed. Westport, Conn.: Praeger. 209–217.

Simmel, G. 1971. *On Individuality and Social Forms: Selected Writings*. Ed. Donald N. Levine. Chicago: University of Chicago Press.

Streib, H., and B. Keller. 2004. "The Variety of Deconversion Experiences—Contours of a Concept in Respect to Empirical Research." *Archive for the Psychology of Religion* 26, no. 1: 180–200.

Theodorou, A. 2014., "Which countries still outlaw apostasy and blasphemy?" Pew Research Center, 28 May. www.pewresearch.org/fact-tank/2016/07/29/which-countries-still-outlaw-apostasy-and-blasphemy.

Weiss, R. S. 1975. *Marital Separation*. New York: Basic Books.

Wilson, S. G. 2004. *Leaving the Fold: Apostates and Defectors in Antiquity*. Minneapolis: Fortress Press.

Wright, S. A. 1991. "Reconceptualizing Cult Coercion and Withdrawal: A Comparative Analysis of Divorce and Apostasy." *Social Forces* 70, no. 1: 125–145.

———. 1998. "Exploring Factors That Shape the Apostate Role." In *The Politics of Religious Apostasy*. David G. Bromley, ed. Westport, CT: Praeger. 95–114.

Yip, A. K. T. 2000. "Leaving the Church to Keep My Faith: The Lived Experiences of Non-Heterosexual Christians." In *Joining and Leaving Religion: Research Perspectives*. Leslie J. Francis and Yaacov J. Katz, eds. Leominster: Gracewing. 129–145.

Zuckerman, P. 2009. "Atheism, Secularity, and Well-Being: How the Findings of Social Science Counter Negative Stereotypes and Assumptions." *Sociology Compass* 3, no. 6: 949–971.

THIRTEEN

RELIGIOUS SKEPTICISM AND NONBELIEVING IN EGYPT

KARIN VAN NIEUWKERK

During the past few years in Egypt, particularly after the ousting of President Mohamed Mursi in 2013, there has been remarkable attention paid in the Egyptian state media to a "new" phenomenon: young people abandoning Islam. Several TV channels covered the issue by framing these skeptics and nonbelievers as a threat to the moral, social, and political fabric of society that needs to be combated.

The Mehwar channel broadcast a show on the topic called the "Secret World of Atheists" as did the Al-Qahira wa al-Nas' program "Secrets under the Bridge." Anchor Riham Saʿid dedicated two episodes of her popular talk show to skeptics: one with the ex-Coptic humanist Ayman Ramzi, who afterward faced dismissal from his job and trial (Whitaker 2015), and the other with a Salafi-turned-agnostic lady, Dr. Nuha. The anchor could not handle the topic and felt so hurt by Dr. Nuha's opinions that she finally threw out her guest. She even publicized the Facebook page of Dr. Nuha, who had been covered with a face veil in the talk show to conceal her identity.[1] The program *The Open Door* tried to cover the topic in a less sensational way, but the presenter still felt the need to guide her audience and wished her guests and audience spiritual guidance.[2] The religious channel Misr 25[3] hosted a four-episode debate on "Islam and Atheism" between the Muslim thinker and writer Dr. ʿAmr Sherif and the atheist journalist and writer Bassam al-Baghdady.[4] The live debate, with al-Baghdady on Skype, covered topics such as the Big Bang theory, intelligent design, evolution, as well as logic and science. Although it was moderated in a 10-minutes-each fashion, the atheist position was misrepresented several times by the moderator, and al-Baghdady was entirely absent in the final episode. The popular preacher Habib ʿAli al-Jofri even had a thirty-episode Ramadan series on the topic "A Moment of Tranquility" in 2014.[5] Most episodes started with a critique or question raised by an atheist, which was then answered in a relaxed and friendly way by the preacher in the studio setting, taking his time to explain the misunderstanding of Islam by the nonbelievers. The channel The Alternative showed a more sympathetic image by portraying eight young nonbelievers and letting them speak without a voiceover.[6] The Christian channel al-Karama TV even provided a platform for the vocal ex-Salafist-turned-atheist Ahmad Harqan, who had been interrupted and marginalized in several of the above-mentioned programs, to voice his views in detail.[7]

Skeptics and nonbelievers also created their own media. They have been active on Facebook and have several pages[8] and a magazine,[9] and they have also opened their own video channels, like the ones by Alber Saber,[10] George Paul,[11] Masry Mulhid/the Egyptian Atheist,[12] and Masry Pharaon/the Egyptian Pharao, the latter taking his Egyptian identity from pre-Arab and pre-Muslim times.[13] In addition to the Arab Atheist Broadcasting Channel,[14] the Egyptian online channel *al-Batt al-Iswid/The Black Duck* is especially productive.[15] It uploaded its first video in August 2013 and has produced over 200 episodes at the time of writing. The host, Ismail Muhammad, interviews ex-Muslim and ex-Christian nonbelievers and agnostics or members of minority groups from Egypt and other Arab countries. According to the official website, the channel aims to "achieve a secular society in the Middle East and North Africa. Another goal is to offer solace and courage to those who are atheists in secrecy so they may know they are not alone in the world."[16] Although some of his guests reveal their identity, others are concealed from view. He discusses their motives for leaving the faith, the reaction of the environment, gender issues, freedom of speech, and recent political events like Charlie Hebdo and Islamic State (IS); three episodes are provided with English subtitles.[17] Together with Ahmad Harqan and George Paul, Ismail Muhammad is also active in Free Mind TV, launched in February 2015, in which activists appear in a more professional studio setting.[18] Ahmad Harqan explained that during those occasions when nonbelievers appear on mainstream media "we always get interrupted and never get a chance to fully convey our message."[19] The manager, Khaldoon al-Ghanimi, is an Iraqi businessman currently living in the United States, where he seeks asylum because of his nonbelief.

There is clearly something going on, and this contestation is not limited to the visual and print media.[20] Several openly atheist youths are persecuted, like Alber Saber, who fled to Switzerland to escape his sentence of three years in prison.[21] Ahmad Harqan, who stayed in Egypt, was also attacked and harassed.[22] On January 10, 2015, Karim al-Banna, a 21-year-old student, was sentenced to three years in prison for writing on Facebook that he was an atheist.[23] The antiblasphemy laws, in particular, have been used to silence nonbelievers. The government closed down Hikayatuna Cafe in downtown

Cairo because the cafe was said to house groups of young atheists. It remains to be seen, though, whether the young people gathering there were atheists or members of oppositional movements.[24] Al-Azhar, the renowned center of religious orthodoxy, recently started a campaign together with the Ministry of Youth to combat atheism. The campaign's goals are to spread awareness of the danger of atheism to society and to launch a dialogue with atheists to give them a chance to come back to religion.[25] Atheists entered the political field as well by asking for removal of the prescribed category of religion from the national ID card. They also met with the Committee of Fifty, which wrote the new Egyptian constitution in 2014, asking for a complete "secularization of the state."[26]

Despite the lively, not to say fierce, debates on disbelieving, not many scholarly works have addressed this "new" phenomenon (Schielke 2012, 2013; Whitaker 2014, 2015).[27] This holds true not only for the Egyptian case but also for the movement out of Islam, which has generally received less attention than "moving in."[28] Even less attention has been given to religious doubt and uncertainty. Convictions, whether strong belief or firm nonbelief, are easier to capture than trajectories of doubt, since "doubt tends to vanish with articulation" and "doubt is always on the move" (Pelkmans 2013: 5, 15). In this chapter, I will dive into the trajectory of doubt among Muslim skeptics and nonbelievers in Egypt and capture some of the reasons for their initial skepticism.

I think trajectories of doubts and "moving out" of Islam in Egypt[29] are not only an important entry into current sociopolitical issues in Egypt; studying how and why people leave Islam can also be a way to redress the dominant way in which Islam is studied. First, as several authors have stressed, the study of Muslim societies suffers from an overemphasis on religion as the most important factor in the lives of Muslims (Schielke 2013; Bowen 2012). In addition, Islam is often conflated with "violence and extremism." In Western media, the question is not whether "Arabs are religious, but rather to what extent this (assumed) religiosity can harm the West."[30] Studying trajectories of doubt and leaving Islam can rectify this image. Second, as far as the topic has been addressed, some particularly vocal ex-Muslims in the West have determined the representation of Muslim skeptics and atheists. Ex-Muslims, particularly those residing in the West, such as Ayaan Hirsi Ali (2007; 2015), Ehsan Jami (2007), Wafa Sultan (2009), and Ibn Warraq (2003), have fostered an anti-Islam discourse. Their plea for the urgency of a Muslim reformation was embraced by Western liberals and conservatives (Mahmood 2009). This discourse is also present among some Egyptian atheists, including Ahmad Harqan. His view that IS is a literal and full implementation of Islamic practices,[31] and limiting the wide variety of positions of skeptics and atheists to this discourse would leave out many voices. Finally, this recent debate in the Egyptian media and the atheists' own media provides an interesting insight in the "silent revolution" taking place in Egypt.[32] Not only is atheism purportedly on the rise; a number of women have taken off the veil,[33] and a trend toward spiritual Sufism is noticeable among Egyptian youths.[34] In his 2015 new year's speech, 'Abd al-Fattah al-Sisi called for a "religious revolution," specifically addressing al-Azhar.[35] Recent explanations for these trends, particularly atheism, point to the January 25 revolution and to the one-year rule of the Muslim Brotherhood. This makes the study of nonbelieving a fertile ground for studying contemporary religious and political transformations in Egypt.

Based upon the above-mentioned state media and ex-Muslim YouTube channels, particularly some episodes of *Black Duck*, as well as interviews with Egyptian atheists and skeptics, in order to cover the less-profiled agnostics and nonbelievers[36] I will address the following questions: First, is there a growing number of skeptics and atheists, and how is this related to the revolution and Muslim Brotherhood rule? Second, how are atheists represented by the Egyptian state media, and why does this issue evoke a "moral panic"? Finally, who are these skeptics and nonbelievers, and what are their main motives for leaving Islam? I will particularly highlight their trajectories of doubt.

THE REVOLUTION, MUSLIM BROTHERHOOD RULE, AND THE GROWING NUMBERS OF MUSLIM SKEPTICS

Although it is impossible to say anything about the number of nonbelievers in Egypt because of the dangers involved in "coming out," it is interesting to look at the attempt to do so, the variety of categorizations of nonbelieving, and particularly the diverse explanation for the "growing" number.

Religious sources such as al-Azhar's Dar al-Ifta reported that Egypt counted exactly 866 atheists out of a population of 87 million. However, the former Grand Mufti 'Ali Goma' said that a study was conducted by al-Azhar among 6,000 youths and 12.5 percent of them turned out to be atheists. He managed to have 10 percent of them revert back to Islam. Sheikh Turki, responsible for the al-Azhar campaign to fight atheism, estimated them at a few thousand, yet he feared nonbelief would spread like an epidemic, thereby explaining the need for such a campaign.[37] However, another sheikh in a media program estimated atheism at 3.7 million, particularly due to people's anger at the Muslim Brotherhood rule.[38] Al-Karama TV described atheism as a new wave of "millions" as well.[39] Atheists themselves mention that "in almost every house there is a nonbeliever."[40] One of the atheists I interviewed remarked: "Most Egyptians lead secret lives, the vast majority of them, whether it is sexually, or religiously, what they choose to believe or even what they like. I have no doubt that there are far more atheists in Egypt than would be publicly counted. And those very atheists would express adamant religious belief in public even though they might be secretly atheists. This is not an environment that would allow expression in any way."[41]

Another question we can raise is: Who counts as an atheist, as a skeptic, or as an agnostic? This question is particularly pertinent in a climate in which nonbelieving is highly politicized, and a secularist can sometimes be labeled an atheist because both positions are perceived as despicable. An interviewer from the Christian al-Karama TV channel remarked: "We got used to a strange culture saying that whoever disagrees with me is considered a *kafir*/ unbeliever or a *mulhid*/atheist or a *mushrik*/polytheist and therefore should not be listened to or dealt with."[42] Age-old discussions about who counts as a real Muslim simmer through the dialogue between the "skeptic" Dr. Nuha, who still identifies as a Muslim, and the anchor, Riham. After hearing her guest's views that the five pillars of Islam are not important and that Muhammad wrote the Qur'an, Riham concludes: "Then you are not a Muslim!"[43]

It is interesting to see the different ways atheism in these media debates is defined and categorized. Several terms are used: *ilhad*, the most common term for atheism, literally "deviance" or "heretic"[44]; *la adriyya*, or agnosticism, literally "I don't know"[45]; *la dini*, or nonreligious, an umbrella term for atheists and agnostics; *kufr*, or unbelief; and *irtidad* or *ridda*,[46] meaning apostasy or abandonment of Islam. The first three labels are used by nonbelievers and skeptics as well, whereas the latter two are used in religious discourses or with regard to the religious punishment for this "deviance."

In the *Oxford Handbook of Atheism*, atheism is broadly defined as "an absence of belief in the existence of a God or gods" (Bullivant 2013: 11). The Egyptian atheist Aly Aly, now living in the United States, closely echoes this definition when he explains the term *ilhad* (atheism) in his video: "Atheism is an answer to one definite question, and it is one question only: 'Do you believe in the existence of God'? Not: 'Does God exist'; No! . . . Atheism does not say anything about the existence or nonexistence of God. It only discusses the belief of a specific person in God's existence, or the lack of his belief in the existence of God."[47] Several nonbelievers stress that it is not a belief in itself but a stance, a viewpoint, or an intellectual position.[48] The agnostic position (*la adriyya*) is a lesser-known stance and for that reason a young Egyptian started the Facebook page Agnostics in Egypt. He explained that "atheists do not believe in any religion or God whereas agnostics say I am not sure about God's existence. I am in between."[49]

In one of the media debates, the scholar ʿAmr Sherif distinguished between strong and weak atheism: whereas the strong ones openly speak out to mock and belittle beliefs, the weak ones keep their ideas to themselves.[50] In another program, Dr. ʿAkasha distinguishes between the atheists who really studied religion and deny the existence of God; born Muslims who do not practice or believe but do not actively distance themselves; and, finally, the spiritual persons for whom a spiritual or godly power exists but who denounce the importance of religious rites, practices, and institutions.[51]

George, an ex-Coptic I interviewed, identified himself as a "proper atheist": "Which is complete skepticism. I think of myself as a complete and absolute skeptic. I believe in nothing supernatural whatsoever."[52] Among his friends he sees two categories of atheism:

> The ones, to put it simply that were angry with God. They were not really atheist to begin with. They are the ones that go through a certain phase of anger. They return very quickly back to religion especially considering the current pervasive pattern in new age Islam, that is, Sufism. There is Sufism now as a cultural trend. A lot of these people were atheist at some point! At least they expressed atheism. I would not call them atheists because as I said they simply expressed anger. I think them referring to themselves as atheists is also incorrect. They are going through a period of agnosticism. The other type is people that go through a pattern of thought.[53]

The idea of a "religious crisis"—a stage many young people go through, not necessarily indicating a final destination as atheist—was common in the interviews I conducted. It was also a convenient way for parents to consider their sons or daughters going through a temporary stage. The flexibility of positions from doubt and anger toward disbelief and (re)turning to positions such as Sufism should caution us in treating atheism as a final and fixed stage.

However, taking into account a historical dimension should also caution us to embrace the media representation of nonbelieving as a "new" phenomenon. Many intellectuals in the 1950s and 1960s had a secular attitude and open or hidden stances of nonbelieving (see Schielke 2014, Whitaker 2015). Also, currently several leftist intellectuals and activists with a secular agenda are not outspoken about their religious views. This is so not out of fear, but, as Milad explained,

> we know that there are a thousand ... atheists in Egypt all the time. At least for me for 15 years I am part of a group in which no one believes, and their fathers and grandfathers did not believe. It is old and normal, but no one is interested in speaking about it.... It is not an issue. [We are] talking about the police torturing people in police stations; that is an issue. Fifty percent of the population under the poverty line; that is an issue, but believing or not believing is not an issue.[54]

Although we simply do not know the number of nonbelievers and skeptics, in its different shades and moments there is a shared feeling that, even though we cannot know whether the trend is growing, it is at least becoming more visible and audible. There is undeniably a lot of attention paid to the topic, and the amount of TV programs, mentioned in the introduction to the chapter, illustrate the public visibility of the topic. There is also a clear campaign among atheists to "come out of the closet"[55] using the slogan "Say it! I am an atheist!"[56] In these media debates as well as the interviews I conducted, explanations for either "growth" or "growing visibility" abound. I will deal with the three most important ones: religious "extremism," particularly Muslim Brotherhood rule; the Arab Spring; and access to social media.

In the state media, reference is often made to the presidency of Mursi, which would have alienated people from religion. This explanation is part of the general "Muslim Brotherhood bashing" that is currently going on in Egypt, in which all evils of the current circumstances are traced back to the one-year rule of the Muslim Brotherhood. In this discourse, which is particularly audible in the state media, something as "hideous as atheism" is to be blamed on that organization. A related idea is that "the more extreme a society gets, the percentage of atheists will rise," as a reporter explained.[57] Also, Thomas Friedman of the *New York Times* related the growth of nonbelieving in the Arab World to horrific acts committed in the name of Islam: "The Islamic State has visibly attracted young Muslims from all over the world to its violent movement to build a caliphate in Iraq and Syria. But here's what's less visible—the online backlash against the Islamic State ... by young Muslims declaring their opposition to rule by Islamic law, or Shariah, and even proudly avowing their atheism."[58] Although the Muslim Brotherhood cannot be compared to IS, the way Islam has been used by the Muslim Brotherhood for political purposes and also the way they have been felt to dictate a certain understanding of Islam evoked a reaction I have heard quite often: "I am a Muslim; you don't need to tell me how to believe."

Yet this latter expression also points to the limits of this explanation. Whereas it might have led to a "countermovement," as George told me,[59] the content of the reaction can be multifarious. It can also be used to explain a significant trend among young people searching for a "spiritual Islam," or Sufism. So Muslim Brotherhood Islam or IS Islam might lead to conscious reflection on and sometimes defecting from Islam. Yet it can as easily result in different forms: "my Islam," "Sufi Islam," as well as "no Islam."

Perhaps more important is the connection between the revolution in Egypt and leaving Islam. This explanation is often used, in a direct or indirect way, by young people involved in the revolution themselves. Several activist nonbelievers were politically engaged before and during the revolution. The ex-Coptic activist Alber Saber said: "I was involved in activism and wanted to join Kefaya and started taking to the streets at the time of the 6 April [strike actions] in 2008. Do you think someone who would take to the streets before the revolution and who chanted against Mubarak would be afraid to reveal their beliefs?"[60] For many activist youths, freedom from religion is a direct result of their fight for the freedom of expression, democracy, and a secular state irrespective of personal beliefs. For instance, *Black Duck* host Ismail Muhammad first fought for Alber Saber's freedom to express his nonbelief, only to start his own search about his own religious background, instigating a process of reflection and eventually abandoning Islam.[61] The failure of religious authorities, whether al-Azhar or the Coptic Church, to connect with the revolutionary forces in the initial stage angered many young people and drove them away from religious institutions.[62]

Claiming freedom of thought and expression, whether during the ousting of Mubarak or of Mursi, has been a watershed experience for many young people. Although the revolution is often seen as a political failure, for many it meant a seminal moment because they took hold of their own thoughts, actions, beliefs, and lives. They started questioning inherited faith and traditions, and they queried the habit of blindly following religious norms, practices, and texts. Above all they questioned forms of authority, whether religious or secular, ruling their lives and prescribing thoughts and actions. This can take several shapes and does not necessarily lead to leaving the faith, but an attitude of skepticism is generally part of resistance toward authorities. I talked with several young women who deliberately took off the veil, not necessarily as a part of a journey toward nonbelieving but to express their feeling that they wanted to rethink whether the decision was theirs or part of an inherited faith and peer pressure.[63] Ibtisam, for instance, explained her trajectory of questioning as follows:

> That is what I like about the revolution. It can be a collective experience and at the same time it is very personal. After the revolution I was still wear-

> ing the *hijab*. Then I started to question not just Islam, but also the idea of God himself. I compared him to the president, to tyranny, God became a tyrant himself. Like somebody in charge all the time. You are not free, even if you think you are free. For me it started with this point.[64]

Conscious reflections on religious practices and refusing to follow blindly the authorities are part of the process unleashed by the upheavals in Egypt. Whereas the rule of authority is square back in Egypt, and freedom of expression is far from lived reality, this does not make the experience and possibility of overthrowing authority less meaningful, at least as far as personal lives and thoughts are concerned. This current is captured in the notion of the "silent revolution."[65] Yet we should keep in mind that this does not necessarily predict the outcome of deliberations and reflections. Ibtisam, for instance, eventually took off the veil, and after her period of "anger at God" she found solace in a spiritual, loving God.

As to the third main explanation, many observers relate the "growth" of atheism to the influence of social media. The revolution itself is often partly ascribed to social media activism, but social media has been instrumental in several other ways as well. Social media is central not only due to the present repressive climate in which it is not wise to express nonbelief; it is also an important source of information about lesser-known stances such as agnosticism. The availability of alternative theories to the religious origins of the universe and the human species was an eye-opening experience as well. Several skeptics and atheists mention the "turning point" of reading about Darwin or the New Atheists, such as Richard Dawkins.[66] Many skeptics and nonbelievers also expressed their happiness when finding out that their doubts and irreverence was shared by many. Yet, again, social media is instrumental to many different currents of thought and not exclusively to atheism but also, for instance, to Salafism. Yet marginal currents and repressed ideas certainly benefit from the relative privacy of the virtual space.

Although all three factors (Muslim Brotherhood rule; the revolution; and access to social media) help explain part of the conditions under which the current visibility and debate about skepticism and atheism might thrive, they explain insufficiently the motives of skeptics and nonbelievers themselves. To understand personal motivations we have to look more specifically at the individual trajectories of doubt. Before I return to the reasons for leaving Islam, I first look at the media representation of atheism and the "moral panic" it unleashed (McRobbie and Thornton 1995) in order to convey a sense of the social context in which individuals embark on a journey of doubt and nonbelief.

ATHEISM AND "MORAL PANIC" IN EGYPTIAN STATE MEDIA

"Let's not grant very precious time on air to certain groups to broadcast deformed ideas that eventually deform an entire generation."[67] This comment, from a caller during a program by the Mehwar channel, summarizes some of the main points behind the fear of atheism. It also points to the question of whether this topic should be broadcast at all. Most moderators are very ambivalent as to how to properly deal with nonbelief. They make great efforts to distance themselves from the topic they professionally have to introduce in a somewhat objective way. Some of them ask for God's guidance in dealing with this topic properly.[68] This ambivalent position among moderators is sometimes used by religious guests to gain more airtime than the opponent. For instance, the preacher Sherif al-Sawy tells the moderator: "You have to let me finish. . . . This has a very negative effect on society."[69] The attitude of the preacher is not hostile to the atheist Ahmad Harqan in trying to save his soul: "I swear to God (3x) it seems to me if I invested my whole life to save you from what you are in now, and bring you back to the Islam you belonged to, I would not hesitate for a second."[70] Sheikh Salim, who had been with Ahmad in another program, called him "brother" and "friend" and kissed him,[71] but he regretted and later apologized for this mistake during a phone call on another program "because my presence with him gave him value he does not deserve."[72] It is clear that when channels choose to broadcast atheists they feel a heavy responsibility to contain the danger they themselves might unleash. I will not go into media strategies (such as the way atheists are interrupted, silenced, and belittled, as well as the gloomy sounds accompanying reports), but I will present the underlying images they try to create about atheists as a way of combating this danger.

First, atheists are presented as deviants. A moderator told the atheist Ismail Muhammad: "You are the abnormal one. You are the one who deviated from society's norms. Therefore I have the right to ask."[73] As mentioned above, *ilhad* (the Arabic word commonly used for "atheism") can be traced to the Qur'an, where it means "deviance" (Schielke 2013: 639). The media accordingly delve into the "deviants'" family background and private lives to see whether some crisis—financial, social, or moral—can explain their deviation. In one program, Ismail Muhammad's mother was called to express how distressed she is by her son's nonbelief. Ismail got annoyed by this strategy and observed: "You did not ask the professor [the other guest in the program] about his family life."[74] They thus try to portray nonbelievers as marginalized and deprived youths, not as representatives of a way of thinking that might be present among all groups and classes. This evoked a remark by Ismail: "We have atheist university professors.... Atheists belong to various social groups as well as age groups."[75] The media tries to contain this "danger" by showing that atheists are exceptional, deviant, abnormal, and belong to marginal groups in society. In fact, many atheists, after being exposed as such, are ostracized and become outcasts.

Second, atheists are presented as belonging to a "secret society" with "imported ideas," possibly paid from "outside." The titles of some programs such as "The Secret World of Atheism" point at this representation. Questions such as "Who leads you today in Egypt?"[76]; "Where did you get your ideas from?"; "Who pays you?"; or remarks like "certain cells are being imported from abroad to propagate certain ideas"[77] expose traces of generally widespread conspiracy theories in Egypt. The disappointed Sheikh Salim, who thought that talking with atheist Ahmad Harqan "would put him on the right path again and restore his sanity," concluded: "Rather he wanted to propagate an idea that is imposed on him. He is paid to propagate such an idea."[78] Also, a link to communism is sometimes created to show the foreign and dangerous nature of such thought.[79] It is no wonder, then, that atheists have a strong discourse on being Egyptians and citizens, similar to Ismail Muhammad, who exclaimed: "No! We are young Egyptian citizens, not spies and traitors!"[80] Yet several atheists, after becoming publicly known, including Alber Saber and Aliya al-Mahdi, seek refuge abroad.

Third, atheism is sometimes portrayed as a disease or mental illness. It is not uncommon to invite a psychiatrist or psychologist to reflect on atheism. The Misr 25 channel invited a Saudi "specialist in the psychology of atheists" to reflect on the possible "Obsessive Compulsive Disorder" of atheists.[81] The specialist defined them as psychologically unstable persons who adopted a defective way of thinking. According to him, atheists may have an identity crisis or a personality problem: "Then, this atheist does not discuss an idea, but discusses his existence.... So, instead of fixing it from the inside, they try to fix it by adopting other ideas to achieve such peace of mind." Often the profiled atheists are represented not only as unstable and feeble minded but also as "attention seeking."[82] In fact, many young people experiencing doubts or a "religious crisis" are sent to either a psychiatrist or a sheikh.[83]

This brings us to the fourth representation in the media: atheists are ill-guided. They have supposedly been exposed to wrong ideas about Islam (e.g., by extremists and the Muslim Brotherhood). By providing them with a correct and moderate form of Islamic preaching, they might revert back. This representational strategy ties in with the attempt to instigate a "religious revolution" and attempts to win the hearts and minds of nonbelievers. The sheikhs debating with atheists make an effort in that direction, and so do some of the moderators. The anchor Riham Sa'id, for instance, invites a Muslim child to recite the Qur'an and explain his unshakable belief in Allah to convince the ex-Coptic humanist guest on her show at least to believe in the existence of God. However, the general response to religious doubt is repression, denial, and silencing. Asking questions is *haram* (forbidden in Islam) since "God knows best," and doubt is considered the work of the devil.[84]

Religious scholars invited to the shows warn other religious authorities and parents against not dealing properly with religious doubt. Azhar Sheikh Sayyid Zayid says: "We used to hear philosophers say 'I doubt therefore I am' ... Doubt is the first step towards certainty. However, to deny for the sake of denial and fame—for a personal need, the one who denies, is pitied."[85] Rarely one finds sheikhs on TV acknowledging that "they don't know."[86] The Yemeni preacher Habib 'Ali al-Jofri opened the way for questioning: "Doubt is reality ... it is not optional and one cannot say I choose to doubt or not to doubt." The preacher explains Ahmad Harqan's case—that any discourse that forbids doubting and raising questions would push someone to leave Islam because of the accumulative burden of guilt. Questions lead to knowledge, and there is no knowledge without questioning. Yet some questions are from Satan, when the aim is not knowledge but trying to be able to keep indulging certain sins. "Yes," he replies to Ahmad, "in all religions and ideologies there can be some inconsistencies." Al-Jofri is rather exceptional in this stance; most religious scholars deny or try to explain away contradictions.[87]

In addition, atheism is represented as illogical. Much effort is spent in showing how atheists deny the "logic" accepted by all times and all human societies, that is, the existence of God. Human beings are born with the innate disposition (*fitra*) to submit to God, the original meaning of Islam. Atheists are portrayed as refusing to acknowledge "the logic of their minds."[88] The fact that religion is of all times and places confirms the idea of the natural state of religiosity, and the idea that God created both religion and science, show that they cannot be contradictory, Sheikh Salim argued.[89] Generally they aim to show that the existence of God is not merely a "theological" stance but a "logical" position.[90] Atheists are blamed for lacking scientific evidence when they deny God's existence. In addition, the discourse about the scientific character of the Qur'an, or Bucailleism,[91] is used to convey the importance of science and logic as natural partners in faith. Sometimes great scholars and atheists who are finally said to have acknowledged the existence of God, such as Anthony Flew and Jean-Paul Sartre, are quoted.[92] Many debates revolve around the (in)compatibility of science and faith, from both the religious media and atheists.

Finally, atheists are frequently represented as immoral. They are often questioned about their moral ideas and actions. When the mother of the atheist Ismail Muhammad calls in during the show and Ismail expresses concern for her distress, the moderator asks him: "Why do you do that? Taking care of your parents is something religion calls for."[93] Questions such as "Would you accept if I propagate prostitution?" and "Are you now sleeping with your mother and sister?" are often directed at atheists.[94] Atheists are perceived to be driven by lust and to reject religion because it limits their lust.[95] This conveys the idea that there is no moral framework outside the religious scope, defining nonbelievers automatically as immoral. Dr. Bakr Zaki Awad, dean of the faculty of theology at al-Azhar University, was allowed to conclude the show—after Ismail decided to leave the show, as he was not allowed to express himself—by saying:

> Without religion, there is no right or wrong. Atheists do not believe in the wrong at all. Therefore, it's okay for an atheist to marry his sister or his daughter or his mother. For them this is allowed, because they don't believe anything is forbidden. When they deny the existence of God, they deny the existence of what is forbidden. They don't watch what they do or say, whether in public or private. His God becomes his mind. In their faith, they don't believe in hell or heaven. There is death and it ends there. So they are entitled to enjoy life as much as they want in their lifetime. There is no payback or punishment. They allow themselves to satisfy their needs and their interest whatever way possible.[96]

This accusation of immorality makes leaving Islam even more sensitive for women. Different ways of grounding morality and gender issues are among the most important bones of contention between believers and nonbelievers.

MUSLIM SKEPTICS' TRAJECTORIES AND MOTIVES TO LEAVE ISLAM

We have seen that nonbelievers are represented in the media as misguided, marginal, mentally sick, and immoral persons, an image shared by society at large. It must thus be very difficult to embark on this journey, let alone to come out of the closet. What are their motives and reasons for leaving Islam, and how did their trajectory unfold? I will go into the process of loss of faith and the period of doubt, although becoming a nonbeliever also entails developing new ideas and practices (Schielke 2013). As we have seen above, how to deal with religious doubt is contested among preachers. For the skeptics, this period of doubt was a crucial and painful stage.

I base this analysis on my own interviews as well as some *al-Batt al-Iswid* interviews that provide more in-depth biographical material. This material consists of twenty-one Muslim skeptics and nonbelievers, of whom eight are women and thirteen men, six of them are currently living abroad.[97] Most of them are well educated young men and women, in their twenties or early thirties. Those living abroad have more or less come out for their nonbelieving, whereas nine of those living in Egypt did not disclose their ideas except to some very intimate friends.

In general, many of the skeptics' and nonbelievers' trajectories of doubt started with theological and existential questions with regard to the existence of God. They perceived contradictions in the Qur'an, doubted the exemplary character of the Prophet, and were confronted with scientific theories that contradicted religious explanations—issues that the "scientific miracles" in the Qur'an could not settle for them. In particular, perceived "injustice," whether with regard to women, minorities, or nonbelievers—sometimes born out of personal experiences—raised serious doubts that, when expressed, were often silenced, further encouraging investigation.

For many skeptics and nonbelievers their journey started at a young age with the basic questions about God: how to know God and how to know he really exists. "I can't see Him, how do I know He really exists?" asked the young agnostic Sarah.[98] Aly Aly in his YouTube lecture about how to define atheism states that for him there is no answer to the question about God's existence. "The answer is we don't know. I can't believe in a thing from which I basically know there is no answer. So that is the way I reached atheism."[99] Sami explains that as a 14-year-old he was confused about why the almighty God does not know how to get his message across, requiring three messages that still need explanation, whereas he could have just directly spoken to humans.[100] The blogger Khalid Diab mockingly suggests that God should use "Faithbook" to connect to humanity directly instead of relying on prophets and scripture.[101] A recurrent issue was the identified inability of the omnipotent God to stop violence, war, and injustice from continuously spreading all over the world. Besides, the image of God they were taught, through lessons or sermons, about torments in the grave, cruel punishment in hell, and violent conduct against enemies and nonbelievers conveyed to them an image of a frightening, violent, cruel God they eventually dared to challenge.

This image of violence and cruelty is also what speaks to them from the Qur'an, raising questions about its holiness. For some Salafis turned atheists it was the perceived contradictions in the Qur'anic verses that instilled a journey of skepticism and apostasy. As Ahmad Harqan explains: "It's about the Qur'an as a whole, being a reason to become an atheist."[102] "I left Islam due to the contradictions in the verse of the Qur'an itself, the Qur'an that I memorize like my own name!"[103] The answer he received—that contradictory elements should be understood metaphorically or symbolically—was apparently making things worse for him: "But those who say it is symbolic have an even larger problem. I then have no way to measure what is true and what is symbolic."[104] Also, Rania told in different episodes of *Black Duck* how her religious eagerness and scrutiny of the Qur'an and other religious sources eventually caused her faith to crumble. It is not my intention to elaborate on the content of these perceived contradictions and the religious rebuttal of them. These debates are intricate and lengthy. It suffices to note that, especially for those inclined to a Salafist literal reading of texts, the identified contradictions were an explosive experience.

Also, the expected exemplary role model of the Prophet lost its appeal after finding out deeds they attributed to the Prophet and experienced as reprehensible. "How can you marry someone who is 9 years old, have 4 wives and make war with another country and take their wives as well?!" expressed the agnostic Momi during the interview I had with his group of friends.[105] Hayat was confused and shocked when she read about Prophet Muhammad marrying Aisha at nine, but when someone came to ask for his daughter's hand at a similar young age, he refused. This not only sharpened her sense of unfairness toward women; it also highlighted for her the apparent arbitrariness of some of his deeds.[106] Several skeptics expressed doubts about several revelations of God to the Prophet that in fact suited his own interest all too well. The loss of such an iconic role model was a shocking experience for them.

Several skeptics and nonbelievers explained how their initial "childish" questions about God's existence slumbered but were awakened when they went to college, started reading, and encountered scientific theories. Several of my interlocutors echo the experience of the blogger Al-Hussein: "The discovery of the elementary notion of evolution was mind-blowing. Books like Dawkins's *The God Delusion* and Darwin's *The Origin of Species* opened my eyes to a whole new paradigm."[107] 'Aziz similarly explained how his education in college in the department of computer science and artificial intelligence changed his paradigm. He concluded from his studies that things are digital: either right or wrong. To him religion showed many contradictions and contradictory explanations were perceived as inconsistent. "Some argue

Big Bang is supported by the Qur'an, others deny this."[108] This opened his way to skepticism. For others, it was the theory of "the scientific miracles in the Qur'an," or the inimitability of the Qur'an (*ʿigaz ʿilmi*), and the idea of the Qur'an itself as a linguistic miracle that lost their foothold. The theory of the scientific miracles mentioned in the Qur'an is often used to bring science into the fold of religion instead of representing them as opposing fields. For the atheist ʿAmru, reading a book by an Egyptian Muslim scholar who believed in God but denied the scientific miracles of the Qur'an shattered his convictions. "I was raised my whole life with the idea of the scientific miracles, I was totally convinced of them, and now it is wrong. That means that there can be many mistakes in other aspects as well."[109] In another episode of *Black Duck* (no. 38), he explains why he does not consider the Qur'an inimitable and argues that the Qur'an contains not only scientific errors but also that the knowledge deemed a miracle—for instance, about the process of pregnancy and growth of the embryo—was available at the Prophet's time.

A prominent theme among trajectories to leave Islam is related to perceived injustice. Particularly women's issues were frequently evoked, not only by female skeptics and nonbelievers but also by men. For the Femen activist Aliya al-Mahdi the position of women was a major theme. She recollects the start of her trajectory of doubt when a discussion at home evolved around a couple who both went to a dating site secretly, only to bump into each other again. Whereas the woman was heavily criticized, no objections were raised about the man's behavior.[110] Others expressed their experience of unequal treatment in comparison to their brothers at home being religiously legitimated by their family. Whereas, for instance, Zuzu first thought that perhaps this inequality was to blame on human errors and not religiously ordained, her quest led her to understand the opposite.[111] A group of four young male and female skeptics and atheists I interviewed together all mentioned the position of women as their primary motive to leave Islam. Mona, the oldest of the group, related her personal experience of marrying young into a Salafi community, getting pregnant for a second time, being denied an abortion on religious grounds, and having to wear a *niqab* while witnessing all kinds of "hypocritical sexual behavior" within this Salafi community. She finally broke out, took off her *hijab*, and tried to rebuild her life as a single mother back in her parental home.[112] Rania, not from her personal experience but out of her eagerness to read profoundly about Islam, discovered to her great amazement that female slaves were treated as "objects that could be touched and sold."[113]

The trigger that starts the trajectory of doubt can be manifold. In addition to existential questions that can begin at a young age, and awake during college or intensive reading, or personal experiences perceived as unjust, travelling abroad or meeting with alternative ideas and lifestyles can prompt a search. Mahmud, for instance, having already left Salafi circles, turned into a skeptic after meeting a British volunteer in the development association he was working in. She challenged his preconceptions; although she was not a believer, she was highly moral and spiritual. "So according to the Islamic theology disbelievers will go to hell. But this girl is someone who works for the environment, for Greenpeace, she is actually better in every way than all the people I know who supposedly were going to heaven. In every way! I could not accept this concept, that according to religion she is going to hell. And there is no justification for this. This actually made me a skeptic."[114] Also, the realization that it is a mere geographical coincidence, rather than a matter of choice, that one happens to be born in the Muslim faith—supposedly the only one true religion—could be an initial starting point for doubt and research.[115]

The religious backgrounds of the nonbelievers were varied; most described their families as "religiously moderate," although some labeled their families as strict, "fundamentalist" (*usuliyin*), or Salafi. Although five of them described themselves as former strict or Salafi Muslims, most were "moderate," somewhat "lazy," "negligent," or "sometimes praying sometimes not." Magdi, although from a "normal" family, was living in Saudi Arabia for a while, "thus becoming acquainted with a violent Wahhabi Islam."[116] ʿAziz, the computer science skeptic, was not only troubled by the contradictions he perceived; he increasingly felt religion as a "burden": many things you had to do while it was not clear why. Questioning the need of religious practices such as prayer and fasting led, in his view, to contradictory answers. Why would God bother about such minor issues as praying five times a day? Almsgiving he deemed logical and beneficial, but he could not figure out a higher purpose behind praying. Besides, he admitted that he was fond of smoking hash with his friends.[117] Many a religious scholar or believer would rush to point out that these youngsters did "not have real understanding of religion" and therefore "were not Muslims in the first place,"[118] but most searched and initially felt the urge to go deep into religion before eventually—after a mostly painful trajectory—renouncing faith.

Whatever the initial point, for most it was not a sudden awakening: "You don't wake up as an atheist one day,"[119] "it is an accumulation,"[120] "It does not come overnight."[121] Also Dr. Nuha refuses the conversion idiom, the "defining moment" forced upon her by the presenter Riham, explaining that it is not a moment but a journey.[122] ʿAmru turns the conversion idiom that "everyone is born as a Muslim" (Van Nieuwkerk 2006) upside down by claiming that all people are born as nonbelievers: "All people are born as atheists, they do neither believe in God, nor in religion, paradise and hell, devils and angels. Today I am like that again."[123] Just as it is the process of upbringing and socialization within the family that makes one a believer, it is a journey of unlearning religious thought and acts as well as learning new paradigms when one leaves the faith.

For some, particularly those leaning toward literalist interpretations and after discovering contradictions in the Qur'an, the process of unlearning might be short but explosive. Rania, for instance, "deconverted" in two months,[124] relating that: "They would even call me a '*sheikha*.' They used to tell me I would have a great future in Islam, but I am really happy that I got to know the truth.... I left Islam, because one small mistake is enough to destroy it completely. There are so many mistakes in Islam."[125] Hussein explained how he—as not a very outgoing type, lacking connection to peers in the university—became attracted to the serious studious atmosphere of brotherhood in the Salafi movements. Although he went deep into it for several years, it was an ideological attraction rather than a religious feeling or deeply felt piety. "I took the topic more ideologically ... the level of spirituality was not very high ... I prayed on time but there was no *khusu*ʿ, God fearing."[126] The internal discussion among Salafi sheikhs sowed his initial doubt, particularly regarding the different interpretations of the Hadith, reporting the conduct of the Prophet (Sunnah). He therefore decided to denounce the Hadith and became "Quraniyya" but realized that the Qur'an without the Sunnah is difficult: "How do you know how to pray?" When his faith in the scientific miracles of the Qur'an was crushed, he was a deist (*rububi*) for some time, but eventually his intellectual journey led him to the position of nonbeliever.

Ahmad Harqan gives insight into how his intellectual journey—eventually stumbling over inconsistencies and becoming a vocal atheist who speaks out against Islam—was invested with deep emotional anguish and pious fear. Ahmad grew up in a very religious family. His father's ambition was not to educate his son to become a doctor or engineer but for him to become a great religious scholar. Ahmad memorized the Qur'an as a child, and it "was my foundation and everything in my life.... Religion was the center of my life."[127] At an early age, confusion and doubt took hold of him, a skepticism that he tried to dispel: "I didn't want to lose my religion or anger Allah and as a result I began to blame myself and spent more time in worshipping so God would drive away my doubt."[128] He studied in Mecca and often made the pilgrimage. He would make extra circumbulations (*tawwaf*) to keep his doubts away and also tried to keep himself busy with prayer. Also his supplication, asking God "you change hearts and minds, keep me on your religion," was to no avail.[129] His whole life he had been close to doubts. Finally giving in to his qualms and acknowledging the "contradictions" and "scientific errors" "was the hardest that can be."[130] Until the age of 27 he tried to dispel doubts but now perceives doubt "as the beginning of knowledge."

Mahmud similarly explains how hard it was to finally let go of his fears and denounce his faith. After leaving Salafism and turning skeptic, it still was hard to let it go totally. The final step for him was coming across evolution theory introduced to him by a friend. After searching and reading about it he said:

> I could not deny it. I was convinced. And then it hit me: God can send me to hell for something I did not choose to do, because I did not choose this conviction. Conviction happens because of the evidence. The conviction was forced upon me because of readings and evidence. You cannot choose it. And that is the only thing that God hates. God will not tolerate this conviction. If I steal or do anything he can tolerate this, but he cannot tolerate this conviction.... I was convinced but I did not dare to take the step. To declare to myself, at least to myself, I could not do it! It was very hard. Because once you do it, there is a lot of work you have to do! You have to define right and wrong again from the start.

Once he had "figured out" that God "wants us to believe without conviction," he declared himself, only for himself, an atheist.[131]

The period of doubt, the torturing prospect that you might be wrong or that "the devil is playing with you ... you don't know for sure whether you are right or wrong," was "of course a black period," Zuzu explains.[132] Hayat, having denounced institutional religion, is going through a period of doubt regarding God's existence. She related:

> I don't know whether there is a God or not.... Sometimes I think he is present, He is an oppressor (*zalim*) and I will curse him when I am angry. Sometimes, when I have moments which are not nice, then I feel He is present because He does something good, He soothes me (*yitabtab ʿalayya*). Sometimes I feel He is present because I need him to be present to talk to me. I ask him things like a superhero, but there is nothing.... And there are times that I see he is not present, then I think it is impossible that someone Big can make all this. The idea is not logical to me.... If I do not see you, you are not present.... I asked for you, nine years I talk to you and never did you answer me. If you are present you would have at least talked to me once. So no, you are not present! I hesitate between these two thoughts and currently I don't know He is present or not.

> Sometimes I am relaxed with the idea of his presence and sometimes not. And sometimes I hate him, but that still means that He is present because you have feelings towards him. But the times I see that He is not present I feel more relaxed.[133]

Hayat's doubts continue, but in the meantime she took off her veil, moved out of her parental home when she was 30, and lives a "secret" life with her Christian boyfriend.

CONCLUSION

Hayat's contemplation neatly captures "the doubting moment" (Pelkmans 2013: 4). Doubt is often pressing for a resolution. Which direction her doubt will move is not yet certain, but when it further evolves in the direction of complete skepticism or nonbelief this will entail more than losing faith. It also involves working out new paradigms, lifestyles, forging new relationships, rethinking the building blocks for ethical behavior outside the religious frame, dealing with questions about hiding and revealing nonbelief, and playing along or challenging religion. Whereas some became activists, most hid their serious doubts and their new convictions. Even the activist Ahmad Harqan cautions: "It is not easy for someone young who still lives with his parents to announce atheism and openly refuse religion because he still depends on his parents who will oppose him. So if a young man or woman who is still dependent upon their families discusses their atheism openly, it will result in too much trouble." He continues: "But with an independent person who is scared or ashamed to openly say that he is an atheist, he should not be scared or ashamed." Harqan concluded as follows: "Atheism is an honor and it should be the believers who would be ashamed of believing in a myth that has no logical or scientific proof."[134]

Whereas the narrative of pride about leaving Islam (see Davidman and Greil 2007) is shared by some or is expressed as a discourse of claiming citizenship, such as Ismail Muhammad, keeping a low profile is not illogical in view of society's condemnation and perception of atheists as ill-guided, mentally sick, and amoral. The aura of ambivalent skepticism, without revealing the full extent of it, suits Mahmud. His family is divided between Mursi and al-Sisi loyalists. The two sides of the family are not on speaking terms and avoid each other at family occasions. Mahmud, as "the revolution guy," is accepted by both sides, poking daring questions at each of them.[135] For some it is not only about fear of condemnation by society or relatives or not wanting to hurt the feelings of loved ones; over time it can also become a less pressing issue. While meeting Momi and Magdi for a second time, two years after the first interview, it appeared that they had more urgent matters to attend to. Politics had worn them out. While Momi was busy with work and less active with the agnostic website, Magdi was preparing his flat in order to marry. It was evident that not only political projects but also personal trajectories had moved on in new directions.[136]

NOTES

1. www.youtube.com/watch?v=VX-hscY3ApY.

2. 1/3 www.youtube.com/watch?v=duofaE2WG6c; 2/3www.youtube.com/watch?v=7YlH3Utbxvo; 3/3 www.youtube.com/watch?v=7YlH3Utbxvo.

3. The name of the channel refers to the January 25 revolution.

4. www.youtube.com/watch?v=JUS3GrhYyRQ.

5. www.youtube.com/watch?v=iQqIZ1-p5L4.

6. www.youtube.com/watch?v=BY4tnYkZIvA.

7. www.youtube.com/watch?v=1WF7HXsB2kk. No longer available (accessed July 11, 2015). Several channels and Facebook pages by atheists are blocked since around December 2017. For that reason they are no longer available. They might reappear at another URL.

8. For instance "Egyptians without Religion"; "Agnostics in Egypt"; "Arab Atheist Library."

9. Secular Magazine. www.facebook.com/31manya20. No longer available (accessed December 2015).

10. www.youtube.com/user/AlberEgypte1.

11. www.youtube.com/user/drmeky85/videos.

12. www.youtube.com/channel/UCEGdwhyVrEW-ZzqPow2m_Qg.

13. www.youtube.com/channel/UCP3f3OIUCrySHyysHf49srA/videos.

14. www.arabatheistbroadcasting.com/program/programs/podcast.

15. www.youtube.com/channel/UCQuIoUMMoWaUXnlyEuo-6Ng/videos.

16. www.youtube.com/channel/UCQuIoUMMoWaUXnlyEuo-6Ng/about.

17. Episodes 102, 103, and 108.

18. www.youtube.com/watch?v=h8tOu1r9Xf4&list=PL3UWYjowlv43_QeSTtmqu7MfLQXp2m2iP.

19. www.al-monitor.com/pulse/originals/2015/05/egypt-radio-channel-online-religion-atheism-us-media.html#.

20. At the 2015 Cairo book fair, I came across M. Adib, *al-Ilhad/Atheism* (Cairo: Nashrit al-Tawziʿ, 2013); M. Dawud, *ʿAzizit al-Mulhid / Dear Atheist* (Cairo: Dar al-Nahda Masr, 2015); K. Farhat, *Lassit Mulhidan ... Limadha? [I am not an atheist ... Why?]* (Cairo: Dar al-Nahda Masr, 2014); and A. Sherif, *Khurafit al-Ilhad [The Myth of Atheism]* (Cairo: Maktabat al-Shuruq al-Dawliyya, 2014).

21. Sources at www.al-monitor.com/pulse/originals/2014/05/atheism-egypt-criticism-law.html; and www.dailynewsegypt.com/2013/01/27/alber-saber-brotherhood-will-drive-the-people-to-secularism.html. Both no longer available (accessed June 10, 2015).

22. english.ahram.org.eg/News/120204.aspx.

23. www.eutopiamagazine.eu/en/ayman-abdelmeguid/columns/egypt's-silent-revolution.html. No longer available (accessed June 10, 2015).

24. www.al-monitor.com/pulse/originals/2015/01/egypt-crackdown-atheism-cafes.html.

25. www.al-monitor.com/pulse/originals/2014/07/egypt-govemment-fears-atheism.html. No longer available. See also www.youtube.com/watch?v=Gut38V94toU&feature=em-subs_digest-vrecs. No longer available (accessed July 13, 2015). For further information see also IHEU freedom of thought report online at freethoughtreport.com.

26. chronikler.com/middle-east/egypt/atheists-out-closet; and www.youtube.com/watch?v=KfPEXqiXfMg.

27. More information is available about blasphemy, apostasy, and (Islamic) law or specific cases such as Nasr Abu Zaid (see Peters and De Vries 1976–1977; O'Sullivan 2003; and Olsson 2008).

28. For "moving in" see extensive literature, e.g.: Allievi (1998); Van Nieuwkerk (2006); Gooren (2012); Özyürek (2015). For moving out see Cottee (2015); Crimp and Richardson (2008); and Khalil and Bilici (2007).

29. The issue is not confined to Islam, and several Coptic Christians are abandoning the faith as well. In the first two sections I will go into the debates around Egyptian nonbelievers in general. In the final section on trajectories of doubt, I will limit myself to leaving Islam.

30. www.newrepublic.com/article/121559/rise-arab-atheists.html.

31. *Black Duck* episode 108 is available online.

32. www.eutopiamagazine.eu/en/ayman-abdelmeguid/columns/egypt's-silent-revolution.html.

33. My main source is interviews and fieldwork. See also www.nytimes.com/2015/04/11/opinion/mona-eltahawy-my-unveiling-ceremony.html?_r=0.

34. My main source for this observation is fieldwork and interviews.

35. Memri TV clip 4704. www.memritv.org/clip/en/4704.htm.

36. Next to the sixteen media debates, I transcribed twenty-eight episodes of *al-Batt al-Iswid* and two of *Aly Aly*. In addition, I conducted sixteen interviews with skeptics or on the topic of atheism. Twelve of them self-identified as skeptic or atheist, including four Christians. The remaining four interviews were on religious views of atheism, Sufism, and (two) on taking off the veil. I interviewed seven women and nine men.

37. english.ahram.org.eg/News/120204.aspx.

38. www.youtube.com/watch?v=0TGTaJtA30A.

39. www.youtube.com/watch?v=1WF7HXsB2kk. No longer available (accessed June 10, 2015).

40. www.youtube.com/watch?v=KfPEXqiXfMg.

41. Interview, February 8, 2015.

42. www.youtube.com/watch?v=1WF7HXsB2kk. No longer available (accessed June 10, 2015).

43. www.youtube.com/watch?v=VX-hscY3ApY.

44. www.brill.com/products/reference-works.

45. www.brill.com/products/reference-works.

46. www.brill.com/products/reference-works.

47. www.youtube.com/watch?v=2NAybCnZz8U.

48. *Al-Batt al-Iswid*, episodes 38 and 61.

49. Interview, July 2, 2013.

50. www.youtube.com/watch?v=JUS3GrhYyRQ.

51. www.youtube.com/watch?v=7YlH3Utbxvo.

52. Interview, February 8, 2015.

53. Interview, February 8, 2015.

54. Interview, February 17, 2015.

55. Some of the terminology in Egypt to denote and represent atheists is also used to describe homosexuals.

56. www.youtube.com/watch?v=yDHO3qz7LbI. No longer available (accessed July 14, 2015).

57. www.youtube.com/watch?v=Gk2uwSv4tGk&list=PL3UWYjowlv408sEWlHQajtuvVTCaBpV-g. No longer available (accessed July 14, 2015).

58. www.nytimes.com/2014/12/07/opinion/sunday/thomas-l-friedman-how-isis-drives-muslims-from-Islam.html. No longer available (accessed June 10, 2015).

59. Interview, February 8, 2015.

60. www.dailynewsegypt.com/2013/01/27/alber-saber-brotherhood-will-drive-the-people-to-secularism.html. No longer available (accessed June 10, 2015).

61. www.youtube.com/watch?v=KfPEXqiXfMg. See also *al-Batt al-Iswid*, episode 12.

62. Interviews with George, February 8, 2015; Milad, February 17, 2015; Hayat, February 15, 2015; Imad, February 2, 2015; and Ibtisam, February 13, 2015.

63. Interviews with Hayat, February 15, 2015; Ibtisam, February 13, 2015; Soʿad, January 29, 2015, and February 2, 2015; and Soheir, February 29, 2015. See also www.nytimes.com/2015/04/11/opinion/mona-eltahawy-my-unveiling-ceremony.html?_r=0.

64. Interview, February 13, 2015.

65. www.eutopiamagazine.eu/en/ayman-abdelmeguid/columns/egypt%E2%80%99s-silent-revolution. No longer available (accessed July 14, 2015).

66. See the last section, on trajectories of doubt.

67. www.youtube.com/watch?v=JUS3GrhYyRQ.

68. www.youtube.com/watch?v=Ozn9q3TTcbE.

69. www.youtube.com/watch?v=WqG9KJPH6do. No longer available (accessed July 14, 2015).

70. www.youtube.com/watch?v=WqG9KJPH6do. No longer available (accessed July 14, 2015).

71. www.youtube.com/watch?v=Uvgm1wv5pDs.

72. www.youtube.com/watch?v=WqG9KJPH6do. No longer available (accessed July 14, 2015).

73. www.youtube.com/watch?v=KfPEXqiXfMg.

74. www.youtube.com/watch?v=KfPEXqiXfMg.

75. www.youtube.com/watch?v=KfPEXqiXfMg.

76. www.youtube.com/watch?v=Gk2uwSv4tGk. No longer available (accessed July 14, 2015).

77. www.youtube.com/watch?v=KfPEXqiXfMg.

78. www.youtube.com/watch?v=WqG9KJPH6do. No longer available (accessed July 14, 2015).

79. www.youtube.com/watch?v=Gk2uwSv4tGk. No longer available (accessed July 14, 2015).

80. www.youtube.com/watch?v=KfPEXqiXfMg.

81. Dr. Tarek Al-Habib, an attending psychiatrist at the University of King Saud. He is specialized in the psychology of atheists. www.youtube.com/watch?v=Ozn9q3TTcbE.

82. www.youtube.com/watch?v=Gk2uwSv4tGk. No longer available (accessed July 14, 2015).

83. www.youtube.com/watch?v=6LediogocuY. Interview with Yusif, February 13, 2015. See further the final section, on trajectories of doubt.

84. E.g., *al-Batt al-Iswid*, episodes 6, 24, 85.

85. www.youtube.com/watch?v=Gk2uwSv4tGk. No longer available (accessed July 14, 2015).

86. Episode 4: www.youtube.com/watch?v=iQqIZ1-p5L4&list=PL9ZuXv4q1CBJMgg3vb9Tc9q8M5NHmNwsv.

87. Episodes 1 and 4: www.youtube.com/watch?v=iQqIZ1-p5L4&list=PL9ZuXv4q1CBJMgg3vb9Tc9q8M5NHmNwsv.

88. www.youtube.com/watch?v=Ozn9q3TTcbE.

89. www.youtube.com/watch?v=Uvgm1wv5pDs.

90. Particularly in the four episodes of the Misr 25 debate. See, e.g., www.youtube.com/watch?v=JUS3GrhYyRQ.

91. The term "Bucailleism" is derived from Maurice Bucaille, who published the book *The Bible, the Qur'an and Science* in 1976. In this book he argued that the Qur'an contains no statements contradicting established scientific facts.

92. www.youtube.com/watch?v=Ozn9q3TTcbE.

93. www.youtube.com/watch?v=KfPEXqiXfMg.

94. www.youtube.com/watch?v=KfPEXqiXfMg. See also *al-Batt al-Iswid*, episodes 24, 26, and 111.

95. *Al-Batt al-Iswid*, episode 63.

96. www.youtube.com/watch?v=KfPEXqiXfMg.

97. I will leave out six portrayals of former Christians for this section.

98. Interview, July 2, 2013.

99. www.youtube.com/watch?v=2NAybCnZz8U.

100. *Al-Batt al-Iswid*, episode 26.

101. chronikler.com/reflections/belief/faithbook.

102. www.youtube.com/watch?v=1WF7HXsB2kk. No longer available (accessed July 11, 2015).

103. www.youtube.com/watch?v=Uvgm1wv5pDs.

104. www.youtube.com/watch?v=Uvgm1wv5pDs.

105. Interview, July 2, 2013.

106. Interview, February 15, 2015.

107. www.newrepublic.com/article/121559/rise-arab-atheists.

108. Interview, February 20, 2015.

109. *Al-Batt al-Iswid*, episode 24.

110. *Al-Batt al-Iswid*, episode 3.

111. *Al-Batt al-Iswid*, episode 6.

112. Interview, July 2, 2013.

113. *Al-Batt al-Iswid* 37.

114. Interview, February 14, 2015.

115. *Al-Batt al-Iswid*, episode 34.

116. Interview, July 2, 2013.

117. Interview, February 20, 2015.

118. Interview, February 13, 2015.

119. *Al-Batt al-Iswid*, episode 61.

120. www.youtube.com/watch?v=WqG9KJPH6do. No longer available (accessed July 14, 2015).

121. www.youtube.com/watch?v=KfPEXqiXfMg.

122. www.youtube.com/watch?v=VX-hscY3ApY.

123. *Al-Batt al-Iswid*, episode 24.

124. *Al-Batt al-Iswid*, episode 37.

125. *Al-Batt al-Iswid*, episode 39.

126. *Al-Batt al-Iswid*, episode 8.

127. www.youtube.com/watch?v=1WF7HXsB2kk. No longer available (accessed July 11, 2015).

128. www.youtube.com/watch?v=1WF7HXsB2kk. No longer available (accessed July 11, 2015).

129. www.youtube.com/watch?v=BY4tnYkZIvA.

130. www.youtube.com/watch?v=BY4tnYkZIvA.

131. Interview, February 14, 2015.

132. *Al-Batt al-Iswid*, episode 6.

133. Interview, February 15, 2015.

134. *Al-Batt al-Iswid*, episode 103.

135. Interview, February 14, 2015.

136. Interview, February 11, 2015.

REFERENCES

Allievi, Stephano. 1999. *Les convertis à l'islam. Les nouveaux musulman d'Europe*. Paris: L'Harmattan.

Bowen, J. R. 2012. *A New Anthropology of Islam*. Cambridge: Cambridge University Press.

Bullivant, S. 2013. "Defining 'Atheism.'" *The Oxford Handbook of Atheism*. S. Bullivant and M. Ruse, eds. Oxford: Oxford University Press. 11–22.

Cottee, S. 2015. *The Apostates: When Muslims Leave Islam*. London: Hurst.

Crimp, S., and J. Richardson. 2008. *Why We Left Islam: Former Muslims Speak Out*. Los Angeles: WND Books.

Gooren, H. 2010. *Religious Conversion and Disaffiliation: Tracing Patterns of Change in Faith Practices*. London and New York: Macmillan Palgrave.

Hirsi Ali, A. 2007. *Infidel*. New York: Free Press.

———. 2015. *Heretic: Why Islam Needs a Reformation Now*. New York: HarperCollins.

Ibn Warraq. 2003. *Leaving Islam: Apostates Speak Out*. New York: Prometheus.

Jami, E. 2007. *Het recht om ex-moslim te zijn [The right to be an Ex-Muslim]*. Kampen: Uitgeverij Ten Have.

Khalil, M. H., and M. Bilici. 2007. "Conversion Out of Islam: A Study of Conversion Narratives of Former Muslims." *The Muslim World* 97, no. 1: 111–124.

McRobbie, A., and S. L. Thornton. 1995. "Rethinking 'Moral Panic' for Multi-Mediated Social Worlds." *British Journal of Sociology* 46, no. 4: 559–574.

Mahmood, S. 2009. "Feminism, Democracy, and Empire: Islam and the War on Terror." In *Gendering Religion and Politics. Untangling Modernities*. H. Herzog and A. Braude, eds. New York: Palgrave MacMillan US. 193–216.

Olsson, S. 2008. "Apostasy in Egypt: Contemporary Cases of *Hisbah*." *The Muslim World* 98, no. 1: 95–116.

O'Sullivan, D. 2003. "Egyptian Cases of Blasphemy and Apostasy against Islam: Takfir al-Muslim." *International Journal of Human Rights* 7, no. 2: 97–137.

Özyürek, E. 2015. *Becoming Muslim: Race, Religion, and Conversion in the New Europe*. Princeton and Oxford: Princeton University Press.

Pelkmans, M. 2013. "Outline for an Ethnography of Doubt." In *Ethnographies of Doubt: Faith and Uncertainty in Contemporary Societies*. M. Pelkmans, ed. London: I. B. Tauris. 1–42.

Peters, R., and G. J. J. De Vries. 1976–1977. "Apostasy in Islam." *Die Welt des Islams* 17, no. 1/4: 1–25.

Schielke, S. 2012. "Being a Nonbeliever in a Time of Islamic Revival: Trajectories of Doubt and Certainty in Contemporary Egypt." *International Journal of Middle East Studies* 44, no. 2: 301–320.

———. 2013. "The Islamic World." In *The Oxford Handbook of Atheism*. S. Bullivant and M. Ruse, eds. Oxford: Oxford University Press. 638–651.

Schielke, S., and L. Debevec, eds. 2012. "Introduction." In *Ordinary Lives and Grand Schemes: An Anthropology of Everyday Religion*. New York: Berghahn.

Sultan, W. 2009. *A God Who Hates*. New York: St. Martin's Griffin.

Van Nieuwkerk, K. 2006. "'Islam is your birthright.' Conversion, Reversion, and Alternation: The Case of New Muslimas in the West." In *Cultures of Conversion*. J. N. Bremmer, W. van Bekkum, and A. L. Molendijk, eds. Leuven: Peeters.

Van Nieuwkerk, K., ed. 2006. *Women Embracing Islam: Gender and Conversion in the West*. Austin: University of Texas Press.

Whitaker, B. 2014. *Arabs without God: Atheism and Freedom of Belief in the Middle East*. CreateSpace Independent Publishing Platform (ebook).

———. 2015. "The Rise of Arab Atheism." *The New Humanist*, June 29, 2015. newhumanist.org.uk/articles/4898/the-rise-of-arab-atheism.

FOURTEEN

"GOD NEVER EXISTED, AND I WAS LOOKING FOR HIM LIKE CRAZY!"

Muslim Stories of Deconversion

TEEMU PAUHA AND ATEFEH AGHAEE

INTRODUCTION

Conversion, or the adoption of a new religious identity, has been among the phenomena most studied in the psychology of religion. Almost every classic of the discipline, from William James to G. Stanley Hall, has in some way or another commented on the topic. Deconversion, or the abandonment of a previous religious identity, in contrast, has been largely neglected as a research topic. Conversion to one faith, however, typically involves deconversion from another faith (Streib et al. 2009: 17–19). The understanding of deconversion is therefore essential for the understanding of conversion.

Not everyone who deconverts from a faith commits to another one, however, but many of the deconverts remain unaffiliated with any religion. Even though it has become clear that religion as a whole is not disappearing, as the original theories of secularization predicted, it is also clear that the religious landscape is witnessing a major transformation. Even despite "the global resurgence of religions" (Huntington 1996: 64), atheists seem to be growing in number (Zuckerman 2007: 59). Furthermore, the number of those unaffiliated with religious organizations is on the rise because of New Age spiritualities of life that are spreading, at least in the Western world (cf. Heelas 2006: 47).

Streib and Keller (2004: 182–183) describe deconversion as typical of modern religiosity: they describe the generations born after World War II as generations of "seekers" who do not commit themselves to any single institution but instead "shop around" to fulfill their spiritual needs. For these spiritual seekers, the experience of deconversion is at least as familiar as the experience of conversion (Streib and Keller 2004: 182–183).

In their article, as well as in their subsequent book *Deconversion: Qualitative and Quantitative Results from Cross-Cultural Research in Germany and the United States of America* (Streib et al. 2009), Streib and Keller rely on data gathered in Western Europe and North America. But how about the rest of the world and religions other than Christianity?

In their book on apostasy and freedom of religion in Islam, Abdullah and Hassan Saeed (2004: 110) acknowledge the general dearth of research on leaving Islam. According to Saeed and Saeed (2004: 110), the whole subject is taboo for Muslims, many of whom consider Islam self-evidently true and apostasy, therefore, as incomprehensible. Saeed and Saeed (2004: 110–116) also propose a list of reasons for leaving Islam, but for the aforementioned reasons the list is somewhat provisional and not based on empirical research (see the section "Reasons for leaving Islam" below).

In this chapter, we examine the stories of roughly fifty Iranians who have left Islam. The stories were originally written for an internet discussion group, and we have analyzed them with a combination of grounded theory approaches and statistical analysis. By identifying common aspects and the general pattern of the stories, we construct four "paths out of faith" that those who wrote the stories have followed.

BEING IRRELIGIOUS IN IRAN

The term "deconversion" is relatively unknown, even within the study of religion. It is telling that the only reference book devoted to the psychology of religion, *Encyclopedia of Psychology and Religion* (Leeming, Madden, and Marlan 2010), does not have a separate entry for deconversion, and the term does not appear in any of the other entries.

Streib et al. (2009: 17) acknowledge the unfamiliarity of the term "deconversion" but nevertheless encourage its use instead of more widely known terms such as "apostasy" or "defection." First, "deconversion" provides a more neutral alternative to the more widespread (and negative) terms. Second, "deconversion" makes explicit reference to "conversion," thus linking these two phenomena (Streib et al. 2009: 17; see also Račius, this volume).

In Islamic theology, a distinction is made between several terms that are related to deconversion. These include "apostasy" (*riddah*), "blasphemy" (*sabb Allah* and *sabb al-rasul*), "heresy" (*zandaqah*), "hypocrisy" (*nifaq*), and "unbelief" (*kufr*). The distinction, however, may be more important in theory than in practice. Because of conceptual vagueness, the same act of dissent could potentially be classified into any of the aforementioned categories. Furthermore, most interpretations of Islamic law advocate the same sentence for different forms of deconversion, and apostasy, blasphemy, heresy, and hypocrisy may all be punishable by death (Saeed 2011: 32; Saeed and Saeed

2004: 35). Most jurists, however, make an exception if the apostate is a minor, mentally ill, or otherwise incapable of making an informed and voluntary decision. Some jurists exempt as well those who commit apostasy while intoxicated or prohibit the execution of women. These, however, are not universal views in Islamic jurisprudence (Saeed and Saeed 2004: 51–52). As of 2014, apostasy was illegal in twenty-five countries,[1] all of which, except for India, have a Muslim majority (Theodorou 2016).

The Iranian context adds an interesting feature to the study of deconversion from Islam. As the country's official name—the Islamic Republic of Iran—suggests, Islam is tightly interwoven with the Iranian national culture. Since the Islamic Revolution of 1979, Iranian society has gone through a comprehensive process of Islamization and desecularization: legal, political, cultural, and economic institutions have been largely reorganized according to the so-called Islamic principles (Kazemipur and Rezaei 2003: 348). Indeed, according to Abdolmohammad Kazemipur and Ali Rezaei (2013: 348), "the 1979 Islamic Revolution made Iran perhaps the only country in today's world with the so-called caesaropapist embrace of throne and altar." The Iranian constitution lists Islam as the official state religion and "belief in the One God" as the first foundational principle of the state. Furthermore, all laws and regulations have to be based on Islamic tenets. This has resulted, for example, in the banning of "corrupt" music, the enforcement of a "modest" dress code, and gender segregation in public transportation and other public places (Kazemipur and Rezaei 2003: 348).

In Iran, the penal code itself does not criminalize apostasy, but the courts may nevertheless punish it on the grounds of *Shariʿah* law. In fact, Iran is the only modern country that, according to a report by the Law Library of Congress, has executed a person for apostasy (Law Library of Congress 2014).

Islam influences not only the politics and legislation of Iran but also the everyday lives of its citizens. Close to 100 percent of Iranians are, at least nominally, Muslim, and over 80 percent report Islam to be an important part of their daily lives (Central Intelligence Agency 2018; Crabtree and Pelham 2009). Based on their analysis of survey data from Iran, Kazemipur and Rezaei (2013: 354–355) have made a distinction between four aspects of Iranian religiosity. Three of these (collective practices, individual practices, and individual beliefs) can be easily observed in just about any religious setting. According to the researchers, the fourth component (collective or "religio-political" beliefs) is more unique to the Iranian situation. Such collective beliefs concern the political role played by religion—for example, whether atheists should be allowed to hold public offices or express their views publicly. For many Iranian believers, faith is not only a private but also to a large extent a public matter. In line with this, freedom of expression and the right to stand for office are not considered rights but privileges that are to be granted on the basis of one's religious belonging (Kazemipur and Rezaei 2003: 354–356).

Despite the heavy attempts at Islamization—or even because of them—Iranian society is showing some signs of secularization. More specifically, even though the level of private religiosity seems to have remained constant, the participation in collective religious practices has actually decreased since the revolution of 1979. Furthermore, the majority of the Iranian population perceives the importance of religion to be waning in society. This is particularly true for the younger generation (Kazemipur and Rezaei 2003: 351–353). Kazemipur and Rezaei (2013: 357–358) consider these developments to be a counterreaction to the enforced Islamization of Iranian society: before the revolution, political Islam provided an alternative to the secular nationalist ethos of the ruling regime. After the revolution, Islam became the official narrative of the regime and, consequently, could no longer serve as an instrument of resistance. Today, more and more Iranians are using, for example, art or sport as a resource for social criticism.

In this chapter, we argue that atheism may similarly serve as a form of resistance to a theocratic regime. This atheism of those that we will call "rebels" may be a specifically Iranian phenomenon (see also Van Nieuwkerk, this volume, on the Egyptian Muslim Brotherhood as possible cause of rising atheism). Besides it, however, there are also other—and possibly more global—types of atheism in Iran.

REASONS FOR LEAVING ISLAM

The data used in this study was collected from a social network (Google+) where young Iranians shared their stories of apostasy to tell each other how they deconverted from hereditary religion. The idea was initiated by one user who started to tell his story first, and the rest followed and wrote about themselves as well. The whole content is freely accessible online. However, users' consent was asked for the use of their stories in studies. The initiator of the idea also aimed to provide some good social data on Iranian atheists, as there is not much data about it inside the country for the use of researchers on the subject. The stories belong to a hundred male and female, mostly young (20–30 years old) Iranians who live in Iran (some reside outside, though).

The research process began with the second author, Aghaee, reading all the stories and choosing the fifty-two that explicitly describe a personal deconversion experience. She then translated the stories (which were originally written in Persian) into English. The analyses focus on these fifty-two stories.

As with grounded theory generally, we began our analysis with an open coding of the data. That is, we read the data repeatedly and tried to classify its contents under descriptive labels, or codes (cf. Charmaz 2000: 515; Corbin and Strauss 2008: 160). In the first stage, we assigned a code for each line of text, but as the analysis progressed, we constantly compared our codes with each other and with the data to combine the codes into higher-order categories (cf. Charmaz 2003: 96 and 2000: 515; Corbin and Strauss 2008: 159–160, 165; Strauss and Corbin 1998: 113).

Before discussing the results of our analysis, we would like to make a few observations regarding the data: several previous works on atheism and deconversion have devoted space to reasons for leaving faith. Therefore, we would also like to make a brief excursion into the reasons mentioned in our data and compare them to those mentioned in previous studies.

We mentioned previously Abdullah and Hassan Saeed's (2004: 110–114) list of reasons for leaving Islam. The list contained a number of possible reasons for deconversion, some of which also appeared in this study. Limitations on the scope of choices, state misuse of religion, increasing contact with other traditions, and the influence of the discourse on human rights, for example, were among the overarching themes in the data. In many stories, feelings of resentment toward religious limitations and state authorities were described. They were also well informed about alternative worldviews and fundamental human rights such as gender equality.

Some other reasons mentioned by Saeed and Saeed (2004: 110–112), in contrast, were largely absent from our data. These include missionary activities, Westernization, and marriage or change in personal status. A reason for the absence may be the demographic composition of those behind the stories. In Iran, the overarching majority of Google+ users are young (18–24 years old), male, and single.[2] They are also fairly urbanized, with over 50 percent of users living in Tehran, and well educated, with over 90 percent being university alumni. Because the deconverts in our study are probably predominantly from the middle class, it is reasonable to assume that "material support given by missionaries" (Saeed and Saeed 2004: 111) has not been a central motivating factor in their deconversion. According to Saeed and Saeed (2004: 111), the goal of being granted a divorce might also motivate Muslim women to deconvert, but this is understandably a minor issue in a population dominated by single men.

Globalization and new information technologies have dramatically increased the flow of ideas around the globe, atheist ideas being no exception. Translations of Bertrand Russell, Carl Sagan, and Richard Dawkins[3] are circulated in the internet communities of Arabic-speaking atheists. For many Muslims, the first step on the road to atheism is the contact with other religions, either on the internet or while living abroad (Whitaker 2014: 30, 82–89). To some extent, deconversion is a transnational phenomenon, and it is thus important to compare the reasons mentioned in our data to those that have been documented in other contexts.

In his book, Phil Zuckerman (2012: 154–163) lists reasons that the people who participated in his study had for apostasy. All these reasons were also prevalent in the stories that we have analyzed. In table 14.1, we summarize the reasons described by Zuckerman (2012: 154–163), together with examples from our own data. The stories in our data show motives similar to those mentioned by the American deconverts in Zuckerman's (2012) study. It thus appears that deconversion is, at least to some extent, motivated by similar factors in different contexts. In the rest of this chapter, we contend that it is also a process that takes similar forms in various settings.

THE FOUR GROUPS OF DECONVERTS

Toward the end of the open coding, our growing impression was that the stories could be divided into roughly two groups. For one group, the main problem with religion is that it is naïve and irrational, and in these stories religion is portrayed as a kind of superstition that is unacceptable for a rational mind. For the other group, the problem is not so much the irrationality of religion but the damage it causes, both to individuals and to society as a whole. People are hurt and their rights are violated in the name of religion. Thus, depending on the group, religion is described either as "stupid" or as "vicious." We initially referred to these two ways of portraying religion as "intellectual" (or "philosophical") atheism and "social" atheism, respectively.

Despite Glaser and Strauss's (2009: 17–18) insistence that a grounded theory does not require statistical validation, we felt that we would be more confident if we could find some statistical support for our claims. Thus, after finishing the open coding, we entered the data into SPSS statistics software and ran a hierarchical cluster analysis to see whether we could statistically substantiate the distinctive nature of these two groups. As expected, the data clustered neatly into two groups that closely resembled the two hypothesized groups: intellectual atheism and social atheism. What was not expected, however, was that the intellectual group appeared to further divide into three smaller groups, each of which has its own distinctive features. After investigating the statistical properties of the four clusters, we started to reread the data once again, finally coming to the conclusion that the four-cluster solution makes both statistical and theoretical sense.

We named the four groups that we delineated: "seekers," "rationalists," "disillusioned," and "rebels." Of the fifty-two stories that we analyzed in depth, nineteen were classified as seekers, twelve as rationalists, nine as disillusioned, and eleven as rebels. One of the stories was left unclassified.

When analyzing the stories more thoroughly, we paid increased attention to the gender aspects within them. In other words, we examined how gender is made salient in the stories. Some of them contain overt references to the gender of the narrator. Such is, for example, Story #27: "The fact is that I was a beautiful girl who was interested in music, poem, and love, but being in a religious family made a depressed girl out of me."

Besides such explicit self-identifications, there are also less overt references to gender. These are often linked to gender-specific religious practices, such as clothing. The author of the Story #38, for example, confesses to have been "an atheist in veil, with *chador*."

It is worth noting that the four groups are, in a way, ideal types. Many of the stories in the data can be easily classified and represent one of the groups in more or less "pure" form, but there are also stories that have elements from more than one group. Furthermore, we do not regard the deconversion narratives as objective descriptions of events as they have actually occurred. Instead, they are templates that can be employed to structure a wide variety of experiences. A template gives meaning to those experiences and renders them understandable.

The relationship between the template and the actual experience is more or less uncertain, and deconversion stories are best seen as seamless fusions of real-life events and narrative material derived, for example, from media products and stories of other deconverts. This has consequences for our study, because the stories were from the same internet source and they were written in response to each other. Thus, it is possible—even probable—that the stories have influenced one another. We do not consider this a problem, however, because a likely effect of such influence is the convergence of the stories to certain common patterns. Therefore, the joint origin of the stories may actually crystallize the common patterns of an Islamic deconversion narrative.

TABLE 14.1. THE REASONS FOR DECONVERSION IN ZUCKERMAN (2012: 154–163) AND DECONVERSION STORIES GATHERED FROM A HUNDRED IRANIAN GOOGLE+ USERS

1.	*Parents* Because of parental influence on the religiosity of the offspring, having a nonbelieving parent increases the likelihood of apostasy.
2.	*Education* Higher education forces many to scrutinize their beliefs and worldviews, which in turn may lead to apostasy.
3.	*Misfortune* Experiencing pain or loss may cause one to question God's goodness or even God's existence.
4.	*Other cultures, other religions* Getting acquainted with people who do not share one's worldview may be a reason for questioning the justification of one's beliefs.
5.	*Friends, colleagues, lovers* Besides parents, other social intimates have also influence on one's religiosity or irreligiosity.
6.	*Politics* Because strong religiosity is associated with political conservatism, liberal people may experience alienation in a religious community.
7.	*Sex* Religious restrictions on sexuality may come into a conflict with one's own sexual desires.
8.	*Satan and hell* Religious communities use the fear of hell to keep people in the fold, but for some people this fear is a cause of distress, trauma, and, ultimately, apostasy.
9.	*Malfeasance of religious associates* Encountering religious people with compromised morals may cause disappointment and disillusionment with religion altogether.

"I was born in a normal family and in my family, moralities were prior to religion. My dad didn't say prayers and my mom only prayed in Ramadan" (Story #8).

"When I entered university, I found that this religion is all about insult to human beings and doesn't really help people in life" (Story #44).

"My brother-in-law had a stroke because of fasting and his God didn't help him" (Story #34).

"The first doubts started when I saw how Muslims face other religions and think they are the only ones on the right way. I was thinking what if the others are right" (Story #43)?

"Now I owe to my same classmate because he made me go and study and ask questions! He gave me the courage to do that" (Story #26).

"I would hear the attorneys of the Islamic Republic and then comparing the theory and practice made me question many issues" (Story #31).

"I was a live devil because I enjoyed my body, I was supposed to go to hell because I was in love with a boy" (Story #36).

"Religious and theology books always made me question rather than believe. I would ask why we should go to hell? Can't God help me not to burn in fire" (Story #42)?

"I found that there is no God and even if he exists, he is not a good God because his most religious people are the worst ones" (Story #27).

Seekers

Of all the four groups, the seekers (n=19) used to be "true believers." In complete opposition to rebels—whose recollections of childhood religiosity are riddled with trauma—many of the seekers have fond memories of their former faith. Accordingly, they are the group to which the experience of losing faith appears to have been the most difficult. The dramatic structure in many of these stories is that of a regressive or tragic narrative (cf. Gergen and Gergen 1983: 260–262). They describe a downward trajectory, in which good things turn bad. A good example:

> I was born in a religious family. . . . I was very religious among my brothers and sisters. . . . I felt so close to God and I was upset for those who were atheist and nonreligious and would pity for them and how hopeless they are. All these passed and I found that the more I read Quran, the less I understand it. I thought the problem is with me not the great God. . . . I tried to justify myself. It was a mistake, I told myself. It was hard to forget about all those lovely years. . . . Deconverting from religion and leaving all those beliefs we were taught from childhood needs one thing and that is COURAGE! The courage of confronting with reality (Story #1).

The seekers describe their deconversion as a long and arduous process. The process begins when the person, after a devout childhood, starts to read or otherwise look deeper into religion and, as a result, encounters problems and contradictions—things that he or she cannot understand. Often, such problems are of a moral nature. More specifically, a rift appears between religious norms and one's personal morality. To quote Story #16: "I remember sometimes I said to myself that even I am more beneficent than God."

Religious morals are portrayed as too petty and human to be of divine origin. The deconverts are not convinced that an almighty God would be so interested in human affairs.

> Being familiar with psychology also helped me to simply conclude that the probability that humans have created God from their own image is very high. I left religion completely, but not God. A God that did not have hell and heaven was not so cheap to send life instructions for people. A God that was not a decorated image of human being, and humans were not his most important business in the world (Story #16).

Relatedly, moral problems arise as certain aspects of Islamic dogma are experienced as incompatible with the idea of an all-good God. Of the reasons listed in table 14.1, "Satan and hell" are a problem especially for the seekers. For them, it is simply unacceptable that a being of total goodness would punish someone with eternal suffering.

> One more important thing that made me sure about this was the concept of hell. Not the fear of hell, but its concept. The fact that the beneficent benevolent kind and all those good adjectives God would be so revengeful to punish people like that, the eternal torture, was not acceptable (Story #16).

> Thinking of a kind beneficent God who had a counter on the shoulders of the people whom he was loving, to count their sins and masturbations, to punish them was very contrary to me (Story #22).

Problems and contradictions, in turn, launch a cycle of questioning, doubting, and searching for answers. At times, the seeker feels that he or she has found a way to hold on to the precious beliefs, only to be disappointed again.

At the time of their writing, some of the seekers still seemed to be in the cycle of doubting, searching, questioning, and believing, while others had found some kind of a resolution. For some, the resolution was leaving faith altogether, and for some others it was developing a faith of their own. All the mystics and those who confessed a belief in God but not in religion belong to this group. An example of such an individualized belief system is provided in the following excerpt:

> The God introduced to us was a developed version of Robin Hood, but my God is the collection of goodness, lights and knowledge that I felt. Its name isn't important, whatever! The God shown to us was a God of revenge who [is] in need of humans but my real God is the God of relief and consciousness (Story #5).

Gender appears to play only a minor role in the stories of the seekers on the whole. Besides a passing reference to *hijab* in two stories, gender is made salient by only one writer, who describes the puzzlement he experienced because of being allowed to see the hair of his sister but not that of his brother's wife.

The seekers' path out of faith thus goes from childhood religious upbringing and comforts of faith to doubts and questions, and finally to either a loss of faith or some kind of private spirituality. This process is summarized in figure 14.1.

Rationalists

Rationalists (n=12), like seekers, write about religious socialization. Unlike seekers, however, they do not describe themselves as serious practitioners or "true believers." In their stories, religion is a childhood habit—something that is taken for granted until one is mature enough to question it. Religion is a sign of naïveté that cannot withstand rational analysis. Accordingly, the rationalists deconvert on intellectual grounds, whereas the seekers' reasons for deconversion tend to be moral:

> I read the translation of Plato works and went to the world of philosophy and among philosophical discussions, I found that the rationale on the existence of God are all incomplete and all can be criticized (Story #11).

> From last year, by reading philosophy and reading their criticism, I saw that I have no reason to believe in God and decided that I wouldn't believe in him unless there is a strong reason for that (Story #26).

> But today, thanks to science, all the questions which made religions come to existence have been answered (Story #12).

Compared to seekers, rationalists also write relatively little about abandoning religious practices. The reason may be that rationalists were not that active religious practitioners to begin with. Perhaps that is also why they appear to cope better with the loss of faith than do the seekers. Unlike many seekers, who describe religion as comforting and godlessness as burdensome, rationalists portray deconversion as relieving: "I am free now and I am lighter than any time because I do not carry any certainty. I have accepted life the way it is" (Story #51).

Accordingly, the narrative structure in rationalist stories is typically a progressive one and describes an upward trend in which things turn for the better: "I then changed the dark gloomy world of religion with music and paintings. I escaped . . . from childhood" (Story #42).

The stories of the rationalists and the seekers are thus in many respects different. What they share, however, is the emphasis on the search for truth and answers. In order to satisfy their need for answers, the majority of both

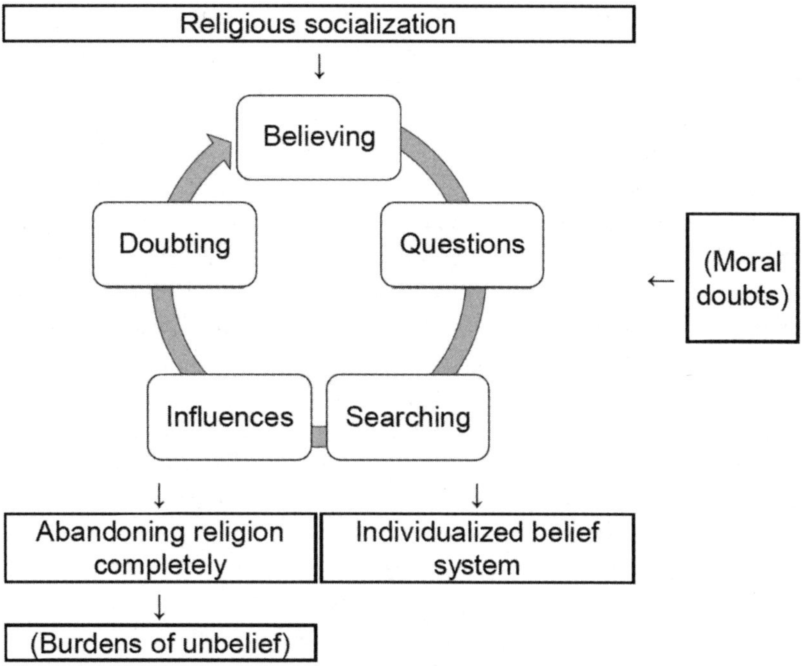

FIGURE 14.1.
Seekers' path out of faith.

rationalists and seekers have turned to reading, and their stories often list an impressive array of influences. Besides sources more specific to the Iranian context, such as the Qur'an, Ali Shariati, and Abdolkarim Soroush, the stories also mention international atheist best sellers and classic works of science and philosophy. *The God Delusion* by Richard Dawkins (2006) appears to be especially popular, as are the likes of Nietzsche and Darwin.

Given the rationalists' emphasis on science and reason, it is noteworthy that education (cf. table 14.1) is seldom mentioned as a reason for deconversion. This may be due to the religious character of the Iranian education system. In fact, one of the rationalists hints at this: "I saw how the education system make[s] people to follow and not to think and question" (Story #49). Instead of education, the rationalists emphasize individual learning and discussions with other nonbelievers (cf. "Friends, colleagues, lovers" in table 14.1).

> Somebody in a social network introduced some sources and books to me and I went to study them. From Islam to Darwin.... From the history of

civilization to the history of Shia and Islam and generally all religions. I found the truth (Story #40).

Only a few rationalists make gender salient in their stories. Out of the five that do so, two are women and three are men. The two female writers make their gender explicit in the context of expressing their frustration at the Islamic dress code. Other examples include a childhood fear of being in contact with the opposite sex: "Why shouldn't I play with girls? What was the problem? . . . During teenage hood, I fell in love with a girl in our neighborhood. The fear of God didn't let me make friends with her" (Story #26). All in all, as with the seekers, gender aspects appear to be a rather minor concern in the rationalist stories.

The rationalists' stories are thus a kind of coming-of-age narrative that describes a progressive trajectory from ignorance to enlightenment. Learning about science and philosophy is often named as the prime mover for growth. The process is summarized in figure 14.2.

Disillusioned

The disillusioned (n=9) are a heterogeneous lot. What is common to all of them is that, unlike seekers and rationalists, they do not so much disagree with the principles of faith as feel unimpressed on a more personal level. On one hand, some of the disillusioned admit to never having been religious. In the stories of this group, there are statements such as "God never had an important role in my life" (Story #48), "I never had religion" (Story #52), or "religion was not important to me" (Story #50). On the other hand, some of the disillusioned structure their story around a major disappointment with faith. They sought help from God in times of trouble, but God let them down (cf. "Misfortune" in table 14.1). As a result, they gave up God and religion. In both kinds of stories, the key aspect is the irrelevance of religion: for the nonreligious ones, faith in general is unimportant. For the disappointed ones, faith has proven to be useless against life's tragedies, and investing in religion is therefore just a waste of time.

The gender of a disillusioned author is brought to the fore in four out of nine stories. In all these four, the author is a woman. Besides an individual complaint about Islamic women's dress, gender is mentioned only incidentally.

Unlike with the other groups, the stories of the disillusioned do not reveal a clear pattern that could be put into a process graph. In fact, in some of the stories, deconversion does not appear as a process at all; religion has, quite

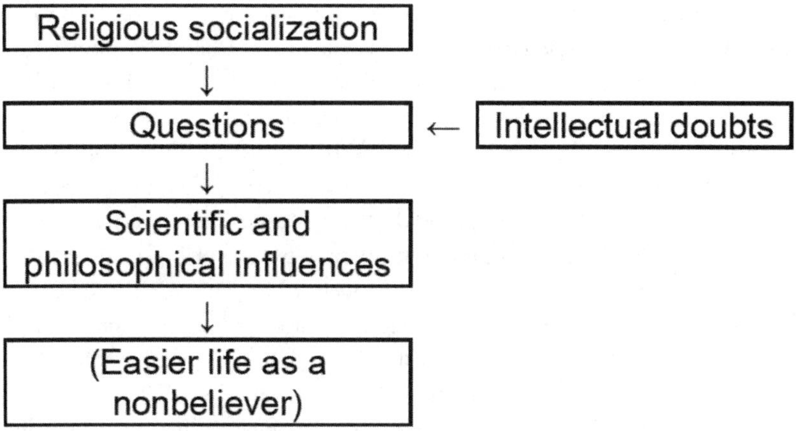

FIGURE 14.2.
Rationalists' path out of faith.

simply, always been meaningless. Not surprisingly, the stories of the disillusioned were, on average, the shortest in the data.

In his book *Faith No More: Why People Reject Religion*, Phil Zuckerman (2012: 166–169) proposes a hypothesis that some people may be naturally predisposed toward irreligion, or "secular by nature." For such people, deconversion is simply a matter of accepting their true identity, something that they are at heart. Many of the disillusioned among our data display characteristics that connect them with the inborn atheists in Zuckerman's study. They may strive to believe, or at least go through the motions of believing, but in the end it is not who they truly are: "I was an actress, a professional one. I even went to Mecca and some other pilgrimages but religion isn't my thing" (Story #52).

Rebels

The disillusioned are unimpressed by the inability of religion to save one from pain and suffering. The rebels (n = 11), in contrast, accuse religion of causing the pains that they have suffered. Their accounts are full of descriptions of both physical and psychological violence perpetrated by religious people. Like seekers, rebels depict religion as an epitome of immorality. Unlike seekers, however, rebels do not write about the immorality of abstract dogma but rather about the cruel and brutal behavior of believers. Rebels have turned into atheists not because of a disagreement over values but because of being traumatized by "unhealthy superstition" or having seen friends beaten and tortured in the name of religion.

> When I entered university, I found that this religion is all about insult to human beings and doesn't really help people in life. I decided to leave it because it only had bad feelings and fear and downgrade for me. It was difficult to do that because I was living in an Islamic country. When my close friend in prison said that her torturer had Vozoo [washing for praying] before beating her because he said it has points in front of God, I found that I shouldn't be indifferent. You should respect to other's beliefs as far as it's personal and only for them, not when they've made a hell of your life. I became against religion and this phase happens when you live in the society which is affected by the rules and educations of the religion and puts you under pressure (Story #44).

It is thus not at all surprising that many of the rebels express a deep grudge against religious authorities and society in general. For the rebels, religion represents archaic brutality and oppression, whereas atheism is about humanity, liberation, and modernity.

> If I had a power to help humanity, I would forbid all kinds of religious teachings around the world. I believe religion is one of the biggest barriers [to] the development of humanity. Humanity meaning the belief of equality and respect for the basic rights of all humans. The teachings that give the fake feeling of superiority or inferiority to people and give them a certain way of life as the best one, only leads to superstition and hindering the development of the curious mind of human beings (Story #25).

Like rationalists, rebels thus associate atheism with liberation. For rationalists, however, the liberation is about personal freedom from religious restrictions, and it is thus accomplished by their deconversion. As a result, the rationalist stories are often marked by a certain positivity. The rebels, in contrast, perceive the liberation as a social matter; in short, the whole society needs to be liberated from the tyranny of religion. Unlike rationalists, then, the rebels have not yet reached their liberation, which is a clear cause of grudges and agony for them.

> I am full of agony and hatred, I know it is neither my right nor my place, but this was not my choice. I had to grow up not to have fear and to be able to defend myself. I had to think independently and have my own thoughts. I thought more of the creation and the whys and hows of it. My life has its own rules now. I am not a defenseless girl now. I am imprisoned in this traditional society (Story #9).

The gender of the rebel author is made salient in five out of eleven stories. In all these instances, the author is a woman. References to gender were often accompanied by arguments familiar from such feminist critics of religion as Ayaan Hirsi Ali. Islam is accused, for example, of privileging men and oppressing women. Female writers are resentful of being forced to wear a *hijab*, of being taught to submit to men, and, even more important, of being filled with depression and self-hatred. Such sentiments are expressed, for example, in the following story:

> Because I was a girl, I had hijab from the first year of elementary school and went to religious ceremonies with mom and I found that every string of my hair will take me to hell. I cut my bangs then. I was hating myself even more as I grew older. I was a live devil because I enjoyed my body, I was supposed to go to hell because I was in love with a boy (Story #36).

The rebel path thus proceeds from childhood religiosity to a social awakening in which the harm inherent to religion is understood. This, in turn, causes a longing for a society free from religious tyranny. Of the reasons listed in table 14.1, "Politics," "Sex," and "Malfeasance of religious associates" are all typical for the rebels. The rebel path out of faith is illustrated in figure 14.3.

BRINGING THE PATHS TOGETHER

In the previous section, we presented a fourfold typology of deconversion trajectories. However, it is worth noting that the division of the stories into types is not always clear-cut. Certain aspects of the stories tend to appear together, but that does not imply, for example, that intellectual doubts are exclusive to those categorized as rationalists. Instead, individual stories often display some combination of several types, with one type being more dominant. Therefore, in the last phase of our analysis (the selective coding), we tried to combine the outcomes of the previous stages into a more comprehensive picture of the central phenomenon under study: deconversion from Islam (cf. Luomanen 2010: 364–366). The following flowchart (figure 14.4) presents a synthesis of different deconversion trajectories.

As a number of scholars have noted, parents are the single-most important factor affecting children's religiosity. Children do not usually reflect on their religious socialization but tend to uncritically adopt the religious practices of their primary caregivers. As a person matures, however, he or she usually begins to construct his or her own worldview and, relatedly, to reexamine the

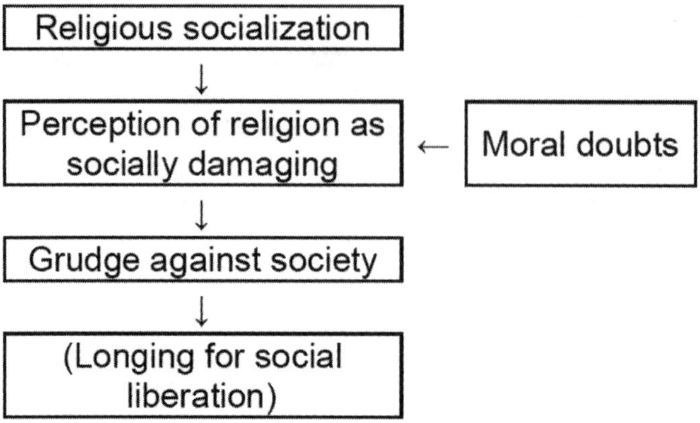

FIGURE 14.3.
Rebels' path out of faith.

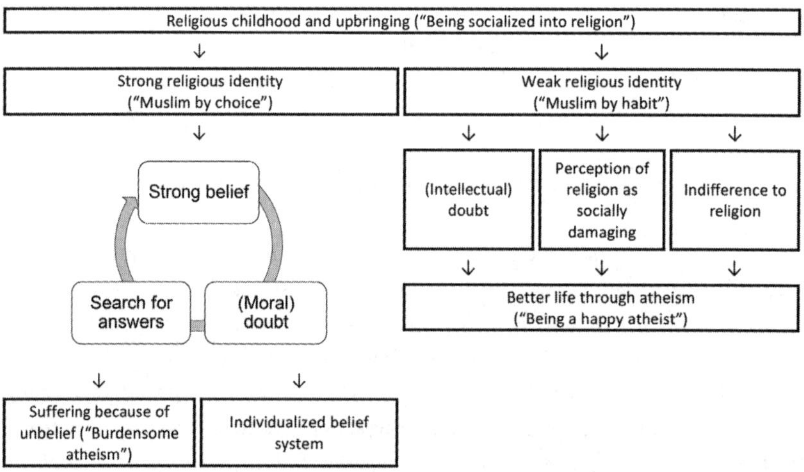

FIGURE 14.4.
Variety of deconversion trajectories.

things that were previously taken for granted. In some cases, this may lead to the rejection of the childhood faith (see, e.g., Zuckerman 2012: 100–101).

Most, though by no means all, stories in our data refer to growing up in a religious family.[4] For some writers, this led to an internalized religious identity and deeply held faith. For others, religion remained an outward habit that never was a central part of their self-conception. They may have been going through the motions of their religion, but it appears that their hearts were not really in it.

In the stories of the "true believers," deconversion appears as a lengthy and arduous process in which moments of doubt alternate with moments of certainty. Finally, however, doubt wins the day, and the deconvert is forced to either painfully acknowledge the nonexistence of God or reinterpret her or his faith in a way that avoids the previous problems. Most often, such reinterpretation leads to a mystical worldview that denies obsolete dogma. Examples of this include Stories #5 and #16 (quoted above).

For the ones whose religious identities were not that strong to begin with, deconversion appears to be an easier process: either religion has always been something irrelevant to them (in which case there is not really much process to leaving the faith) or, alternatively, they abandon their religion right after confronting the irrationality and social harm it represents. For these "happy atheists," nonbelief is a joyful state of being that constitutes liberation from torment and oppression.

However, a simple division between "happy" versus "tormented" atheists needs to be further qualified. As mentioned previously, liberation and its associated happiness are still unattained goals for many rebels, and some of the disillusioned feel rather indifferent about all things religious. To make a crude division, the happiest atheists are often rationalists and the angriest are rebels. The saddest and the most longing, in turn, are found among the seekers.

The role of literary influences is also a factor that differentiates the groups. As mentioned, the stories of the rationalists and seekers are often thick with references to atheist best sellers and other scientific or philosophical works. These are also named as a major reason for the deconversion:

> The last bullet to the respected God was reading "The God Delusion" by Dawkins. I think Dawkins had a great impact on me because he was a biologist and he referred to the concepts I had read about in childhood (Story #22).

> Then I read Dawkins's books and also Sam Harris's books[.] I organized my thoughts and decided that I should leave feelings and fear. So thanks

to Islamic republic, Quran, life problems, Philosophy and Mr. Dawkins, I changed from the most religious person in [the] family to the most non-religious one (Story #24).

The reasons cited by the rebels and the disillusioned, in contrast, are more related to events in their life histories. Instead of books, the two latter groups refer to personal experiences to account for their deconversion. Put somewhat simplified, deconversion is a theoretical and philosophical issue for the rationalists and seekers, but not so for the other two groups. Instead, the rebels and the disillusioned have left the faith because it has proved to be useless or even harmful for people.

This distinction between theory and experience also differentiates between two kinds of moral issues raised in the stories. Especially for many seekers, the moral problem with religion is related to the idea of hell or some other theological concept. Rebels, in contrast, are typically not concerned with abstract teachings but instead with the immorality and social damage caused by religious people. The difference is illustrated with the two quotes below:

Moral doubt	Perception of religion as socially damaging
"I was a teenager who never did anything wrong to anyone, but I still had to be careful to avoid hell and fight with my nature which that fake God had created himself to make God happy. This sadistic nature of God and religion was the most unacceptable thing for me" (Story #27).	"I felt the brutality and aggression of religion in my religious family from childhood. My mother's grandfather was Ayatollah, and was said to be a good man but I didn't see a good person in all his children. Poverty and religion ruin your soul. When my brother was little, I would grab him by feet and pound his head on the ground. The effect of religion and aggression is so bad" (Story #27).

Our findings contain an interesting parallel to those of Phil Zuckerman (2012: 35), who, in an extensive study of American deconversion stories, observes a distinction between two kinds of doubt. First, there is the "acquired incredulity syndrome," in which the religious belief system stops making sense because of contradictions with modern science. In the second kind of syndrome, the loss of faith is due to contradictions with one's own morality. This kind of apostate simply cannot believe in a God that is described as commanding his followers to kill nonbelievers or sentence them to damnation.

Both types of doubt were present in our data. Interestingly, however, they appeared to be linked to different deconversion processes: Disillusionment with religious morality was especially typical of seekers and, to some extent, rebels; however, the rationalists were strictly on the side of science against religion. The difference is, again, illustrated with two quotes:

Moral doubt	Intellectual doubt
"My biggest problem with God in childhood was his interference with my private issues. I think it is a sick tendency to see others wherever they are and whatever they do" (Story #25).	"I realized that the existence of God of the faithful people cannot be proved through rationality and faith doesn't have a logical relationship with logical certainty" (Story #11).

DISCUSSION

God, religion, and atheism

In table 14.2, we have summarized the common ways in which the four groups depict religion, God, and atheism.

Of the four groups considered here, the seekers are generally the most positive toward God and religion. In contrast to the powerless God of the disillusioned and the despotic God of the rebels, the God of the seekers is a magnificent and positive force, even if beyond human comprehension. Some of the seekers experience God as distant, but for them distance is associated with sublimity. The rationalists and the disillusioned, in turn, associate God's distance with His illusoriness or insignificance, and the rebels greet the absence of the tyrannical God with relief.

The views of the writers on atheism and religion mirror their views on God: for many seekers faith is soothing and unbelief painful. For rebels, it is the other way around. Rationalists and the disillusioned, in contrast, have a less emotional attitude toward both religion and irreligion. For them, religion is simply outdated or futile—something that a rational person quite naturally gives up. Accordingly, neither having nor losing faith seems to involve strong emotions for them.

The stories of the seekers and rationalists are, for the most part, not manifestly gendered. In their writings, most references to gender are passing remarks that do not have much significance with regard to the overall story.

Gender is made salient in approximately half of the disillusioned and rebel stories. In all these cases, the writer is a female. Especially in the rebel stories,

TABLE 14.2. FOUR VIEWS OF RELIGION, GOD, AND ATHEISM

	Seekers	*Rationalists*
Religion	ethically questionable but comforting	naïve, ignorant
God	1) distant OR 2) beyond the grasp of religious dogma	figment of imagination
Atheism	burdensome	rational

the gender aspect is pronounced, and Islam is heavily criticized for being oppressive to women. Thus, it would appear that gender (and particularly female gender) is an especially central issue for "social" atheists—in other words, those who have deconverted because of the individual or social harm caused by religion.

Comparing the four types with other typologies

It is fruitful to contrast our fourfold typology with other typologies proposed in the field of deconversion research. Armand Mauss (1969; see also Zuckerman 2012: 5), for example, has divided types of apostasy into three main classes on the basis of motives behind the deconversion act: "intellectual" apostasy (incapability to believe in the articles of faith); "social" apostasy (loss of social relationships within a religious community); and "emotional" apostasy (apostasy as an emotional reaction to disappointment in the religious community). In our data, there are examples of all three motives. However, it is typical for a single story to reflect more than one type. Even if certain motives are more pronounced than others (e.g., intellectual motives in the case of rationalists, or emotional motives in the case of many rebels), most of the stories make references to several of Mauss's categories.

Another sociologist of religion, Phil Zuckerman (2012: 6–7), has made a distinction, on the one hand, between "shallow" apostasy and "deep" apostasy, and, on the other, between "mild" apostasy and "transformative" apostasy. In Zuckerman's terminology, shallow apostates are those who reject religion but nevertheless consider themselves "spiritual" (or at the very least shun the label "atheist"), whereas deep apostates are thoroughly committed to secularity and nonbelief. Deep apostasy dominates our data, but there are also some seekers

	Disillusioned	*Rebels*
Religion	useless	corrupting, enslaving, traumatizing, patriarchal
God	impotent	angry, sadistic and vengeful
Atheism	natural, act of independence	liberating

that would fit the description of shallow apostates. Mild apostasy (i.e., rejecting religion without being deeply committed to it in the first place), in contrast, is especially typical for the disillusioned, whereas the seekers have typically experienced transformative apostasy or turned from a true believer into an unbeliever.

A third typology worth noting is provided by the Bielefeld-Based Cross-Cultural Study on Deconversion, the major research project on the psychology of deconversion, which studied a number of North American and German people who had deconverted from a broad range of religious traditions. The researchers in this project (Streib et al. 2009) also arrived at a fourfold typology of deconversion trajectories that bears both similarities and differences to the classification proposed here.

The first of the trajectories was characterized by "pursuit of autonomy"—that is, leaving behind a once taken-for-granted tradition in order to find one's own individuality. Accordingly, the trajectory was often narrated as a coming-of-age story. Especially for some American respondents, deconversion was a natural accompaniment of growing up and did not appear to be experienced as a crisis.

The taken-for-granted nature of religion, as well as the ease of the deconversion process, links the "pursuit of autonomy" trajectory with the rationalist and the disillusioned groups in our study. However, the emphasis given to autonomy brings the trajectory closer to the group of rebels.

Those deconverts who Streib et al. (2009) characterized as "debarred from paradise" had been deeply committed to their faith. They had invested a lot in their religion, only to be disappointed. This, in turn, parallels the emotional severity of the seekers' deconversion process.

The third deconversion trajectory delineated by Streib et al. (2009), in contrast, has no equivalent in our data. Those for whom deconversion was about "finding a new frame of reference" deconverted only to reconvert to another, and often more controversial, faith. Such deconversions, however, were completely absent in our data. The same applies to the fourth trajectory introduced by Streib et al. (2009), that is, to the "life-long quest." A life-long quest involved a number of consecutive deconversions as the deconvert sought a community that would cater for his or her spiritual needs. These deconversions typically led the deconvert from a more mainstream religious community into a more marginalized one. Even though some seekers described being engaged in a spiritual quest, they expressed neither a commitment to any community nor a desire for such a commitment. On the contrary, they appeared to be content to continue their quest outside of religious communities.

Four types as a global phenomenon?

The people whose deconversion stories we have analyzed are by no means representative of Iranians or Muslims at large. Despite this, our analysis demonstrates that the rise of New Atheism[5] is not merely a phenomenon of the Christian West; it has a more global effect—at least on those who are active in the internet. The Iranian ex-Muslims in our study told deconversion stories, many of which could as well have been told by ex-Christians from Germany or Finland.[6] Themes such as the moral superiority of atheism, science as the foundation of the worldview, and apostasy as liberation are prominent in both the stories of our data and such American deconversion stories as analyzed, for example, by Smith (2011) and Zuckerman (2012). The stories refer time and again to atheist best sellers, such as Dawkins's *The God Delusion*, that are widely known among nonbelievers all around Europe and North America (cf. Smith 2011: 223). Thus, our study demonstrates that deconversion narratives are in many ways similar across both national and religious borders.

The writers to whom we initially referred as "intellectual" atheists were especially reminiscent of previous models of deconversion. It is likely that the rebels' type of atheism is a markedly Iranian phenomenon because of strong linkages between religion and the Iranian state. Perhaps apostasy is less often associated with social critique in the more secularized nations of Western Europe and North America.

In sum, it would appear that the stories analyzed here bear noteworthy similarities to deconversion stories gathered in other contexts (e.g., Europe and North America). However, this does not mean that context is meaningless. It may well be that the unique aspects of Islamic theology or Iranian society have a bearing on the details of the deconversion process. At this point, our data is insufficient to make generalizations about either the universality or nonuniversality of our deconversion typology. It remains to be seen whether this possible universality is because of transnational influences or underlying similarities in human psychology.

NOTES

1. Afghanistan, Bahrain, Brunei, Comoros, Egypt, India, Iraq, Iran, Jordan, Kuwait, Malaysia, Maldives, Mauritania, Morocco, Nigeria, Oman, Pakistan, Qatar, Saudi Arabia, Somalia, Sudan, Syria, United Arab Emirates, Western Sahara, and Yemen.

2. Statistics about Google+ users are from the website www.plusdemographics.com/country_report.php?cid=Iran. The site is no longer available (date of access 08-16-2013).

3. The philosopher Bertrand Russell, the astronomer Carl Sagan, and the biologist Richard Dawkins have become famous as advocates of scientific thinking and as critics of religion. Some of their key writings have been made available in *The Portable Atheist* (2007), edited by Christopher Hitchens.

4. Interestingly, even though describing religious upbringing, several of the seekers and the disillusioned also referred to a nonreligious person in the family, usually either a mother or father. Indeed, according to Phil Zuckerman (2012: 139–141), a loss of faith is especially likely if at least one of the parents is nonreligious.

5. The term "New Atheists" is used in reference to a group of high-profile authors such as Sam Harris, Richard Dawkins, Daniel Dennett, and Christopher Hitchens, who in the early twenty-first century published a number of atheist best sellers. What is common to them is a critique of religion on both rational and moral grounds: On the one hand, religion is considered to be indefensible in light of natural science; on the other, it is portrayed as socially destructive (Taylor n.d.).

6. An interesting, even if nonacademic, parallel to our model is provided by the renowned atheist writer Adam Lee, who has gathered testimonials from a number of former believers and used them to formulate a four-stage model of deconversion. According to Lee (n.d.), "The process of becoming an atheist follows a surprisingly predictable pattern" that begins with Exaltation (that is, a joyful and strong confidence in one's faith) and continues through Doubt and Darkness into Illumination.

REFERENCES

Central Intelligence Agency. 2018. *The World Factbook*. www.cia.gov/library/publications/resources/the-world-factbook/geos/ir.html.

Charmaz, K. 2000. "Grounded Theory: Objectivist and Constructivist Methods." In *Handbook of Qualitative Research*. N. K. Denzin and Y. S. Lincoln, eds. Thousand Oaks: Sage. 509–535.

———. 2003. "Grounded theory." In *Qualitative Psychology: A Practical Guide to Research Methods*. J. A. Smith, ed. London: Sage. 81–110.

Corbin, J., and A. Strauss. 2008. *Basics of Qualitative Research. Techniques and Procedures of Developing Grounded Theory*. Los Angeles: Sage.

Crabtree, S., and B. Pelham. 2009. *What Alabamians and Iranians Have in Common*. www.gallup.com/poll/114211/alabamians-iranians-common.aspx.

Dawkins, R. 2006. *The God Delusion*. London: Bantam Press.

Gergen, K. J., and M. M. Gergen. 1983. "Narratives of the Self." In *Studies in Social Identity*. T. R. Sarbin and K. E. Scheibe, eds. New York: Praeger. 254–273.

Glaser, B. G., and A. L. Strauss. 1999. *The Discovery of Grounded Theory: Strategies for Qualitative Research*. New York: Aldine de Gruyter.

Heelas, P. 2006. "Challenging Secularization Theory: The Growth of 'New Age' Spiritualities of Life." *Hedgehog Review* 8, no. 1–2: 46–58.

Hitchens, C., ed. 2007. *The Portable Atheist: Essential Readings for the Nonbeliever*. Cambridge, MA: Da Capo Press.

Huntington, S. 1996. *The Clash of Civilizations and the Remaking of World Order*. New York: Simon & Schuster.

Iran—Constitution. www.servat.unibe.ch/icl/ir00000_.html.

Kazemipur, A., and A. Rezaei. 2003. "Religious Life under Theocracy: The Case of Iran." *Journal for the Scientific Study of Religion* 42, no. 3: 347–361.

Lee, A. n.d. *Into the Clear Air*. www.patheos.com/blogs/daylightatheism/essays/into-the-clear-air.

Leeming, D. A., K. Madden, and S. Marlan, eds. 2010. *Encyclopedia of Psychology and Religion*. New York: Springer.

Luomanen, J. 2010. "Straussilainen grounded theory—menetelmä." In *Haastattelun analyysi*. J. Ruusuvuori, P. Nikander, and M. Hyvärinen, eds. Tampere: Vastapaino. 351–371.

Mauss, A. 1969. "Dimensions of Religious Defection." *Review of Religious Research* 10, no. 3: 128–135.

Saeed, A. 2011. "Ambiguities of Apostasy and the Repression of Muslim Dissent." *Review of Faith & International Affairs* 9, no. 2: 31–38.

Saeed, A., and H. Saeed. 2004. *Freedom of Religion, Apostasy, and Islam*. Aldershot: Ashgate.

Smith, J. M. 2011. "Becoming an Atheist in America: Constructing Identity and Meaning from the Rejection of Theism." *Sociology of Religion* 72, no. 2: 215–237.

Strauss, A., and J. Corbin. 1998. *Basics of Qualitative Research. Techniques and Procedures of Developing Grounded Theory*. Thousand Oaks, CA: Sage.

Streib, H., et al. 2009. *Deconversion: Qualitative and Quantitative Results from Cross-cultural Research in Germany and the United States of America*. Göttingen: Vandenhoeck & Ruprecht.

Streib, H., and B. Keller. 2004. "The Variety of Deconversion Experiences. Contours of a Concept in Respect to Empirical Research." *Archive for the Psychology of Religion* 26, no. 1: 181–200.

Taylor, J. E. n.d. "The New Atheists." *Internet Encyclopedia of Philosophy*. J. Fieser & B. Dowden, eds. www.iep.utm.edu/n-atheis.

The Law Library of Congress. 2014. "Laws Criminalizing Apostasy." In *Selected Jurisdictions*. www.loc.gov/law/help/apostasy/apostasy.pdf.

Theodorou, A. E. 2016. *Which Countries Still Outlaw Apostasy and Blasphemy?* www.pewresearch.org/fact-tank/2016/07/29/which-countries-still-outlaw-apostasy-and-blasphemy.

Whitaker, B. 2014. *Arabs Without God: Atheism and Freedom of Belief in the Middle East*. North Charleston, SC: CreateSpace.

Zuckerman, P. 2007. "Atheism: Contemporary Rates and Patterns." In *The Cambridge Companion to Atheism*. M. Martin, ed. pp. Cambridge: Cambridge University Press. 47–68.

———. 2012. *Faith No More: Why People Reject Religion*. New York: Oxford University Press.

SECTION V

DEBATING APOSTASY AND DECONVERSION

FIFTEEN

FAITH NO MORE

The Views of Lithuanian Converts to Islam on Deconversion

EGDŪNAS RAČIUS

Because conversion can be regarded as one phase in the process of religious activities (Gooren 2007: 337), it is not unthinkable to presume that some of those who had at one point in their life converted to Islam later moved on—that is, they "moved out" of it. Though the topic of moving out of Islam, or apostasy, has been addressed by numerous authors (Alalwani 2011; see also Cottee; Larsson; Van Nieuwkerk; and Pauhu and Aghaee, all in this volume) from various perspectives (from that of the legal consequences more so than others), historically, but even up to the present day, they would deal mostly with cases of born Muslims who for one reason or another chose to abandon an inherited faith. Apostasy of converts, or deconversion (e.g., those who had earlier consciously chosen Islam, that is to say, had first "moved in") hardly gets any public attention (see Alyedreessy, this volume). This may be so partially because convert-apostates tend to move out of Islam quietly, often having previously moved into it as noiselessly, and shun publicity; consequently, any reporting, let alone serious research, on them is hard to pursue.

This chapter explores how Lithuanian convert Muslims view disaffiliation/apostasy/deconversion—not least how they explain the possible causes, motives, triggers, circumstances, and conditions for moving out of Islam; its stages and consequences; and also what they think should be done with apostates, if anything at all. The research indirectly tests if converts are familiar with the Islamic jurisprudence on *irtidad* (apostasy, literally, "rejection of faith") and whether they side with it. It also inquires about the converts' personal experiences—whether they know of any deconverts and how this might have affected their relations with and views of such people. It is hoped that the research results, no matter how tentative, may contribute, particularly from an intracommunity dynamics perspective, not only to the field of studies of moving out of Islam among European converts but also to the wider field of "conversion careers" (Gooren 2007: 348–351).

The research is based on three primary sources: the material gathered on the online forum at islam_ummah.lt/islamforum, discussion in a Facebook group, and answers to a questionnaire distributed among Lithuanian converts both through the targeted (sent directly) and the snowball principles.

Islam_ummah.lt/islamforum has been a major congregating point for Lithuanian-speaking Muslims since late 2010 until it finally gave way to other forms of communication, namely, Facebook, at the end of 2015. The majority of the forum's members (431 as of September 2015) appear to have been converts, though a fair share were non-Muslims who for whatever reason were interested in Islam. The forum has accumulated more than 41,000 messages on a variety of Islam-related issues. Apostasy was one, albeit, admittedly, minor, of the topics dealt with by its members. The Facebook group *Salaf Kelio Seserys* (Sisters of the *Salaf* Path), comprising some of the same members as the forum, also had a brief discussion on apostasy in mid-2014.

The questionnaire I designed contained twenty-two open questions, of which sixteen were devoted to the general understanding and perception of disaffiliation/deconversion/apostasy from Islam and the remaining six to respondents' personal experiences. The questionnaire was directly sent to roughly thirty individuals who were known to have converted to Islam. It was also placed on the forum, and one of the converts placed it on Facebook group pages. The return rate was, unfortunately, low—just ten filled out questionnaires. Another dozen or so converts expressed their position on apostasy-related matters in the online forum and the Facebook group discussion. Therefore, ultimately, the research results can be treated as only provisional.

The chapter has three sections. The first familiarizes readers with the more than 600-year-long continuous presence of a Muslim community in Lithuania. The second section provides a critical theoretical background to conceptualizing such key terms as "disaffiliation," "deconversion" and "apostasy." The final section is an account of the findings of the qualitative research on the views of Lithuanian converts to Islam on deconversion.

THE LITHUANIAN MUSLIM LANDSCAPE

Historically, Islam in Lithuania has been represented by the so-called Lithuanian Tatars (Račius 2013b), who came to settle the territories of what then was the Grand Duchy of Lithuania (comprising today the sovereign states of Lithuania, Belarus, and Poland) between the fourteenth and sixteenth centuries. Though the estimated numbers of Tatar Muslims in the Grand

Duchy never exceeded 100,000, their community, though radically diminished, managed to survive into the present. At the end of 2017, there were some 3,000 Tatars in Lithuania. During the interwar period (1918–1941), Lithuanian Tatars still made up the bulk (some 90 percent) of Lithuania's Muslim community; however, the Soviet occupation (1944–1990) opened the way for "colonists" from all over the Soviet Union, Muslims among them, to come and permanently settle in Lithuania. By the late 1980s, Lithuania had up to 10,000 inhabitants originally hailing from Muslim-majority areas of the Soviet Union. With Lithuania's independence, however, their numbers dwindled as a significant number chose to repatriate to their ancestral lands or Russia; Lithuanian Tatars once again became the nominal numerical majority in the Muslim community in Lithuania.

Since this research does not focus on Tatars or their relationship to Islam, it suffices to note here that around half of Tatars living in Lithuania at the time of the most recent population census (in 2011) did not self-identify as Muslims. Muslim leadership in Lithuania, however, themselves also of the Tatar ethnicity, would routinely claim that even those Tatars who did not identify with Islam during the census data collection are still to be counted as Muslims, for being a Tatar in Lithuania by default implies being a Muslim. In this regard, local Muslim leaders implicitly deny the option of Tatars having moved out of Islam, at least en masse. And they are not put off by the fact that very few Tatars go to their own mosques and prayer halls for either daily or communal Friday prayers. Tatar leaders defend the absence of Tatars during the prayers by referring to "working hours," though the mosque in Kaunas and the praying hall in the capital, Vilnius, are packed with working-age worshippers of foreign backgrounds on Friday afternoons. It may also be noted that Lithuanian converts to Islam under investigation in this research abstained from identifying Tatars as apostates, though elsewhere (Račius 2013a) some have seen them as having almost apostated. In any case, the issue of Tatars "moving out" of Islam will have to be dealt with elsewhere (see Górak-Sosnowska and Łyszczarz, this volume, for the case of Polish Tatars).

Until the collapse of the Soviet Union, there were virtually no Lithuanian converts to Islam, though some individuals and small groups did sympathize with variations of (neo)Sufism. Soon after the restitution of the independent Lithuanian nation-state, however, the first instances of Lithuanians converting to Islam appeared. Several early converts, chiefly males (who, the anecdotal evidence suggests, have abandoned it later), opted for esoteric Islamic traditions and offshoots; others, namely, young females, discovered Islam through a significant other (i.e., future husbands). However, it is only after the turn of the century, and especially with Lithuania's accession to the European Union in 2004, that the number of converts reached the critical level where one could start talking of a convert element within the general Muslim community in Lithuania hitherto dominated by Lithuanian Tatars. Still, as places of worship were and still are few and tiny, and most of the converts were young females, they rarely were visible at communal prayers or in public. Soon, with the ascent of internet communication, online forums run by converts and devoted to Islam were created, and this has lead to forming a sort of digital community (Račius 2013a), bringing together Lithuanian-speaking converts to Islam, residing both inside and outside Lithuania. The online interaction has in due time also lead to in-person meetings and communal activities in several places of concentration for converts, most notably in the greater London area and Vilnius.

By 2017, the number of Lithuanian citizens who had converted to Islam could have surpassed 700. This estimate is based on a two-decades-long observation by the author and at least in part can be supported by the census figures. In 2011, 374 inhabitants of Lithuania (up from 185 in 2001) claimed to be ethnic Lithuanian Sunni Muslims, of whom the majority must have been converts and their progeny. The total number of Sunni Muslims (there is no official public data on Shiʿas) in Lithuania for 2011 was recorded at 2,727 (down from 2,860 a decade earlier). As the census counted Lithuanian residents only, Lithuanian converts and their offspring who permanently lived outside of Lithuania were not included.

The publicly available data suggests that the overwhelming majority of Lithuanian converts to Islam are females who converted to Islam in their late teens and early twenties.[1] A fairly large number of them converted while already living abroad, and many of those who had converted in Lithuania have also left it. Though there are no reliable figures on the geographical distribution of Lithuanian converts to Islam, based on the information available on the online forums islamas.lt (operational between 2004 and 2010) and islam-ummah.lt (2011–2015), it can be fairly safely argued that no less than 400 Lithuanian converts to Islam permanently live outside their homeland. According to the UK Office for National Statistics, in England and Wales alone 535 Muslims hailing from Lithuania lived at the time of the 2011 census, many, if not most, of whom must have been converts and their progeny. Of some 200 Lithuanian converts to Islam in the database of the author, as of the end of 2017, three-quarters lived outside Lithuania, with a quarter based in the greater London area. About half of the converts in this research also lived outside Lithuania at the time.

WAYS TO MOVE OUT: DISAFFILIATION, DECONVERSION, AND APOSTASY

If entering into a religious fold can be regarded as almost by default a conscious and decisive act, though possibly with a protracted pre-entering period, often solemnized with a particular one-time religious initiating ritual (christening, public declaration of *shahada*, etc.), leaving one's religion can be much more complex and not as decisive (or visible). In contemporary religious studies, especially the psychology of religion but also the sociology of religion, however, apostasy is usually substituted with less value-loaded terms like "disaffiliation" or "deconversion." Nevertheless, instead of treating these terms a synonyms, I propose to see them as subsequent stages in the process of loosing one's religion, of moving out. Disaffiliation, understood here also as "distancing," precedes deconversion and happens gradually as the individual ceases to identify with the community of believers, abandons performance of (obligatory) religious duties, and starts doubting the validity of religious dogmas. Although it may happen overnight, usually this takes time, and a person may remain in this state all her/his life. As Streib et al. (2009: 22) argue, "'disaffiliation' can consist of a withdrawal from participation in meetings or in a retreat from observance of religious practices; this is especially important in regard to religious orientations without formal membership such as Islam." In the eyes of the others, the "disaffiliate" may be seen as a "lapsed" believer.

The next stage in this process of moving out of religion is a conscious decision to forsake one's faith altogether and terminate one's relationship to it in all respects. In the case of converts (i.e., someone who had earlier consciously converted to the religion under question), this act could rightfully be called "deconversion." However, unlike disaffiliation, deconversion "is the change of a person's religious orientation in a specific biographical time which involves re-writing one's religious identity, revising one's system of beliefs and world views, and re-structuring one's way of thinking, moral judgment, and dealing with authority—with a special focus on the act of leaving the old" (Streib et al. 2009: 23).

Streib et al. (2009: 17) contend that:

> Even though "deconversion" is not a term very commonly and widely used, we claim that there are good reasons for using the word. "Deconversion" avoids the negative connotations which are almost unavoidable in "apostasy" or "defection"—terms which associate blaming the individual for a break of loyalty. "Deconversion" allows for less prejudice and suggests

> that deconversion has similar legitimacy as conversion. Further, labeling the process under investigation as conversion with a negative prefix, as a conversion in the opposite direction, suggests that both could possibly have comparable dynamics in biographical change. Thus understanding [of] deconversion is associated with the discussion and the results about conversion. Deconversion research has emerged from conversion research.

As the term "deconversion" semantically implies a U-turn from what one had earlier consciously through conversion turned to, it can be meaningfully applied only to ex-converts, with "apostasy" being the correct term to label the act of moving out by those born into tradition. So, while deconversion is also apostasy—"the term apostate is similar to deconvert" (Streib and Klein 2013: 714)—not all apostasy is deconversion. In any case, in both instances the person becomes an apostate.

There is a qualitative difference between apostasy of converts and that of those born into tradition. The major analytical distinction is the presence of what James T. Richardson (1978) labeled as "conversion career"—only converts to a religious tradition may be assigned this feature; those born into a religious tradition who choose to abandon it still do not qualify as having a career in conversion. Only by virtue of converting to another religion would they earn this attribute. Streib (2014: 271) is right when he concludes:

> It is no longer possible to ignore the fact that a growing number of people choose to convert more than once in their lifetime; multiple conversions are unavoidable in cultures in which religion is no longer a single tradition in a mono-religious environment but plural in a pluralistic environment. Multiple conversions, however, involve deconversion(s) as well as conversions.

Streib et al. propose a set of five characteristics of deconversion: (1) "loss of specific religious experiences"; (2) "intellectual doubt, denial, or disagreement with specific beliefs"; (3) "moral criticism"; (4) "emotional suffering"; and (5) "disaffiliation from the community" (Streib et al. 2009: 22). However, I find this set deficient in that it lacks the final, even if only declarative, characteristic—conscious (and possibly public) termination of the relation to the religious tradition as such. As Streib himself correctly concludes, deconversion is "intellectual, experiential, emotional and moral disengagement from a religion which, in most cases, leads to termination of membership" (Streib 2009: 13). However, Cottee (2015; see also this volume) distinguishes between "closeted" and "open" apostates. When interviewing ex-Muslims (as he did), such a distinction becomes very apparent. However, this distinction can also be utilized as an analytical tool when discussing the disaffiliates (lapsed believers) from the outsider's perspective. So long as a disaffiliate does not openly confess to having definitely moved out, one can only suspect him/her of being a closeted deconvert/apostate. In other words, physically observed disaffiliation might in the end turn to be "closeted" apostasy. Therefore, Brinkerhoff and Mackie (1993: 236) may be right in arguing that apostasy should

> be conceptualized as the multidimensional process of disengagement from the two major elements of religion. One of these elements—religiosity—refers to the embracement of a set of beliefs. The other—communality—refers to the feeling of belonging or Gemeinschaft which grows around a theological doctrine and is most often linked to a denominational organization. In the words of Caplovitz and Sherrow (1977: 31), apostasy "indicates not only a loss of religious belief, but rejection of a particular ascriptive community as a basis for self-identification."

The actual physicality of moving out of religion may not be that clear-cut or even visible. In this regard, the process of moving out may never become a fait accompli and instead remain in the state of permanent disaffiliation not amounting to definite apostasy.

So, to sum up, my argument is that the terms "disaffiliation" and "apostasy/deconversion" should be treated as denoting different subsequent stages in one's moving out of religion, while the term "deconversion," which by default is apostasy, should be used only in regard to ex-converts and not those born into tradition.

PERCEPTION OF AND REACTIONS TO DECONVERSION OF LITHUANIAN CONVERTS TO ISLAM

This section presents the results of the qualitative research, itself based on a questionnaire; its structure follows the clusters of questions in the questionnaire. I start with the broadest ones (on possible conditions and circumstances of deconversion), followed by those on when deconversion becomes a fait accompli and what follows it. I end with a brief discussion on Lithuanian converts' personal encounters with disaffiliates and deconverts.

The scholarly apparatus in the Lithuanian language is not developed enough to distinguish between "deconversion" and "apostasy"; they are not synonyms but rather overlapping concepts. Consequently, in the common language it is even more problematic to grasp the difference between the two. Therefore, there was no easy way to ask respondents if they felt a difference. Apparently, both words would be translated into common Lithuanian as *atsimetimas* (literally, "renouncement," "relapse"). The Lithuanian equivalent of "disaffiliation" is *nutolimas* (literally, "distancing, moving away"), while there are also several words for "moving out"—*apleidimas* (literally, "abandonment") and *pasišalinimas* (literally, "withdrawal"). I did my best to reconcile this semantic limitation by making explicit if I was asking about apostasy in general or the "apostasy of converts"—that is, "deconversion."

Conditions and circumstances of disaffiliation and deconversion

Though who can be considered (or even declared) an apostate is naturally the most central issue in the deliberations on moving out of Islam, as this tends to be the most contested aspect, it may be left for a later discussion. One can thus start with the question What could facilitate a Muslim to abandon his or her faith?

Answers to this question by Lithuanian converts to Islam suggest a number of causes, reasons, and motives for such a move. As may be expected, weak belief (*iman*) is often cited as the primary cause for distancing oneself from performing religious duties and the possible outright moving out of Islam. Here is Kelrodė Šviesa: "It is terrible . . . this happens because of the weakening of *iman* (belief), and this happens due to various reasons, unfortunately."[2] Some attribute this weakness to the whisperings (*waswas*) of Satan: "If a person sincerely professed Islam and then rejected it, this, according to my deep conviction, was the impact of long-standing non-practicing and whispering and enticement by the Satan" (Umm_Aisha[3]; also Rano[4]). Pavasario Snaigė also sees Satan's hand in this: "I think, this distancing also depends on whether out of laziness or because of Satan's *waswas*."[5]

On a more rational level, some converts contend that the weakness of faith may be caused by ignorance such as "incomplete comprehension of the Islamic principles, incomplete awareness of the perception of God in Islam, [and] reception of wrong information" (Lidija).[6] Furthermore, it may be caused by a personal crisis involving doubts

> which we all have, bigger or smaller, temporary or permanent. . . . But not all manage to keep them inside, it happens that some open to their close circle. And such secrets and doubts in a group have a risk of receiving support, alas, someone will also feel more courageous to share them, then the person feels no more alone, they will engage in discussing those doubts

more often and so on. I know a real case when through such a collective way, one may say, the elite members of our *umma* (community), the pioneers and authorities among the Lithuanian converts went down (Pavasario Snaigė).[7]

Rimantė also contends that even "strong" Muslims may go on a distancing path: "To say that for a strong Muslim it is impossible to distance from religion, I think, is not correct.... Our *iman*, belief, as it was given so it can be taken away, therefore, we are left to only beg to die Muslim."[8] Likewise, UmmJumana argues that "our faith is in Allah's hands and we have to realize that it was not us who led ourselves into Islam but Him,... and we completely depend on Him, our bodies and our souls."[9] By forwarding this somewhat fatalist reasoning, Rimantė and UmmJumana actually reveal an otherwise rather common notion among Muslims that the strength or weakness of the faith depends on God himself. One is left to wonder whether, if pushed to the extreme, such a view would not make the discussion on apostasy obsolete.

The possibility of the fall of "strong" Muslims suggests, even if indirectly, that some may become disappointed with Islam. To this the respondents generally reacted by admitting such a possibility but sometimes in connection with weak faith (Umm_Aisha[10]) or ignorance (Lidija, Mariam, also Dovilė).[11] Umm-Harun[12] even thinks that "converts get disappointed with Islam much more often than the Muslim-borns" though, like Umm_Aisha[13] and Dovilė, she reasons that this happens due to their unpreparedness before and during the conversion to Islam. Anonimas (also Vika, Mariam, Rano),[14] however, suggests making distinction between getting disappointed with Muslims and getting disappointed with Islam: "People often get disappointed with surrounding Muslims, their behavior, which often has nothing to do with religion, and attribute that to Islam."[15]

Some of the converts contend that in cases of conversion to Islam in order to please a significant other (arguably an intermittent case among Lithuanian converts to Islam), the very act of moving in has the contagion of failure. As Stefano Allievi (2002: 1) has noted, this type of conversion can be called "relational," and "conversion under these circumstances is a means to reach another aim (marriage), not an end in itself." Umm_Aisha reasons that "it may happen that a girl having fallen in love with a Muslim guy accepts Islam only 'for the eyes' (dressing-up) and later, with the relationship having fallen apart, she rejects also the faith. But in principle, that was not even a real conversion to Islam" (Umm_Aisha,[16] also Rano[17]). Conversion that is not "real" would imply that the apostasy is not "real" either and does not count as such. Since a fairly large number of Lithuanian females indeed had moved into Islam through the significant other, having an "affectional motivational experience" (Lofland and Skonovd 1981: 373–385), their possible distancing from Islam can rightfully be viewed in this perspective. Unfortunately, there is no data on how many Lithuanian converts of this "type" have later disaffiliated or even deconverted.

Aside from the weakness of faith or maybe because of it, the non-Muslim social environment appears to be recognized by Lithuanian converts as playing a role in one's spiritual journey. However, as suggested by converts, it may lead to two opposing paths. The first, naturally, implies that Muslims living in a non-Muslim environment are susceptible to its trappings that may lead them astray and all the way into deconversion. Lidija: "I think, that if a Muslim's faith is weak, [his/her] comprehension of Islam is weak, then non-Islamic society may exercise pressure, especially on a convert."[18] However, she also cautions that she is not sure whether this could be the main reason for apostasy. UmmJumana, who has been living in the Middle East for a decade, also sees the dangers of the non-Muslim social environment for the commitment of Muslims to the tenets of their religion:

> The Prophet has said that Shaitan comes to him who remains alone and the community is extremely important in Islam. . . . Muslims are commanded to perform *hijra* [emigration] in the name of Allah, death in a non-Muslim land is considered a bad death. . . . Islam is a religion of communality. . . . It is dangerous for a Muslim to stay alone and he always has to strive to remain with the community and emigrate to *dar al Islam* [Muslim lands]. And remaining alone in a non-Islamic country, and especially [one] such as Lithuania, is very dangerous.[19]

Indeed, the discussions on the two online forums would often invoke the need for "religious" emigration from Lithuania to a more Islamic environment. Like UmmJumana, some respondents (Umm_Harun, Mariam, Rano)[20] would also emphasize that in order to remain fully committed to their religion Muslims should live, if not in an Islamic or Muslim-majority state, then at least in a Muslim community, something that admittedly is nonexistent in Lithuania due to small numbers of Muslims and their dispersal throughout the country. A closer social environment, like family, is also seen by some respondents as a possible factor in the weakening of faith and leading to deconversion: "If there is a permanent psychological/emotional pressure (through bullying and teasing, exclusively negative talking, comparisons of religions and their believers and the like) from the domestic environment, in the family, from parents, husband or wife, I think their role may be very important in that the Muslim may decide to renounce, leave Islam" (Mariam,[21] also Anonimas[22]).

However, there are also others, like Umm_Aisha,[23] who would argue that if the faith is strong the environment has no bearing on such Muslims, as they arguably can perform the pillars of Islam unhindered basically in any environment. She further reasons that "I do not think that a convert for whom a new world has opened, who has discovered the true new path of life, would go for compromises because of the environment, old non-believer attitudes" (Umm_Aisha).[24] Very much in the same vein, Vika argues that "a strongly believing person will not change his beliefs because of the social environment, it is more likely he will change the environment."[25] The ultimate alternative is that a non-Muslim social environment facilitates the strengthening of the commitment to one's newly found faith. Rimantė tells that she has "noticed that those sisters who blame the environment, most often even when they have changed it, when they go abroad, still remain there where they had been. For me personally, the more unwelcoming the environment, the bigger the desire to practice more, to abide by stricter verdicts."[26] Umm_Aisha, building on Rimantė's position, argues that "then such an opposition rises and a desire to hold firmer onto that what is true and to be a stronger Muslim."[27]

Most of the respondents (Anonimas, Geltona Spalva, Grazkebraske, Lidija, Umm_Harun)[28] admit that moving out of Islam is more a process than a momentous act of outright deconversion. Here is Lidija: "I would say, it is more of a process. I think, a not insignificant part of Muslims encounter doubts which some are able to brush away through deepening their knowledge of Islam or by looking for the answers to the questions that cause their doubts. There are those who do not look for the answers, live with doubts which get deeper until they become dissatisfaction and unbelief."[29] To some, the process implies levels of moving out. As Rano reasons, "Satan works in deceptive ways, little by little, and I would relate this gradual [process] to this."[30] However, others, like Dovilė, argue that "a Muslim may not be partially apostate, for he either believes in Allah or he does not believe," though she allows that distancing from God, in the form of not praying, is possible, which, however, is not considered by her as deconversion but as a sin. Grazkebraske also admits that practicing religion may be measured in levels, but "faith as such is an inner feeling which cannot be measured so simply."

As converts in this research did not allow themselves to be drawn into any deeper considerations of the distinction between disaffiliation and deconversion, Streib's (2014: 271–272) observation comes in as handy, and not only in regard to the gradation of the moving out: "Disaffiliation from the community does not exclusively mean the termination of membership; for example, it can consist of total withdrawal from participation without formally terminating the membership." Apparently, some of the converts do not regard temporary disaffiliation (referred to by them as "distancing") due to doubts leading to failure to perform certain duties (Islamic pillars) without their denial as amounting to deconversion. Disaffiliation as nonperformance and nonparticipation is excusable as long as it is not coupled with loss of faith, which is the definite criteria for deconversion. Yet, as has been pointed out earlier, the loss of faith as an "invisible act," if not made public, may never be realized and recognized by others.

Formalization of deconversion and its aftereffects

Though the circumstances leading to or accompanying moving out of Islam are undoubtedly significant, still, the question of when that process reaches its end-stage and moving out becomes a fait accompli (e.g., at what point one becomes a definite apostate—*murtad*, in the parlance of Islamic jurisprudence) is of utmost importance. Does one have to (publicly) declare his/her apostasy, or does it suffice that he/she does or does not do certain things? If there is no public admittance of apostasy by the concerned person, who can decide whether he/she has become an apostate? These and similar questions have been tackled by Muslim jurists for basically the entire history of Islam. As this chapter does not seek to find any "correct" answers to such questions, in the following pages the answers provided by converts in the research are not judged against possible approaches by Muslim jurists (see Larsson, this volume, for a brief overview). Instead, the research aims plainly at collecting the opinions of Lithuanian converts to Islam on apostasy-related matters.

Stopping believing in Allah and public admittance of this were seen by converts to be the major milestones when moving out of Islam. To the question What makes one an apostate? Dovilė plainly replies: "If a person claims to have ceased believing in Allah."[31] Likewise, Mariam argues that whoever "publicly declares to be leaving Islam and that he is no more a Muslim" becomes an apostate; "and also if one declares not to believe in any God."[32] ViVi also reasons that, in her opinion,[33] "the person has to publicly tell all this for if he hides it then certainly no one will get into his heart, [to find out if] he believes or not."[34] Grazkebraske, Anonimas, and Lidija speak in more or less the same words, though they also admit that certain acts (such as the denial of duties, the prophethood of Muhammad, or the divine nature of the Qur'an) indicate that the person is not Muslim any more. Geltona Spalva, Pavasario Snaigė[35] and Umm_Harun contend that it suffices for a person to negate the pillars of faith like praying, fasting, and the like to become an apostate. According to Umm_Harun, "He does not have to announce that publicly, this can be his inner state."[36]

However, if the person in question does not publicly declare or admit to have apostasized, who is authorized to decide on the matter—to pronounce him or her an apostate? Rimantė quotes Muhammed Ibn Abdul Wahabb's list of actions that "annul" Islam and then adds that, according to him, "only Allah knows if the person is a believer or a disbeliever. Thus Muslims have to be cautious when declaring someone *kafir* (disbeliever) or *fasik* (sinful)."[37] Some other converts also caution against *takfir* (pronouncing someone a nonbeliever): "We cannot do *takfir* against them. *Takfir* is done by scholars and they base [their decisions] on knowledge. It is *shirk* [polytheism] that leads out of Islam. . . . Also, the person who does *shirk* out of ignorance does not become a *kafir*, he is just *jahil* [ignorant] and he is in need of *daʿwa* [proselytism]. *Allahu Aalem*" (UmmJumana).[38]

The overwhelming majority of replies to the questionnaire were in virtual agreement that no one may decide on whether a person has become an apostate. Anonimas, for instance, was firm on this: "No one. Only the person himself may decide and announce or not announce."[39] Grazkebraske: "I do not think that any person has a right to judge if someone else has apostasized or not."[40] Lidija[41] and Dovilė[42] are also of practically the same opinion, while Mariam goes even further: she also thinks "that no one should decide on this, so long as the person has not announced that publicly," and states that she "totally objects to the practice of those Muslim countries, where Sharia is institutionalized, to officially establish if the person is an apostate or not."[43] Umm_Harun,[44] whose position is quite contrary to the majority's position, identifies *ulama* (the learned men) as those who may (or, according to her, are the *only* people who may) decide on the matter. Geltona Spalva,[45] in line with Umm_Harun, talks of the court in an Islamic state as the authorized institution that would decide and also accords such a right to a *mufti* (juristconsul).

Disaffiliation (and even more so apostasy) from a religious community as a rule is not welcomed by the in-group, and some faith communities may even have preventive measures. In the face of apostasy, many faith communities practice excommunication, which in addition to excluding a former member from communal religious practices often encompasses social ostracizing, effectively pushing the apostate outside the geographical boundaries of the community. In the most extreme cases, however, apostasy has been criminalized. Such, arguably, is the case of Islam, where, according to most jurists, abandoning Islam is regarded as one of the gravest crimes to be firmly punished. In some Muslim-majority countries—for instance, in Afghanistan, Iran, Saudi Arabia, and Kuwait—apostasy remains part of the penal code to this day (Račius 1999).

In the online forum islam-ummah.lt, a brief discussion on the question of the penalty for apostasy, under the title "Death upon rejection of Islam," gathered half a dozen forum members, some of whom have been the most active contributors to all topics. The topic was initiated by lidovskaja, who lamented having had problems explaining to her non-Muslim father why, according to Islamic regulations, apostates deserve the death penalty: "I had a very difficult discussion with my father. I did not know how to answer about the argument that in Islam the person who has abandoned Islam has to be killed. I do not know how to explain such [a] thing [as] why God has ordered to kill. . . . I know that this is the worst sin one may commit but why is this given over to people for judgment?" (lidovskaja).[46] UmmJumana reacted to lidovskaja's plea by simply providing a link (islamqa.info/en/696) to an online *fatwa* "Punishment of the one who leaves Islam." This *fatwa*, as might be expected, confirms the general classical Islamic judicial position regarding apostasy: the apostate is to be put to death.

The converts in the research appear to fall into two distinct categories regarding both the existence of an official Islamic ban on apostasy and their personal position on the issue—those who, as might be expected, support, even if only in principle, the ban and the ensuing death penalty versus those who dismiss the existence of such a ban and consequently the punishment. The first camp is well represented by Lidija (also Geltona Spalva[47]) who confirms: "Yes, there is a prohibition to renounce Islam. In the Quran and the *hadiths* (I know [of this] in the collections of Bukhari and Muslim) it is said that who renounces Islam, punishment awaits him, that is ordered to be killed."[48] Some, like Selma (also UmmJumana,[49] Umm_Harun[50]), reason that "all questions and crimes have to be decided by sharia courts and the caliph of the country,"[51] though she immediately admits that "they do not exist in our times. Therefore, the execution of punishment is also impossible."[52] In contrast, Pavasario Snaigė, when arguing in favor of both the ban and the punishment, draws in an unusual aspect—the "domino" (though called by her "snowball") effect: "If an authority falls, or a very close person, as much as I have seen, there will always be a group of 'fallers.' Maybe because of this apostasy is such a heavy crime and punishable by death, for it is a very big negative influence on *umma*, a true *fitna* [social disorder]."[53]

The other side comprises those who vehemently oppose any punishment. For instance, Mariam reasons that "the renouncer has a right to renounce Islam freely, freedom to choose, to renounce is secured in the Quran. No, the renouncer should not be punished."[54] Vika likewise argues that, in her opinion, "faith is a person's free choice and no-one should be punished for this. I think [such] punishments may be administered in some countries more out of long-standing traditions than out of the Islamic practice. . . . I think, the non-believer has to be left solely to the God's judgment."[55] Grazkebraske is also of the opinion that the apostate should not be punished. Such an approach to apostasy is, even if indirectly, conducive of the "conversion career" mentioned earlier in the chapter and supports Streib's (2014: 271) reflection that "multiple conversions are unavoidable in cultures in which religion is no longer a single tradition in a mono-religious environment but plural in a pluralistic environment." And although this (one may say liberal) approach among some of the converts, due to the research limitations, should not be seen as representative of, and less so dominant, among Lithuanian converts to Islam, it nonetheless should be taken as indicative of the spectrum of their positions.

Asked if Muslims are to shun deconverts and not interact with them, most respondents tended to be on a pro-engagement side, with only several being reserved. Dovilė places herself squarely on the pro-interaction end by arguing that "just because the person is not a Muslim does not mean that he is our enemy. A Muslim has to be noble and loving with all people."[56] Vika also argues that "through interaction one may make influence, thus it is logical to think that through interaction one may precisely help the person to come back to Islam."[57] Umm_Harun, however, after having stated that apostates become *kafir* (disbelievers), contends that "we may interact with disbelievers but not closely."[58]

Some of the converts when discussing the apostasy issue are aware of a procedure to be followed upon learning of one's apostasy, namely, allocation of time for the apostate to reconsider his/her decision. Moreover, they argue that the provided time has to be used proactively, that is, to try and pull the apostate back into the fold of Islam through what is generally referred to as "*daʿwah*": "As far as I know, when a Muslim rejects Islam, one needs to try to bring [him] back to Islam, to do *daʿwah*" (Nelli,[59] also Rano[60]). However, who exactly is supposed to engage in this post-apostasy *daʿwah*? Vika maintains that "to try to return the person to Islam is every decent Muslim's duty—to try as much as one's strength, circumstances, possibilities allow."[61] Anonimas thinks that it could be "the family, relatives, the religious community that one has moved out [of]."[62] Geltona Spalva, though allowing that it can be "anyone who wants and is able," also adds that the "community leader is probably responsible."[63]

Others are also in favor of *daʿwah*, however, as Grazkebraske reasons: "Not everyone may engage in *daʿwa*. . . . Ill-informed persuasion simply distances even further."[64] UmmJumana is also of the view that "in the beginning *daʿwa* needs to be done—and done very seriously, such a person has to be shown that he is mistaken and only scholars may decide if enough was explained to him."[65] Mariam opines that "*daʿwa* to apostates should be done by rather well-trained Muslims not only in the religion of Islam but also in psychological, emotional, spiritual aspects related to believers, their behavior. By those who would not traumatize the renouncer even further but help him. It should be Muslim persons empowered and trained by official institutions, mosques, centers of Islamic learning."[66] Kelrodė Šviesa is even more precise: "'*Ulama*' [those knowledgeable in Islam] should interact with such a person for three days and answer his questions, enlighten him, urge him, that is give him a chance to return to Islam. If not [successful], after the three days the death penalty should be administered to him."[67] Finally, Umm_Harun[68] makes a distinction between the function of *ulama* in an Islamic country and the place of *daʿwah* in a non-Islamic environment:

> According to Sharia, before announcing the sentencing and punishment Islamic theologists consult and invite the person back to Islam. But in the countries where there is no Sharia, we deal with the renouncer like with any other non-believer: we do *daʿwa*—that is, we invite [him] to Islam with the same means, though naturally emphasizing more the things because of which Islam was abandoned.

Though, as shown earlier, many among the converts in the research contend that Muslims have a right to apostasy and there is no punishment for it, while some others maintain that there is such a ban with an ensuing punishment, the overwhelming majority also thinks that it is not only not forbidden for Muslims to engage apostates but that it is even advisable to do *daʿwah* to them with the objective of giving it a try to return them to the fold of Islam. However, practical experiences with disaffiliates/deconverts add an additional flavor to how one perceives them. The final section of this chapter is devoted to this intimate side of encountering deconversion among former brothers and sisters in faith.

Personal experience

Though a number of converts under research admitted knowing of those from among Lithuanian Muslims who do not practice Islam any more (Rimantė,[69]

Pavasario Snaigė,[70] Ieva[71]), most abstained from judging if they have deconverted or merely disaffiliated (literally, "distanced" themselves from Islam). Apart from noticing changes in behavior, converts also spoke of disaffiliates' changes in communication with Muslims, sometimes amounting to termination of it: "As a rule, apostates rush to as quickly as possible terminate all the relationships with the *umma* [Lithuanian convert Muslim community] and particularly with those from whom they would expect moralizing and condemnation" (Umm_Harun).[72]

Most of the converts abstained from sharing the information on disaffiliates or deconverts they personally know or their own feelings about them. Rimantė, who is one of the most vocal converts, acknowledges that upon learning of someone's deconversion she becomes angry and is disappointed by that person "both religiously and humanly" and cannot make herself keep up the relations. According to her, it becomes "even more difficult if those persons start disseminating their new worldview, if there appear their followers, like-minded people, if someone falls off [deconverts] as a consequence of their big authoritativeness."[73] With this she indirectly expresses the other converts' worry indicated above that deconverts may be a danger not only for themselves but for other, especially spiritually weak, converts. In contrast, Umm_Aisha argues that "by meeting little practicing, openly sinning Muslims there is no big danger to relapse from Islam. Maybe even to the contrary, the will to be more exemplary strengthens."[74] However, she also admits that she seeks to avoid being in contact with such people.

The converts noted that although they have attempted to approach disaffiliates with the aim of persuading them to remain Muslim, those have been futile efforts: "If you try to look for, to renew the contact, [they] do not wish [it] any more, do not go into conversation, [and] after some time you (accidentally) notice that that person is already leading a completely different life"[75] (Rimantė, also Pavasario Snaigė[76] and Umm_Harun[77]). The failure of this sort of *daʿwah* as explained by converts themselves is predetermined by either the very nature of conversion—it is those "who came to Islam with the intention to please someone, to be liked, to try something new and try on" (Rimantė,[78] also Dia[79])—or spiritual weakness: "They were susceptible to influence by others, were not keen on going deep into the faith, did not raise questions, did not look for answers, or to the contrary—were lost among faiths, went through a number, jumped from one onto another because they would always find something more beautiful, easier, better, though they would not remain in any of them and did not fully practice, did not try to get to the core" (Ieva).[80] Ieva's reasoning here resonates with the conversion career concept noted above—indeed, a number of Lithuanians who at one point have embraced Islam are "conversion careerists" the way Ieva described them.

Finally, when asked if anything could make them consider deconversion, all the converts rejected such a possibility, though some admitted that they have experienced pressure, albeit usually indirect, to be less of a Muslim. Nonetheless, many did concede that there may be or even have been times when they had doubts about their faith or were lenient toward their Islamic duties. One even confessed having been on the verge of deconversion—she then changed her Islamic orientation from Sunni to Sufi and has been continuing to live as a Muslim.

CONCLUDING OBSERVATIONS

Investigating apostasy from a sociological and anthropological perspective, as has been so skillfully shown by Cottee (2015; see also this volume), may be a daunting and rewarding task. Apostates, due to numerous reasons, may not want to be dragged into the spotlight and scrutinized by outsiders. As there are apparently very few Lithuanian Muslim deconverts, the focus of this chapter was not on deconverts themselves but on what the remaining converts think about apostasy from Islam in general and deconversion from Islam by fellow Lithuanians. It, however, proved to be not an easy endeavor either. Many of the approached converts were wary of engaging the researcher, and most of those who went along chose to be both brief and cautious. Asked why this is the case, Rimantė answered by saying that "I think that this is a sort of half taboo topic, because those who have not directly encountered this [deconversion/ apostasy] likely think that this is not possible (to renounce Islam having converted to it). And those, who have encountered this, avoid talking even in abstract terms or hypothetically, so that inadvertently not to say too much, not to become [an object of] slander" (Rimantė).[81]

The process of moving out of religion is as a rule a protracted one and involves at least several stages (see also Alyedreessy, this volume), one of which is disaffiliation (in the Lithuanian language, "distancing"), arguably preceding the actual act of abandoning one's faith, whether it is called "apostasy" or "deconversion." It, however, became apparent during the investigation that for the Lithuanian converts disaffiliation and what Cottee (2015) has labeled "closet apostates" are barely distinguishable. The Lithuanian converts accepted only an open declaration of abandoning of religion as apostasy/deconversion. In such a case, some of the converts supported the principle of strict physical punishment in the form of the death penalty (though some admitted that under the current circumstances this can hardly be administered due to the lack of proper Islamic jurisdiction), while several thought such punishment to be obsolete—if anything, God will punish the apostates in the Hereafter.

As a consequence, nondeclaration or nonadmission of deconversion would be treated by converts as good enough ground to still consider the person a Muslim, albeit lapsed. Most of the converts abstained from what Rimantė called "personal *takfir*,"[82] that is, judging on whether one has deconverted. In contrast, many converts admitted knowing other converts who appear to be on the way of moving out. In such cases some of the converts indicated that they attempted some sort of counseling, or *daʿwah*, but it was admittedly futile as the disaffiliates shunned the topic or interaction with remaining converts altogether.

The results of this research, due to its small sample size and the sensitivity of the topic among the Lithuanian converts to Islam, may be treated as only tentative and not necessarily representative of the entire Lithuanian convert Muslim segment, let alone the Lithuanian Muslim community. There is still much to investigate in this totally new field. Even so, it is hoped that this research and its findings may meaningfully contribute to the wider field of research on "moving in and out" of religion in general and in the European Muslim landscape in particular.

NOTES

1. Lithuanians do not appear to be unique in this regard. Other research (Köse and Loewenthal 2000; Jensen 2006) have found similar tendencies.

2. www.facebook.com/groups/406366666119537/?fref=ts. Group: salaf kelio seserys, 06-18-2014, last accessed 12-15-2016, not accessible any more.

3. islam-ummah.lt, last accessed 12-15-2016, not accessible any more.

4. Answer to the questionnaire.

5. www.facebook.com/groups/406366666119537/?fref=ts. Group: salaf kelio seserys, 06-18-2014, last accessed 12-15-2016, not accessible any more.

6. Answer to the questionnaire.

7. www.facebook.com/groups/406366666119537/?fref=ts. Group: salaf kelio seserys, 06-18-2014, last accessed 12-15-2016, not accessible any more.

8. islam-ummah.lt, 07-19-2014, last accessed 12-15-2016, not accessible any more.

9. islam-ummah.lt, 07-21-2014.; also Nelli, islam-ummah.lt, 11-14-2011, last accessed 12-15-2016, not accessible any more.

10. islam-ummah.lt, 07-14-2014, last accessed 12-15-2016, not accessible any more.

11. Answers to the questionnaire.
12. Answer to the questionnaire.
13. islam-ummah.lt, 07-14-2014, last accessed 12-15-2016, not accessible any more.
14. Answers to the questionnaire.
15. Answer to the questionnaire.
16. islam-ummah.lt, 07-18-2014, last accessed 12-15-2016, not accessible any more.
17. Answer to the questionnaire.
18. Answer to the questionnaire.
19. islam-ummah.lt, 07-21-2014, last accessed 12-15-2016, not accessible any more.
20. Answers to the questionnaire.
21. Answer to the questionnaire.
22. Answer to the questionnaire.
23. islam-ummah.lt, 07-18-2014, last accessed 12-15-2016, not accessible any more.
24. islam-ummah.lt, 07-21-2014, last accessed 12-15-2016, not accessible any more.
25. Answer to the questionnaire.
26. islam-ummah.lt, 07-21-2014, last accessed 12-15-2016, not accessible any more.
27. islam-ummah.lt, 07-21-2014, last accessed 12-15-2016, not accessible any more.
28. Answers to the questionnaire.
29. Answer to the questionnaire.
30. Answer to the questionnaire.
31. Answer to the questionnaire.
32. Answer to the questionnaire.
33. In fact, converts use "in my opinion" and its variants quite often. This may be indicative of their wish to make a conscious distinction between an authoritative position, to which they do not aspire, and merely their personal, and possibly "wrong," opinion.
34. islam-ummah.lt, 11-14-2011, last accessed 12-15-2016, not accessible any more.
35. www.facebook.com/groups/406366666119537/?fref=ts. Group: salaf kelio seserys, 06-18-2014, last accessed 12-15-2016, not accessible any more.
36. Answer to the questionnaire.
37. islam-ummah.lt, 02-15-2013), last accessed 12-15-2016, not accessible any more.
38. islam-ummah.lt, 11-14-2011, last accessed 12-15-2016, not accessible any more.
39. Answer to the questionnaire.
40. Answer to the questionnaire.
41. Answer to the questionnaire.
42. Answer to the questionnaire.
43. Answer to the questionnaire.
44. Answer to the questionnaire.
45. Answer to the questionnaire.
46. islam-ummah.lt, 10-23-2011, last accessed 12-15-2016, not accessible any more.
47. Answer to the questionnaire.
48. Answer to the questionnaire.
49. islam-ummah.lt, 11-14-2011, last accessed 12-15-2016, not accessible any more.

50. Answer to the questionnaire.

51. islam-ummah.lt, 11-13-2011, last accessed 12-15-2016, not accessible any more.

52. Answer to the questionnaire.

53. www.facebook.com/groups/406366666119537/?fref=ts. Group: salaf kelio seserys, 06-18-2014, last accessed 12-15-2016, not accessible any more.

54. Answer to the questionnaire.

55. Answer to the questionnaire.

56. Answer to the questionnaire.

57. Answer to the questionnaire.

58. Answer to the questionnaire.

59. islam-ummah.lt, 11-13-2011, last accessed 12-15-2016, not accessible any more.

60. Answer to the questionnaire.

61. Answer to the questionnaire.

62. Answer to the questionnaire.

63. Answer to the questionnaire.

64. Answer to the questionnaire.

65. islam-ummah.lt, 11-14-2011, last accessed 12-15-2016, not accessible any more.

66. Answer to the questionnaire.

67. www.facebook.com/groups/406366666119537/?fref=ts. Group: salaf kelio seserys, 06-18-2014, last accessed 12-15-2016, not accessible anymore; see also Geltona Spalva (answer to the questionnaire).

68. Answer to the questionnaire.

69. www.facebook.com/groups/406366666119537/?fref=ts. Group: salaf kelio seserys, 06-18-2014, last accessed 12-15-2016, not accessible any more.

70. www.facebook.com/groups/406366666119537/?fref=ts. Group: salaf kelio seserys, 06-18-2014, last accessed 12-15-2016, not accessible any more.

71. www.facebook.com/groups/406366666119537/?fref=ts. Group: salaf kelio seserys, 06-18-2014, last accessed 12-15-2016, not accessible any more.

72. Answer to the questionnaire.

73. islam-ummah.lt, 07-19-2014, last accessed 12-15-2016, not accessible any more.

74. islam-ummah.lt, 07-21-2014, last accessed 12-15-2016, not accessible any more.

75. www.facebook.com/groups/406366666119537/?fref=ts. Group: salaf kelio seserys, 06-18-2014, last accessed 12-15-2016, not accessible any more.

76. www.facebook.com/groups/406366666119537/?fref=ts. Group: salaf kelio seserys, 06-18-2014, last accessed 12-15-2016, not accessible any more.

77. Answer to the questionnaire.

78. islam-ummah.lt, 07-19-2014, last accessed 12-15-2016, not accessible any more.

79. Answer to the questionnaire.

80. www.facebook.com/groups/406366666119537/?fref=ts. Group: salaf kelio seserys, 06-18-2014, last accessed 12-15-2016, not accessible any more.

81. islam-ummah.lt, 07-19-2014, last accessed 12-15-2016, not accessible any more.

82. islam-ummah.lt, 07-19-2014, last accessed 12-15-2016, not accessible any more.

REFERENCES

Alalwani, T. J. 2011. *Apostasy in Islam: A Historical and Scriptural Analysis*. Herndon: International Institute of Islamic Thought.

Allievi, S. 2002. "Converts and the Making of European Islam." *ISIM Newsletter* 11: 1, 26.

Brinkerhoff, M. B., and M. M. Mackie. 1993. "Casting Off the Bonds of organized Religion: A Religious-Careers Approach to the Study of Apostasy." *Review of Religious Research* 34, no. 3: 235–258.

Caplovitz, D., and F. Sherrow. 1977. *The Religious Drop-Outs: Apostasy among College Graduates*. Beverly Hills, CA: Sage.

Cottee, S. 2015. *The Apostates: When Muslims Leave Islam*. London: Hurst.

Gooren, H. 2007. "Reassessing Conventional Approaches to Conversion: Toward a New Synthesis." *Journal for the Scientific Study of Religion* 46, no. 3: 337–353.

Jensen, T. G. 2006. "Religious Authority and Autonomy Intertwined: The Case of Converts to Islam in Denmark." *The Muslim World* 96, no. 4: 643–660.

Köse, A., and K. M. Loewenthal. 2000. "Conversion Motifs among British Converts to Islam." *International Journal for the Psychology of Religion* 10, no. 2: 101–110.

Lofland, J., and N. Skonovd. 1981. "Conversion Motifs." *Journal for the Scientific Study of Religion* 20, no. 4: 373–385.

Račius, E. 1999. "Limits of Application of the Shariʿa in Modern Kuwait: The Case Study of Apostasy of Hussein Qambar Ali, a Convert from Islam to Christianity." *Studia arabistyczne i islamistyczne* 7: 5–21.

Račius, E. 2013a. "A 'Virtual Club' of Lithuanian Converts to Islam." In *Muslims and the New Information and Communication Technologies*. T. Hoffman and G. Larsson, eds. Dordrecht: Springer Verlag. 31–47.

———. 2013b. "Both Muslim and European? An Inquiry into the Case of the Muslim Community in Lithuania." *Journal of Muslims in Europe* 2, no. 2: 165–185.

Streib, H. 2014. "Deconversion." In *Oxford Handbook on Religious Conversion*. L. R. Rambo and C. E. Farhadian, eds. Oxford: Oxford University Press. 271–296.

Streib, H., and C. Klein. 2013. "Atheists, Agnostics, and Apostates." In *APA Handbook of Psychology, Religion, and Spirituality*, vol. 1. K. I. Pargament, J. J. Exline, and J. W. Jones, eds. Washington, DC: American Psychological Association. 713–728.

Streib, H., et al. 2009. *Deconversion: Qualitative and Quantitative Results from Cross-Cultural Research in Germany and the United States of America*. Göttingen: Vandenhoeck & Ruprecht.

SIXTEEN

LET'S TALK ABOUT APOSTASY!

Swedish Imams, Apostasy Debates, and Police Reports on Hate Crimes and (De)conversion[1]

GÖRAN LARSSON

This chapter focuses on one sensitive question: Is it dangerous for Muslims in Sweden to leave Islam? Although the notion that it is highly dangerous to leave Islam seems to be primarily produced by former Muslims who have done so and who feel an urgent need to voice strong criticism of their former beliefs, or by Christian leaders who have baptized former Muslims (see, e.g., Naskret 2016), several individuals have actually testified that they have been threatened because they have changed their religious belief or belonging (Naskret 2016; Daniel 2014 and Björk 2014).

Without saying that these voices are incorrect, there is, however, a frequent tendency for these narratives to be reproduced uncritically by the media (Naskret 2016), leaving little room for more liberal opinions about apostasy on the part of Muslims. As noted earlier, ex-Muslims who receive threats should be taken seriously, but it is also important to underscore that they have the potential to produce and reproduce an understanding of Islam that is not upheld by all Muslims. As a consequence, they block out more liberal positions upheld by theologians like, for example, Taha Jabir Alalwani, Abdullah Saeed, Abdullahi Ahmed an-Naʿim, and Tariq Ramadan, to whom I will return below.

Although a growing number of academic studies have addressed Muslim theological debates and case studies concerning apostasy accusations and trials in the Muslim world both past and present,[2] there is hardly any data on how imams in Europe view individuals who have left Islam. The first aim of this chapter is therefore to present data on this topic. My sample consists of field data collected during 2015 and 2016 showing how six imams in Sweden talk about and understand the question of Muslims leaving Islam. However, the imams in the sample are mainly talking about individuals who have decided to leave the community and stopped calling themselves Muslims; they rarely use the word "apostate."[3]

Since it is often argued in both media reporting and by ex-Muslims that it is impossible or highly dangerous to leave Islam, the second aim of this chapter is to describe and analyze police records from Sweden containing information about hate crimes directed against individuals who have converted from one religion to another religion or to a different worldview (e.g., atheism). The material I have used for this task consists of data collected by the Swedish National Council for Crime Prevention (Brottsförebyggande rådet, abbreviated as Brå in Swedish) for the years 2010 to 2012.

The central questions for this chapter are accordingly the following: How do certain Swedish imams talk about the issues of apostasy and of people moving away from Islam? Do the existing police records on religiously motivated hate crimes include any references that can be related to apostasy, conversion, or deconversion?

ISLAM AND APOSTASY: A SHORT OVERVIEW

When talking about "apostasy," it should be realized that it is a negative term in the history of religions, mainly used to condemn individuals who have left the community because of their thoughts or actions. However, in both past and present it is a common strategy to label one's opponents or enemies heretics or apostates, though it is seldom if ever the case that those who are branded with this label look upon themselves as such—quite the contrary. Nevertheless, using this identification has often made it legitimate for those in power to initiate a process against those who have deviated in thought or action or are regarded as having done so. The implication of this procedure is that it is possible to punish and to bring the so-called heretic or apostate back into line (cf. Watt 1964).

In Islamic discourses, apostasy is explicitly linked to the Arabic root consonant *r-d-d*, which has a wide range of connotations (cf. Larsson 2015). However, derived terms like *irtidad* and *murtadd* refer more commonly to a return to a previous state (i.e., to go back to a previous condition, or a former belief). Even though the Qur'an contains many strong condemnations of those who commit error and sin and who stray from the righteous path, few Muslim theologians appear to argue that the Qur'an contains an explicit reference to punishment for abandoning Islam (cf. Hallaq 2001). In the Qur'an the punishment for apostasy is, rather, postponed to the next life (cf. Q 9:74).

In order to find explicit references and even recommendations that apostates from Islam should be punished in this life, it is necessary to turn to the prophetic literature and subsequent juridical discussions. For example, one of the most famous *hadiths* dealing with this question comes from al-Bukhari's collection. It reads:

> Narrated ʿAbdullāh: Allāh's Messenger said, "The blood of a Muslim who confesses that *Lā ilāha illallāh* (none has the right to be worshipped but Allāh) and that I am the Messenger of Allāh, cannot be shed except in three cases: (1) Life for life, (in cases of intentional murders without right, i.e., in *Qiṣāṣ*—Law of Equality in punishment), (2) a married person who commits illegal sexual intercourse, and (3) the one who turns renegade from Islām (apostate) and leaves the group of Muslims (by innovating heresy, new ideas and new things, etc. in the Islāmic religion." (Bukhari, *Sahih*, 9: 20)

While it is beyond question that many Muslim theologians, as well as so-called ordinary Muslims, have interpreted this passage as proof of the obligation to punish or kill apostates from Islam and the legality of doing so, other theologians argue that God has given humanity free will. Because of this emphasis, they argue further that there is no compulsion in the religion (cf. Q 2:25). For example, contemporary theologians like Taha Jabir Alalwani, Abdullah Saeed, Abdullahi Ahmed an-Naʿim, and Tariq Ramadan have all questioned the claim that apostates from Islam should be killed. According to their understanding, it is only apostates who pose a real threat to the social order who should be punished—that is, it is the act of rebellion and not the change in religious status that constitutes a problem (see, e.g., Kraemer 1980). Without going into any historical debates or source-critical discussions (for more information, see Cook 2006 and Kraemer 1980), one can find several different and even contradictory opinions about apostasy among Muslim theologians.

The fact that individuals can suffer hate crimes and harassment in connection with conversion or deconversion is true for many individuals in both Sweden and many other parts of the world, especially in countries and regions that generally lack freedom with respect to religion and basic human rights. Consequently, it is quite easy to find modern cases where apostates from Islam have been severely punished or even killed in countries like, for example, Saudi Arabia, Iran, and Sudan (cf. Peters 2003: 177). Also, groups like Islamic State, Boko Haram, and Harakat al-Shabaab stress that it is proper to kill individuals who have changed their religion or whom they regard as apostates. This has also had a deadly impact on many Sunni and Shiʿa Muslims who disagree with the views of the groups mentioned above.

Thus, without ignoring the fact that individuals can be and are persecuted or even killed because of their convictions in many parts of the world, it is important to investigate the alternative interpretations that exist among Muslims and theologians and to analyze how imams talk about apostasy in the West. In the third section ("Let's talk about apostasy"), I will show how a small number of Swedish imams understand the question of apostasy and the fundamental right to be able to choose or discard a religious belief in the Western context. I will then turn to police reports on hate crimes and try to see what they say about the threats and harassment that may follow conversion. First, however, I would like to discuss some methodological and ethical questions.

METHODOLOGICAL AND ETHICAL QUESTIONS

The six imams included in the study were selected as representative of different ethnic backgrounds. Consequently, they belong to various Muslim organizations, including major Sunni Muslim and Shiʿa groups, as well as other minority Muslim groups. The interviews were conducted by either telephone or email or by personally visiting informants. The telephone interviews were recorded, and those conducted in mosques were either recorded on a smart phone or by handwritten notes. The length of the interviews varied from twenty minutes to approximately one hour. In order to make the information comparable, all imams were asked the same questions, but I was also able to ask follow-up questions, and informants were also free to develop the conversation and explore other questions if necessary.

Even though imams can rightly be seen as representatives of Muslim organizations or mosques, the voices included in the chapter are anonymous, and I created aliases for the imams. I have provided dates only for the interviews, and included no information about place or locality, in order to protect the imams as much as possible.

In assessing whether conversion from one religion to another can put the individual concerned in a vulnerable situation, it is important to stress that Sweden does not keep any record of religious belonging. Consequently, it is not possible to estimate how many or under what circumstances individuals choose to change religious belonging or to stop being religious in the first place. As the fourth section ("Is it dangerous to leave Islam?") will show, it is very hard to find police records describing cases where individuals have been harassed and threatened after they have left a religious community. This lacuna could be due to the difficulty in accessing police records that contain information about these questions. Moreover, these kinds of offenses may be filed under many different categories of crime. It is also likely that hate crimes and harassment related to conversion or deconversion are not being reported to the police, with this underreporting causing a large lacuna in the available data set. Nonetheless, it is vital to conduct a systematic analysis of harassment and threats to individuals who express their freedom of religion by choosing a new religion or by leaving a particular form of religious life.

LET'S TALK ABOUT APOSTASY

According to the imams I interviewed, it is not common for Muslims to denounce and reject their faith publicly: most of the imams thought that those who become disinterested just drop out and stop visiting the mosque for prayers or other activities. In other words, these Muslims simply become nominal Muslims, and this is likely the most common way of being Muslim, according to the imams. However, these "passive" Muslims are generally not looked upon as individuals who have left Islam.

As with other religious communities, it is common for Muslims to express different levels of attachment and engagement over time. A more profound interest in religion is often related to life-cycle patterns (e.g., marriage, childbirth, divorce, sicknesses, and finally death) or recurring holidays and festivities (e.g., Ramadan, the two *ʿids*, ʿAshura, or the celebration of the birth of the Prophet Muhammad). Even those who have dropped out of their religious tradition and left the communal life may show up at major religious festivities. Such occasional attendance most likely has more to do with social bonding and identity than religious beliefs. However, this nonreligious attachment to a religious tradition or practice is a topic about which there is very little research in Sweden (one important exception being Otterbeck 2010).

While some of the imams in the sample stress that they have never met anyone who has left Islam (e.g., Imam Mustafa), others indicated that they have at least heard of such cases. Imam Husain, for example, claimed to have met a family that has left the mosque and the religion, although he is not sure, and some informants have even been in contact with individuals who openly express a desire to leave Islam. One of the imams, Imam Tariq, stressed that some of those who have left Islam also have a strong urge to be provocative and to tease the imam and anybody else who follows Islam. This group can sometimes cause problems for the imam, as well as distress among former fellow Muslims. According to Imam Abdullah, losing an individual who decides to leave Islam is a great sorrow. For him this is therefore a matter of grief, but not of violence, hatred, or revenge.

However, it was Imam Rahman who provided the most vivid outline of an encounter with someone who has left Islam. This encounter was exceptional, for Rahman explained that he has met only one individual who told him openly that he wanted to leave Islam during his eighteen years as an imam in Sweden. This particular case concerned a non-Muslim man who became engaged to a Muslim woman from Algeria. Since she realized that the man would have to become a Muslim in order to be permitted to marry her as a Muslim woman (a basic requirement in Islamic law; see, e.g., Doumato 1995: 52), he decided to investigate the possibility of him converting to Islam. In his first conversations with the man, Rahman stressed: "You [i.e., the man who wanted to convert] will have to choose this [i.e, convert to Islam] from your heart and not because of the marriage." After affirming that this was his choice and that it had nothing to do with his love for or attraction to the woman, he converted, and they got married in a mosque in Sweden. The problem was that the woman was not serious about the marriage, and difficulties emerged soon after the wedding. After they divorced, the man decided that he also wanted to leave Islam, but he felt bad about his earlier decision to become a Muslim. To remedy his error, the man (i.e., the former Muslim) wanted to contact a mosque in order to let them know that he had left Islam. The former Muslim said to Rahman: "Now I feel guilt for calling an imam and tell him that I have left Islam," Rahman told him that he was mixing up marriage and Islam, but the man was persistent and said that he wanted to leave both (i.e., both his wife and Islam). Rahman replied: "It is up to you to decide, and no one can force you to remain a Muslim." However, the imam advised the man not to get in touch with the mosque in which he had converted to Islam. Rahman explained that the man had no obligation to return the written paper issued by the mosque when he had become a Muslim some time earlier:[4] It was enough that the man had contacted him as an imam, and there was no obligation in Islam to return such a paper. This conversation is interesting because it shows that converts as well as those who decide to leave a religious community can cause ethical dilemmas for religious leaders. As a further example, in Sweden today there is a debate among some Christian priests and pastors as to how they should treat migrants and asylum-seekers from a Muslim cultural background who want to abandon Islam and convert to Christianity. This is a sensitive question because of the belief among some would-be converts that a conversion would, for example, guarantee the emigrant or asylum-seeker staying in Sweden after becoming Christian. Since a conversion does not automatically provide any such guarantee, this is potentially an ethical dilemma for many priests and pastors in Sweden today. Another reading of this episode is that the imam was afraid that members of his congregation would not be as tolerant and liberal as he himself was.

No matter what their personal experiences, the imams I interviewed are more or less united in their opinion about what they think Islam says on the question of apostasy. For example, Tariq says: "Islam clearly says in the Qur'an, *la ik'raha fi al-din*," that is, there is no compulsion in religion (Q 2:256). He continues by stressing that the belief is situated in the heart, and according to him the heart is composed of "conviction, love and faith." In Tariq's understanding, God does not accept any action if it is not situated in the heart, and every action should therefore be honest and sincere. According to Tariq, God has given humanity the freedom to choose. Consequently, it becomes a violation to force a person to adopt a certain belief or to remain in a condition that the individual wants to leave. Furthermore, it is argued that the Qur'an provides examples showing that individuals were actually able to change their opinions about religion during the formative history of Islam—explaining why conversion and deconversion are not problematic for Imam Rahman. For example, both Imam Rahman and Imam Mustafa refer to the following verse in the Qur'an in stressing that it is not forbidden to change your religion:

> Those who believe, then disbelieve, then believe again, then disbelieve and then increase in their disbelief—God will never forgive them nor guide them to the path (Q 4:137).

Although this quotation indicates that the apostate will be punished, this passage from the Qur'an does not prescribe a punishment in this life but instead hints that it will be postponed to the next life. Furthermore, the passage also suggests that one can change one's belief and then return to one's former belief. Hence for the majority of imams, there is no support in the Qur'an for punishing those who leave Islam in this life. For example, Imam Mustafa stresses that "the law about *irtidad* [apostasy] has nothing to do with Islam at all"; nor does this interpretation have anything to do with how Muhammad looked upon these questions. The so-called obligation to kill apostates from Islam is nothing but a human invention, according to Imam Mustafa. However, all the imams were aware that support for the punishment and even the killing of apostates can be found in the *hadith* literature and that some Muslims see it as obligatory to kill anyone who leaves Islam (see the first section above). Although all imams are well aware of these prophetic traditions, it is clear that they have different ways of analyzing and explaining passages that can be read as providing support for the killing of apostates. While Imam

Tariq and Imam Mustafa stress the necessity of submitting the *hadith* literature to a source-critical analysis, Imam Rahman, for example, stresses that the authenticity of some of these *hadiths* is questionable according to the rules of *ʿilm al-hadith* and *usul al-fiqh*. Without going into any detail about these genres or the hermeneutical and source-critical approaches that underpin them in Islamic literary genres (Ziadeh 1995), most of the imams in my sample argue that the *hadith* literature must be linked to the political context and the circumstances that prevailed when Muhammad uttered these sayings.

For example, Imam Rahman argued that the three *hadiths* (i.e., the most common prophetic traditions that are said to support the killing of apostates—see Bukhari, *Sahih* 5: 383–384; 9: 20; and 9: 31–34) must be related to the prevailing circumstances at the time of the Prophet Muhammad and that those who left Islam were also seen as rebels threatening the social order. Hence, it is not the act of apostasy per se that is the reason they should be killed but their rebellion or treason against the Muslim community.[5] Consequently, the prescription to kill apostates must be understood against the backdrop of a specific political context. According to Imam Rahman, one should remember that the early Muslim community was very fragile, that many people who were branded as hypocrites said one thing and acted in another way, and that this was a serious problem for the community. This is the main reason why the *hadith* literature prescribes a harsh punishment for those who leave the community, but this *hadith* should not be read ahistorically: the prescription that apostates be killed is not a universal one that is applicable to all times and places, according to Imam Rahman. This way of arguing is not unique to this imam: contemporary theologians such as, for example, Taha Jabir Alalwani (2011) and Tariq Ramadan (2007; 2008) argue along similar lines.

Most of the imams in my sample stress that, even though there may be a basis in Islamic tradition or Islamic jurisprudence (e.g., within the law schools) in favor of apostates being killed, this is not applicable in a non-Islamic context such as Sweden. To follow this ruling, the state must be governed entirely by *Shariʿa* law, and the apostate should be tried in court under that law before he or she is punished. Since this condition is not met in Sweden or in the Western world, or in most countries that are governed by or influenced by Islamic legal principles, this way of handling apostasy is not applicable today. However, some of the imams in the sample (e.g., Imam Mustafa) stress that imams and Muslims who blindly follow tradition, also known as *taqlid*,[6] might have greater problems in dealing with apostasy since the punishment for those who leave Islam is established in the tradition (i.e., in the *hadith* literature). Thus, in order to avoid such a blind following of the law schools or a literal reading of the *hadith* texts, the sources must be interpreted and contextualized with the help of *ijtihad*, that is, independent reasoning (Peters 1989). In this way, religious scholars and imams can be directed to readings that lead to a renewal of how Islam can be applied and interpreted in present-day society (cf. Ramadan 2008). It is therefore important for Tariq to stress that the founder of the four Sunni schools of law were humans and therefore that, if their opinions about a particular matter are not supported or contradicted by the Qur'an, it is important to follow the latter. With regard to the question of apostasy, this is important because the Qur'an does not provide any support for the killing of those who leave Islam, according to Imam Rahman and Imam Mustafa.

Sweden is a country that enshrines freedom of religion. Consequently, those who decide to leave a religious tradition or embrace a new tradition cannot be prosecuted or punished (Swedish Constitution, Instrument of Government, Chapter 2). According to both Imam Abdullah and Imam Mustafa, the Swedish law guaranteeing freedom of religion is clearly in line with the essence of Islam, and they even describe this law as being Islamic in nature. In discussing this issue, Rahman stressed the paradox of Muslim leaders on the one hand accepting that individuals are permitted to embrace Islam by conversion and on the other hand not accepting that individuals can also leave Islam. Accordingly, in an open and democratic society that upholds the principle of freedom of religion, individuals must be able to both convert and leave a religious tradition, this being a matter of personal choice that Muslim leaders and imams have to accept, according to Imam Rahman.

As has become clear in this section, the imams in this study are more liberal than they are usually portrayed in the media. In the next section I will investigate whether the idea, commonly expressed in the media, that leaving Islam is dangerous is warranted.

IS IT DANGEROUS TO LEAVE ISLAM?

As already indicated, it is very hard to find data on how many individuals are harassed or threatened when they leave Islam, convert to another religious tradition, or take up a nonreligious worldview, or how frequent this is. Whereas former Muslims who have publicly criticized Islam (see, e.g., Larsson 2016) argue that it is quite common for individuals who convert from Islam to Christianity to be bullied and threatened, it is often hard to substantiate this claim. For example, the Swedish National Council for Crime Prevention (Brå), which among many other things has a responsibility to collect

TABLE 16.1. REPORTED INCIDENTS THAT ARE RELATED TO CONVERSION FOR THE YEARS 2010–2012

Conversion to	*2010*	*2011*	*2012**
Christianity	11	21	10
Judaism	X	0	0
Islam	X	5	23
Other/no information	0	4	4
Total	*16*	*30*	*37*

x = Less than 4.

*The numbers for 2012 have been estimated on the basis of a random check.

Source: *Främlingsfientliga handlingar mot trossamfund. En kartläggning av religiösa grupper och individers utsatthet i Sverige 2014*, 30.

data on hate crimes, does not include any information about reported crimes that can be related to conversion or changes to religious belonging in its annual report. However, in 2004 Brå was asked by the Commission for Government Support for Faith Communities (SST), the governmental body that organizes financial support for faith communities in Sweden, to look for such information in their earlier records (*Främlingsfientliga handlingar mot trossamfund. En kartläggning av religiösa grupper och individers utsatthet i Sverige 2014*: 30–35). To the best of my knowledge this is the first time that information on reported crimes has been linked to conversion and been systematically collected. The results for the years 2010–2012 are presented in table 16.1.

The data in table 16.1 includes eighty-three individuals who have changed their religious belonging or who are about to change it. According to Brå it is likely that the perpetrators of these crimes viewed the "potential" converts as a threat and that the convert was not acting according to the prescribed norms and behavior. One individual in Brå's sample also changed religion (or maybe congregation or place of worship) because he or she was a homosexual, and this was not liked. This indicates that "conversion" can also include those who would like to remain religious but who need to change congregation or "religion" in order to be able to continue to be openly both homosexual and a believer. However, validating this conclusion is difficult since the data do not provide any explanation for why the individual was threatened or harassed in the first place or what victims imply when they have changed religion. However, table 16.1 shows convincingly that it is not only individuals who convert from Islam to another religion (predominantly to Christianity) who have suffered from some kind of discrimination or threat. It seems that adopting a new form of religious belonging may cause stress and hard feelings among various religious groups.

From table 16.2, it is possible to deduce that fifty-five individuals (66 percent) received threats after or during their conversion to a new religious tradition. Eight individuals (10 percent) were victims of crimes of violence, twelve (14 percent) experienced intimidation because of their conversion, and five (6 percent) felt that they had been targets of incitement to racial hatred. Since the focus of the police is on actions and not experiences and feelings, it is much harder to demonstrate a connection between defamation and incitement to racial hatred and hate crimes (on this problem, see Larsson and Sander 2015).

TABLE 16.2. NUMBER OF REPORTED INCIDENTS THAT INCLUDE IDENTIFIED CONVERTS, SUBDIVIDED BY CRIME CATEGORY FOR THE YEARS 2010–2012

Crime category	*Total number*	*Percentage*
Crime of violence*	8	10
Illegal threat/molestation	55	66
Defamation	12	14
Incitement to racial hatred	5	6
Illegal discrimination	0	0
Other crimes**	2	2
Total	*83*	*100*

The figures for 2012 are based on a selection. Because of rounding up, the summary in the table does not match the estimated total figure (83).

* The category "crime of violence" includes assault and battery, murder/manslaughter, and violence against a civil servant. The period 2010–2011 could maybe also include isolated cases of harassment of women (*kvinnofridsbrott*), robbery, and rape.

** The category "other crimes" includes damage and graffiti.

Source: *Främlingsfientliga handlingar mot trossamfund. En kartläggning av religiösa grupper och individers utsatthet i Sverige 2014*, 31.

From the data presented, it is also possible to obtain an impression of where identified converts are harassed and where they suffered from hate crimes. Table 16.3 contains information about the place of the assault. The most common "place" for threats are telephone or text messages or via the internet, but eleven individuals (13 percent) also reported that they have been victims in their own homes. Table 16.4, which includes information about the relationship between perpetrators and victims, supports the view that the home can be a vulnerable place. Among other things, the data shows that thirty-nine individuals (47 percent) reported being threatened or harassed by individuals with whom they have an intimate or close relationship.

According to Brå's sample, it is not uncommon for converts to be harassed or physically attacked by relatives or close friends in their own homes (as

TABLE 16.3. REPORTED CASES THAT INCLUDE CONVERTS AND PLACE OF ASSAULT, 2010–2012

Place	*Number*	*Percentage*
Telephone/text message	18	22
Public place	12	14
Home	11	13
Another place*	11	13
Internet	7	8
School	4	5
Other place category**	5	6
Public transport	0	0
Place for amusement	0	0
No information	14	17
Number of converts 2010–2012	*83*	*100*

* "Another place" includes, for example, a house that belongs to another person, laundry room, shop, shopping mall, or fast-food restaurant.

** "Other place category" is an allocated category that consists of places with low numbers: media, workspaces, or religious room.

*** The figures for 2012 are based on a selection. Because of rounding up, the summary in the table does not match the estimated total figure (83).

Source: *Främlingsfientliga handlingar mot trossamfund. En kartläggning av religiösa grupper och individers utsatthet i Sverige 2014*, 32.

TABLE 16.4. REPORTS CONCERNING IDENTIFIED CONVERTS THAT INCLUDE INFORMATION ABOUT THE PERPETRATORS' RELATIONSHIP TO THE VICTIM, 2010–2012

Relation	*Number*	*Percentage*
Intimate/close	*39*	*47*
Married/partner/sambo/ex-partner	3	4
Relatives	26	31
Friend/acquaintance	10	12
Superficial acquaintance	*15*	*18*
A person/group who is known by name or looks	9	11
Other superficial acquaintance*	6	7
Unknown	*27*	*33*
Customer/client	0	0
Service personnel	4	5
Unknown person	23	28
No information	*1*	*1*
*Number of converts, 2010–2012***	*83*	*100*

* Neighbors, colleges, or school friends.

** The figures for 2012 are based on a selection. Because of rounding up, the summary in the table does not match the estimated total figure (83).

Source: *Främlingsfientliga handlingar mot trossamfund. En kartläggning av religiösa grupper och individers utsatthet i Sverige 2014*, 33.

shown in table 16.3). In total, thirty-nine individuals (47 percent) reported having been victims of hate crimes to the police and stated that these crimes were committed by intimate or close friends or family members. By contrast, in total twenty-three individuals (28 percent) were attacked by unknown assailants. Even though the figures are small, the results indicate that family members or close friends can react strongly when a family member or friend decides to convert to a new religious affiliation or adopt a new view on religion (e.g., by becoming an atheist).

ANALYSIS

Contrary to how public debates and some ex-Muslims publicly voicing strong criticisms of Islam frame the question of the danger of leaving the religion, my sample shows that imams have different opinions about individuals who actually leave Islam. Without denying that individuals can be threatened in connection with conversion or deconversion, the results indicate that some imams in Sweden also hold more liberal views. Besides a description of the various opinions that can be found among Swedish imams, this chapter also contains a critical discussion of apostasy and threats. While it is common to find individuals prepared to testify that they have been threatened after having left Islam (especially if we turn to public critics of Islam who call themselves ex-Muslims), it is not easy to find police reports with information about this social problem. This lacuna is most likely related to the fact that individuals seldom report having been threatened or harassed, and our knowledge about such events suffers from underreporting. However, even though the available records indicate that a change of religion could result in threats and growing pressure from peer groups, it is clear that this problem is not unique to those who leave Islam. The small sample collected by the Swedish National Council for Crime Prevention shows that this is a general problem.

To summarize the hate crimes that can be related to conversion would not be enough to form a general conclusion. The findings are not statistically representative, and consequently there is a need for further data collection in order to be able to say whether it is dangerous for an individual to change his or her religious affiliation and, if so, to what extent. But the available data from the Swedish National Council for Crime Prevention does not point in a direction that can convincingly be read as supporting the claim that someone who leaves Islam in order to join another religious tradition is more likely to be harassed and abused than someone who converts to Islam (or to any other religion, for that matter). Rather, it seems that conversion can expose the person to a stressful and vulnerable situation and that in the worst case the decision to change one's view of religion or religious belonging can be dangerous for the individual. But yet again it is necessary to stress that the quality of the data does not say how frequent this danger is. Consequently, there is a great need to collect more data on conversion, deconversion, and exit processes leading to changes in religious belonging in Sweden. Irrespective of the lack of empirical data, however, it is hardly bold to argue that it is quite safe to change opinions about religion or religious belonging in Sweden today. In order to test this conclusion (or, rather, hypothesis) it is, of course, necessary to collect more data and to look more deeply into police records that might contain data on threats that can be related to conversion or a change of worldview.

The imams I interviewed were more or less united in their opinions about apostasy. Contrary to both Muslims and non-Muslims who argue that it is impossible to leave Islam, these imams stress that faith is a matter of choice and personal conviction. According to the imams there is no compulsion in religion, and the prophetic texts (see the third section) that can be read as expressing support for the killing of those who leave Islam must be situated in a historical context and should be exposed to a source-critical test. It is only imams who blindly follow and imitate the law schools who are likely to argue in favor of this punishment for those who leave Islam. However, to be able to put this interpretation into practice, the imams also argue that it is necessary to live in a country governed by Islamic laws and backed up by a functioning Islamic legal system. Since this is not the case for Sweden, this part of the Islamic legal system is not applicable according to the imams, and, more important, they are happy to follow the law concerning freedom of religion in Sweden. However, the imams in my sample indicate that knowledge about this fact (i.e., that it is legal and acceptable to change religious belonging) may be low among the Muslim laity, and two of them (Imam Rahman and Imam Mustafa) complained that the Muslims in their congregations are often uninterested in these questions. For example, whenever Imam Rahman organizes lectures on so-called sensitive topics (including apostasy), the interest among his fellow Muslims has been low, and when Imam Mustafa has published texts in both print and social media, he has received almost no response from other Muslims. The imams complain about this situation, and without touching upon this sensitive topic, they seem to indicate that knowledge about Islam is generally very low among the Muslim laity. This, according to Imam Rahman, is one potential reason why some young Muslims harass individuals who have decided to leave Islam. Unlike those Muslim theologians who blindly follow the law schools of Islam, the imams in my sample follow the principle of *itjihad*. As a result, they have no problem in saying that there is no support in the Qur'an for the killing of apostates. For example, five of the six imams I interviewed stated explicitly that it is not possible to find any support for the killing of those who leave Islam and that, in Imam Rahman's words, "there is no strong evidence in the Qur'an that says that it is not allowed to do it [i.e., leave Islam or change religion]." It was only Imam Safet who explained that "the juridical punishment [according to Islam] is actually death" for those who leave Islam, but he also stated that this legal ruling is not applicable in Sweden, since this country is not governed by Islamic laws and regulations.

Although my findings indicate that the imams in the sample have no or very few problems with the fact that some Muslims leave Islam, the quality of the sample could be called into question for two reasons. First, there is the question of whether it includes a representative number of imams and whether the selected imams represent what imams in general think about apostasy. Although there is no exact figure for the number of imams in Sweden or how different Muslim groups define who should be seen as an authoritative imam or not, the sample is very small. From this point of view it is not statistically representative and should therefore be seen primarily as a snapshot of how six Swedish imams look upon and understand apostasy. In order to obtain a more representative picture, more interviews need to be conducted and more quantitative data on imams in Sweden collected. However, already after six interviews it is clear that the variations in the answers were not infinite and hardly any new aspects emerged. This could, of course, be seen as an indication that the imams in the sample shared more or less the same views. Although this is a correct observation, it is important to stress that the imams in the sample belong to various traditions and that it would be unusual for them to agree on ways of understanding Islam. Furthermore, we do not know the extent to which the Muslim laity actually listens to and follows the interpretations provided by the imams. For example, this concern became apparent when one of the imams in my sample stressed that it is not necessary for an ex-Muslim to pay a visit to his former congregation in order to explain why he has left Islam.

A second criticism has to do with the quality of the information. To put it very bluntly, can I trust what the imams tell me about their views on apostasy? This problem is, of course, not unique to this question, but since apostasy could be a sensitive issue for the imams, it is necessary to be aware of it. By addressing this methodological problem I am not saying that I am genuinely distrustful of my informants, but since Swedish television, for example, has reported that Swedish imams have been caught saying one thing to non-Muslims (journalists) and something else to Muslims (i.e., believers) after the recording equipment has been turned off, it is essential to address this question.[7] The quality of the media reportage that has focused on this problem can, of course, be questioned, and some of the programs have also received heavy criticism for having biased views of Islam and Muslims in general (see Holmqvist 2012). Still, this is a problem the reader should be aware of, and in the discussion and analysis I have treated the information as trustworthy. Following a good academic standard that should be applied to any research (no matter what its subject or content), I have tried as much as possible to find data that could call the opinions of the imams into question.

CONCLUSION

In conclusion, this chapter indicates that there seems to be a gap between public perceptions (i.e., that it is dangerous or even impossible to leave Islam) and what the imams I interviewed think about apostasy. Furthermore, it is generally hard to find police records showing that apostates are suffering from discrimination and hate crimes, though the data is most likely suffering from underreporting. As noted earlier, this should not automatically be taken as an indication that converts or ex-Muslims are not suffering from harassment and hatred—quite the contrary. All violations of the principles of freedom of religion and freedom of speech should be taken seriously in an open and democratic society. Still, it is vital to ask: Why does it seem to be so hard for Muslim theologians to communicate liberal interpretations of Islam that correspond to the values of the liberal society? In both public perceptions and media outlets, it seems to be easier to communicate an image of Islam as a harsh, punitive, and intolerant religion or "Islam" as the main or sole explanation for why Muslims are supposed to act in a certain way (for a critical discussion of these explanations, see Mahmood 2008; Shooman and Speilhaus 2010; Bayoumi 2010). One explanation is, of course, the situation in the world (e.g., the current refugee crisis, the war on terror, and the growing nationalism in Europe and North America) and especially the rise of violence and terror in the name of Islam. But this does not explain why plural and more liberal voices are being silenced and often left out of public debates in the West. Does this problem tell us more about Muslim communities, or does it reveal more about the current media and political climate in the West? This is an open question that calls for more empirically and critically driven research in the future.

NOTES

1. This study was conducted within the framework of a larger research project titled "Leaving Islam: Apostasy, Freedom of Religion and Conflicts in a Multireligious Sweden" and funded by the Swedish Research Council (Vetenskapsrådet).

2. Detailed overviews of the literature on apostasy from Islam can be found in Peters and De Vries (1976–1977), O'Sullivan (2001), Ahmedov (2006), and Cook (2006). A growing number of academic publications document and analyze cases in which alleged apostates from Islam have been punished by excommunication, legal penalties, and even death; see, for example, Peters (2003).

3. As just noted, those who exit Islam most likely do not look upon themselves as heretics or apostates. As researchers such as Streib (2014) and Zuckerman (2012) have shown, there are many different paths that can lead to one leaving a religious tradition. However, since this study focuses only on imams and how they talk about apostasy, I will not go into any details about why individuals leave Islam or how these individuals narrate or view their way out of Islam.

4. As far as I know, it is not common practice to give converts to Islam a piece of paper that indicates that they have embraced Islam.

5. On the importance of community in Islamic history, see, for example, Watt (1964); cf. also Kraemer (1980).

6. For more information on this concept, see, for example, Peters (1980).

7. The television program on the imams is still available to watch online at www.svt.se/ug/muslimska-ledare-uppmanar-kvinnor-till-underkastelse; parts of this material are also available in English at www.svt.se/ug/undercover-report-muslim-leaders-urges-women-to-total-submission.

REFERENCES

Ahmedov, A. 2006. "Religious Minorities and Apostasy in Early Islamic States: Legal and Historical Analysis of Sources." *Journal of Islamic State Practices in International Law* 2, no. 3: 1–17.

Alalwani, T. J. 2011. *Apostasy in Islam: A Historical and Scriptural Analysis*. London and Washington, DC: International Institute of Islamic Thought.

Bayoumi, M. 2010. "The God That Failed: The Neo-Orientalism of Today's Muslim Commentators." In *Islamophobia/Islamophilia: Beyond the Politics of Enemy and Friend*. A. Shryock, ed. Bloomington and Indianapolis: Indiana University Press. 79–93.

Björk, F. 2014. "Hotades efter att ha konverterat." *SVT.SE*, 2014-04-17. www.svt.se/nyheter/lokalt/vast/hotades-efter-att-ha-konverterat.

Björk, E. 2014. "Hon blev hotad och bespottad." *Göteborgs-Posten*, 2014-10-16. www.gp.se/nyheter/göteborg/hon-blev-hotad-och-bespottad-1.246520.

Bukhari. 1997. *Sahih al-Bukhari*. (Arabic-English edition). Dr. Muhammad Muhsin Khan, ed. Vols. 1–9. Riyadh: Darussalam.

Cook, D. 2006. "Apostasy from Islam: A Historical Perspective." *Jerusalem Studies in Arabic and Islam* 31: 248–288.

Daniel, H. 2014. "Trakaserier mot kristna konvertiteter." *SVT.SE*, 2014-01-15. www.svt.se/nyheter/utrikes/allt-fler-konverterar-fran-islam-till-kristendomen.

Doumato, E. A. 1995. "Marriage and Divorce: Modern Practice." In *The Oxford Encyclopedia of the Modern Islamic World*, vol. 3. J. L. Esposito, ed. Oxford: Oxford University Press. 50–54.

Främlingsfientliga handlingar mot trossamfund. En kartläggning av religiösa grupper och individers utsatthet i Sverige 2014. Stockholm: Nämnden för Statligt Stöd till Trossamfund, SST.

Hallaq, W. 2001. "Apostasy." In *Encyclopaedia of the Qur'an*, vol. 1. J. D. McAuliffe, ed. Leiden and Boston: Brill. 119–122.

Holmqvist, A. 2012. "'De har klippt och klistrat' Imamernas kritiska till inslag i SVT:s Uppdrag Granskning." *Aftonbladet*, 2012-05-16. www.aftonbladet.se/nyheter/article14837150.ab.

Kraemer, J. L. 1980. "Apostates, Rebels, and Brigands." *Israel Oriental Studies* 10: 34–73.

Larsson, G. 2015. "En semantisk och lexical analys av roten R-D-D i svenska översättningar av Koranen." *CHAOS: Skandinavisk tidskrift for religionshistoriske studier* 64, no. 2: 72–78.

Larsson, G. 2016. "Most Muslims are like You and I, but the 'real' Muslims ... Ex-Muslims and anti-Muslim sentiments." *Journal of Muslims in Europe* 5: 205–223.

Larsson, G., and Å. Sander. 2015. "An Urgent Need to Consider How to Define Islamophobia." *Bulletin for the Study of Religion* 44, no. 1: 13–17.

Mahmood, S. 2008. "Feminism, Democracy, and Empire: Islam and the War on Terror." In *Women's Studies on the Edge*. J. Wallach Scott, ed. Durham and London: Duke University Press. 81–114.

Naskret, P. 2016. "Stora risker för dem som lämnar islam." *SVT.SE*, 2016-08-29. www.svt.se/nyheter/lokalt/jonkoping/stora-risker-for-de-som-lamnar-islam.

"Ny lag i Iran: Dödsstraff för alla som lämnar islam." *Dagen*, 2008-09-16. www.dagen.se/ny-lag-i-iran-dodsstraff-for-alla-som-lamnar-islam-1.192783.

O'Sullivan, D. 2001. "The Interpretation of Qur'anic Text to Promote or Negate the Death Penalty for Apostates and Blasphemers." *Journal of Qur'anic Studies* 3, no. 2: 63–93.

Otterbeck. J. 2010. *Samtidsislam. Unga muslimer i Malmö och Köpenhamn*. Stockholm: Carlssons.

Peters, R. 2003. *Crime and Punishment in Islamic Law: Theory and Practice from the Sixteenth to the Twenty-first Century*. Cambridge: Cambridge University Press.

Peters, R. 1980. "*Idjtihād* and *Taqlīd* in 18th and 19th Century Islam." *Die Welt des Islams* 20, no. 3/4: 131–145.

Peters, R., and G. J. J. De Vries. 1976–1977. "Apostasy in Islam." *Die Welt des Islams* 17, no. 1/4: 1–25.

Ramadan, T. "Muslim Scholars Speak Out." *Newsweek Washington Post*, July 25, 2007. tariqramadan.com/english/muslim-scholars-speak-out/ (no page number).

Ramadan, T. 2008. *Radical Reform: Islamic Ethics and Liberation*. Oxford: Oxford University Press.

Shooman, Y., and R. Spielhaus. "The Concept of the Muslim Enemy in the Public Discourse." In *Muslims in the West after 9/11: Religion, Politics, and Law*. J. Cesari, ed. London and New York: Routledge. 198–228.

Staten och Imamerna. Religion, integration, autonomi. 2009. (SOU: 52). Stockholm: Fritzes.

Streib, H. 2014. "Deconversion." In *The Oxford Handbook of Religious Conversion*. L. R. Rambo and C. E. Farhadian, eds. Oxford: Oxford University Press. 271–296.

Watt, M. W. 1964. "Conditions of Membership of the Islamic Community." *Studia Islamica*, no. 21: 5–12.

Zetterman, J. 2011. "Dödshot mot konvertiter i Sveriges Radio." *Dagen*, 2011-09-07. www.dagen.se/dodshot-mot-konvertiter-i-sveriges-radio-1.130565.

Ziadeh, F. J. 1995. "Uṣūl al-fiqh." In *The Oxford Encyclopedia of the Modern Islamic World*, vol. 4. J. L. Esposito, ed. Oxford: Oxford University Press. 298–300.

Zuckerman, P. 2012. *Faith No More: Why People Reject Religion*. Oxford: Oxford University Press.

Interviews with imams

Abdullah (personal visit, April 14, 2016)
Husain (personal e-mail, May 5, 2016)
Mustafa (telephone, October 14, 2015)
Rahman (telephone, October 14, 2015)
Safet (telephone, March 21, 2016)
Tariq (personal visit, January 14, 2016)

CONTRIBUTORS

ATEFEH AGHAEE is an independent researcher currently based in Finland. She holds a master's degree in intercultural communication from the University of Jyväskylä. Her research interests include comparative religion, education, and migrant adaptation.

MONA ALYEDREESSY is a British Arab sociologist who received her PhD from Kingston University, London, in 2016. Her research is primarily connected to the personal and social issues that many British Muslim converts face during their religious conversion journey to Islam and deconversion trajectories from Islam within a Western context. She is currently training to become a personal counselor to those who are or have previously been victims of social and personal abuse connected to conversion to or deconversion from Islam.

WILLIAM BARYLO is an independent researcher focusing on the articulations between diasporic cultures, religions, and hyper-modernity from a decolonial and restorative perspective. He is an awarded photographer and filmmaker, having directed the documentary *Polish Muslims: An Unexpected Meeting*, which premiered at the Polish Embassy in London. He is the author of *Young Muslim Change-Makers: Grassroots Charities Rethinking Modern Societies* (2017), published by Routledge. His recent articles include "Appropriating Islam as a Matrix" (2017) and "Neo-liberal Not-for-Profits: The Embracing of Corporate Culture by European Muslim Charities" (2016). He is also a blogger for the Huffington Post UK.

SIMON COTTEE is a senior lecturer in criminology at the University of Kent, UK. He is the author of *The Apostates: When Muslims Leave Islam* (Hurst, 2015) and the editor, with Thomas Cushman, of *Christopher Hitchens and His Critics: Terror, Iraq, and the Left* (New York University Press, 2008). He is a contributing writer to *The Atlantic* and a regular contributor to *Foreign Policy*, the *Los Angeles Times*, and Vice.

MARTIJN DE KONING is an anthropologist. He teaches at the Department of Islam Studies at Radboud University Nijmegen in the Netherlands and is engaged in research on lifestyles, identities, and memories of Dutch Muslims in the UK. He is a postdoctoral researcher at the Department of Anthropology at the University of Amsterdam, where he is currently involved in the NWO-funded project Forces That Bind and/or Divide (on how Muslims claim a voice in the public debates on Islam), and in the ERC-funded program Problematizing "Muslim Marriages": Ambiguities and Contestations. Martijn de Koning has published on Moroccan-Dutch youth and identity formation, radicalization, Salafism, Islamophobia, racialization, and activism among Muslims in the Netherlands, Germany, and Belgium. He maintains his own weblog (CLOSER) at religionresearch.org/closer.

DANIEL ENSTEDT is a senior lecturer in religious studies at the University of Gothenburg, Sweden. Enstedt's research focuses mainly on contemporary religion and the sociology of religion. He received his PhD in 2011 with the completion of a thesis on the reception of the Church of Sweden's decision to introduce a special blessing ceremony for same-sex unions. Since then he has been working on two research projects: "Leaving Islam: Apostasy, Freedom of Religion, and Conflicts in a Multireligious Sweden," together with professor Göran Larsson, and "The Good Life: Contemporary Views on Family Life and Life at Work." Enstedt coedited the *Annual Review of the Sociology of Religion*, vol. 6, "Religion and Internet" (2015) with Göran Larsson and Enzo Pace.

JULIETTE GALONNIER is a postdoctoral fellow at INED (Institut National d'Études Démographiques) in Paris. She studies the social construction of race and how it intersects with religion. She received in 2017 a double PhD in sociology from both Northwestern University and Sciences Po. Her dissertation "Choosing Faith and Facing Race: Converting to Islam in France and the United States" provides a comparative analysis of the experiences of converts to Islam on the two sides of the Atlantic. On this topic, she has published several book chapters and articles in academic journals such as *Sociology of Religion*, *Social Compass*, and *Tracés*.

KATARZYNA GÓRAK-SOSNOWSKA is an associate professor at the Department of Political Studies and vice dean for master studies at the Warsaw

School of Economics in Poland. She is also the head of two projects: EU—Muslim Minorities and the Refugee Crisis in Europe (cofunded by Erasmus+ Programme), and Contested Identity: The Case of Polish Female Converts to Islam (funded by the National Science Centre in Poland). She earned her PhD in economics and habilitation in the study of religion with the focus on Islam in Europe. She is the author of several books; those in English include *Deconstructing Islamophobia in Poland* (2014) and *Muslims in Poland and Eastern Europe* (editor, 2011).

HAIFAA JAWAD is senior lecturer in Islamic and Middle Eastern studies, Department of Theology and Religion, University of Birmingham. She is also the director of the Centre of Islamic and Middle Eastern Studies. She has specialized in the sociopolitical study of Islam, modern and contemporary Islamic thought, women in Islam, Islam and the West, interreligious relations, especially Christian-Muslim relations, British Islam, especially new Muslims, and Middle East politics. She has personal interest in Islamic spirituality and ethics. She was the holder of the Fulbright/American University of Beirut scholarship in contemporary Islam at the University of Alabama (2004) and held visiting lectureship positions in Lancaster University and Trinity College, Dublin. Among her recent publications are: "A Muslim Response to the Christian Theology of Religions," in Paul Hedges et al. (eds.), *Twenty-First Century Theologies of Religions: Retrospection and New Frontiers* (Brill, 2016), *Women, Islam, and Resistance in the Arab World* (with Holt; Lynne Rienner, 2013), and *Towards Building a British Islam: New Muslims' Perspectives* (Continuum International, 2011).

GÖRAN LARSSON is professor in religious studies at the University of Gothenburg, Sweden. Larsson's research is focused mainly on the study of Islam and Muslims in Europe in both history and contemporary times. His most recent publication is *Annotated Legal Documents on Islam in Europe: Sweden* (together with Mosa Sayed; Brill 2017). He has directed the research project "Leaving Islam: Apostasy, Freedom of Religion, and Conflicts in a Multireligious Sweden," funded by the Swedish Research Council (Vetenskapsrådet).

MICHAŁ ŁYSZCZARZ is a sociologist and political scientist. He works as adjunct at the Department of Sociology, University of Warmia and Mazury, in Olsztyn, Poland. He is the author of the book *Young Generation of Polish Tatars: The Study of Youth Generational Changes in the Context of Muslim Religiosity and Ethnic Identity* (in Polish) (Olsztyn-Białystok, 2013). In English he published "Perspectives on Muslim Dress in Poland: A Tatar View" (with coauthor Katarzyna Górak Sosnowska) in *Islamic Fashion and Anti-Fashion. New Perspectives from Europe and North America*, edited by E. Tarlo and A. Moors (London, 2013); "Generational Changes among Young Polish Tatars," in *Muslims in Poland and Eastern Europe. Widening the European Discourse on Islam*, edited by Katarzyna Górak-Sosnowska (Warsaw, 2011); and "(Un-)Islamic Consumers? The Case of Polish Tatars" (with coauthor: Katarzyna Górak-Sosnowska) in *Muslim Societies in the Age of Mass Consumption: Politics, Culture, and Identity between the Local and Global*, edited by J. Pink (Newcastle, 2009).

ESRA ÖZYÜREK is an Associate Professor and Chair for Contemporary Turkish Studies at the European Institute, London School of Economics. She is a political anthropologist who seeks to understand how Islam, Christianity, secularism, and nationalism are dynamically positioned in relation to each other in Turkey and in Europe. Her most recent book, *Being German, Becoming Muslim: Race, Religion, and Conversion in the New Europe*, was published by the Princeton University Press (2014). Her previous book *Nostalgia for the Modern: State Secularism and Everyday Politics in Turkey* was published by Duke University Press (2007). She also is the editor of *Politics of Public Memory in Turkey* (Syracuse University Press, 2007).

TEEMU PAUHA is a PhD candidate in the study of religions at the University of Helsinki. His research concentrates on Islam, and especially young Muslims, in Finland. At the moment, he is studying the social psychology of religious prejudice. Pauha serves also as the Finnish contributor to the *Yearbook of Muslims in Europe*. Besides his research, Pauha is working as a clinical psychologist in a child psychiatric clinic.

GABRIEL PIRICKÝ is an Islamologist, Arabist, and Turcologist based at the Institute of Oriental Studies of the Slovak Academy of Sciences in Bratislava, Slovakia. He is the author of several publications in the Slovak and Czech languages, including *Turkey—A Short History* (Praha: Libri, 2006) and *Islam in Turkey* (Trnava: Univerzita sv. Cyrila a Metoda, 2004). He coedited the following books in Slovak: *Fascination and (Un)Understanding: West-East Cultural Encounters* (Bratislava: Chronos, 2003, with M. Slobodník); *Contemporary Manifestations of Sufism from the Balkans to China* (Bratislava: Univerzita Komenského, 2010, with D. Deák and M. Slobodník), and *Forms of Globalisation in Orient* (Bratislava: Ústav orientalistiky SAV, 2015, with M. Bucková). He is also the chairman of the Slovak Oriental Society.

EGDŪNAS RAČIUS (PhD in Arabic and Islamic studies, University of Helsinki, 2004) is professor of Middle Eastern and Islamic studies at the Department of Area Studies of Vytautas Magnus University, Kaunas, Lithuania. He is the reviews editor of the *Journal of Muslims in Europe* and a coeditor of the *Yearbook of Muslims in Europe* (both by Brill). His research interests encompass Eastern European Muslim communities as well as Muslim revivalist movements. Račius is a coeditor (together with Antonina Zhelyazkova) of *Islamic Leadership in the European Lands of the Former Ottoman and Russian Empires: Legacy, Challenges, and Change* (Brill, 2018) and the author of *Muslims in Eastern Europe* (Edinburgh University Press, 2018).

YAFA SHANNEIK is lecturer in Islamic studies at the University of Birmingham, UK. She researches the dynamics and trajectories of gender in Islam within the context of contemporary diasporic and transnational Muslim women's spaces. She also has a particular research interest in the authority and leadership of Muslim women and the changing nature of women's participation in religious practices in Europe and the Middle East. She has published several articles on gender and Islam and migrant identities in Europe, including "Remembering Karbala in the Diaspora: Religious Rituals among Iraqi Shii Women in Ireland" (in *Religion*, 2015) and "Religion and Diasporic Dwelling: Algerian Muslim Women in Ireland" (in *Religion and Gender*, 2012).

KARIN VAN NIEUWKERK is an anthropologist and professor of contemporary Islam in Europe and the Middle East at the Radboud University Nijmegen in the Netherlands. She is the author of *'A Trade like Any Other': Female Singers and Dancers in Egypt* (1995) and *Performing Piety: Singers and Actors in Egypt's Islamic Revival* (2013). She is also editor of *Women Embracing Islam: Gender and Conversion in the West* (2006) and *Muslim Rap, Halal Soaps, and Revolutionary Theatre: Artistic Developments in the Muslim World* (2011). She coedited *Islam and Popular Culture* (2016) with Mark LeVine and Martin Stokes. All books were published by University of Texas Press.

OLEG YAROSH is an associate professor and senior researcher at the Institute of Philosophy of National Academy of Sciences of Ukraine. He is a religious studies scholar focusing on Islam in Muslim-minority countries and Western Sufism. He is the author of several articles and book chapters on Sufism and coedited *Sufism and the Muslim Spiritual Tradition: Texts, Institutions, Ideas, and Interpretations* (St. Petersburg, Russia, 2013) with Alexander Knysh and Denys Brylov.

INDEX